C A REFERENCE MANUAL

C A REFERENCE MANUAL

Fourth Edition

Samuel P. Harbison

Tartan, Inc.

Guy L. Steele Jr.

Thinking Machines, Inc.

Prentice Hall, Englewood Cliffs, New Jersey 07632

Library of Congress Cataloging-in-Publication Data

Harbison, Samuel P.
C, a reference manual / Samuel P. Harbison, Guy L. Steele Jr. --
4th ed.
p. cm.
Includes bibliological references and index.
ISBN: 0-13-326232-4 (case)
ISBN: 0-13-326224-3 (pbk)
1. C (Computer program language)/ I. Steele, Guy.
II. Title.
QA76.73.C15H38 1995
005.13'3--dc20 94-22308
CIP

Acquisitions editor: MARCIA HORTON
Production editor: IRWIN ZUCKER
Copy editor: BOB LENTZ
Buyer: LORI BULWIN
Editorial assistant: DOLORES MARS

Printed in the United States of America

10 9 8 7 6 5 4 3 2

ISBN 0-13-326232-4 {CASE}

ISBN 0-13-326224-3 {PBK}

Prentice-Hall International (UK) Limited, London
Prentice-Hall of Australia Pty. Limited, Sydney
Prentice-Hall Canada Inc., Toronto
Prentice-Hall Hispanoamericana, S.A., Mexico
Prentice-Hall of India Private Limited, New Delhi
Prentice-Hall of Japan, Inc., Tokyo
Simon & Schuster Asia Pte. Ltd., Singapore
Editora Prentice-Hall do Brasil, Ltda., Rio de Janeiro

For Diana, Drew, and Michael Harbison

Contents

List of Tables

Preface to the Fourth Edition

This Fourth Edition of *C: A Reference Manual* brings the text up to date with two important developments. First, I've added a description of ISO C Amendment 1 (1994), which specifies new facilities for writing portable, international programs in C. Second, I've added a discussion of how to write C programs that are compatible with C++—in fact, how to write programs that are valid both as C programs *and* as C++ programs. These "Clean C" programs will be maximally portable and reusable in C and C++ environments.

As usual, I've taken advantage of the new edition to make a number of improvements in the presentation of the older material, fixing all the known bugs and hopefully not introducing too many more. Second Edition readers will be pleased to see that I have put back Guy Steele's excellent bit set example in Chapter 7.

ISO C AND AMENDMENT 1

Readers familiar with the Third Edition of *C:ARM* will notice that I have replaced all references to "ANSI C" with "ISO C." Since 1990, the C language has had an International Standard which supersedes the US standard. Except for minor editorial changes, the International Standard, ISO/IEC 9899:1990, is identical to the earlier American National Standard X3.159–1989. The terms "ISO C," "ANSI C," and "Standard C" all refer to the same language.

The increased international attention given to C did reveal some weaknesses in the standard language. Although ISO C introduced into C the important concepts of multibyte characters and wide characters, experience showed that the facilities were not rich enough to permit the development of portable international programs. Therefore, the committees responsible for the standard have specified some additions to ISO C, collecting them in *Amendment 1 (1994)* to ISO/IEC 9899:1990. These additions are all upward compatible. Except for possible name clashes, programs written for an ISO C implementation should behave the same when the implementation is upgraded to Amendment 1.

THE C++ LANGUAGE

The past few years have seen the C++ language rapidly gaining "mind share" among C programmers. Thanks to Borland, Microsoft, and the Free Software Foundation (GNU), most C programmers now have C++ implementations at hand. C++ includes many improvements over C that programmers need for large applications, including improved type checking and better support for data abstraction. However, C++ is also one of the more complex object-oriented programming languages, built around concepts that are still unfamiliar to many. C++ is presently undergoing international standardization, with the first public review of the draft standard scheduled to appear in 1995.

C++ is nearly—but not exactly—a superset of ISO C. It is possible to write C code in the common subset of the ISO C and C++ languages, so that the code can be compiled either as a C program or as a C++ program. This new dialect of C—called *Clean C* by some—is important for several reasons:

- Clean C code must follow certain restrictions—such as using prototypes in function declarations—that tend to make the C code safer and more readable. Clean C is a kind of "strict ISO C," without some of the anachronisms kept for compatibility.
- Clean C code is portable across C and C++ implementations, so it can be used alongside C++ code, or it can be the starting point of a gradual transition into C++. This adds value to the C code and expands its potential customer base.
- There is no important functionality that is lost in Clean C, and converting code is fairly easy. If you already use prototypes, most of the work will involve renaming objects to avoid collisions with the new C++ reserved words.

ACKNOWLEDGMENTS

The corrections to the Third Edition were largely made possible by the contributions of many people in the C programming community. I would like to thank Aurelio Bignoli, Steve Clamage, Arthur Evans Jr., Roy J. Fuller, Morris M. Kessan, George V. Reilly, Mark Lan, Mike Hewett, Charles Fischer, Kevin Rodgers, Tom Gibb, David Lim, Stavros Macrakis, Steve Vegdahl, Christopher Vickery, Peter van der Linden, and Dave Wilson for reporting problems. I especially want to thank Steve Vinoski, who proofread the entire Third Edition after its publication and reported many problems.

For assistance with the Fourth Edition, I would especially like to thank Jeffrey Esakov, Rex Jaeschke, Debra Martin, and P. J. Plauger.

The use of "I" instead of "we" in this Preface reflects the fact that Guy Steele's work load prevented him from being an active contributor to this new edition. The text still reflects his clear and rigorous analysis of the C language, but he can't be held responsible for any new problems in this edition.

C: A Reference Manual is now over ten years old. Its entire life has been under the careful guidance of Marcia Horton at Prentice-Hall and the love and support of Diana Harbison at home.

Sam Harbison
Pittsburgh, PA

Preface

This text is a reference manual for the C programming language. Our aim is to provide a complete discussion of the language, the run-time libraries, and a style of C programming that emphasizes correctness, portability, and maintainability.

We expect our readers to already understand basic programming concepts, and many will have previous experience with C. In keeping with a reference format, we have presented the language in a "bottom-up" order: the lexical structure, the preprocessor, declarations, types, expressions, statements, functions, and the run-time libraries. We have included many cross-references in the text so that readers can begin at any point.

With the Third Edition of *C: A Reference Manual* we have fully integrated the descriptions of "traditional C" and the American National Standard X3.159–1989—"ANSI C." Many popular C compilers—including, for example, Microsoft C for the IBM PC—have been moving toward the ANSI C language for some time. Even if these compilers are not fully ANSI conforming as we write this, programmers using them are better served by books that fully cover ANSI C.

For the majority of programmers still using non-ANSI conforming implementations, we have not short-changed traditional C. We have retained the descriptions of various shortcomings and variations in pre-ANSI compilers so that programmers may avoid the less portable language areas if desired. We have been careful to note where ANSI C and traditional C differ and have given suggestions for writing programs that are portable between the two languages.

We have also taken the opportunity afforded by this edition to make more extensive changes in the text. We added study problems to most chapters in Part 1 so that readers may test their understanding of the language. We added various tables to highlight language features and make the text more readable. Finally, we added many examples that illustrate the use of the library facilities in Part 2. To keep the book to a reasonable length, we shortened some tedious discussions of minor technical points, and we eliminated two chapters at the end of Part 1 that contained a separate discussion of ANSI C and a large C example program. The ANSI C description is now integrated into the main text, and there are many software engineering textbooks that treat the problems of building large software systems in more depth.

This book grew out of our work at Tartan Laboratories developing a family of C compilers for a wide range of computers, from micros to supermainframes. We wanted the compilers to be well documented, to provide precise and helpful error diagnostics, and to generate exceptionally efficient object code. A C program that compiles correctly with one compiler must compile correctly under all the others, insofar as the hardware differences allow.

In spite of C's popularity, and the increasing number of primers and introductory texts on C, we found that there was no description of C precise enough to guide us in designing the new compilers. Similarly, no existing description was precise enough for our programmer/customers, who would be using compilers that analyzed C programs more thoroughly than was the custom. In this text we have been especially sensitive to language features that affect program clarity, object code efficiency, and the portability of programs among different environments, both UNIX and non-UNIX.

Acknowledgments

This edition was greatly improved by comments from reviewers Jeffrey Esakov of the University of Pennsylvania, Alan J. Filipski of Arizona State University, and Frank J. Wagner of the University of Cincinnati. Marcia Horton at Prentice Hall has been an excellent guide for the book and the authors over the past seven years.

We also wish to thank our colleagues who helped in the writing, editing, and production of this book in its various editions: Michael Angus, Mady Bauer, Larry Breed, Sue Broughton, Alex Czajkowski, Robert Firth, David Gaffney, Steve Gorman, Dennis Hamilton, Chris Hanna, Ken Harrenstien, Rex Jaeschke, Don Lindsay, Tom MacDonald, Peter Nelson, Joe Newcomer, Kevin Nolish, David Notkin, Peter Plamondon, P. J. Plauger, Roger Ray, Larry Rosler, David Spencer , and Barbara Steele.

This printing includes corrections to the original Third Edition suggested by Steve Vinoski of HP Apollo Division, and Aurelio Bignoli, Steve Clamage, Roy J. Fuller, Morris M. Kessan, George V. Reilly, Mark Lan, Mike Hewett, Charles Fischer, Kevin Rodgers, Tom Gibb, David Lim, Stavros Macrakis, Steve Vegdahl, Christopher Vickery, Peter van der Linden, and Dave Wilson.

Some of the example programs in this book were inspired by algorithms appearing in the following works, which we recommend to anyone seriously interested in programming: Beeler, Michael, Gosper, R. William, and Schroeppel, Richard, *HAKMEM*, AI Memo 239 (Massachusetts Institute of Technology Artificial Intelligence Laboratory, February 1972); Bentley, Jon Louis, *Writing Efficient Programs* (Prentice-Hall, 1982); Bentley, Jon Louis, "Programming Pearls" (monthly column appearing in *Communications of the ACM* beginning August 1983); Kernighan, Brian W., and Ritchie, Dennis M., *The C Programming Language* (Prentice-Hall, 1978); Knuth, Donald E, *The Art of Computer Programming* Volumes 1–3 (Addison-Wesley, 1968, 1969, 1973, 1981); and Sedgewick, Robert, *Algorithms* (Addison-Wesley, 1983). We are indebted to these authors for their good ideas.

Sam Harbison
Guy Steele

PART 1
The C Language

1

Introduction

C is a member of the "ALGOL family" of algebraic programming languages, and is more similar to languages such as PL/I, Pascal, and Ada, and less similar to BASIC, FORTRAN, or Lisp. A collection of papers, *Comparing & Assessing Programming Languages Ada, C, and Pascal*, edited by Alan R. Feuer and Narain Gehani (Prentice-Hall, 1984) discusses the similarities and differences found in C, Pascal, and Ada.

Dennis Ritchie designed the C language at Bell Laboratories in about 1972, and its ancestry dates from ALGOL 60 (1960), through Cambridge's CPL (1963), Martin Richards's BCPL (1967) and Ken Thompson's B language (1970) at Bell Labs. Although C is a general-purpose programming language, it has traditionally been used for systems programming. In particular, the popular UNIX operating system is written in C. Now widely available on both UNIX and non-UNIX systems, C is increasingly popular for applications that must be ported to different computers.

C's popularity is due to several factors. First, C provides a fairly complete set of facilities for dealing with a wide variety of applications. It has all the useful data types, including pointers, structures, and strings. There is a rich set of operators and control structures. C also has a standard run-time library that includes useful functions for input/output, storage allocation, string manipulation, and other purposes.

Second, C programs are efficient. C is a small language, and its data types and operators are closely related to the operations provided directly by most computers. Said another way, there is only a small "semantic gap" between C and the computer hardware.

Third, C programs are generally quite portable across different computing systems. Although C allows the programmer to write nonportable code, the uniformity of most C implementations makes it relatively easy to move applications to different computers and operating systems.

Finally, there is a growing number of C programs and C programmers. The UNIX operating system provides a large set of tools that improve C programming productivity and can serve as starting points for new applications. Because UNIX has been used in universities for several years, many students have C and UNIX experience.

Unfortunately, some of the very characteristics of C that account for its popularity can also pose problems for programmers. For example, C's smallness is due in large part to its lack of "confining rules," but the absence of such rules can lead to error-prone programming habits. To write well-ordered programs, the C programmer often relies on a set of stylistic conventions that are not enforced by the compiler. As another example, to allow C compilers to implement operations efficiently on a variety of computers, the precise meaning of some C operators and types is intentionally unspecified. This can create problems when moving a program to another computer.

In spite of the inelegancies, the bugs, and the confusion that often accompany C, it has withstood the test of time. It remains a language in which the experienced programmer can write quickly and well. Millions of lines of code testify to its usefulness.

1.1 LANGUAGE STANDARDS

Although there were many introductions to C at the time we wrote the First Edition of this book, there were no detailed descriptions of the C language.

1.1.1 Traditional C

The traditional (pre-standard) language reference is the book *The C Programming Language*, by Brian Kernighan and Dennis Ritchie (Prentice-Hall, 1978). In fact, it is not uncommon to see references to "K&R C." However, after the book was published the language continued to evolve in small ways; some features were added and some were dropped. Usually a consensus was reached on these features, although this consensus was not always documented. Many new implementations of C added their own variations to the language. When we use the phrase "the original definition of C" in this book, we mean specifically Kernighan and Ritchie's definition, before the post-1978 changes. When we speak of "traditional C," "classic C," or "pre-ISO C," we include the generally accepted extensions in use just prior to the ANSI standard. Kernighan and Richie produced a Second Edition of *The C Programming Language* in 1988 which describes ANSI C.

1.1.2 ANSI C, ISO C, Standard C

In 1982 the American National Standards Institute (ANSI) formed a technical subcommittee to propose a standard for the C language and run-time libraries. The X3J11 committee, chaired by Jim Brodie, produced a standard that was formally adopted in 1989 as *American National Standard X3.159-1989*, referred to as "ANSI C" or more informally as "Standard C". The standardization effort involved a large number of commercial C implementors—including ourselves—and their discussions helped to clarify existing practices as well as to map out some new features. Many parts of this book have benefited from these discussions.

Recognizing that programming is an international activity, an international standardization effort was begun as ANSI C was completed. The ISO/IEC JTC1/SC22/WG14

(C) committee, chaired by P. J. Plauger, converted the ANSI standard to an international standard, ISO/IEC 9899:1990, making only minor editorial changes. WG14 is now the official home of the common C standard ("ISO C"), with X3J11 having important influence representing the U. S. programming community—although, in fact, X3J11's membership is international also.

Because there is no technical difference between ISO C and the earlier ANSI C, both may be referred to as Standard C. In this book, we refer to this common language as "ISO C."

It would be difficult to list all the changes from traditional C to ISO C, but some of the changed areas include:

- New preprocessor commands and features.
- Function prototypes, which let you specify the argument types in a function declaration.
- Some new keywords, including **`const`**, **`volatile`**, and **`signed`**.
- Wide characters, wide strings, and multibyte characters.
- Many smaller changes and clarifications to conversion rules, declarations, and type checking.

1.1.3 Amendments and Corrigenda

In 1994, WG14 produced the first extensions to the ISO C standard. *Amendment 1* includes additional facilities to support international use of C, including more library support for foreign character sets, multibyte characters and wide characters. We have incorporated the extensions of Amendment 1 into this book, and have designated them as such in the descriptions. It may be some time before all Standard C compilers incorporate the extensions in the Amendment. The additions in Amendment 1 include:

- three new standard header files: **`iso646.h`**, **`wctype.h`**, and **`wchar.h`**
- several new tokens and macros used as replacements for operators and punctuation characters that are not found in some countries' character sets
- some new formatting codes for the **`printf/scanf`** family of functions
- a large number of new functions, plus some types and constants, for multibyte and wide characters

Also in 1994, WG14 produced the first correction to ISO C. *Technical Corrigendum 1* to ISO C is not an extension, but is rather a "bug fix." It specifies 35 small changes to the standard which resolve inconsistencies or errors. Because these corrections affect more the exposition than the intent of the Standard, we have not explicitly noted them in this book. Of course, we have reviewed the text to be sure our interpretations are consistent with the Corrigendum.

1.1.4 Other Variations on C

Many groups have experimented with extensions to C. There is Concurrent C, with parallel processing features, and there is Numerical C, with some extensions designed for scientific programmers and others with particular concerns about complex numbers, arrays, floating-point arithmetic, etc. Objective C introduced object-oriented programming features to the language. These variations all have limited use so far, and we do not consider them in this book.

1.1.5 C++

The term "limited use" certainly does not apply to the programming language that started as an extension to C: C++, designed by Bjarne Stroustrup at AT&T Bell Labs. The past few years have seen the C++ language rapidly gaining "mind share" among C programmers. Thanks to Borland, Microsoft, and the Free Software Foundation ("GNU"), most C programmers now have C++ implementations at hand. C++ includes many improvements over C that programmers need for large applications, including improved type checking and better support for data abstraction. However, C++ is also one of the more complex object-oriented programming languages, built around concepts that are still unfamiliar to many.

C++ is nearly—but not exactly—a superset of ISO C. It is possible to write C code in the common subset of the ISO C and C++ languages—called *Clean C* by some—so that the code can be compiled either as a C program or as a C++ program. Since C++ generally has more strict rules than ISO C, Clean C tends to be a good, portable subset to write in. The major changes you must consider when writing Clean C are:

- Clean C programs must use function prototypes; old-style declarations are not permitted in C++.
- Clean C programs must avoid using names that are reserved words in C++, like **`class`** and **`virtual`**.

There are several other rules and differences, but they are less likely to cause problems.

Unfortunately, we can't be as precise when speaking about C++ as we can about ISO C. The C++ language has not yet been standardized, and many current C++ implementations differ in significant ways. C++ is presently undergoing international standardization, with the first public review of the draft standard scheduled to appear in 1995. The ISO C++ committee working on the standard has introduced changes which have not yet found their way into commercial implementations. Finally, the draft of the future ISO C++ standard is still changing in significant ways. When explaining how to write Clean C, we will be talking about the version C++ as specified in the Working Draft of ISO C++ at the beginning of 1994.

In this book, we will explain how to write ISO C code so that it is acceptable to C++ compilers. We will not discuss features of C++ that are not available in ISO C. (Which, of course, includes almost everything interesting in C++.)

1.1.6 The Future of C

In accordance with ISO policies on timely reexamination of standards, WG14 will consider whether a major revision of ISO C is necessary beginning in 1995. It is too soon to tell in what direction WG14 will seek to evolve C, but it is possible that the committee will recommend adopting some of the more conservative features of C++ and perhaps some numerical extensions that have been worked on by subgroups of the standards committees.

It is unlikely that WG14 will recommend abandoning C in favor of C++. Most people believe that C and C++ address different programming problems, and that there is merit in both languages.

1.1.7 This Text

This book describes the two major variations of C: ISO C and traditional C. It also describes two variations on ISO C: the additional features in Amendment 1, and the Clean C subset of C and C++. ISO C gives implementors some freedom in how they implement the language, and so we try to describe the common variations. We also try to indicate how to write "good" C programs—programs that are readable, portable, and maintainable.

1.2 CONFORMANCE

Both C programs and C implementations can *conform* to ISO C. A C program is said to be *strictly conforming* to ISO C if that program uses only the features of the language and library described in the Standard. The program's operation must not depend on any aspect of the C language that the Standard characterizes as unspecified, undefined, or implementation-defined. There are several ISO C test suites available that help establish conformance to the standard.

There are two kinds of conforming implementations—hosted and freestanding. A C implementation is said to be a *conforming hosted implementation* if it accepts any strictly conforming program. A *conforming freestanding implementation* is one that accepts any strictly conforming program that uses no library facilities other than those provided in the header files **float.h**, **iso646.h** (Amendment 1), **limits.h**, **stdarg.h**, and **stddef.h**. (Chapter 10 lists the contents of these header files.) This kind of conformance is meant to accommodate C implementations for embedded systems or other target environments with minimal run-time support. (For example, such systems may have no file system.)

A *conforming* program is one that is accepted by a conforming implementation. Thus, a conforming program can depend on some nonportable, implementation-defined features of a conforming implementation, whereas a strictly conforming program cannot depend on those features (and so is maximally portable).

Conforming implementations may provide extensions that do not change the meaning of any strictly conforming program. This allows implementations to add library routines and define their own **#pragma** directives, but not to introduce new reserved identifiers or change the operation of standard library functions.

Compiler vendors continue to provide non-conforming extensions that their customers have grown used to. Compilers enable (or disable) these extensions with special switches.

1.3 WHICH DIALECT OF C SHOULD YOU USE?

Which dialect of C you use depends on what implementation(s) of C you have available and on how portable you want your code to be. Your choices are one *or more* of:

1. Standard (ANSI, ISO) C, possibly with the ISO C Amendment 1 extensions.
2. Traditional C. (Watch out for minor variations across implementations!)
3. Clean C, compatible with C++.

Unfortunately, you can't write much C code that is compatible with all three of these dialects unless you use conditional compilation. Consider function prototypes, for example. They are optional in ISO C, forbidden in traditional C, and required in C++. Fortunately, you can use the C preprocessor to alter your code depending on which implementation is being used—and even on whether your ISO C includes the Amendment 1 extensions. Therefore, your C programs can remain compatible with all dialects. We explain how to use the preprocessor to do this in Chapter 3. An example appears on page 63.

If you are not limited by your compiler or an existing body of C code, you should definitely use ISO C as your base language. ISO C compilers are now almost universally available. The free C compilers that come with UNIX tend to be non-ISO compilers, but commercial ISO C compilers are available for UNIX systems, and the Free Software Foundation's GNU C (**`gcc`**) is a free, ISO C implementation (with many extensions).

A compiler and run-time library conforming to ISO C will have consistent behavior, whereas non-ISO implementations often exhibit unwelcome variations. In large part, ISO C codified existing practice by traditional C programmers and did not invalidate the large body of C programs. If you are a "traditional C" programmer, do not be discouraged. The vast majority of C programs use well-understood language features and will port to ISO C with little or no changes. ISO C allows—but does not require—a programmer to write more portable programs.

1.4 AN OVERVIEW OF C PROGRAMMING

We expect most of our readers to be familiar with programming in a high-level language such as C, but a quick overview of C programming may be helpful to some.

A C *program* is composed of one or more *source files*, or *translation units*, each of which contains some part of the entire C program—typically some number of external functions. Common declarations are often collected into *header files* and are included into the source files with a special **`#include`** command (section 3.4). One external function must be named **`main`** (section 20.1); by convention this will be the first function executed.

A C compiler independently processes each source file and translates the C program text into instructions understood by the computer. The compiler "understands" the C program and analyzes it for correctness. If the programmer has made an error the compiler can detect, the compiler issues an error message. Otherwise, the output of the compiler is usually called *object code* or an *object module*.

When all source files are compiled, the object modules are given to a program called the *linker*. The linker resolves references between the modules, adds functions from the standard run-time library, and detects some programming errors such as the failure to define a needed function. The linker is typically not specific to C; each computer system has a standard linker that is used for programs written in many different languages. The linker produces a single executable program, which can then be invoked, or "run."Although most computer systems go through these steps, they may appear different to the programmer. In this book we are not concerned with the details of building C programs; readers should consult their own computer system and programming documentation.

Example

Suppose a program to be named **prog** consists of the two C source files **proga.c** and **progb.c**. (The "**.c**" extension in the file names is a common convention for C source files.) The file **proga.c** might contain these lines:

```
#include <stdio.h>
void hello(void)
{
    printf("Hello!\n");
}
```

The header file for **proga.c**, named **proga.h** (also by convention), contains:

```
extern void hello(void);
```

File **progb.c** contains the main program, which simply calls function **hello**:

```
#include "proga.h"
int main(void)
{
    hello();
    return 0;
}
```

On a UNIX system, compiling, linking, and executing the program takes only two steps:

```
% cc -o prog proga.c progb.c
% prog
```

The first line compiles and links the two source files, adds any standard library functions needed, and writes the executable program to file **prog**. The second line then executes the program, which prints:

```
Hello!
```

Other, non-UNIX implementations may use different commands. Increasingly, modern programming environments present an integrated, graphical interface to the programmer. Building a C application in such an environment requires only selecting commands from a menu or clicking a graphical button.

1.5 SYNTAX NOTATION

This text makes use of a stylized notation for expressing the form of a C program. When specifying the C language grammar, terminal symbols are printed in fixed type and are to appear in the program exactly as written. Nonterminal symbols are printed in italic type; they are spelled beginning with a letter and can be followed by zero or more letters, digits, or hyphens:

expression *argument-list* *declarator*

Syntactic definitions are introduced by the name of the nonterminal being defined followed by a colon. One or more alternatives then follow on succeeding lines:

character :
    printing-character
    escape-character

When the words "one of" follow the colon, this signifies that each of the terminal symbols following on one or more lines is an alternative definition:

digit : one of
    `0 1 2 3 4 5 6 7 8 9`

Optional components of a definition are signified by appending the suffix *opt* to a terminal or nonterminal symbol:

enumeration-constant-definition :
    enumeration-constant $enumeration\text{-}initializer_{opt}$

initializer :
    expression
    `{` *initializer-list* $,_{opt}$ `}`

2

Lexical Elements

This chapter describes the lexical structure of the C language—that is, the characters that may appear in a C source file and how they are collected into lexical units, or tokens.

2.1 CHARACTER SET

A C source file is a sequence of characters selected from a character set. C programs are written using the following characters (which ISO C requires):

1. the 52 uppercase and lowercase alphabetic characters:

```
A B C D E F G H I J K L M N O P Q R S T
U V W X Y Z a b c d e f g h i j k l m
n o p q r s t u v w x y z
```

2. the 10 decimal digits:

```
0 1 2 3 4 5 6 7 8 9
```

3. the space, horizontal tab, vertical tab, and form feed characters
4. the 29 graphic characters shown in Table 2–1.

There must also be some way of dividing the source program into lines; this can be done with a character or character sequence or with some mechanism outside the source character set (for example, an end-of-record indication).

Some countries have national character sets that do not include all the graphic characters in Table 2–1 on page 12. ISO C defines trigraphs and token respellings (Amendment 1) to allow C programs to be written in the ISO 646-1083 Invariant Code Set.

Table 2–1 Graphic characters

Char	Name	Char	Name	Char	Name
!	exclamation pt.	+	plus	"	double quote
#	number sign	=	equal	{	left brace
%	percent	~	tilde	}	right brace
^	circumflex	[	left bracket	,	comma
&	ampersand	]	right bracket	.	period
*	asterisk	\	backslash	<	less than
(	left parenthesis	|	vertical bar	>	greater than
)	right parenthesis	;	semicolon	/	slash
-	hyphen or minus	:	colon	?	question mark
_	underscore	'	apostrophe		

Additional characters are sometimes used in C source programs, including:

1. formatting characters such as the backspace and carriage return characters.
2. extra graphic characters not needed in the basic character set, including the characters **$** (dollar sign), **@** (at-sign), and ` (accent grave).

The formatting characters are treated as spaces and do not otherwise affect the source program. The extra graphic characters may appear only in comments, character constants, and string constants.

As will be seen from the previous discussion, C has a much larger source character set than do most other programming languages.

References character constants 2.7.3; comments 2.2; character encoding 2.1.3; character escape codes 2.7.6; execution character set 2.1.1; string constants 2.7.4; token respellings 2.4.1; trigraphs 2.1.4

2.1.1 Execution Character Set

The character set interpreted during the execution of a C program is not necessarily the same as the one in which the C program is written. Characters in the execution character set are represented by their equivalents in the source character set or by special character escape sequences that begin with the backslash (\ ) character.

In addition to the standard characters mentioned above, the execution character set must also include:

1. a null character that must be encoded as the value 0
2. a newline character, that is used as the end-of-line marker
3. the alert, backspace, and carriage return characaters

The null character is used to mark the end of strings; the newline character is used to divide character streams into lines during input/output. (It must appear to the programmer as if this newline character were actually present in text streams in the execution environment. However, the run-time library implementation is free to simulate them. For instance, newlines could be converted to end-of-record indications on output, and end-of-record indications could be turned into newlines on input.)

As with the source character set, it is common for the execution character set to include the formatting characters backspace, horizontal tab, vertical tab, form feed, and carriage return. Special escape sequences are provided to represent these characters in the source program.

These source and execution character sets are the same when a C program is compiled and executed on the same computer. However, occasionally programs are cross-compiled; that is, compiled on one computer (the host) and executed on another computer (the target). When a compiler calculates the compile-time value of a constant expression involving characters, it must use the target computer's encoding, not the more natural (to the compiler writer) source encoding.

References character constants 2.7.3; character encoding 2.1.3; character set 2.1; constant expressions 7.11; escape characters 2.7.5; text streams Ch. 15

2.1.2 Whitespace and Line Termination

In C source programs the blank (space), end-of-line, vertical tab, form feed, and horizontal tab (if present) are known collectively as whitespace characters. (Comments, discussed below, are also whitespace.) These characters are ignored except insofar as they are used to separate adjacent tokens or when they appear in character or string constants. Whitespace characters may be used to lay out the C program in a way that is pleasing to a human reader.

The end-of-line character or character sequence marks the end of source program lines. In some implementations, the formatting characters carriage return, form feed, and (or) vertical tab additionally terminate source lines and are called line break characters. Line termination is important for the recognition of preprocessor control lines. The character following a line break character is considered to be the first character of the next line. If the first character is itself a line break character, then another (empty) line is terminated, and so forth.

A source line can be continued onto the next line by ending the first line with a backslash (\) character or with the ISO C trigraph `??/`. The backslash and end-of-line marker are removed to create a longer, *logical source line*. This convention has always been valid in preprocessor command lines and within string constants, where it is most useful and portable. ISO C, and many non-ISO implementations, generalize it to apply to any source program line. This splicing of source lines conceptually occurs before preprocessing and before the lexical analysis of the C program.

Example

Even tokens may be split across lines in ISO C. The two lines:

```
if (a==b) x=1; el\
se x=2;
```

are equivalent to the single line

```
if (a==b) x=1; else x=2;
```

If an implementation treats any nonstandard source characters as whitespace or line breaks, it should handle them exactly as it does blanks and end-of-line markers, respectively. ISO C suggests that an implementation do this by translating all such characters to some canonical representation as the first action when reading the source program. However, programmers should probably beware of relying on this by, for example, expecting a backslash followed by a form feed to be eliminated.

Most C implementations impose a limit on the maximum length of source lines both before and after splicing continuation lines. ISO C requires implementations to permit logical source lines of at least 509 characters.

References character constants 2.7.3; preprocessor lexical conventions 3.2; string constants 2.7.4; tokens 2.3; trigraphs 2.1.4

2.1.3 Character Encoding

Each character in a computer's (execution) character set will have some conventional encoding—that is, some numerical representation on the computer. This encoding is important because C converts characters to integers, and the values of the integers are the conventional encoding of the characters. All of the standard characters listed earlier must have distinct, nonnegative integer encoding.

A common C programming error is to assume a particular encoding is in use when, in fact, another one holds.

Example

The C expression `'Z'-'A'+1` computes one more than the difference between the encoding of `Z` and `A` and might be expected to yield the number of characters in the alphabet. Indeed, under the ASCII character set encoding the result is 26, but under the EBCDIC encoding, in which the alphabet is not encoded consecutively, the result is 41.

References source and execution character sets 2.1.1

2.1.4 Trigraphs

A set of trigraphs is included in ISO C so that C programs may be written using only the ISO 646-1083 Invariant Code Set, a subset of the seven-bit ASCII code set and a code set that is common to ISO 646 national character sets. The trigraphs, introduced by two consecutive question mark characters, are listed in Table 2–2. (Trigraphs are not customary in non-ISO compilers.) Amendment 1 to ISO C also provides for respelling of some tokens (section 2.4.1).

Table 2–2 ISO trigraphs

Trigraph	Replaces	Trigraph	Replaces
`??(`	`[`	`??)`	`]`
`??<`	`{`	`??>`	`}`
`??/`	`\`	`??!`	`|`
`??'`	`^`	`??-`	`~`
`??=`	`#`		

The translation of trigraphs in the source program occurs before lexical analysis (tokenization) and before the recognition of escape characters in string and character constants. Only these exact nine trigraphs are recognized; all other character sequences (e.g., **`??&`**) are left untranslated. A new character escape, **`\?`**, is available to prevent the interpretation of trigraph-like character sequences.

Example

If you want a string to contain a 3-character sequence that would ordinarily be interpreted as a trigraph, you must use the backlash escape character to quote at least one of the trigraph characters. Therefore, the string constant **`"What?\?!"`** actually represents a string containing the characters **`What??!`**.

To write a string constant containing a single backslash character, you must write two consecutive backslashes. (The first quotes the second.) Then, each of the backslashes can be translated to the trigraph equivalent. Therefore, the string constant **`"??/??/"`** represents a string containing the single character **`\`**.

References character set 2.1; escape characters 2.7.5; string concatenation 2.7.4; token respellings 2.4.1

2.1.5 Multibyte Characters and Wide Characters

In order to accommodate foreign alphabets that may contain a very large number of characters, ISO C introduces wide characters and wide strings. In order to represent wide characters and strings in the external, byte-oriented world, the concept of multibyte characters is introduced. Amendment 1 to ISO C expands the facilities for dealing with wide characters and multibyte characters.

Wide characters and strings A *wide character* is a binary representation of an element of an *extended character set*. It has the integer type **`wchar_t`** declared in header file **`stddef.h`**. Amendment 1 to ISO C adds type **`wint_t`**, must be able to represent all values of type **`wchar_t`**, plus except an additional, distinguished, non-wide character value denoted **`WEOF`**. ISO C does not specify any encoding for wide characters, but the value zero is reserved as a "null wide character." Wide-character constants can be specified with special character constants (section 2.7.3).

Example

> It is typical for a wide character to occupy 16 bits, so **`wchar_t`** could be represented as **`short`** or **`unsigned short`** on a 32-bit computer. If **`wchar_t`** were **`short`**, and the value –1 were not a valid wide character, then **`wint_t`** could be **`short`** and **`WEOF`** could be –1. However, it's more typical for **`wint_t`** to be **`int`** or **`unsigned int`**.
>
> If an implementor chooses not to support an extended character set—which is common among the U.S. C vendors—then **`wchar_t`** can be defined as **`char`**, and the "extended character set" is the same as the normal character set.

A *wide string* is a contiguous sequence of wide characters, ending with a null wide character. The *null wide character* is the wide character whose representation is 0. Other than this null wide character, and the existence of **`WEOF`**, ISO C does not specify the encoding of the extended character set. Wide-string constants can be specified with special string constants (section 2.7.4).

Multibyte characters Wide characters may be manipulated as units within a C program, but most external media (e.g., files), and the C source program itself, are based on byte-sized characters. Programmers experienced with extended character sets have devised *multibyte encoding*, which are locale-specific ways to map between a sequence of byte-sized characters and a sequence of wide characters.

A *multibyte character* is the representation of a wide character in either the source or execution character set. (There may be different encoding for each.) A multibyte string is therefore a normal C string, but whose characters can be interpreted as a series of multibyte characters. The form of multibyte characters and the mapping between multibyte characters and wide characters is implementation-defined. This mapping is performed for wide-character and wide-string constants at compile time, and the standard library provides functions that perform this mapping at run time.

Multibyte characters might use a *state-dependent encoding*, in which the interpretation of a multibyte character may depend on the occurrence of previous multibyte characters. Typically such an encoding makes use of *shift characters*, control characters which are part of a multibyte character and which alter the interpretation of the current and subsequent characters. The current interpretation within a sequence of multibyte characters is called the *conversion state* (or *shift state*) of the encoding. There is always a distinguished, *initial conversion (shift) state* that is used when starting a conversion of a sequence of multibyte characters, and which frequently is returned to at the end of the conversion.

Example

> *Encoding A*—a hypothetical encoding that we will use in examples—is state-dependent, with two shift states, "up" and "down." The character ↑ changes the shift state to "up" and the character ↓ changes it to "down." In the down state, which is the initial state, all non-shift characters have their normal interpretation. In the up state, each multibyte character consist of a pair of alphanumeric characters that define a wide character in a manner that we do not specify.

The following sequences of characters each contain three multibyte characters under Encoding A, beginning in the initial shift state.

abc **ab↑e3** **↑ab↓b↑23** **↓a↓b↓c**

The last string includes shift characters that are not strictly necessary. If redundant shift sequences are permitted, multibyte characters may become arbitrarily long, e.g., ↓↓...↓**x**. Unless you know what the shift state is at the start of a sequence of multibyte characters, you cannot parse a sequence like **abcdef**, which could represent either three or six wide characters.

The sequence **ab↑?x** is invalid under Encoding A because a nonalphanumeric character appears while in the up shift state. The sequence **a↑b** is invalid because the last multibyte character ends prematurely.

Multibyte characters might also use a *state-independent encoding*, in which the interpretation of a multibyte character does not depend on previous multibyte characters. (Although you may have to look at a multibyte sequence from the beginning in order to locate the beginning of a multibyte character in the middle of a string.) For example, the syntax of C's escape characters (section 2.7.5) represents a state-independent encoding for type **char**, since the backslash character (****) changes the interpretation of one or more following characters to form a single value of type **char**.

Example

Encoding B—another hypothetical encoding—is state-independent, and uses a single special character, which we will denote ∇, to change the meaning of the following nonnull character. The following sequences each contain three multibyte characters under Encoding B:

abc **∇a∇b∇c** **∇∇∇∇∇∇** **a∇bc**

On the other hand, the sequence ∇∇∇ is not valid under Encoding B, because a nonnull character is missing at the end.

ISO C places some restrictions on multibyte characters:

1. All characters from the standard character set must be present in the encoding.
2. In the initial shift state, all single-byte characters from the standard character set retain their normal interpretation and do not affect the shift state.
3. A byte containing all zeroes is taken to be the null character regardless of shift state. No multibyte character can use a byte containing all zeroes as its second or subsequent character.

Together, these rules ensure that multibyte sequences can be processed as normal C strings (e.g., they will not contain embedded null characters), and that a C string without special multibyte codes will have the expected interpretation as a multibyte sequence.

Source and execution uses of multibyte characters Multibyte characters may appear in comments, preprocessor header names, string constants, and character constants. They are written with characters from the source character set. Each comment, header name, string constant, or character constant must begin and end in the initial shift state, and must consist of a valid sequence of multibyte characters.

Example

A Japanese text editor might allow Japanese characters to be written in string constants and comments. When the text was written to a file, the Japanese characters would be translated to multibyte sequences, which would be acceptable to—and, in the case of string constants, understood by—an appropriate ISO C implementation.

During processing, characters appearing in string constants and character constants are translated to the execution character set before they are interpreted as multibyte sequences. Therefore, escape sequences (section 2.7.5) can be used in forming multibyte characters. Comments are removed from a program before this stage, so escape sequences in multibyte comments may not be meaningful.

Example

If the source and execution character sets are the same, and if `'a'` has the value 141_8 in the execution character set, then the string constant `"∇aa"` contains the same two multibyte characters as `"∇\141\141"` (Encoding B).

References character constant 2.7.3; comments 2.2; multibyte conversion facilities 11.7, 11.8; string constants 2.7.4; `wchar_t` 11.1; `WEOF` 11.1; wide character 2.7.3; wide string 2.7.4; `wint_t` 11.1

2.2 COMMENTS

A comment in a C program begins with an occurrence of the two characters `/*`—not within a character or string constant—and ends with the first subsequent occurrence of the two characters `*/`. Comments may contain any number of (multibyte) characters and are always treated as whitespace.

Example

The following program contains six valid C comments:

```
/*******************************************/
/*/ Program to compute the squares of    /*/
/*/ the first 10 integers                /*/
/*******************************************/
void Squares()   /* no arguments */
{
    int i;
    /*
        Loop from 1 to 10,
        printing out the squares
    */
    for (i=1; i<=10; i++)
        printf("%d squared is %d\n",i,i*i);
}
```

Comments are removed by the compiler before preprocessing or lexical analysis, so line breaks inside comments do not terminate preprocessor commands.

Example

The two **#define** commands below have the same effect:

```
#define ten (2*5)

#define ten /* ten:
               one greater than nine
            */ (2*5)
```

ISO C specifies that all comments are to be replaced by a single space character for the purposes of further translation of the C program, but many current implementations do not insert any white space. This affects the behavior of the preprocessor and is discussed in section 3.3.9.

A few non-ISO C implementations implement "nestable comments," in which each occurrence of **/*** inside a comment must be balanced by a subsequent ***/**. This implementation is not standard, and programmers should not depend on it. For a program to be acceptable to both implementations of comments, no comment should contain the character sequence **/*** inside it.

Example

To cause the compiler to ignore large parts of a C program, it is best to enclose the parts to be removed with the preprocessor commands

```
#if 0
...
#endif
```

rather than to insert comment delimiters. This avoids having to worry about comments in the enclosed source text (unless the comments span the preprocessor commands).

References **#if** preprocessor command 3.5.1; preprocessor lexical conventions 3.2; whitespace 2.1

2.3 TOKENS

The characters making up a C program are collected into lexical tokens according to the rules presented in the rest of this chapter. There are five classes of tokens: operators, separators, identifiers, reserved words, and constants.

The compiler always forms the longest tokens possible as it collects characters in left-to-right order, even if the result does not make a valid C program. Adjacent tokens may be separated by whitespace characters or comments. To prevent confusion, an identifier, reserved word, integer constant, or floating-point constant must always be so separated from a following identifier, reserved word, integer constant, or floating-point constant.

The preprocessor has slightly different token conventions. In particular, the ISO C preprocessor treats **#** and **##** as tokens; they would be invalid in traditional C.

Example

Characters	C Tokens
`forwhile`	`forwhile`
`b>x`	`b`, `>`, `x`
`b->x`	`b`, `->`, `x`
`b--x`	`b`, `--`, `x`
`b---x`	`b`, `--`, `-`, `x`

In the fourth example, the sequence of characters `b--x` is invalid C syntax. The tokenization `b`, `-`, `-`, `x` would be valid syntax, but that tokenization is not permitted.

References comments 2.2; constants 2.7; identifiers 2.5; preprocessor tokens 3.2; reserved words 2.6; token merging 3.3.9; whitespace characters 2.1

2.4 OPERATORS AND SEPARATORS

The operator and separator (punctuator) tokens in C are usefully divided into several groups, as shown in Table 2–3.

Table 2–3 Operators and separators

<table>
<tr><th>Token class</th><th>Tokens</th></tr>
<tr><td>Simple operators</td><td><code>! % ^ & * - + =</code>
<code>~ | . < > / ?</code></td></tr>
<tr><td>Compound assignment operators</td><td><code>+= -= *= /= %=</code>
<code><<= >>= &= ^= |=</code></td></tr>
<tr><td>Other compound operators</td><td><code>-> ++ -- << >></code>
<code><= >= == != && ||</code></td></tr>
<tr><td>Other separator characters</td><td><code>( ) [ ] { } , ; :</code></td></tr>
</table>

In traditional C, the compound assignment operators are considered to be two separate tokens—an operator and the equals sign—which can be separated by whitespace. In ISO C the operators are single tokens.

References compound assignment operators 7.9.2

2.4.1 Token Respellings

Amendment 1 to ISO C provides six new tokens that are convenient when writing source programs in restricted character sets (such as the ISO 646-1083 Invariant Code Set). The respellings (Table 2–4) are more readable than the equivalent form using trigraphs, and they may be used wherever the customary tokens are permitted.

Table 2–4 ISO C Amendment 1 token respellings

Respelling	Traditional	Respelling	Traditional
`<:`	`[`	`<%`	`{`
`:>`	`]`	`%>`	`}`
`%:`	`#`[a]	`%:%:`	`##`[a]

[a] Preprocessor token

In rare circumstances, the addition of the `%:` and `%:%:` preprocessing tokens can change the meaning of pre-Amendment programs. For example, the preprocessor command `#include <:file:>` would be interpreted as specifying a file named "`:file:`" in a pre-Amendment program, but it would be considered ill-formed by an implementation conforming to the Amendment.

In addition to the new tokens, Amendment 1 specifies a new header file, `iso646.h`, which introduces macros that rename these operators:

```
&&   &=   &   |   ~   !   !=   ||   |=   ^   ^=
```

References `iso646.h` 11.9; preprocessor tokens 3.2; trigraphs 2.1.4

2.5 IDENTIFIERS

An identifier, or *name*, is a sequence of letters, digits, and underscores. An identifier must not begin with a digit, and it must not have the same spelling as a reserved word:

identifier :
    underscore
    letter
    identifier following-character

following-character :
    letter
    underscore
    digit

letter : one of

```
A B C D E F G H I J K L M
N O P Q R S T U V W X Y Z
a b c d e f g h i j k l m
n o p q r s t u v w x y z
```

underscore :

```
_
```

digit : one of

```
0 1 2 3 4 5 6 7 8 9
```

Two identifiers are the same when they are spelled identically, including the case of all letters. That is, the identifiers **abc** and **aBc** are distinct.

In addition to avoiding the spelling of the reserved words, a C programmer must guard against inadvertently duplicating a name used in the standard libraries. ISO C specifically reserves these identifiers for their indicated uses, and further reserves for implementations all names beginning with an underscore; programmers should avoid creating such identifiers.

The original description of C specified that two identifiers spelled identically up to the first eight characters would be considered the same even if they differed in subsequent characters. ISO C requires implementations to permit a minimum of 31 significant characters in identifiers. This limit is met or exceeded by many non-ISO C implementations.

Example

In a pre-ISO implementation that limited the length of identifiers to 8 characters, the identifiers **countless** and **countlessone** would be considered the same identifier.

Longer names tend to improve program clarity and thus reduce errors. The use of underscores and mixed letter case make long identifiers more readable:

```
averylongidentifer
AVeryLongIdentifier
a_very_long_identifier
```

An external identifier—one declared with storage class **extern**—may be subject to additional restrictions on particular computer systems. These identifiers have to be processed by other software, such as debuggers and linkers, which may have more restrictive limits on identifiers. ISO C states that implementations must consider as unique those external identifiers whose spellings differ in the first six characters, *not* counting letter case. (Notice is also given that future versions of the standard could increase this limit.) However, by far the majority of implementations allow external names of at least 31 characters.

Example

When a C compiler permits long internal identifiers but the target computer requires short external names, the preprocessor may be used to hide these short names. In the code below, an external error-handling function has the short and somewhat obscure name **eh73**, but the function is referred to by the more readable name **error_handler**. This is done by making **error_handler** a preprocessor macro that expands to the name **eh73**.

```
#define error_handler eh73
extern void error_handler();
...
error_handler("nil pointer error");
```

Some compilers permit characters other than those specified above to be used in identifiers. The dollar sign (**$**) is often allowed in identifiers so that programs can access special non-C library functions provided by some computing systems.

References **#define** command 3.3; external names 4.2.9; **extern** storage class 4.3; reserved words 2.6

2.6 RESERVED WORDS

The identifiers listed in Table 2–5 have been reserved in various versions of the C language and must not be used as program identifiers when they are reserved. Some C

Table 2–5 C reserved words

asm[a]	default	float	register	switch
auto	do	for	return	typedef
break	double	fortran[a]	short	union
case	else	goto	signed[b]	unsigned
char	entry[a]	if	sizeof	void[c]
const[b]	enum[c]	int	static	volatile[b]
continue	extern	long	struct	while

[a] Traditionally reserved, but omitted from ISO C.
[b] New to ISO C.
[c] In most modern compilers, and ISO C.

implementations have additional reserved words, but this is not permitted in ISO conforming implementations, because it could cause a conforming program to become invalid. A reserved word may be used as a preprocessor macro name, although doing so is usually poor style.

Example

The following code is one of the few cases in which using a macro with the same spelling as a reserved word is useful. The definition allows the use of **void** in a program built with a non-ISO compiler.

```
#ifndef __STDC__
#define void int
#endif
```

References **#define** command 3.3; identifiers 2.5; **#ifndef** command 3.5; **__STDC__** 11.3; **void** type specifier 5.9

2.7 CONSTANTS

The lexical class of constants includes four different kinds of constants: integers, floating-point numbers, characters, and strings:

constant :
integer-constant
floating-constant
character-constant
string-constant

Such tokens are called literals in other languages, to distinguish them from objects whose values are constant (that is, not changing) but that do not belong to lexically distinct classes. An example of these latter objects in C is enumeration constants, which belong to the lexical class of identifiers. In this book, we use the traditional C terminology of "constant" for both cases.

Every constant is characterized by a value and a type. The formats of the various kinds of constants are described in the following sections.

References character constant 2.7.3; enumeration constants 5.5; floating-point constant 2.7.2; integer constant 2.7.1; string constant 2.7.4; tokens 2.3; value 7.3

2.7.1 Integer Constants

Integer constants may be specified in decimal, octal, or hexadecimal notation:

integer-constant :
decimal-constant integer-suffix$_{opt}$
octal-constant integer-suffix$_{opt}$
hexadecimal-constant integer-suffix$_{opt}$

decimal-constant :
nonzero-digit
decimal-constant digit

octal-constant :
0
octal-constant octal-digit

hexadecimal-constant :
  0x *hex-digit*
  0X *hex-digit*
  hexadecimal-constant hex-digit

digit : one of
  0 1 2 3 4 5 6 7 8 9

nonzero-digit : one of
  1 2 3 4 5 6 7 8 9

octal-digit : one of
  0 1 2 3 4 5 6 7

hex-digit : one of
  0 1 2 3 4 5 6 7 8 9
  A B C D E F a b c d e f

integer-suffix :
  long-suffix unsigned-suffix$_{opt}$
  unsigned-suffix long-suffix$_{opt}$

long-suffix : one of
  l L

unsigned-suffix : one of (ISO C)
  u U

These are the rules for determining the radix of an integer constant:

1. If the integer constant begins with the letters **0x** or **0X**, then it is in hexadecimal notation, with the characters **a** through **f** (or **A** through **F**) representing 10 through 15.
2. Otherwise, if it begins with the digit **0**, then it is in octal notation.
3. Otherwise, it is in decimal notation.

An integer constant may be immediately followed by the one of the letters **l** or **L** to indicate a constant of type **long**. (The lowercase letter **l** can be easily confused with the digit **1** and should be avoided.) ISO C also permits the suffix letters **u** or **U** to indicate an unsigned constant. Originally, C also allowed the digits **8** and **9** in octal constants, but they are invalid in ISO C.

The type of an integer constant depends on its size, on its radix, on whether a suffix letter is present, and on type representation decisions made by the particular C implementation. Furthermore, the rules for determining the type are different in ISO C. Both the traditional and new rules are shown in Table 2–6.

The value of an integer constant is always nonnegative in the absence of overflow. If there is a preceding minus sign, it is taken to be a unary operator applied to the constant, not part of the constant itself.

Table 2–6 Types of integer constants

Constant	Conventional type[a]	ISO C type[a]

dd...d	`int`
	`long int`
		`int`
		`long int`
		`unsigned long int`

0dd...d
0Xdd...d
	`unsigned int`
	`long int`
		`int`
		`unsigned int`
		`long int`
		`unsigned long int`

dd...dU 0dd...dU 0Xdd...dU	*not applicable*	`unsigned int` `unsigned long int`
dd...dL 0dd...dL 0Xdd...dL	`long int`	`long int` `unsigned long int`
dd...dUL 0dd...dUL 0Xdd...dUL	*not applicable*	`unsigned long int`

[a] The chosen type is the first one from the appropriate group that can represent the value of the constant without overflow.

The ISO C rules differ subtly from those found in most current implementations: under the new rules constants without suffixes may have an unsigned type and therefore force expressions to use unsigned arithmetic.

Example

If type **`long`** has a 32-bit, two's-complement representation, the following program determines the rules in effect:

```
#define K 0xFFFFFFFF /* -1 in 32-bit, 2's compl. */
int main()
{
    if (0<K) printf("K is unsigned (ISO C)\n");
    else printf("K is signed (traditional C)\n");
    return 0;
}
```

To illustrate some of the subtleties of integer constants, assume that in some implementation type **`int`** uses a 16-bit two's-complement representation, and that type **`long`** uses a 32-bit two's-complement representation. We list in Table 2–7 some interesting integer constants, their true mathematical values, their types—conventional and under the ISO rules—and the actual C representation used to store the constant.

If the value of an integer constant exceeds the largest integer representable in type **`unsigned long`**, the result is undefined. Many C compilers will silently substitute another value for the constant. In ISO C, integer type representational information is provided in the header file **`limits.h`**.

Table 2–7 Assignment of types to integer constants

C constant notation	True value	Conventional type	ISO C type	Actual representation
`0`	0	`int`	`int`	`0`
`32767`	$2^{15}-1$	`int`	`int`	`0x7FFF`
`077777`	$2^{15}-1$	`int`	`int`	`0x7FFF`
`32768`	2^{15}	`long int`	`long int`	`0x00008000`
`0100000`	2^{15}	`int`[a]	`unsigned int`	`0x8000`
`65535`	$2^{16}-1$	`long int`	`long int`	`0x0000FFFF`
`0xFFFF`	$2^{16}-1$	`int`[a]	`unsigned int`	`0xFFFF`
`65536`	2^{16}	`long int`	`long int`	`0x0001FFFF`
`0x10000`	2^{16}	`long int`	`long int`	`0x0001FFFF`
`2147483647`	$2^{31}-1$	`long int`	`long int`	`0x7FFFFFFF`
`0x7FFFFFFF`	$2^{31}-1$	`long int`	`long int`	`0x7FFFFFFF`
`2147483648`	2^{31}	`long int`[a]	`unsigned long int`	`0x80000000`
`0x80000000`	2^{31}	`long int`	`unsigned long int`	`0x80000000`
`4294967295`	$2^{32}-1$	`long int`[a]	`unsigned long int`	`0xFFFFFFFF`[a]
`0xFFFFFFFF`	$2^{32}-1$	`long int`[a]	`unsigned long int`	`0xFFFFFFFF`
`4294967296`	2^{32}	undefined	undefined	`0`
`0x100000000`	2^{32}	undefined	undefined	`0`

[a] This type cannot represent the value, causing overflow.

An interesting point to note from this table is that integers in the range 2^{15} through $2^{16}-1$ will have positive values when written as decimal constants but negative values when written as octal or hexadecimal constants (and cast to type **`int`**). In spite of these anomalies, the programmer will rarely be "surprised" by the values of integer constants because the representation of the constants is the same even though the type is in question.

References conversions of integer types 6.2.3; integer types 5.1; **`limits.h`** 5.1.1; overflow 7.2.2; unary minus operator 7.5.3; unsigned integers 5.1.2

2.7.2 Floating-point Constants

Floating-point constants may be written with a decimal point, a signed exponent, or both. A floating-point constant is always interpreted to be in decimal radix. ISO C allows a suffix letter (*floating-suffix*) to designate constants of types **`float`** and **`long double`**. Without a suffix the type of the constant is **`double`**:

floating-constant :
  digit-sequence exponent floating-suffix$_{opt}$
  dotted-digits exponent$_{opt}$ *floating-suffix*$_{opt}$

floating-suffix : one of (ISO only)
f F l L

exponent :
e *sign-part*$_{opt}$ *digit-sequence*
E *sign-part*$_{opt}$ *digit-sequence*

sign-part : one of
+ -

dotted-digits :
digit-sequence **.**
digit-sequence **.** *digit-sequence*
. *digit-sequence*

digit-sequence :
digit
digit digit-sequence

digit : one of
0 1 2 3 4 5 6 7 8 9

The value of a floating-point constant is always nonnegative in the absence of overflow. If there is a preceding minus sign, it is taken to be a unary operator applied to the constant, not part of the constant itself. If the magnitude of the floating-point constant is too great or too small to be represented, the result is unpredictable. Some compilers will warn the programmer of the problem, but most will silently substitute some other value that can be represented. In ISO C the floating-point limits are recorded in the header file **float.h**.

Example

These are valid floating-point constants: **0.**, **3e1**, **3.14159**, **.0**, **1.0E-3**, **1e-3**, **1.0**, **.00034**, **2e+9**. These additional floating-point constants are valid in ISO C: **1.0f**, **1.0e67L**, **0E1L**.

References **double** type 5.2; **float.h** 5.2; overflow and underflow 7.2.2; sizes of floating-point types 5.2; unary minus operator 7.5.3

2.7.3 Character Constants

A character constant is written by enclosing one or more characters in apostrophes. A special escape mechanism is provided to write characters or numeric values that would be inconvenient or impossible to enter directly in the source program. ISO C allows the character constant to be preceded by the letter **L** to specify a wide character constant:

character-constant :
' *c-char-sequence* **'**
L' *c-char-sequence* **'** (ISO C)

c-char-sequence :
    c-char
    c-char-sequence c-char

c-char :
    any source character except the apostrophe (`'`), backslash (`\`), or newline
    escape-character

The apostrophe, backslash, and newline characters may be included in character constants by using escape characters, as described in section 2.7.5. It is a good idea to use escapes for any character that might not be easily readable in the source program, such as the formatting characters. Character constants containing more than a single character or escape are called multibyte characters.

Character constants not preceded by the letter **L** have type **int**. It is typical for such a character constant to be a single character or escape code (section 2.7.7), and the value of the constant is the integer encoding of the corresponding character in the target character set or the value of the numeric escape code. The resulting integer value is computed as if it had been converted from an object of type **char**. For example, if type **char** were an 8-bit signed type, the character constant **'\377'** would undergo sign extension and thus have the value **-1**. The value of a character constant is implementation-defined if:

1. there is no corresponding character in the target character set,
2. more than a single character appears in the constant, or
3. a numeric escape has a value not represented in the target character set.

Example

Here are some examples of single-character constants along with their (decimal) values under the ASCII encoding.

Character	Value	Character	Value
`'a'`	97	`'A'`	65
`' '`	32	`'?'`	63
`'\r'`	13	`'\0'`	0
`'"'`	34	`'\377'`	255
`'%'`	37	`'\23'`	19
`'8'`	56	`'\\'`	92

ISO C wide character constants, designated by the prefix letter **L**, have type **wchar_t**, an integral type defined in the ISO C header file **stddef.h**. Their purpose is to allow C programmers to express characters in alphabets (e.g., Japanese) that are too large to be represented by type **char**. Wide character constants typically consist of a sequence of characters and escape codes that together form a single multibyte character. The mapping from the multibyte character to the corresponding wide character is implementation-defined. (The **mbtowc** function performs that conversion at run time.) The value of a wide character constant is implementation-defined if it contains more than a single multibyte character. If multibyte characters use a shift-state encoding, then the wide character constant must begin and end in the initial shift state.

Multicharacter constants Some C implementations permit character constants that contain more than a single character. (In ISO C, this is permitted and its effect is implementation-defined.) Since most computers represent integers in a storage area big enough to hold several characters, character constants such as **`'ABCD'`** can be a convenient way to specify a complete integer. The use of this feature, if available, can result in portability problems, not only because integers have different sizes on different computers but also because computers differ in their "byte ordering," that is, the order in which characters are packed into words.

Example

> In an ASCII implementation with 4-byte integers and left-to-right packing, the value of **`'ABCD'`** would be 41424344_{16}. (The value of **`'A'`** is **`0x41`**, **`'B'`** is **`0x42`**, etc.) However, if right-to-left packing were used, the value of **`'ABCD'`** would be 44434241_{16}.

References ASCII characters App. A; byte order 6.1.2; character encoding 2.1; **`char`** type 5.1.3; escape characters 2.7.5; formatting characters 2.1; **`mbtowc`** facility 11.7; multibyte characters 2.1.5; **`wchar_t`** 11.1

2.7.4 String Constants

A string constant is a (possibly empty) sequence of characters enclosed in double quotes. The same escape mechanism provided for character constants can be used to express the characters in the string:

string-constant :
  `"` *s-char-sequence*$_{opt}$ **`"`**
  `L"` *s-char-sequence*$_{opt}$ **`"`** (ISO C)

s-char-sequence :
  s-char
  s-char-sequence s-char

s-char :
  any source character except the double quote **`"`**,
    backslash **`\`**, or newline character
  escape-character

The double quote, backslash, and newline characters may be included in character constants by using escape characters, as described in section 2.7.5. It is a good idea to use escapes for any character that might not be easily readable in the source program, such as the formatting characters.

Example

Five string constants are listed below.

```
""
"\""
"Total expenditures: "
"Copyright 1994 \
Tartan, Inc. "
"Comments begin with '/*'.\n"
```

The fourth string above is the same as `"Copyright 1994 Tartan, Inc."`; it does not contain a newline character.

For each string constant of n characters (not prefixed by the letter `L`) there will be at run time a statically allocated block of $n+1$ characters whose first n characters are initialized with the characters from the string and whose last character is the null character, `'\0'`. This block is the "value" of the string constant, and its type is "`char [`*n*`+1]`."

Example

The `sizeof` operator returns the size of its argument, whereas the `strlen` function (section 13.4) returns the number of characters in a string. Therefore, `sizeof("abcdef")` is 7, not 6, and `sizeof("")` is 1, not 0. On the other hand, `strlen("abcdef")` is 6 and `strlen("")` is 0.

If a string constant appears anywhere except as an argument to `sizeof` or as an initializer of a character array, then the conversions that are usually applied to arrays come into play, and those conversions change the string from an array of characters to a pointer to the first character in the string, which has type "`char *`" or "pointer to `char`."

Example

This conversion means that strings can and do appear in contexts that require character pointers. The declaration `char *p = "abcdef";` results in the pointer `p` being initialized with the address a block of memory in which are stored the seven characters `'a'`, `'b'`, `'c'`, `'d'`, `'e'`, `'f'`, and `'\0'`, respectively.

The value of a single-character string constant and the value of a character constant are quite different. The declaration `int X = (int) "A";` results in `X` being initialized with (the integer value of) a pointer to a two-character block of memory containing `'A'` and `'\0'`; but the declaration `int Y = (int) 'A';` results in `Y` being initialized with the character code for `'A'` (`0x41` in the ISO 646 and ASCII encoding).

Storage for string constants You should never attempt to modify the memory that holds the characters of a string constant, since that memory may be "read-only," that is, physically protected against modification. Some functions (e.g., `mktemp`) expect to be passed pointers to strings that will be modified in place; do not pass string constants to those functions. Instead, initialize an array of characters to the contents of the string constant and pass the address of the array.

Example

Consider these three declarations:

```
char p1[]        = "Always writable";
char *p2         = "Possibly not writable";
const char p3[] = "Never writable"; /* ISO C only */
```

The values of **p1**, **p2**, and **p3** are all strings (pointers to character arrays), but they differ in their writability. The assignment **p1[0]='x'** will always work; **p2[0]='x'** may work, or may cause a run-time error; and **p3[0]='x'** will always cause a compile-time error, because of the meaning of **const**.

Also, do not depend on all string constants being stored at different addresses. ISO C allows implementations to use the same storage for two strings that contain the same characters. Older C implementations traditionally have allocated a distinct block of storage for every string constant.

Example

Here is a simple program that discriminates the various implementations of strings. The assignment to **string1[0]** could cause a runtime error if string constants are allocated in read-only memory.

```
char *string1, *string2;
int main() {
    string1 = "abcd"; string2 = "abcd";
    if (string1==string2) printf("Strings are shared.\n");
    else printf("Strings are not shared.\n");
    string1[0] = '1'; /* RUN-TIME ERROR POSSIBLE */
    if (*string1=='1') printf("Strings writable\n");
    else printf("Strings are not writable\n");
    return 0;
}
```

Continuation of strings A string constant is normally written on one source program line. If a string is too long to fit conveniently on one line, all but the final source lines containing the string can be ended with a backslash character, ****, in which case the backslash and end-of-line character(s) are ignored. This allows string constants to be written on more than one line. (Some older implementations also remove leading whitespace characters from the continuation line, although it is incorrect to do so.)

ISO C automatically concatenates adjacent string constants and adjacent wide string constants, placing a single null character at the end of the last string. Therefore, an alternative to using the **** continuation mechanism in ISO C programs is to break a long string into separate strings. A wide string constant and a normal string constant cannot be concatenated in this way.

Example

The string initializing **s1** is acceptable to ISO and pre-ISO C compilers, but the string initializing **s2** is allowed only in ISO C:

```
char s1[] = "This long string is acc\
eptable to all C compilers.";
char s2[] = "This long string is permissible "
            "in ISO C.";
```

A newline character (i.e., the end of line in the execution character set) may be inserted into a string by putting the escape sequence **\n** in the string constant; this should not be confused with line continuation within a string constant.

Wide strings A string constant prefixed by the letter **L** is an ISO C wide string constant and is of type "array of **wchar_t**." It represents a sequence of wide characters from an extended target character set, such as might be used for a language like Japanese. The characters in the wide string constant are a multibyte character string, which is mapped to a sequence of wide characters in an implementation-defined manner. (The **mbstowcs** function performs a similar function at run time.) If multibyte characters use a shift-state encoding, the wide string constant must start and end in the initial shift state.

References array types 5.4; **const** type specifier 4.4.4; versions from array types 6.2.7; escape characters 2.7.5; initializers 4.6; **mbstowcs** facility 11.8; **mktemp** facility 15.16; multibyte characters 2.1.5; pointer types 5.3; preprocessor lexical conventions 3.2; **sizeof** operator 7.5.2; **strlen** facility 13.4; whitespace characters 2.1; usual unary conversions 6.3.3, **wchar_t** 11.1

2.7.5 Escape Characters

Escape characters can be used in character and string constants to represent characters that would be awkward or impossible to enter in the source program directly. The escape characters come in two varieties: "character escapes," which can be used to represent some particular formatting and special characters, and "numeric escapes," which allow a character to be specified by its numeric encoding:

escape-character :
  **** *escape-code*

escape-code :
  character-escape-code
  octal-escape-code
  hex-escape-code (ISO C)

character-escape-code : one of
  n t b r f
  v \\ ' "
  a ? (ISO C)

octal-escape-code :
  octal-digit
  octal-digit octal-digit
  octal-digit octal-digit octal-digit

hex-escape-code :
  x *hex-digit*
  hex-escape-code hex-digit (ISO C)

The meanings of these escapes are discussed in the following sections.

If the character following the backslash is neither an octal digit, the letter **x**, nor one of the character escape codes listed above, the result is undefined. (In traditional C, the backslash was ignored.) In ISO C, all lowercase letters following the backslash are reserved for future language extensions. Uppercase letters may be used for implementation-specific extensions.

2.7.6 Character Escape Codes

Character escape codes are used to represent some common special characters in a fashion that is independent of the target computer character set. The characters that may follow the backslash, and their meanings, are listed in Table 2–8.

Table 2–8 Character escape codes

Escape code	Translation	Escape code	Translation
a[a]	alert (e.g., bell)	**v**	vertical tab
b	backspace	****	backslash
f	form feed	**'**	single quote
n	newline	**"**	double quote
r	carriage return	**?**[a]	question mark
t	horizontal tab		

[a] ISO C addition.

The code **\a** is typically mapped to a "bell" or other audible signal on the output device (e.g., ASCII control-G, whose value is 7). The **\?** escape is needed to obtain a question mark character in the rare circumstances in which it might be mistaken as part of a trigraph.

The quotation mark (**"**) may appear without a preceding backslash in character constants, and the apostrophe (**'**) may appear without a backslash in string constants.

Example

To show how the character escapes can be used, here is a small program that counts the number of lines (actually, the number of newline characters) in the input. The function **getchar** returns the next input character until the end of the input is reached, at which point **getchar** returns the value of the macro **EOF** defined in **stdio.h**:

```
#include <stdio.h>
main()     /* Count the number of lines in the input. */
{
    int next_char;
    int num_lines = 0;
    while ((next_char = getchar()) != EOF)
        if (next_char == '\n')
            ++num_lines;
    printf("%d lines read.\n", num_lines);
}
```

References character constants 2.7.3; **EOF** 15.1; **getchar** facility 15.6; **stdio.h** 15.1; string constants 2.7.4; trigraphs 2.1.4

2.7.7 Numeric Escape Codes

Numeric escape codes allow any value of type **unsigned char** to be expressed by writing the value directly in octal or—in ISO C—hexadecimal notation. (ISO C prohibits values outside the range of **unsigned char**.) Up to three octal digits or any number of hexadecimal digits may be used to express the encoding. (The octal notation is sufficient for characters represented by up to nine bits on the target computer.) For instance, under the ASCII encoding, the character **'a'** may be written as **'\141'** and the character **'?'** as **'\77'**. The null character, used to terminate strings, is always written as **\0**. The value of a numeric escape that does not correspond to a character in the execution character set is implementation-defined.

Example

The following short code segment illustrates the use of numeric escape codes. The variable **inchar** has type **int**.

```
for (;;) {
    inchar = receive();
    if (inchar == '\0') continue;          /* Ignore */
    if (inchar == '\004') break;           /* Quit */
    if (inchar == '\006') reply('\006'); /* ACK */
    else reply('\025');                    /* NAK */
    }
```

There are two reasons for the programmer to be cautious when using numeric escapes. First, of course, the use of numeric escapes may depend on character encoding and therefore be nonportable. It is always much better to hide escape codes in macro definitions so that they are easy to change:

```
#define NUL '\0'
#define EOT '\004'
#define ACK '\006'
#define NAK '\025'
```

Second, the syntax for numeric escapes is very delicate; an octal escape code terminates when three octal digits have been used or when the first character that is not an octal digit is encountered. Therefore, the string `"\0111"` consists of two characters, `\011` and `1`, and the string `"\090"` consists of three characters, `\0`, `9`, and `0`. Hexadecimal escape sequences also suffer from the termination problem, especially since they can be of any length; to stop an ISO C hexadecimal escape in a string, break the string into pieces:

```
"\xabc"      /* This string contains one character. */
"\xab" "c"   /* This string contains two characters. */
```

Some non-ISO C implementations provide hexadecimal escape sequences that, like the octal escapes, permit only up to a fixed number of hexadecimal digits.

References character constant 2.7.3; **`#define`** 3.3; macro definitions 3.3; null character 2.1; string constant 2.7.4; target character set 2.1

2.8 C++ COMPATIBILITY

This section lists the lexical differences between C and C++.

2.8.1 Character Sets

The token respellings and trigraphs in ISO C and Amendment 1 will be part of the ISO C++ standard, but they are not common in pre-ISO C++ implementations.

2.8.2 Comments

In C++, the characters `//` begin a comment that extends to the end of the current source line. C's traditional commenting style (`/*...*/`) is also recognized. The `//` comment is not recognized inside `/*...*/` in C++. Although this change is mostly upward compatible, there is a rare case in which a valid ISO C program will be unacceptable to C++ because of the new comment style (section 2.9, problem 6).

2.8.3 Operators

There are three new compound operators in C++:

```
.*    ->*    ::
```

Since these combinations of tokens would be invalid in ISO C programs, there is no impact on portability from C to C++.

2.8.4 Identifiers and Reserved Words

In C++, all characters making up an identifier are significant. That is, C++ implementations cannot ignore differences after 31 characters, as ISO C implementations are permitted.

Because of the obvious possibility for confusing the reader, C programs should always be written as if all characters of an identifier were significant.

A more common and bothersome problem with C++ compatibility stems from the fact that C++ has a number of additional reserved words, listed in Table 2–9. When writing C++-compatible C, you must avoid using these reserved words.

Table 2–9 Additional C++ reserved words

asm	**false**[a]	**private**	**throw**
bool	**friend**	**protected**	**true**[a]
catch	**inline**	**public**	**try**
class	**mutable**[a]	**reinterpret_cast**[a]	**typeid**[a]
const_cast[a]	**namespace**[a]	**static_cast**[a]	**using**[a]
delete	**new**	**template**	**virtual**
dynamic_cast[a]	**operator**	**this**	

[a] New to ISO C++; rare in previous versions of C++.

2.8.5 Character Constants

Single-character constants have type **int** in C, but have type **char** in C++. Multicharacter constants—which are implementation-defined—have type **int** in both languages. In practice, this makes little difference, since in C++ character constants used in integral contexts are promoted to **int** under the usual conversions. However, **sizeof('c')** is **sizeof(char)** in C++, whereas it is **sizeof(int)** in C.

2.9 EXERCISES

1. Which of the following are lexical tokens?
   (a) reserved words
   (b) comments
   (c) whitespace
   (d) hexadecimal constants
   (e) trigraphs
   (f) wide string constants
   (g) parentheses
2. Assume the following strings of source characters were processed by an ISO C compiler. Which strings would be recognized as a sequence of C tokens? How many tokens would be found in each case? (Don't worry if some of the token sequences could not appear in a valid C program.)
   (a) **X++Y**
   (b) **-12uL**
   (c) **1.37E+6L**
   (d) **"String ""FOO"""**
   (e) **"String+\"FOO\""**
   (f) **x**2**
   (g) **"X??/"**
   (h) **B$C**
   (i) **A*=B**
   (j) **while##DO**
3. Eliminate all the comments from the following C program fragment.

```
/**/*/*"*/*/*"//*//**/*/
```

4. An ISO C compiler must perform each of the following actions on an input program. In what order are the actions performed?
   collecting characters into tokens
   removing comments
   converting trigraphs
   processing line continuation
5. Some poor choices for program identifiers are shown below. What makes them poor choices?
   (a) **`pipesendintake`**
   (b) **`Const`**
   (c) **`lO`**
   (d) **`077U`**
   (e) **`SYS$input`**
6. Write some simple code fragments in ISO C that would be invalid, or interpreted differently, in C++ for the reason listed:
   (a) `//`-style comments
   (b) identifier length
   (c) reserved word conflicts
   (d) type of constants

3

The C Preprocessor

The C preprocessor is a simple macro processor that conceptually processes the source text of a C program before the compiler proper reads the source program. In some implementations of C, the preprocessor is actually a separate program that reads the original source file and writes out a new "preprocessed" source file that can then be used as input to the C compiler. In other implementations, a single program performs the preprocessing and compilation in a single pass over the source file.

3.1 PREPROCESSOR COMMANDS

The preprocessor is controlled by special preprocessor command lines, which are lines of the source file beginning with the character **#**. Lines that do not contain preprocessor commands are called lines of source program text. The preprocessor commands are shown in Table 3–1 on page 40.

The preprocessor removes all preprocessor command lines from the source file and makes additional transformations on the source file as directed by the commands, such as expanding macro calls that occur within the source program text. The resulting preprocessed source text must then be a valid C program.

The syntax of preprocessor commands is completely independent of (though in some ways similar to) the syntax of the rest of the C language. For example, it is possible for a macro definition to expand into a syntactically incomplete fragment, as long as the fragment makes sense (that is, is properly completed) in all contexts in which the macro is called.

Table 3–1 Preprocessor commands

Command	Meaning	Sec.
#define	Define a preprocessor macro.	3.3
#undef	Remove a preprocessor macro definition.	3.3.5
#include	Insert text from another source file.	3.4
#if	Conditionally include some text, based on the value of a constant expression.	3.5.1
#ifdef	Conditionally include some text, based on whether a macro name is defined.	3.5.3
#ifndef	Conditionally include some text, with the sense of the test opposite that of **#ifdef**.	3.5.3
#else	Alternatively include some text, if the previous **#if**, **#ifdef**, **#ifndef**, or **#elif** test failed.	3.5.1
#endif	Terminate conditional text.	3.5.1
#line	Supply a line number for compiler messages.	3.6
#elif[a]	Alternatively include some text based on the value of another constant expression, if the previous **#if**, **#ifdef**, **#ifndef**, or **#elif** test failed.	3.5.2
defined[a]	Preprocessor function that yields 1 if a name is defined as a preprocessor macro and 0 otherwise; used in **#if** and **#elif**.	3.5.5
# operator[b]	Replace a macro parameter with a string constant containing the parameter's value.	3.3.8
## operator[b]	Create a single token out of two adjacent tokens.	3.3.9
#pragma[b]	Specify implementation-dependent information to the compiler.	3.7
#error[b]	Produce a compile-time error with a designated message.	3.8

[a] Not originally part of C, but now common in ISO and non-ISO implementations.
[b] New in ISO C.

3.2 PREPROCESSOR LEXICAL CONVENTIONS

The preprocessor does not parse the source text, but it does break it up into tokens for the purpose of locating macro calls. The lexical conventions of the preprocessor are somewhat different from the compiler proper; the preprocessor recognizes the normal C tokens, and additionally recognizes as "tokens" other characters that would not be recognized as valid in C proper. This enables the preprocessor to recognize file names, the presence and absence of whitespace, and the location of end-of-line markers.

A line beginning with **#** is treated as a preprocessor command; the name of the command must follow the **#** character. ISO C permits whitespace to precede and follow the **#** character on the same source line, but some older compilers do not. A line whose only non-whitespace character is a **#** is termed a "null directive" in ISO C and is treated the same as a blank line. Older implementations may behave differently.

The remainder of the line following the command name may contain arguments for the command if appropriate. If a preprocessor command takes no arguments, then the remainder of the command line should be empty except perhaps for whitespace characters or comments. Many pre-ISO compilers silently ignore all characters following the expected arguments (if any); this can lead to portability problems. The arguments to preprocessor commands are generally subject to macro replacement.

Preprocessor lines are recognized before macro expansion. Therefore, if a macro expands into something that looks like a preprocessor command, that command will not be recognized by the preprocessors in ISO C or in most other C compilers. (Unfortunately, some older UNIX implementations violate this rule.)

Example

For example, the result of the following code is *not* to include the file **math.h** in the program being compiled:

```
/* This example doesn't work as one might think! */
#define GETMATH #include <math.h>
GETMATH
```

Instead, the expanded token sequence

```
# include < math . h >
```

is merely passed through and compiled as (erroneous) C code.

As noted in section 2.1.2, all source lines (including preprocessor command lines) can be continued by preceding the end-of-line marker by a backslash character, ****. If a line ends with a backslash, then the following line will never be treated as a preprocessor command line, even if its first non-whitespace character is **#**.

Example

The preprocessor command

```
#define err(flag,msg)  if (flag) \
   printf(msg)
```

is the same as

```
#define err(flag,msg)  if (flag) printf(msg)
```

If the backslash character below immediately precedes the end-of-line marker, the second **define** command will be ignored:

```
#define BACKSLASH \
#define ASTERISK *
```

As explained in section 2.2, the preprocessor treats comments as whitespace, and line breaks within comments do not terminate preprocessor commands.

References comments 2.2; line termination and continuation 2.1; tokens 2.3

3.3 DEFINITION AND REPLACEMENT

The **#define** preprocessor command causes a name (identifier) to become defined as a macro to the preprocessor. A sequence of tokens, called the body of the macro, is associated with the name. When the name of the macro is recognized in the program source text or in the arguments of certain other preprocessor commands, it is treated as a call to that macro; the name is effectively replaced by a copy of the body. If the macro is defined to accept arguments, then the actual arguments following the macro name are substituted for formal parameters in the macro body.

Example

If a macro **sum** with two arguments is defined by

```
#define sum(x,y)  x+y
```

then the preprocessor replaces the source program line

```
result = sum(5,a*b);
```

with

```
result = 5+a*b;
```

Since the preprocessor does not distinguish reserved words from other identifiers, it is possible, in principle, to use a C reserved word as the name of a preprocessor macro, but to do so is usually bad programming practice. Macro names are never recognized within comments or string constants.

3.3.1 Object-like Macro Definitions

The **#define** command has two forms, depending on whether or not a left parenthesis immediately follows the name to be defined. The simpler, "object-like" form has no left parenthesis:

#define name *sequence-of-tokens*$_{opt}$

An object-like macro takes no arguments. It is invoked merely by mentioning its name. When the name is encountered in the source program text, the name is replaced by the body (the associated *sequence-of-tokens*, which may be empty). The syntax of the **#define** command does not require an equal sign or any other special delimiter token after the name being defined. The body starts right after the name.

The object-like macro is particularly useful for introducing named constants into a program, so that a "magic number" such as the length of a table may be written in exactly one place and then referred to elsewhere by name. This makes it easier to change the number later.

Another important use of object-like macros is to isolate implementation-dependent restrictions on the names of externally defined functions and variables. An example of this appears in section 2.5.

Example

Here are some typical macro definitions:

```
#define BLOCK_SIZE  0x100
#define TRACK_SIZE  (16*BLOCK_SIZE)
#define EOT         '\004'
#define ERRMSG      "*** Error %d: %s.\n"
```

A common programming error is to include an extraneous equal sign:

```
#define NUMBER_OF_TAPE_DRIVES = 5  /* Probably wrong. */
```

This is a valid definition, but it causes the name `NUMBER_OF_TAPE_DRIVES` to be defined as "`= 5`" rather than as "`5`". If one were then to write the code fragment

```
if (count != NUMBER_OF_TAPE_DRIVES) ...
```

it would be expanded to

```
if (count != = 5) ...
```

which is syntactically invalid. For similar reasons, also be careful to avoid an extraneous semicolon:

```
#define NUMBER_OF_TAPE_DRIVES 5 ;  /* Probably wrong. */
```

References compound assignment operators 7.9.2; operators and separators 2.4

3.3.2 Defining Macros with Parameters

The more complex, "function-like" macro definition declares the names of formal parameters within parentheses, separated by commas:

#define *name* **(***name*$_1$**,** *name*$_2$**,** ..., *name*$_n$**)** *sequence-of-tokens*$_{opt}$

The left parenthesis must immediately follow the name of the macro with no intervening whitespace. If whitespace separates the left parenthesis from the macro name, the definition is considered to define a macro that takes no arguments and has a body beginning with a left parenthesis.

The names of the formal parameters must be identifiers, no two the same. There is no requirement that any of the parameter names be mentioned in the body (though normally they all will be mentioned). A function-like macro can have an empty formal parameter list, i.e., zero formal parameters. This kind of macro is useful to simulate a function that takes no arguments.

A function-like macro takes as many actual arguments as there are formal parameters. The macro is invoked by writing its name, a left parenthesis, then one actual argument token sequence for each formal parameter, then a right parenthesis. The actual argument token sequences are separated by commas. (When a function-like macro with no formal parameters is invoked, an empty actual argument list must be provided.) When a macro is invoked, whitespace may appear between the macro name and the left parenthesis or in the actual arguments. (Some older and deficient preprocessor implementations do not permit the actual argument token list to extend across multiple lines unless the lines to be continued end with a \.)

An actual argument token sequence may contain parentheses if they are properly nested and balanced and may contain commas if each comma appears within a set of parentheses. (This restriction prevents confusion with the commas that separate the actual arguments.) Braces and subscripting brackets likewise may appear within macro arguments, but they cannot contain commas and do not have to balance. Parentheses and commas appearing within character-constant and string-constant tokens are not counted in the balancing of parentheses and the delimiting of actual arguments.

Example

Here is the definition of a macro that multiplies its two arguments:

```
#define product(x,y)   ((x)*(y))
```

It is invoked twice in the following statement:

```
x = product(a+3,b) + product (c, d);
```

The arguments to the **product** macro could be function (or macro) calls. The commas within the function argument lists do not affect the parsing of the macro arguments:

```
return product( f(a,b), g(a,b) ); /* OK */
```

Example

The **getchar** macro below has an empty parameter list:

```
#define getchar()   getc(stdin)
```

When it is invoked, an empty argument list is provided:

```
while ((c=getchar()) != EOF) ...
```

(**getchar** is defined in the standard header file **stdio.h**.)

Example

We can also define a macro that takes as its argument an arbitrary statement:

```
#define insert(stmt)   stmt
```

The invocation

```
insert( {a=1; b=1;} )
```

works properly, but if we change the two assignment statements to a single statement containing two assignment expressions:

```
insert( {a=1, b=1;} )
```

then the preprocessor will complain that we have too many macro arguments for insert. To fix the problem we would have to write:

```
insert( {(a=1, b=1);} )
```

Example

Defining function-like macros to be used in statement contexts can be tricky. The following macro swaps the values in its two arguments, **x** and **y**, which are assumed to be of a type whose values can be converted to **unsigned long** and back without change.

```
#define swap(x, y) { unsigned long _temp=x; x=y; y=_temp; }
```

The problem is that it is natural to want to place a semicolon after **swap**, as you would if **swap** were really a function:

```
if (x > y) swap(x, y);        /* Whoops! */
else x = y;
```

This will result in an error, since the expansion includes an extra semicolon (section 8.1). We put the expanded statements on separate lines below to illustrate the problems more clearly:

```
if (x > y) { unsigned long _temp=x; x=y; y=_temp; }
;
else x = y;
```

A clever way to avoid the problem is to define the macro body as a **do-while** statement, which will consume the semicolon (section 8.6.2):

```
#define swap(x, y) \
    do { unsigned long _temp=x; x=y; y=_temp; } while 0
```

When a function-like macro call is encountered, the entire macro call is replaced, after parameter processing, by a processed copy of the body. Parameter processing proceeds as follows. Actual argument token strings are associated with the corresponding formal parameter names. A copy of the body is then made in which every occurrence of a formal parameter name is replaced by a copy of the actual argument token sequence associated with it. This copy of the body then replaces the macro call. The entire process of replacing a macro call with the processed copy of its body is called *macro expansion*; the processed copy of the body is called the *expansion* of the macro call.

Example

Consider this macro definition, which provides a convenient way to make a loop that counts from a given value up to (and including) some limit:

```
#define incr(v,low,high)  \
    for ((v) = (low); (v) <= (high); (v)++)
```

To print a table of the cubes of the integers from 1 to 20, we could write

```
main()
{
    int j;
    incr(j, 1, 20)
        printf("%2d %6d\n", j, j*j*j);
}
```

The call to the macro **incr** is expanded to produce this loop:

```
    for ((j) = (1); (j) <= (20); (j)++)
```

The liberal use of parentheses ensures that complicated actual arguments will not be misinterpreted by the compiler. (See section 3.3.6.)

References **do** statement 8.6.2; statement syntax 8.1; **unsigned long** 5.1.2; whitespace 2.1.2

3.3.3 Rescanning of Macro Expressions

Once a macro call has been expanded, the scan for macro calls resumes at the beginning of the expansion so that names of macros may be recognized within the expansion for the purpose of further macro replacement. Macro replacement is not performed on any part of a **#define** command, not even the body, at the time the command itself is processed and the macro name defined. Macro names are recognized within the body only after the body has been expanded for some particular macro call.

Macro replacement is also not performed within the actual argument token strings of a function-like macro call at the time the macro call is being scanned. Macro names are recognized within actual argument token strings only during the rescanning of the expansion, assuming that the corresponding formal parameter in fact occurred one or more times within the body (thereby causing the actual argument token string to appear one or more times in the expansion).

Example

Given the following definitions:

```
#define plus(x,y)   add(y,x)
#define add(x,y)    ((x)+(y))
```

The invocation

```
plus(plus(a,b),c)
```

is expanded as shown below.

Step	Result
1. (original)	`plus(plus(a,b),c)`
2.	`add(c,plus(a,b))`
3.	`((c)+(plus(a,b)))`
4.	`((c)+(add(b,a)))`
5. (final)	`((c)+(((b)+(a))))`

Macros appearing in their own expansion—either immediately or through some intermediate sequence of nested macro expansions—are not reexpanded in ISO C. This permits a programmer to redefine a function in terms of its old definition. Older C preprocessors traditionally do not detect this recursion, and will attempt to continue the expansion until they are stopped by some system error.

Example

The following macro changes the definition of the square root function to handle negative arguments in a different fashion than is normal:

```
#define sqrt(x)   ((x)<0 ? sqrt(-x) : sqrt(x))
```

This macro would work as intended in ISO C, but might cause an error in older compilers. Similarly:

```
#define char   unsigned char
```

3.3.4 Predefined Macros

Preprocessors for ISO C are required to define certain object-like macros (Table 3–2). The name of each begins and ends with two underscore characters. None of these predefined macros may be redefined by the programmer.

Table 3–2 Predefined macros

Macro	Value
`__LINE__` [a]	The line number of the current source program line, expressed as a decimal integer constant.
`__FILE__` [a]	The name of the current source file, expressed as a string constant.
`__DATE__`	The calendar date of the translation, expressed as a string constant of the form **"Mmm dd yyyy"**. **Mmm** is as produced by **asctime**.
`__TIME__`	The time of the translation, expressed as a string constant of the form **"hh:mm:ss"**, as returned by **asctime**.
`__STDC__`	The decimal constant 1, if and only if the compiler is an ISO conforming implementation.
`__STDC_VERSION__`	If the implementation conforms to Amendment 1 of ISO C, then this macro is defined and has the value **199409L**.

[a] These macros are common in non-ISO implementations also.

The **__LINE__** and **__FILE__** macros are useful when printing certain kinds of error messages. The **__DATE__**, and **__TIME__** macros can be used to record when a compilation occurred. The **__STDC__** and **__STDC_VERSION__** macros are very useful for writing code that is compatible with ISO and non-ISO implementations.

The values of **__TIME__** and **__DATE__** must remain constant throughout the compilation. The values of the **__LINE__** and **__FILE__** macros are established by the implementation but are subject to alteration by the **#line** directive (section 3.6).

Implementations routinely define additional macros to communicate information about the environment, such as the type of computer for which the program is being compiled. Exactly which macros are defined is implementation-dependent, although UNIX implementations customarily predefine **unix**. Unlike the built-in macros, these macros may be undefined. ISO C requires implementation-specific macro names to begin with a leading underscore followed by either an uppercase letter or another underscore. (The macro **unix** does not meet that criterion.)

Example

The predefined macros are useful in certain kinds of error messages:

```
if (n != m)
    fprintf(stderr,"Internal error: line %d, file %s\n",
        __LINE__, __FILE__ );
```

Other implementation-defined macros can be used to isolate host or target-specific code. For example, a compiler targeted to the DEC VAX-11 computer might predefine a macro named **vax** so that the programmer could write

```
#ifdef vax
    VAX-specific-code
#endif
```

The **__STDC__** and **__STDC_VERSION__** macros are useful when writing programs that must adapt to both ISO and non-ISO implementations:

```
#ifdef __STDC__
  #if defined(__STDC_VERSION__) && __STDC_VERSION__>=199409L
    /* ISO C and Amendment 1 conforming */
  #else
    /* ISO C but not Amendment 1 conforming */
  #end
#else
    /* Not ISO C conforming */
#endif
```

References **asctime** facility 20.3; **fprintf** 15.11; **#ifdef** preprocessor command 3.5.3; **#if** preprocessor command 3.5.1; undefining macros 3.3.5

3.3.5 Undefining and Redefining Macros

The **#undef** command can be used to make a name be no longer defined:

```
#undef name
```

This command causes the preprocessor to forget any macro definition of ***name***. It is not an error to undefine a name that is currently not defined. Once a name has been undefined, it may then be given a completely new definition (using **#define**) without error. Macro replacement is not performed within **#undef** commands.

The "benign" redefinition of macros is allowed in ISO C and many other implementations. That is, a macro may be redefined if the new definition is the same, token for token, as the existing definition. The redefinition must include whitespace in the same locations as in the original definition, although the particular whitespace characters can be different. We think programmers should avoid depending on benign redefinitions. It is generally better style to have a single point of definition for all program entities, including macros. (Some older implementations of C may not allow any kind of redefinition.)

Example

In the definitions below, the redefinition of **NULL** is allowed, but neither redefinition of **FUNC** is valid. (The first includes whitespace not in the original definition, and the second changes two tokens.)

```
# define NULL 0
# define FUNC(x) x+4
# define NULL /* null pointer */ 0
# define FUNC(x) x + 4
# define FUNC(y) y+4
```

Example

When the programmer for legitimate reasons can't tell if a previous definition exists, the **#ifndef** command can be used to test for an existing definition so that a redefinition can be avoided:

```
#ifndef MAXTABLESIZE
#define MAXTABLESIZE 1000
#endif
```

This idiom is particularly useful with implementations that allow macro definitions in the command that invokes the C compiler. For example, the following UNIX invocation of C provides an initial definition of the macro **MAXTABLESIZE** as **5000**. The C programmer would then check for the definition as shown above:

```
cc -c -DMAXTABLESIZE=5000 prog.c
```

Although disallowed in ISO C, a few older preprocessor implementations handle **#define** and **#undef** so as to maintain a stack of definitions. When a name is redefined with **#define**, its old definition is pushed onto a stack and then the new definition replaces the old one. When a name is undefined with **#undef**, the current definition is discarded and the most recent previous definition (if any) is restored.

References **#define** command 3.3; **#ifdef** and **#ifndef** command 3.5.3

3.3.6 Precedence Errors in Macro Expansions

Macros operate purely by textual substitution of tokens. Parsing of the body into declarations, expressions, or statements occurs only after the macro expansion process. This can lead to surprising results if care is not taken. As a rule, it is safest to always parenthesize each parameter appearing in the macro body. The entire body, if it is syntactically an expression, should also be parenthesized.

Example

Consider this macro definition:

```
#define SQUARE(x) x*x
```

The idea is that **SQUARE** takes an argument expression and produces a new expression to compute the square of that argument. For example, **SQUARE(5)** expands to **5*5**. However, the expression **SQUARE(z+1)** expands to **z+1*z+1**, which is parsed as **z+(1*z)+1** rather than the expected **(z+1)*(z+1)**. A definition of SQUARE that avoids this problem is:

```
#define SQUARE(x)  ((x)*(x))
```

The outer parentheses are needed to prevent misinterpretation of an expression such as **(short) SQUARE(z+1)**.

References cast expressions 7.5.1; precedence of expressions 7.2.1

3.3.7 Side Effects in Macro Arguments

Macros can also produce problems due to side effects. Because the macro's actual arguments may be textually replicated, they may be executed more than once, and side effects in the actual arguments may occur more than once. In contrast, a true function call—which the macro invocation resembles—evaluates argument expressions exactly once, so any side effects of the expression occur exactly once. Macros must be used with care to avoid such problems.

Example

Consider the macro **SQUARE** from the example above, and also a function **square** that does (almost) the same thing:

```
int square(int x) { return x*x; }
```

The macro can square integers or floating-point numbers; the function can square only integers. Also, calling the function is likely to be somewhat slower at run time than using the macro. But these differences are less important than the problem of side effects. In the program fragment

```
a = 3;
b = square(a++);
```

the variable **b** gets the value 9 and the variable **a** ends up with the value 4. However, in the superficially similar program fragment

```
a = 3;
b = SQUARE(a++);
```

the variable **b** may very well get the value 12 and the variable **a** may end up with the value 5, because the expansion of the last fragment is

```
a = 3;
b = ((a++)*(a++));
```

(We say that 12 and 5 "may" be the resulting values of **b** and **a** because ISO C implementations may evaluate the expression **((a++)*(a++))** in different ways. See section 7.12.)

References increment operator **++** 7.4.4

3.3.8 Converting Tokens to Strings

There is a mechanism in ISO C to convert macro parameters (after expansion) to string constants. Before this, programmers had to depend on a "loophole" in many C preprocessors that achieved the same result in a different way.

In ISO C, the **#** token appearing within a macro definition is recognized as a unary "stringization" operator that must be followed by the name of a macro formal parameter. During macro expansion, the **#** and the formal name are replaced by the corresponding actual argument enclosed in string quotations. When creating the string, each sequence of whitespace in the expansion of the macro formal is replaced by a single space character, and any embedded quotation or backslash characters are preceded by a backslash character to preserve their meaning in the string.

Example

Consider the ISO C definition of macro **TEST**:

```
#define TEST(a,b) printf( #a "<" #b "=%d\n", (a)<(b) )
```

The statements **TEST(0,0xFFFF); TEST('\n',10);** would expand into

```
printf("0" "<" "0xFFFF" "=%d\n", (0)<(0xFFFF) );
printf("'\\n'" "<" "10" "=%d\n", ('\n')<(10) );
```

After concatenation of adjacent strings, these become

```
printf("0<0xFFFF=%d\n", (0)<(0xFFFF) );
printf("'\\n'<10=%d\n", ('\n')<(10) );
```

A number of non-ISO C compilers will substitute for macro formal parameters *inside* string and character constants. ISO C prohibits this.

Example

In these nonconforming C implementations, the **TEST** macro could be written this way:

```
#define TEST(a,b) printf( "a<b=%d\n", (a)<(b) )
```

The result of expanding **TEST(0,0xFFFF)** would resemble the result of stringization:

```
printf("0<0xFFFF=%d\n", (0)<(0xFFFF) );
```

However, the expansion of **TEST('\n',10)** would almost certainly be missing the extra backslash and the output of the **printf** function would be garbled, with unexpected line breaks in the output:

```
printf("'\n'<10=%d\n", ('\n')<(10) );
```

The handling of whitespace in non-ISO implementations is also likely to vary from compiler to compiler—another reason to avoid depending on this feature except in ISO C implementations.

3.3.9 Token Merging in Macro Expansions

Merging of tokens to form new tokens in ISO C is controlled by the presence of a "merging" operator, **##**, in macro definitions. In a macro replacement list—before rescanning for more macros—the two tokens surrounding any **##** operator are combined into a single token. (If they do not form a valid token, the result is undefined.)

Example

Consider this source text:

```
#define TEMP(i)  temp ## i
TEMP(1) = TEMP(2);
```

After preprocessing, this becomes

```
temp1 = temp2;
```

As with the conversion of macro arguments to strings (section 3.3.8), programmers can obtain something like this merging capability through a loophole in many non-ISO C implementations. Although the original definition of C explicitly described macro bodies as being sequences of tokens, not sequences of characters, nevertheless many C compilers expand and rescan macro bodies as if they were character sequences. This becomes apparent primarily in the case where the compiler also handles comments by eliminating them entirely (rather than by replacing them with a space), a situation exploited by some cleverly written programs.

Example

Consider the following example:

```
#define INC ++
#define TAB internal_table
#define INCTAB table_of_increments
#define CONC(x,y) x/**/y
CONC(INC,TAB)
```

ISO C interprets the body of **CONC** as two tokens, **x** and **y**, separated by a space. (Comments are converted to a space). The call **CONC(INC,TAB)** expands to the two tokens **INC TAB**. However, some non-ISO implementations simply eliminate comments and then rescan macro bodies for tokens; these will expand **CONC(INC,TAB)** to the single token **INCTAB**:

Step	ISO C expansion	Possible non-ISO expansion
1	**CONC(INC,TAB)**	**CONC(INC,TAB)**
2	**INC/**/TAB**	**INC/**/TAB**
3	**INC TAB**	**INCTAB**
4	**++ internal_table**	**table_of_increments**

References increment operator **++** 7.5.8

3.3.10 Other Problems

Some implementations of non-ISO C do not perform stringent error checking on macro definitions and calls, including permitting an incomplete token in the macro body to be completed by text appearing after the macro call. The lack of error checking by certain implementations does not make clever exploitation of that lack legitimate. ISO C reaffirms that macro bodies must be sequences of well-formed tokens.

Example

For example, the following fragment in one of these non-ISO implementations:

```
#define FIRSTPART "This is a split
...
printf(FIRSTPART string."); /* Yuk! */
```

will, after preprocessing, result in the source text

```
printf("This is a split string.");
```

3.4 FILE INCLUSION

The **#include** preprocessor command causes the entire contents of a specified source text file to be processed as if those contents had appeared in place of the **#include** command. The **#include** command has the following three forms in ISO C:

 # include < ***h-char-sequence*** **>**
 # include " ***q-char-sequence*** **"**
 # include ***preprocessor-tokens*** **(ISO C)**

h-char-sequence :
any sequence of characters except **>** and end-of-line

q-char-sequence :
any sequence of characters except **"** and end-of-line

preprocessor-tokens :
any sequence of C tokens—or non-whitespace characters
that cannot be interpreted as tokens—that does not begin with **<** or **"**

In the first two forms of **#include**, the characters between the delimiters should be a file name in some implementation-defined format. There should be only whitespace after the closing **>** or **"**. These two forms of **#include** are supported by all C compilers. The file name is subject to trigraph replacement in ISO C and source-line continuation, but no other processing of the characters occurs.

In third form of **#include**, the *preprocessor-tokens* undergo normal macro expansion and the result must match one of the first two forms (including the quotes or angle brackets). This form of **include** is seen less often, and may not be implemented or may be implemented in a different fashion in non-ISO compilers.

Example

Here is one way to use this third form of **include**:

```
#if some_thing==this_thing
#   define IncludeFile "thisname"
#else
#   define Includefile <thatname>
#endif
...
#include Includefile
```

This style can be used to localize customizations, but programmers interested in compatibility with older compilers should instead place **#include** commands at the site of the **#define** commands above:

```
#if some_thing==this_thing
#   include "thisname"
#else
#   include <thatname>
#endif
```

File names delimited by quotes and file names delimited by angle brackets differ in how the specified file is located by the C implementation. Both forms search for the file in a set of (possibly different) implementation-defined places. Typically, the form

#include < *filename* >

searches for the file in certain "standard" places according to implementation-defined search rules. These standard places usually contain the implementation's own header files, such as **stdio.h**. The form

#include " *filename* "

will also search in the standard places, but usually after searching some "local" places, such as the programmer's "current" directory. Often, implementations have some standard way outside of the C language for specifying the set of places to search for these files. The general intent is that the **"..."** form is used to refer to header files written by the programmer, whereas the **<...>** form is used to refer to standard implementation files.

In fact, standard header files like **stdio.h** are treated as special cases in ISO C. Since the format of file names is implementation-defined, names like "**stdio.h**" might not be valid file names in some implementations. Therefore, ISO C requires that implementations recognize the predefined header file names when they appear in **<>**-delimited **#include** commands, but there is no requirement that those names be true file names that are looked up in some standard place. They can be handled as special cases.

An included file may itself contain **#include** commands. The permitted depth of such **#include** nesting is implementation dependent, but ISO C requires support for at least eight levels. The location of included files can affect the search rules for nested files.

Consider the situation depicted in Figure 3–1. We are compiling a C program, **first.c**, in the file system directory **near**. The first included file, **second.h**, is specified to be in another directory, **far**. The header file **second.h** in turn includes a file, **third.h**, with no specified directory. Will the implementation choose the file **third.h** in the original "current" directory, **near**, or will it choose the file with the same name in the directory of the file containing the **#include**—that is, **far**?

Figure 3–1 Include file lookups.

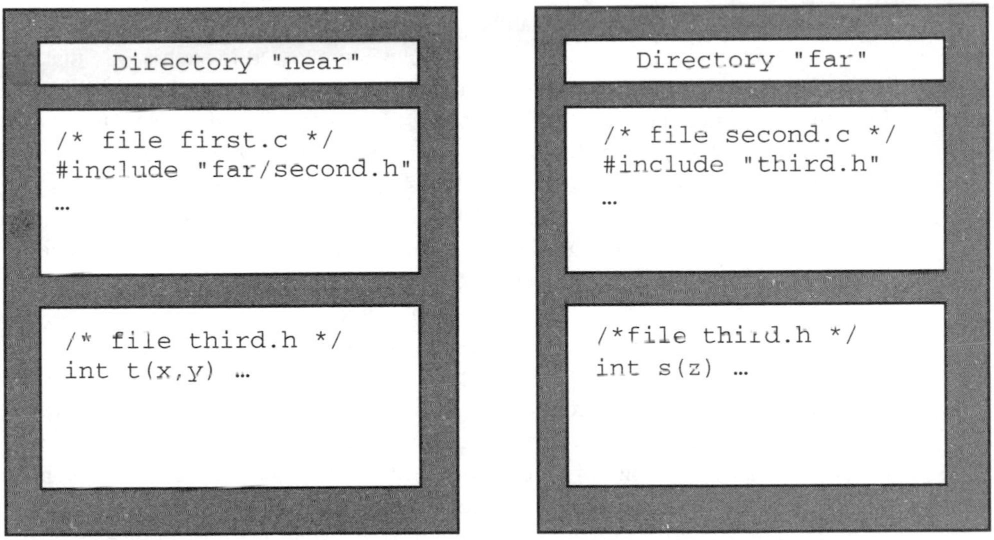

Some UNIX C compilers would find **far/third.h**; the original description of C seems to expect that **near/third.h** should be found. We think **near/third.h** is the better choice for an implementation, but this is not mandated by ISO C.

References string constants 2.7.4; trigraphs 2.1.4

3.5 CONDITIONAL COMPILATION

The preprocessor conditional commands allow lines of source text to be passed through or eliminated by the preprocessor on the basis of a computed condition.

3.5.1 The #if, #else, and #endif Commands

The following preprocessor commands are used together to allow lines of source text to be conditionally included in or excluded from the compilation: **#if**, **#else**, and **#endif**. They are used in the following way:

```
#if constant-expression
    group-of-lines-1
#else
    group-of-lines-2
#endif
```

The *constant-expression* is subject to macro replacement and must evaluate to a constant arithmetic value. Restrictions on the expression are discussed in section 7.11.1. A "group of lines" may contain any number of lines of text of any kind, even other preprocessor command lines, or no lines at all. The **#else** command may be omitted, along with the group of lines following it; this is equivalent to including the **#else** command with an empty group of lines following it. Either group of lines may also contain one or more sets of **#if-#else-#endif** commands.

A set of commands such as shown above is processed in such a way that one group of lines will be passed on for compilation and the other group of lines will be discarded. First the constant-expression in the **#if** command is evaluated. If its value is not 0, then *group-of-lines-1* is passed through for compilation and *group-of-lines-2* (if present) is discarded. Otherwise, *group-of-lines-1* is discarded; and if there is an **#else** command, then *group-of-lines-2* is passed through; but if there is no **#else** command, then no group of lines is passed through. The constant expressions that may be used in a **#if** command are described in detail in sections 3.5.4 and 7.11.

A group of lines that is discarded is not processed by the preprocessor. Macro replacement is not performed and preprocessor commands are ignored. The one exception is that, within a group of discarded lines, the commands **#if**, **#ifdef**, **#ifndef**, **#elif**, **#else**, and **#endif** are recognized for the sole purpose of counting them; this is necessary to maintain the proper nesting of the conditional compilation commands. (This recognition in turn implies that discarded lines are scanned and broken into tokens and that string constants and comments are recognized and must be properly delimited.)

If an undefined macro name appears in the constant-expression of **#if** or **#elif**, it is replaced by the integer constant 0. This means that the commands "**#ifdef** *name*" and "**#if** *name*" will have the same effect as long as the macro name, when defined, has a constant, arithmetic, nonzero value. We think it is much clearer to use **#ifdef** or the defined operator in these cases, but ISO C also supports this use of **#if**.

References **defined** 3.5.5; **#elif** 3.5.2; **#ifdef** 3.5.3

3.5.2 The #elif Command

The **#elif** command is present in ISO C and in the more modern pre-ISO compilers as well. It is convenient because it simplifies some preprocessor conditionals. It is used in the following way:

```
#if constant-expression–1
    group-of-lines–1
#elif constant-expression–2
    group-of-lines–2
...
#elif constant-expression–n
    group-of-lines–n
#else
    last-group-of-lines
#endif
```

A set of commands such as shown above are processed in such a way that at most one group of lines will be passed on for compilation and all other groups of lines will be discarded. First the *constant-expression–1* in the **#if** command is evaluated. If its value is not 0, then *group-of-lines–1* is passed through for compilation and all other groups of lines up to the matching **#endif** are discarded. If the value of the *constant-expression–1* in the **#if** command is 0, then the *constant-expression–2* in the first **#elif** command is evaluated; if that value is not 0, then *group-of-lines–2* is passed through for compilation. In the general case, each *constant-expression–i* is evaluated until one produces a nonzero value; the preprocessor then passes through the group of lines following the command containing the nonzero constant expression, ignoring any other constant expressions in the command set, and discards all other groups of lines. If no *constant-expression–i* produces a nonzero value and there is an **#else** command, then the group of lines following the **#else** command is passed through; but if there is no **#else** command, then no group of lines is passed through. The constant expressions that may be used in a **#elif** command are the same as those used in a **#if** command (see sections 3.5.4 and 7.11).

Within a group of discarded lines, **#elif** commands are recognized in the same way as **#if**, **#else**, and **#endif** commands, for the sole purpose of counting them; this is necessary to maintain the proper nesting of the conditional compilation commands.

Macro replacement is performed within the part of a command line that follows an **#elif** command, so macro calls may be used in the constant-expression.

Example

While the **#elif** command is very convenient when it is appropriate, its functionality can be duplicated using only **#if**, **#else**, and **#endif**. An example is shown in the table below.

Using **#elif**	Without **#elif**
#if *constant-expression–1*	**#if** *constant-expression–1*
group-of-lines–1	*group-of-lines–1*
#elif *constant-expression–2*	**#else**
group-of-lines–2	**#if** *constant-expression–2*
#else	*group-of-lines–2*
last-group-of-lines	**#else**
#endif	*last-group-of-lines*
	#endif
	#endif

3.5.3 The #ifdef and #ifndef Commands

The **#ifdef** and **#ifndef** commands can be used to test whether a name is defined as a preprocessor macro. A command line of the form

#ifdef *name*

is equivalent in meaning to

```
#if 1
```

when *name* has been defined (even with an empty body), and is equivalent to

```
#if 0
```

when *name* has not been defined or has been undefined with the **#undef** command. The **#ifndef** command has the opposite sense; it is true when the *name* is not defined and false when it is.

Note that **#ifdef** and **#ifndef** test names only with respect to whether they have been defined by **#define** (or undefined by **#undef**); they take no notice of names appearing in declarations in the C program text to be compiled. (Some C implementations allow names to be defined with special compiler command-line arguments.)

Example

The **#ifndef** and **#ifdef** commands have come to be used in several stylized ways in C programs. First, it is a common practice to implement a preprocessor-time enumeration type by having a set of symbols of which only one is defined. For example, suppose that we wish to use the set of names VAX, PDP11, and CRAY2 to indicate the computer for which the program is being compiled. One might insist that all these names be defined, with one being defined to be 1 and the rest 0:

```
#define VAX 0
#define PDP11 0
#define CRAY2 1
```

One could then select machine-dependent source code to be compiled in this way:

```
#if VAX
    VAX-dependent code
#endif
#if PDP11
    PDP11-dependent code
#endif
#if CRAY2
    CRAY2-dependent code
#endif
```

However, the customary method defines only one symbol:

```
#define CRAY2 1
    /* None of the other symbols are defined. */
```

Then the conditional commands test whether each symbol is defined:

```
#ifdef VAX
    VAX-dependent code
#endif
#ifdef PDP11
    PDP11-dependent code
#endif
#ifdef CRAY2
    CRAY2-dependent code
#endif
```

Example

Another use for the **#ifdef** and **#ifndef** commands is to provide default definitions for macros. For example, a library file might provide a definition for a name only if no other definition has been provided:

```
#ifndef TABLE_SIZE
#define TABLE_SIZE 100
#endif
...
static int internal_table[TABLE_SIZE];
```

A program might simply include this file:

```
#include <table.h>
```

in which case the definition of **TABLE_SIZE** would be **100**, both within the library file itself and after the **#include**; or the program might provide an explicit definition first:

```
#define TABLE_SIZE 500
#include <table.h>
```

in which case the definition of **TABLE_SIZE** would be **500** throughout.

It is a common C programming error to test whether a name is defined by writing "**#if name**" instead of "**#ifdef name**" or "**#if defined(name)**." The incorrect form often works because the preprocessor replaces any name in the **#if** expression that is not defined as a macro with the constant 0. Therefore, if **name** is not defined, all three forms are equivalent. However, if **name** is defined to have the value 0, then "**#if name**" will be false even though the name is defined. Similarly, if **name** is defined with a value that is not a valid expression, then "**#if name**" will cause an error.

References **#define** 3.3; **defined** operator 3.5.5; **#include** 3.4; preprocessor lexical conventions 3.2; **#undef** 3.3

3.5.4 Constant Expressions in Conditional Commands

The expressions that may be used in **#if** and **#elif** commands are described in section 7.11.1. They include integer constants and all the integer arithmetic, relational, bitwise, and logical operators.

3.5.5 The defined Operator

The **defined** operator, new to C and incorporated into ISO C, can be used in **#if** and **#elif** expressions but nowhere else. An expression in one of the two forms

defined *name*
defined(*name* **)**

evaluates to 1 if *name* is defined in the preprocessor, and 0 if it is not.

Example

The **defined** command allows the programmer to write

```
#if defined(VAX)
```

instead of

```
#ifdef VAX
```

The **defined** operator may be more convenient to use because it is possible to build up complex expressions, such as this:

```
#if defined(VAX) && !defined(UNIX) && debugging
...
```

3.6 EXPLICIT LINE NUMBERING

The **#line** preprocessor command advises the C compiler that the source program was generated by another tool and indicates the correspondence of places in the source program to lines of the original user-written file from which the C source program was produced. The **#line** command may have one of two forms. The form

 # line *n* **"** *filename* **"**

indicates that the next source line was derived from line *n* of the original user-written file named by *filename*. *n* must be an integer constant. The form

 # line *n*

indicates that the next source line was derived from line *n* of the user-written file last mentioned in a **#line** command. Finally, if the **#line** command does not match either of the forms above, it is interpreted as

 # line *preprocessor-tokens*

Macro replacement is performed on the argument token sequence, and the result must match one of the two previous forms of **#line**.

The information provided by the **#line** command is used in setting the values of the predefined macros **__LINE__** and **__FILE__**. Otherwise, its behavior is unspecified and compilers may ignore it. Typically, the information is also used in diagnostic messages. Some tools that generate C source text as output will use **#line** so that error messages can be related to the tool's input file instead of the actual C source file.

Some implementations of C allow the preprocessor to be used independently of the rest of the compiler. Indeed, sometimes the preprocessor is a separate program that is executed to produce an intermediate file that is then processed by the "real" compiler. In such cases the preprocessor may generate new **#line** commands in the intermediate file; the compiler proper is then expected to recognize these even though it does not recognize any other preprocessor commands. Whether the preprocessor generates **#line** commands is implementation dependent. Similarly, whether the preprocessor passes through, modifies, or eliminates **#line** commands in the input is also implementation dependent.

Older versions of C allow simply "**#**" as a synonym for the **#line** command, allowing this form:

*n filename*

This syntax is considered obsolete and is not permitted in ISO C, but many implementations continue to support it for the sake of compatibility.

References **__FILE__** 3.3.4; **__LINE__** 3.3.4

3.7 PRAGMA DIRECTIVE

The **#pragma** command is new in ISO C. Any sequence of tokens can follow the command name:

 # pragma *preprocessor-tokens*

The **#pragma** directive can be used by C implementations to add new preprocessor functionality or to provide implementation-defined information to the compiler. No restrictions are placed on the information that follows the **#pragma** command, and implementations should ignore information they do not understand. The argument to **#pragma** is subject to macro expansion.

There is obviously the possibility that two implementations will place inconsistent interpretations on the same information, so it is wise to use **#pragma** conditionally, based on which compiler is being used.

Example

The following code checks that the proper compiler (**tcc**), computer, and standard-conforming implementation are in use before issuing the **#pragma** command:

```
#if defined(_TCC) && defined(__STDC__) && defined(vax)
#pragma builtin(abs),inline(myfunc)
#endif
```

References **defined** 3.5.3; memory models 6.1.5; **#if** 3.5.1

3.8 ERROR DIRECTIVE

The **#error** directive is new in ISO C. Any sequence of tokens can follow the command name:

error *preprocessor-tokens*

The **#error** directive produces a compile-time error message that will include the argument tokens, which are subject to macro expansion.

Example

The **#error** directive is most useful in detecting programmer inconsistencies and violations of constraints during preprocessing. Here are some examples:

```
#if defined(A_THING) && defined(NOT_A_THING)
#error "Inconsistent things!"
#endif

#include "sizes.h"   /* defines SIZE */
...
#if (SIZE % 256) != 0
#error "SIZE must be a multiple of 256!"
#endif
```

References **defined** 3.5.3; **#if** 3.5.1

3.9 C++ COMPATIBILITY

C++ includes the ISO C preprocessor, so the differences going from C to C++ are minimal.

3.9.1 Predefined Macros

The macro **__cplusplus** is predefined by C++ implementations, and can be used in source files that are meant to be used in both C and C++ environments. The name does not follow ISO C spelling conventions for predefined macros, but rather is compatible with existing C++ implementations.

Whether or not **__STDC__** is defined in C++ environments is—in the current definition of C++—implementation-defined. There are enough differences between ISO C and C++ that it is not clear whether **__STDC__** should be defined or not.

Example

For compatibility with traditional C, ISO C, and C++, you should test the environment in this fashion:

```
#ifdef __cplusplus
    /* It's a C++ compilation */
#else
#ifdef __STDC__
    /* It's an ISO C compilation */
#else
    /* It's a non-ISO C compilation */
#endif
#endif
```

If you know that your C implementations will be ISO C conforming, this can be shortened to

```
#if defined(__cplusplus)
    /* It's a C++ compilation */
#else
    /* It's an ISO C compilation */
#endif
```

You may also wish to test for **__STDC_VERSION__**. It is likely that a new, predefined macro will be introduced to denote an ISO C++-conforming implementation.

References **__STDC__** 3.3.4; **__STDC_VERSION__** 3.3.4

3.10 EXERCISES

1. Which of the following ISO C macro definitions are (probably) wrong? Why? Which definitions might cause problems in traditional C?

   (a) `#define ident (x) x`
   (b) `# define FIVE = 5;`
   (c) `#define PLUS +`
   (d) `#define void int`

2. Below are shown some macro definitions and invocations. How would each macro invocation be expanded by ISO C and by traditional C?

	Definition	*Invocation*
(a)	`#define sum(a,b) a+b`	`sum(b,a)`
(b)	`#define paste(x,y) x/**/y`	`paste(x,4)`
(c)	`#define str(x) # x`	`str(a book)`
(d)	`#define  free(x) x ? free(x) : NULL`	`free(p)`

3. Two header files and a C program file are shown below. If the C preprocessor is applied to the program file, what will be the result?

```
/* File blue.h */
int blue = 0;
#include "red.h"
```

```
/* file red.h */
#ifndef __red__
#define __red__
```

```
/* file test.c */
#include "blue.h"
#include "red.h"
```

```
#include "blue.h"
int red = 0;
#endif
```

4. A friend shows you the following definition for a macro that is supposed to double its numeric argument. What is wrong with the macro? Rewrite the macro so that it operates correctly.

```
#define DBL(a)   a+a
```

5. In the following ISO C program fragment, what is the expansion of `M(M)(A,B)`?

```
#define M(x)       M ## x
#define MM(M,y)    M = # y
M(M)(A,B)
```

6. Write a sequence of preprocessor directives that will cause an ISO C program to fail to compile if the macro **SIZE** has not been defined, or if it has been defined but has a value that is not in the range 1 through 10.

7. Give an example of a sequence of characters that is a single token to the preprocessor but not to the C compiler proper.

8. What is wrong with the following program fragment?

```
if (x != 0)
   y = z/x;
else
   # error "Attempt to divide by zero, line " __LINE__
```

4

Declarations

To *declare* a *name* in the C language is to associate an identifier with some C object, such as a variable, function, or type. The names that can be declared in C are

- variables
- functions
- types
- type tags
- structure and union components
- enumeration constants
- statement labels
- preprocessor macros

Except for statement labels and preprocessor macros, all identifiers are declared by their appearance in C *declarations*. Variables, functions, and types appear in *declarators* within declarations, and type tags, structure and union components, and enumeration constants are declared in certain kinds of *type specifiers* in declarations. Statement labels are declared by their appearance in a C function, and preprocessor macros are declared by the **#define** preprocessor command.

Declarations in C are difficult to describe for several reasons. First, they involve some unusual syntax that may be confusing to the novice. For example, the declaration

```
int (*f)();
```

declares a pointer to a function returning an integer.

Second, many of the abstract properties of declarations, such as scope and extent, are more complicated in C than in other programming languages. Before jumping into the actual declaration syntax, we will discuss these properties in section 4.2.

Finally, some aspects of C's declarations are difficult to understand without a knowledge of C's type system, which is described in Chapter 5. In particular, discussions of type tags, structure and union components, and enumeration constants are left to that chapter, although some properties of those declarations will be discussed here for completeness.

References enumeration type 5.5; **#define** preprocessor command 3.3; statement labels 8.3; structure types 5.6; type specifiers 4.4; union types 5.7

4.1 ORGANIZATION OF DECLARATIONS

Declarations may appear in several places in a C program, and where they appear affects the properties of the declarations. A C source file, or *translation unit*, consists of a sequence of *top-level declarations* of functions, variables, and other things. Each function has *parameter declarations* and a *body*; the body in turn may contain *blocks* (compound statements). A block may contain a sequence of *inner declarations*.

The basic syntax of declarations is shown below. A discussion of function definitions is deferred until Chapter 9.

declaration :
    declaration-specifiers initialized-declarator-list **;**

declaration-specifiers :
    storage-class-specifier declaration-specifiers$_{opt}$
    type-specifier declaration-specifiers$_{opt}$
    type-qualifier declaration-specifiers$_{opt}$

initialized-declarator-list :
    initialized-declarator
    initialized-declarator-list **,** *initialized-declarator*

initialized-declarator :
    declarator initializer-part$_{opt}$

At most one storage class specifier and one type specifier may appear in the *declaration-specifiers*, although a single type specifier may be formed of several tokens (e.g., **unsigned long int**). Each of the two type qualifiers can appear at most once in the *declaration-specifiers*. Within these constraints, type specifiers, storage class specifiers, and type qualifiers can appear in any order in *declaration-specifiers*.

Example

It is customary to put any storage class specifier first, followed by any type qualifiers, and finally the type specifiers. In the following declarations, **i** and **j** have the same type and storage class, but the declaration of **i** is better style.

```
unsigned volatile long extern int const j;
extern const volatile unsigned long int i;
```

References declarators 4.5; expressions ch. 7; function definitions ch. 9; initializers 4.6; statements ch. 8; storage class specifiers 4.3; type specifiers and qualifiers 4.4

4.2 TERMINOLOGY

This section establishes some terminology used to describe declarations.

4.2.1 Scope

The *scope* of a declaration is the region of the C program text over which that declaration is active. In C, identifiers may have one of the six scopes listed in Table 4–1.

Table 4–1 Identifier scopes

Kind	Active region of declaration
Top-level identifiers	Extends from its declaration point (section 4.2.3) to the end of the source program file.
Formal parameters in function definitions	Extends from its declaration point to the end of the function body.
Formal parameters in function prototypes[a]	Extends from its declaration point to the end of the prototype.
Block (local) identifiers	Extends from its declaration point to the end of the block.
Statement labels	Encompasses the entire function body in which it appears.
Preprocessor macros	Extends from the **#define** command that declares it through the end of the source program file, or until the first **#undef** command that cancels its definition.

[a] New in ISO C.

Nonpreprocessor identifiers declared within a function or block are often said to have *block scope*, or *local scope*. Identifiers in prototypes have *prototype scope*. Statement labels have *function scope*. All other identifiers have *file scope*.

The scope of every identifier is limited to the C source file in which it occurs. However, some identifiers can be declared to be *external*, in which case the declarations of the same identifier in two or more files can be linked as described in section 4.8.

References **#define** preprocessor command 3.3; external names 4.8; prototypes ch. 4; **#undef** preprocessor command 3.3

4.2.2 Visibility

A declaration of an identifier is *visible* in some context if a use of the identifier in that context will be bound to the declaration. That is, the identifier will be associated with that declaration. A declaration might be visible throughout its scope, but it may also be *hidden* by other declarations whose scope and visibility overlap that of the first declaration.

Example

In the following program, the declaration of **foo** as an integer variable is hidden by the inner declaration of **foo** as a floating-point variable. The outer **foo** is hidden only within the body of function **main**.

```
int foo = 10;    /* foo defined at the top level */
int main(void)
{
    float foo;    /* this foo hides the outer foo */
    ...
}
```

In C, declarations at the beginning of a block can hide declarations outside the block. For one declaration to hide another, the declared identifiers must be the same, must belong to the same *overloading class*, and must be declared in two distinct scopes, one of which contains the other.

In ISO C, the scope of formal parameter declarations in a function definition is the same as the scope of identifiers declared at the beginning of the block that forms the function body. However, some earlier implementations of C have considered the parameter scope to enclose the block scope.

Example

The following redeclaration of **x** is an error in ISO C, but some older implementations permit it, probably allowing a troublesome programming error to go undetected.

```
int f(x)
    int x;
{
    long x = 34;        /* invalid? */
    return x;
}
```

References block 8.4; overloading class 4.2.4; parameter declarations 9.3; top-level declarations 4.1

4.2.3 Forward References

An identifier may not normally be used before it is fully declared. To be precise, we define the *declaration point* of an identifier to be the position of the identifier's lexical token in its declaration. Uses of the identifier after the declaration point are permitted. In the example below, the integer variable, **intsize**, can be initialized to its own size because the use of **intsize** in the initializer comes after the declaration point:

```
static int intsize = sizeof(intsize);
```

When an identifier is used before it is completely declared, a *forward reference* to the declaration is said to occur. C permits forward references in three situations:

1. A statement label may appear in a **goto** statement before it appears as a label, since its scope covers the entire function body:

```
if (error) goto recover;
...
recover:
    CloseFiles();
```

2. An incomplete structure, union, or enumeration type may be declared, allowing it to be used for some purposes before it is fully defined. See section 5.6.1.
3. A function can be declared separately from its definition, either with a declaration or implicitly by its appearance in a function call. See sections 4.7 and 5.8.

Example

Invalid forward references are illustrated in this example. The programmer is attempting to define a self-referential structure with a **typedef** declaration. In this case, the last occurrence of **cell** on the line is the declaration point, and therefore the use of **cell** within the structure is invalid.

```
typedef struct { int Value; cell *Next; } cell;
```

The correct way to declare such a type is by use of a structure tag, **S**, which is defined on its first appearance and then used later within the declaration:

```
typedef struct S { int Value; struct S *Next; } cell;
```

See also the later discussions of implicit declarations (section 4.7) and duplicate declarations (section 4.2.5).

References duplicate declarations 4.2.5; function types 5.8; **goto** statement 8.10; implicit declarations 4.7; pointer types 5.3; structure types 5.6

4.2.4 Overloading of Names

In C and other programming languages, the same identifier may be associated with more than one program entity at a time. When this happens, we say that the name is *overloaded*, and the context in which the name is used determines the association that is in effect. For instance, an identifier might be both the name of a variable and a structure tag. When used in an expression, the variable association is used; when used in a type specifier, the tag association is used.

There are five *overloading classes* for names in C. (We sometimes refer to them as *name spaces*.) They are listed and described in Table 4–2 on page 70.

These overloading rules differ slightly from those in the original definition of C. First, the original definition of C put statement labels in the same name space as ordinary identifiers, and enough compilers still follow this rule that the programmer should be aware of it and consider not using the same name for a label and a variable.

Second, the original definition of C allocated all structure and union component names from a single name space instead of separate name spaces for each type. Thus, if **x** was a component of one structure type, it couldn't be the member of another structure

Table 4–2 Overloading classes

Class	Included identifiers
Preprocessor macro names	Because preprocessing logically occurs before compilation, names used by the preprocessor are independent of any other names in a C program.
Statement labels	Named statement labels are part of statements. Definitions of statement labels are always followed by **:** (and are not part of **case** labels). Uses of statement labels always immediately follow the reserved word **goto**.
Structure, union, and enumeration tags	These tags are part of structure, union, and enumeration type specifiers and, if present, always immediately follow the reserved words **struct**, **union**, or **enum**.
Component names	Component names are allocated in name spaces associated with each structure and union type. That is, the same identifier can be a component name in any number of structures or unions at the same time. Definitions of component names always occur within structure or union type specifiers. Uses of component names always immediately follow the selection operators **.** and **->**.
Other names	All other names fall into an overloading class that includes variables, functions, **typedef** names, and enumeration constants.

type. There were complicated rules that allowed identifiers to be in more than one structure if their offsets in the structure were identical. Fortunately, this is now rarely seen in C compilers and has been corrected in the current language definitions.

When a name is overloaded with several associations, each association has its own scope and may be hidden by other declarations independent of other associations. For instance, if an identifier is being used both as a variable and a structure tag, an inner block may redefine the variable association without altering the tag association.

C++ injects structure and union tags into the "other" name space. See section 4.9.2.

References component names 5.6.3; duplicate definition 4.2.5; enumeration tags 5.5; **goto** statement 8.10; selection operators 7.4.2; statement labels 8.10; structure tags 5.6; structure type specifiers 5.6; **typedef** names 5.10; union tags 5.7; union type specifiers 5.7

4.2.5 Duplicate Declarations

It is invalid to make two declarations of the same name (in the same overloading class) in the same block or at the top level. Such declarations are said to *conflict*.

Example

The two declarations of **howmany**, below, are conflicting but the two declarations of **str** are not (because they are in different name spaces).

```
extern int howmany;
extern char str[10];
typedef double howmany();
extern struct str {int a, b;} x;
```

There are two exceptions to the prohibition against duplicate declarations. First, any number of external (*referencing*) declarations for the same name may exist, as long as the declarations assign the same type to the name in each instance. This exception reflects the belief that declaring the same external library function twice should not be invalid.

Second, if an identifier is declared as being external, that declaration may be followed with a *definition* (section 4.8) of the name later in the program, assuming that the definition assigns the same type to the name as the external declaration(s). This exception allows the user to generate valid forward references to variables and functions.

Example

We define two functions, **f** and **g**, that reference each other. Normally, the use of **f** within **g** would be an invalid forward reference. However, by preceding the definition of **g** with an external declaration of **f**, we give the compiler enough information about **f** to compile **g**. (Without the initial declaration of **f**, a one-pass compiler could not know when compiling **g** that **f** returns a value of type **double** rather than **int**.)

```
extern double f();

double g(x, y)
    double x, y;
{
    ... f(x-y) ...
}

double f(z)
    double z;
{
    ... g(z, z/2.0) ...
}
```

There is a deficiency in this mechanism. Variables that are the subject of forward references from within the same file must be declared **extern**, when they could otherwise have storage class **static**. Some compilers, when they see an **extern** declaration followed by a **static** definition of the same name, will guess (correctly or not) what is going on and not generate an external reference at link time.

References defining and referencing declarations 4.8; **extern** storage class 4.3; forward references 4.2; overloading class 4.2; **static** storage class 4.3

4.2.6 Duplicate Visibility

Because C's scoping rules specify that a name's scope begins at its declaration point rather than at the head of the block in which it is defined, a situation can arise in which two nonconflicting declarations can be referenced in different parts of the same block.

Example

In the code below there are two variables named **i** referenced in the block labeled **B**—the integer **i** declared in the outer block is used to initialize the variable **j**, and then a floating-point variable **i** is declared, hiding the first **i**.

```
{
    int i = 0;
    ...
    B: {
            int j = i;
            float i = 10.0;
            ...
        }
}
```

The reference to **i** in the initialization of **j** is ambiguous. Which **i** was wanted? Most compilers will do what was (apparently) intended; the first use of **i** in block **B** is bound to the outer definition, and the redefinition of **i** then hides the outer definition for the remainder of the block. We consider this usage to be bad programming style; it should be avoided.

4.2.7 Extent

Variables and functions, unlike types, have an existence at run time—that is, they have storage allocated to them. The *extent* of these objects is the period of time that the storage is allocated.

An object is said to have *static extent* when it is allocated storage at or before the beginning of program execution and the storage remains allocated until program termination. In C, all functions have static extent, as do all variables declared in top-level declarations. Variables declared at the beginning of blocks may have static extent, depending on the declaration.

An object is said to have *local extent* when it is created upon entry to a block or function and is destroyed upon exit from the block or function. If a variable with local extent has an initializer, the variable is initialized each time it is created. Formal parameters have local extent, and variables declared at the beginning of blocks may have local extent, depending on the declaration. A variable with local extent is called *automatic* in C.

Finally, it is possible in C to have data objects with *dynamic extent*—that is, objects that are created and destroyed explicitly at the programmer's whim. However, dynamic objects must be created through the use of special library routines such as **malloc** and are not viewed as part of the C language itself.

References **auto** storage class 4.3; initializers 4.6; **malloc** function 16.1; **static** storage class 4.3; storage allocation functions ch. 16

4.2.8 Initial Values

Allocating storage for a variable does not necessarily establish the initial contents of that storage. Most variable declarations in C may have *initializers*, expressions used to set the initial value of a variable at the time that storage is allocated for it. If an initializer is not specified for a variable, its value after allocation is unpredictable.

It is important to remember that a static variable is initialized only once and that it retains its value even when the program is executing outside its scope.

Example

In the following code, two variables, **L** and **S**, are declared at the head of a block and both are initialized to 0. Both variables have local scope, but **S** has static extent while **L** has local (automatic) extent. Each time the block is entered, both variables are incremented by one and the new values printed.

```
{
    static int S = 0;
    auto int L = 0;
    L = L + 1;
    S = S + 1;
    printf("L = %d, S = %d\n", L, S);
}
```

What values will be printed? If the block is executed many times, the output will be this:

```
L = 1, S = 1
L = 1, S = 2
L = 1, S = 3
L = 1, S = 4
...
```

There is one dangerous feature of C's initialization of automatic variables declared at the beginning of blocks. The initialization is guaranteed to occur only if the block is entered normally—that is, if control flows into the beginning of the block. Through the use of statement labels and the **goto** statement, it is possible to jump into the middle of a block; if this is done, there is no guarantee that automatic variables will be initialized. (In fact, most ISO and non-ISO implementations do *not* initialize them.) The same is true when **case** or **default** labels are used in conjunction with the **switch** statement to cause control to be transferred into a block.

Example

The initialization of variable **sum**, below, will (probably) not occur when the **goto** statement transfers control to label **L**. This will cause **sum** to begin with an indeterminate value.

```
goto L;
...
{
    static int vector[10] = {1,2,3,4,5,6,7,8,9,10};
    int sum = 0;
L:
    /* Add up elements of "vector". */
    for ( i=1; i<10; i++ ) sum += vector[i];
         printf("sum is %d", sum);
}
```

References **goto** statement 8.10; initialization of variables 4.6; storage classes 4.3; **switch** statement 8.7

4.2.9 External Names

A special case of scope and visibility is the *external* variable or function. An external object is treated just like a static object in the file containing its declaration. However, an identifier declared to be external is *exported* to the linker, and if the same identifier is similarly declared in another program file, the linker will ensure that the two files reference the same object (variable or function).

External names are usually declared at the top level of a C program and therefore have file scope. However, pre-ISO implementations differ on how external names declared within a block are handled.

Example

The following program fragment is acceptable to many C compilers; it declares an external name within a block and then uses it outside the block:

```
{
    extern int E;
    ...
}
E = 1;
```

According to normal block-scoping rules the declaration should not be visible outside the block, but many implementations of C implicitly give **E** file scope and so compile this fragment without error. ISO C requires the declaration to have block scope, but does not state that the above fragment should be invalid. Technically, the behavior of an implementation in this case is undefined, thus permitting a conforming implementation to accept the program. We think programmers should treat this fragment as a programming error even if the compiler accepts it and the run-time behavior is correct.

It is indisputably an error if two external declarations (in the same file or different files within the same program) specify different types for the same identifier.

Example

In the following program, the two declarations of **X** do not conflict in the source file, although their behavior at run-time is undefined:

```
int f()    { extern int X;    return X; }
double g() { extern double X; return X; }
```

References external name conventions 2.5; external name definition and reference 4.8; scope 4.2.1; visibility 4.2.2

4.2.10 Compile-time Objects

So far the discussion has focused mainly on variables and functions, which have an existence at run time. However, the scope and visibility rules apply equally to identifiers associated with objects that do not necessarily exist at run time: **typedef** names, type tags, and enumeration constants. When any of these identifiers are declared, their scope is the same as that of a variable defined at the same location.

References enumeration constants 5.5; scope 4.2.1; structure type 5.6; **`typedef`** name 5.10; visibility 4.2.2

4.3 STORAGE CLASS SPECIFIERS

We now proceed to examine the pieces of declarations: storage class specifiers, type specifiers, declarators, and initializers.

A storage class specifier determines the extent of a declared object (except for **`typedef`**, which is special). At most one storage class specifier may appear in a declaration. It is customary for storage class specifiers (if any) to precede type specifiers or qualifiers (if any) in declarations. In fact, both ISO and traditional C allow them to occur in any order, although ISO C considers this to be an obsolescent feature.

storage-class-specifier : one of
  `auto` **`extern`** **`register`** **`static`** **`typedef`**

The meanings of the storage classes are given in Table 4–3. Note that not all storage classes are permitted in every declaration context.

Table 4–3 Storage class specifiers

Specifier	Usage
`auto`	Permitted only in declarations of variables at the heads of blocks. It indicates that the variable has local (automatic) extent. (Because this is the default, **`auto`** is rarely seen in C programs.)
`extern`	May appear in declarations of external functions and variables, either at the top level or at the heads of blocks. It indicates that the object declared has static extent and its name is known to the linker. See section 4.8.
`register`	May be used for local variables or parameter declarations. It is equivalent to **`auto`**, except that it provides a hint to the compiler that the object will be heavily used and should be allocated in a way that minimizes access time.
`static`	May appear on declarations of functions or variables. On function definitions, it is used only to specify that the function name is not to be exported to the linker. On function declarations, it indicates that the declared function will be defined—with storage class **`static`**—later in the file. On data declarations, it always signifies a defining declaration that is not exported to the linker. Variables declared with this storage class have static extent (as opposed to local extent, signified by **`auto`**).
`typedef`	Indicates that the declaration is defining a new name for a data type, rather than for a variable or function. The name of the data type appears where a variable name would appear in a variable declaration, and the data type itself is the type that would have been assigned to the variable name. (See section 5.10.)

ISO C allows **register** to be used with any type of variable or parameter, but it is not permitted to compute the address of such an object, either explicitly (with the **&** operator) or implicitly (e.g., by converting an array name to a pointer when subscripting the array). Many non-ISO C compilers behave differently:

- They may restrict the use of **register** to objects of scalar types.
- They may permit the use of **&** on **register** objects.
- They may implicitly widen small objects declared with **register**, e.g., treating the declaration **register char x** as if it were **register int x**.

Implementations are permitted to treat the **register** storage class specifier the same as the **auto** specifier. However, programmers can expect the use of **register** on one or two heavily used variables in a function to increase performance. Using **register** on many declarations is likely to be ineffective or counterproductive. The use of **register** with highly optimizing compilers is likely to have less effect, since those compilers already allocate variables to registers as necessary.

References address operator **&** 7.5.6; formal parameter declarations 9.3; initializers 4.6; subscripts 7.4.1; top-level declarations 4.1; **typedef** names 5.10

4.3.1 Default Storage Class Specifiers

If no storage class specifier is supplied with a declaration, one will be assumed based upon the declaration context, as shown in Table 4–4.

Table 4–4 Default storage class specifiers

Location of declaration	Kind of declaration	Default storage class
Top level	All	**extern**
Function parameter	All	**none** (that is, "not **register**")
Block head	Functions	**extern**
Block head	Non-functions	**auto**

Omitting the storage class specifier on a top-level declaration may not be the same as supplying **extern**, as discussed in section 4.8. As a matter of good programming style, we think programmers should supply the storage class **extern** when declaring an external function inside a block. The **auto** storage class is rarely seen in C programs; it is usually defaulted.

References blocks 8.4; parameter declarations 9.3; top-level declarations 4.1, 4.8

4.3.2 Examples of Storage Class Specifiers

An implementation of the heapsort algorithm is shown below. It is beyond the scope of this book to explain how it works in detail.

Example

The algorithm regards the array as a binary tree such that the two subtrees of element **b[k]** are elements **b[2*k]** and **b[2*k+1]**. A *heap* is a tree such that every node contains a number that is no smaller than any of the numbers contained by that node's descendants.

```
static void adjust (int v[], int m, register int n)
/*  If v[m+1] through v[n] is already in heap form,
    this puts v[m] through v[n] into heap form. */
{
    register int *b, j, k, temp;
    b = v - 1; /* b is "1-origin", customary in heapsort,
                  i.e., v[j] is the same as b[j-1] */
    j = m;
    k = m * 2;
    while (k <= n) {
        if (k < n && b[k] < b[k+1]) ++k;
        if (b[j] < b[k]) SWAP(b[j], b[k]);
        j = k;
        k *= 2;
    }
}

#define SWAP(x, y) (temp = (x), (x) = (y), (y) = temp)

/* Sort v[0]...v[n-1] into increasing order. */
void heapsort(int v[], int n)
{
    int *b, j, temp;
    b = v - 1;
    /* Put the array into the form of a heap. */
    for (j = n/2; j > 0; j--) adjust(v, j, n);
    /* Repeatedly extract the largest element and
       put it at the end of the unsorted region. */
    for (j = n-1; j > 0; j--) {
        SWAP(b[1], b[j+1]);
        adjust(v, 1, j);
    }
}
```

The auxiliary function **adjust** does not need to be externally visible, and so it is declared **static**. The speed of the **adjust** function is crucial to the performance of the sort, and so its local variables have been given storage class **register** as a hint to the compiler. The formal parameter **n** is also referred to repeatedly within **adjust**, and so it is also specified with storage class **register**. The other two formal parameters for **adjust** are referred to only once and are defaulted to "not register."

The main function is **heapsort**; it must be visible to users of the sort package, and so it has the default storage class, namely **extern**. The local variables of function **heapsort** do not impact performance; they have been given the default storage class, **auto**.

4.4 TYPE SPECIFIERS AND QUALIFIERS

Type specifiers provide some of the information about the data type of the program identifiers being declared. Additional type information is supplied by the declarators. Type specifiers may also define (as a side effect) type tags, structure and union component names, and enumeration constants.

The type qualifiers, **const** and **volatile**, are new in ISO C and specify additional properties of types that are relevant only when accessing objects of the type through lvalues (section 7.1):

type-specifier :
    enumeration-type-specifier
    floating-point-type-specifier
    integer-type-specifier
    structure-type-specifier
    typedef-name
    union-type-specifier
    void-type-specifier

type-qualifier :
    const
    volatile

Example

Here are some examples of type specifiers:

`void`	`union { int a; char b; }`
`int`	`enum {red, blue, green}`
`unsigned long int`	`char`
`my_struct_type`	`float`

The type specifiers are described in detail in Chapter 5, and we will defer further discussion of particular type specifiers until then. However, a few general issues surrounding type specifiers will be discussed in the following sections.

References declarators 4.5; enumeration type specifier 5.5; floating-point type specifier 5.2; integer type specifier 5.1; lvalue 7.1; structure type specifier 5.6; type qualifiers 4.4.3; **typedef** name 5.10; union type specifier 5.7; **void** type specifier 5.9

4.4.1 Default Type Specifiers

C allows the type specifier in a variable declaration or function definition to be omitted, in which case it defaults to **int**. This is bad programming style in modern C. Older compilers did not implement the **void** type, so a rationale behind omitting the type specifier on function definitions was to indicate to human readers that the function didn't really return a value (although the compiler had to assume that it did).

Example

In pre-ISO C it was common to see function definitions like this:

```
/* Sort v[0]…v[n-1] into increasing order. */
sort(v, n)
   int v[], n;
{
   …
}
```

The modern, ISO C style is to declare those functions with the **void** type:

```
/* Sort v[0]…v[n-1] into increasing order. */
void sort(int v[], int n)
{
   …
}
```

Example

When using a compiler that doesn't implement **void**, it is much nicer to define **void** yourself and then use it explicitly than to omit the type specifier entirely:

```
/* Make "void" be a synonym for "int". */
typedef int void;
```

At least one compiler we know of actually reserves the identifier **void** but doesn't implement it. For that compiler, the preprocessor definition

```
#define void int
```

is one of the few cases in which using a reserved word as a macro name is justified.

Example

The declaration syntax (section 4.1) requires declarations to contain a storage class specifier, a type specifier, a type qualifier, or some combination of the three. This requirement avoids a syntactic ambiguity in the language. If all specifiers and qualifiers were defaulted, the declaration

```
extern int f();
```

would become simply

```
f();
```

which is syntactically equivalent to a statement consisting of a function call. We think that the best style is to always include the type specifier and to allow the storage class specifier to default, at least when it is **auto**.

Example

A final note for LALR(1) grammar aficionados: both the storage class specifier and the type specifier can be omitted on a function *definition*, and this is very common in C programs, as in

```
main() { … }
```

There is no syntactic ambiguity in this case, because the declarator in a function declaration must be followed by a comma or semicolon, whereas the declarator in a function definition must be followed by a left brace.

References declarations 4.1; function definitions 9.1; **`void`** type specifier 5.9

4.4.2 Missing Declarators

The following discussion deals with a subtle point of declarations and type specifiers. Type specifiers that are structure, union, or enumeration definitions have a side effect of defining new types. If you simply want to define a type, it makes sense to omit all the declarators from the declaration and just write the type specifier. The C grammar permits this, and so do all C compilers. However, the grammar also permits some nonsensical declarations, such as omitting the type tag, including nonsensical storage class specifiers, or writing a type specifier that does not create a type as a side effect. Good C compilers will issue warnings when these nonsensical declarations appear.

Example

The following declaration consists of a single type specifier. It defines a new structure type **`S`** with components **`a`** and **`b`**.

```
struct S { int a, b; };    /* Define struct S */
```

The type can be referenced later by using just the specifier

```
struct S x, y, z;          /* Define 3 variables */
```

However, the following declarations are nonsensical:

```
struct { int a, b; };             /* no tag */
int ;                             /* no effect */
static struct T { int a, b; };    /* extra storage class */
```

In the first case, there is no structure tag, so it would be impossible to refer to the type later in the program. In the second case, the declaration has no effect at all. In the third case, a storage class specifier has been supplied, which will be ignored. You might think that a later declaration of the form

```
struct T x, y;
```

will cause **`x`** and **`y`** to have the storage class **`static`**. It won't.

References enumeration types 5.5; declarators 4.5; structure types 5.6; type specifiers 4.4; union types 5.7

4.4.3 Type Qualifiers

The type qualifiers **`const`** and **`volatile`** are new in ISO C. An identifier declared using one or both of these qualifiers is said to have a *qualified type*; there are three different qualified *versions* of each unqualified type, corresponding to the presence of the qualifier **`const`**, **`volatile`**, or both. None of the three qualified versions is compatible with the others or with the unqualified type.

Type qualifiers specify additional properties of types that are relevant only when accessing objects through lvalues with those qualified types. When used in a context that requires a value rather than a designator, the qualifiers are eliminated from the type. That is, in the expression L=R, the type of the right operand of = always has an unqualified type, even if it was declared with type qualifiers. The left operand, however, keeps its qualification, since it is used in lvalue context.

Example

When using a C compiler that does not support type qualifiers, you can supply the following macro definitions so that the use of the type qualifiers will not cause the compilation to fail. Of course, the qualifiers will also have no effect.

```
#ifndef __STDC__
#define const /*nothing*/
#define volatile /*nothing*/
#endif
```

References **#ifndef** 3.5.3; **__STDC__** 11.3; type compatibility 5.11

4.4.4 Const

The type qualifier **const** may be used with other type specifiers and qualifiers—including structure, union, and enumeration type specifiers and **volatile**—or it may be used alone, in which case the additional specifier **int** is assumed. Members of structures can also be qualified with **const**.

An lvalue expression of a **const**-qualified type cannot be used to modify an object. That is, such an lvalue cannot be used as the left operand of an assignment expression or the operand of an increment or decrement operator. The intent is to use the **const** qualifier to designate objects whose value is unchanging, and to have the C compiler attempt to ensure that the programmer does not change the value.

Example

The following declaration specifies that **ic** is to be an integer with the constant value 37:

```
const int ic = 37;
...
ic = 5; /* Invalid */
ic++;   /* Invalid */
```

The **const** qualifier can also appear in pointer declarators, to make it possible to declare both "constant pointers" and "pointers to constant data":

```
int * const const_pointer;
const int *pointer_to_const;
```

The syntax may be confusing: constant pointers and constant integers, for example, have the type qualifier **const** in different locations. The appearance also changes when

typedef names are used—the constant pointer **const_pointer** in the previous example may also be declared like this:

```
typedef int *int_pointer;
const int_pointer const_pointer;
```

This makes **const_pointer** look like a "pointer to constant **int_pointer**," but it isn't—it's still a constant pointer to a (non-constant) **int**. In fact, because the order of type specifiers and qualifiers doesn't matter, the last declaration may be written:

```
int_pointer const const_pointer;
```

You can alter a variable that has type "pointer to constant data," but the object to which it points cannot altered. Expressions with this type can be generated by applying the address operator **&** to values of **const**-qualified types. To protect the integrity of constant data, assigning a value of type "pointer to **const** *T* " to an object of type "pointer to *T* " is allowed only by using an explicit cast.

Example

```
const int *pc;  /* pointer to a constant integer */
int *p, i;
const int ic;
pc = p = &i;     /* OK */
pc = &ic;        /* OK */
*p = 5;          /* OK */
*pc = 5;         /* Invalid */

pc = &i;         /* OK */
pc = p;          /* OK */
p = &ic;         /* Invalid */
p = pc;          /* Invalid */
p = (int *)&ic;  /* OK */
p = (int *)pc;   /* OK */
```

The language rules for **const** are not foolproof—that is, they may be bypassed or overridden if the programmer tries hard enough. For instance, the address of a constant object can be passed to an external function without a prototype, and that function could modify the constant object. However, implementations are permitted to allocate static objects of **const**-qualified types in read-only storage, so that attempts to alter the objects could cause run-time errors.

Example

This program fragment illustrates some dangers is circumventing the **const** qualifier.

```
static const int * pc;
static int * p;
static const int ic = 0;
...
pc = &ic;           /* OK */
p = (int *)pc;      /* Valid, but dangerous */
*p = 5;             /* Valid, but may cause a run-time error */
```

References assignment expression 7.9; increment and decrement expressions 7.4; pointer declarators 4.5.2

4.4.5 Volatile

The type qualifier **volatile** may be used with other type specifiers and qualifiers—including structure, union, and enumeration type specifiers and **const**—or may be used alone, in which case the additional specifier **int** is assumed.

The **volatile** type qualifier informs the ISO C implementation that certain objects can have their values altered in ways not under control of the implementation. That is, any object (strictly speaking, any lvalue expression) of a **volatile**-qualified type should not participate in optimizations that would increase, decrease, or delay any references to, or modifications of, the object.

To be more precise, ISO C introduces the notion of *sequence points* in C programs. A sequence point exists at the completion of all expressions that are not part of a larger expression—that is, at the end of expression statements, control expressions **if**, **switch**, **while**, and **do** statements, each of the three control expressions in the **for** statement, **return** statement expressions, and initializers. Additional sequence points are present in function calls immediately after all the arguments are evaluated, in the logical AND (**&&**) and OR (**||**) expressions, and before the conditional operator (**?:**) and the comma operator (**,**).

References to and modifications of volatile objects must not be optimized across sequence points, although optimizations between sequence points are permitted. Extra references or modifications can be generated at any time.

Example

Consider the following program fragment:

```
extern int f();
auto int i,j;
...
i = f(0);
while (i) {
    if (f(j*j)) break;
}
```

If the variable **i** were not used again during its lifetime, then traditional C implementations would be permitted to rewrite this program fragment as

```
if (f(0)) {
    i = j*j;
    while( !f(i) ) ;
}
```

The first assignment to `i` was eliminated, and `i` was reused as a temporary variable to hold `j*j`, which is evaluated once outside the loop. If the declaration of `i` and `j` were

```
auto volatile int i,j;
```

then these optimizations would not be permitted. However, we could write the loop as shown below, eliminating one reference to `j` before the sequence point at the end of the `if` statement control expression:

```
i = f(0);
while (i) {
    register int temp = j;
    if (f(temp*temp)) break;
}
```

The new syntax for pointer declarators allows the declaration of type "pointer to **volatile** ...." References to this kind of pointer may be optimized, but references to the object to which it points cannot be. Assigning a value of type "pointer to **volatile** *T*" to an object of type "pointer to *T*" is allowed only when an explicit cast is used.

Example

Here are some examples of valid and invalid uses of **volatile** objects:

```
volatile int * pv;
int *p;
pv = p;          /* OK */
p = pv;          /* Invalid */
p = (int *)pv;  /* OK */
```

The most common use of **volatile** is to provide reliable access to special memory locations used by the computer hardware or by asynchronous processes such as interrupt handlers.

Example

Consider the following typical example. A computer has three special hardware locations:

Address	Use
0xFFFFFF20	Input data buffer
0xFFFFFF24	Output data buffer
0xFFFFFF28	Control register

The control register and input data buffer can be read by a program but not written; the output buffer can be written but not read. The third least significant bit of the control register is called "input available"; it is set to 1 when data have arrived from an external source, and it is set to

0 automatically when these data are read out of the input buffer by the program (after which time the contents of the buffer are undefined until "input available" becomes 1 again). The second least significant bit of the control register is called "output available"; when the external device is ready to accept data, the bit is set to 1. When data are placed in the output buffer by the program the bit is automatically set to 0 and the data are written out. Placing data in the output buffer when the control bit is 0 causes unpredictable results.

The function **copy_data** below copies data from the input to the output until an input value of 0 is seen. The number of characters copied is returned. There is no provision for overflow or other error conditions:

```
typedef unsigned long datatype, controltype, counttype;

#define CONTROLLER \
    ((const volatile controltype * const) 0xFFFFFF28)
#define INPUT_BUF \
    ((const volatile datatype * const) 0xFFFFFF20)
#define OUTPUT_BUF \
    ((volatile datatype * const)  0xFFFFFF24)
#define input_ready ((*CONTROLLER) & 0x4)
#define output_ready ((*CONTROLLER) & 0x2)

counttype copy_data(void)
{
    counttype count = 0;
    datatype temp;
    for(;;) {
        while (!input_ready) ;     /* Wait for input */
        temp = *INPUT_BUF;
        if (temp == 0) return count;
        while (!output_ready) ;    /* Wait to do output */
        *OUTPUT_BUF = temp;
        count++;
    }
}
```

References pointer declarators 4.5.2

4.5 DECLARATORS

Declarators introduce the name being declared and also supply additional type information. No other programming language has anything quite like C's declarators:

declarator :
  pointer-declarator
  direct-declarator

direct-declarator :
  simple-declarator
  (*declarator* **)**
  function-declarator
  array-declarator

The different kinds of declarators are described in the following sections.

4.5.1 Simple Declarators

Simple declarators are used to define variables of arithmetic, enumeration, structure, and union types:

simple-declarator :
  identifier

Suppose that *S* is a type specifier and *id* is any identifier. Then the declaration

S id **;**

indicates that *id* is of type *S*. The *id* is called a simple declarator.

Example

Declaration	Type of x
`int x;`	integer
`float x;`	floating-point
`struct S { int a; float b;} x;`	structure of two components

Simple declarators may be used in a declaration when the type specifier supplies all the typing information. This happens for arithmetic, structure, union, enumeration, and void types, and for types represented by **typedef** names. Pointer, array, and function types require the use of more complicated declarators. However, every declarator includes an identifier, and we thus say that a declarator "encloses" an identifier.

References type specifiers 4.4; structure types 5.6; **typedef** names 5.10

4.5.2 Pointer Declarators

Pointer declarators are used to declare variables of pointer types. The *type-qualifier-list* in the following syntax is new in ISO C; in older compilers it is omitted:

pointer-declarator :
  pointer direct-declarator

pointer:
  ***** *type-qualifier-list*$_{opt}$
  ***** *type-qualifier-list*$_{opt}$ *pointer*

type-qualifier-list : (ISO C)
  type-qualifier
  type-qualifer-list type qualifier

Suppose that *D* is any declarator enclosing the identifier *id*, and that the declaration "*S D*;" indicates that *id* has type "… *S*." Then the declaration

```
S *D ;
```

indicates that *id* has type "…pointer to *S*." The optional *type-qualifier-list* in pointer declarators is allowed only in ISO C. When present, the qualifiers apply to the pointer, not to the object pointed to.

Example

In the three declarations of **x** in the table below, *id* is **x**, *S* is **int**, and "…" is, respectively, "", "array of," and "function returning." (It's harder to explain than it is to learn.)

Declaration	Type of x
`int *x;`	pointer to integer
`int *x[];`	array of pointers to integers
`int *x();`	function returning a pointer to an integer

Example

In the following declarations, **ptr_to_const** is a (non-constant) pointer to a constant integer, whereas **const_ptr** is a constant pointer to a (non-constant) integer:

```
const int * ptr_to_const;
int * const const_ptr;
```

References array declarators 4.5.3; **const** type qualifier 4.4.4; function declarators 4.5.4; pointer types 5.3; type qualifiers 4.4.3

4.5.3 Array Declarators

Array declarators are used to declare objects of array types:

array-declarator :
  direct-declarator **[** *constant-expression*$_{opt}$ **]**

constant-expression :
  expression

If *D* is any declarator enclosing the identifier *id*, and if the declaration "*S D*;" indicates that *id* has type "... *S*," then the declaration

```
S (D) [ e ] ;
```

indicates that *id* has type "... array of *S*." (The parentheses may often be elided according to the precedence rules in constructing declarators; see section 4.5.5.) The integer constant expression *e*, if present, specifies the number of elements in the array.

Example

In the three declarations below, *id* is **x**, *S* is **int**, and "..." is, respectively, "", "pointer to," and "array of."

Declaration	Type of x
`int (x)[5];`	array of integers
`int (*x)[5];`	pointer to an array of integers
`int (x[5])[5];`	array of array of integers

Type qualifiers may appear in the declaration of an object of array type, but the qualifiers apply to the elements rather than the array itself. That is, the declaration **const int a[10]** is a declaration of an array of constant integers, not a constant array of integers.

C's arrays are always "0-origin." The number of elements in an array must be greater than 0, although some popular C compilers do not check this. Higher-dimensioned arrays are declared as "arrays of arrays."

Example

The array declaration

```
int A[3];
```

defines the elements **A[0]**, **A[1]**, and **A[2]**. Examples of higher-dimensioned arrays include:

```
int judges_scores[10][2];
int checker_board[8][8];
```

The length of the array, a constant expression, may be omitted as long as it is not needed to allocate storage. It is not needed when:

1. The object being declared is a formal parameter of a function.
2. The declarator is accompanied by an initializer from which the length of the array can be deduced.
3. The declaration is not a defining occurrence—that is, it is an external declaration that refers to an object defined elsewhere.

An exception to these cases is that the declaration of any n-dimensional array must include the sizes of the last n–1 dimensions so that the accessing algorithm can be determined. For more information, see section 5.4.

Example

Here are some examples of using (and omitting) array dimensions.

Declaration	Use of array length
`static int vector[5];`	This is a defining occurrence of the array; the length must be specified.
`char prompt[]="Yes or No?";`	The length (11) is computed from the size of the initializer (including the final `'\0'`).
`extern matrix[][10];`	Although this is not a defining occurrence, the bounds of the subarray are needed for address calculations.

References array types 5.4; constant expressions 7.11; formal parameters 9.3; initializers 4.6; referencing and defining declarations 4.8; type qualifiers 4.4.3

4.5.4 Function Declarators

Function declarators are used to declare or define functions, and to declare types that have function pointers as components:

function-declarator :
  direct-declarator **(** *parameter-type-list* **)** (ISO C)
  direct-declarator **(** *identifier-list*$_{opt}$ **)**

parameter-type-list :
  parameter list
  parameter-list **,** ...

parameter-list :
  parameter-declaration
  parameter-list **,** *parameter-declaration*

parameter-declaration :
  declaration-specifiers declarator
  declaration-specifiers abstract-declarator$_{opt}$

identifier-list :
  identifier
  parameter-list **,** *identifier*

If *D* is any declarator enclosing the identifier *id*, and if the declaration "*S D*`;`" indicates that *id* has type "… *S*," then the declaration

```
S (D)(P) ;
```

indicates that *id* has type "... function returning *S* with parameters *P*." The parentheses around *D* can be omitted in most cases according to the precedence rules in constructing declarators (section 4.5.5). The presence of *parameter-type-list* in the declarator syntax indicates that the declarator is in the form of an ISO C prototype. Without it, the declarator is in traditional form, which is accepted by both traditional and ISO C compilers.

Example

Some examples of function declarators are shown below:

Declaration	Type of **x**
int x();	function with unspecified parameters returning an integer
int x(double, float);	function taking a `double` and a `float` parameter and returning an integer (prototype)
int x(double d, float f);	same as the preceding declarator
int (*x)();	pointer to a function with unspecified parameters returning an integer
int (*x[])(int,...);	array of pointers to functions that take a variable number of parameters beginning with an integer and return an integer (prototype)

Function declarators are subject to several constraints depending on whether they appear in a function definition or as part of an object or function type declaration. Table 4–5 shows the possible forms of a function declarator, indicates whether it is in traditional C form or ISO C prototype form, whether it can appear in a function definition or in a function type declaration, and what parameter information is specified. In the table, the

Table 4–5 Function declarators

Syntax	Form	Appears in	Parameters specified
f()	traditional	definitions	no parameters
f()	traditional	type declarations	any number of parameters
f(x, y,..., z)	traditional	definitions	fixed[a]
f(**void**)	prototype	either	no parameters
f(T_x, T_y,..., T_z)	prototype	type declarations	fixed
f(T_x, T_y,..., T_z**, ...**)	prototype	type declarations	fixed, plus extras[b]
f(T_x x, T_y y,..., T_z z)	prototype	either	fixed
f(T_x x, T_y y,..., T_z z**, ...**)	prototype	either	fixed, plus extras[b]

[a] It is possible to have additional, unspecified parameters, except in ISO C.
[b] The number and type of the extra parameters are unspecified.

notation T_x x refers to the syntax "*declaration-specifiers declarator*;"—that is, a parameter type declaration that includes the parameter name, x. T_x refers to

declaration-specifiers abstract-declarator$_{opt}$

—that is, a parameter type declaration that omits the parameter name.

The declaration and use of functions are discussed in more detail in Chapter 9. Variable-length parameter lists are accessed with the facilities in the **stdarg.h** or **varargs.h** header files.

References abstract declarator 5.12; array declarators 4.5.3; defining and referencing declarations 4.8; function types and declarations 5.8; function definitions 9.1; pointer declarators 4.5; **stdarg.h** and **varargs.h** 11.4

4.5.5 Composition of Declarators

Declarators can be composed to form more complicated types, such as "5-element array of pointers to functions returning **int**," which is the type of **ary** in this declaration:

```
int (*ary[5])();
```

The only restriction on declarators is that the resulting type must be a valid one in C. The only types that are *not* valid in C are:

1. Any type including **void** except in the form of "...function returning **void**" or (in ISO C) "pointer to **void**."
2. "Array of function of ...." Arrays may contain pointers to functions, but not functions themselves.
3. "Function returning array of ...." Functions may return pointers to arrays, but not arrays themselves.
4. "Function returning function of ...." Functions may return pointers to other functions, but not the functions themselves.

When composing declarators, the precedence of the declarator expressions is important. Function and array declarators have higher precedence than pointer declarators, so that "***x()**" is equivalent to "***(x())**" ("function returning pointer ...") instead of "**(*x)()**" ("pointer to function returning ..."). Parentheses may be used to group declarators properly. Early C compilers had an upper limit of 6 on the depth of declarator nesting. Modern C compilers allow at least a depth of 12, which is also the minimum depth that ISO-conforming implementation must provide.

Although declarators can be arbitrarily complex, it is better programming style to factor them into several simpler definitions.

Example

Declaration	Type of x
`int x();`	function returning an integer
`int (*x)();`	pointer to a function returning an integer
`void (*x)();`	pointer to a function returning no result
`void *x();`	function returning "pointer to **void**"

Example

Rather than writing

```
int *(*(*(*x)())[10])();
```

write instead

```
typedef int *(*print_function_ptr)();
typedef print_function_ptr (*digit_routines)[10];
digit_routines (*x)();
```

The variable **x** is a pointer to a function returning a pointer to a 10-element array of pointers to functions returning pointers to integers, in case you wondered.

Example

The rationale behind the syntax of declarators is that they mimic the syntax of a use of the enclosed identifier. To illustrate the symmetry in the declaration and use, if you see the declaration

```
int *(*x)[4];
```

then the type of the expression

```
*(*x)[i]
```

is **int**.

References array types 5.4; function types 5.8; pointer to **void** 5.3.2; pointer types 5.3; **void** type specifier 5.9

4.6 INITIALIZERS

The declaration of a variable may be accompanied by an initializer that specifies the value the variable should have at the beginning of its lifetime. The full syntax for initializers is

initializer :
    assignment-expression
    { *initializer-list* **,** $_{opt}$ **}**

initializer-list :
  initializer
  initializer-list **,** *initializer*

The optional trailing comma inside the braces doesn't affect the meaning of the initializer.

The initializers permitted on a particular declaration depend on the type and storage class of the object to be initialized and on whether the declared object has static or automatic storage class. The options are listed in Table 4–6 and presented in more detail in the following sections. Declarations of external objects should not have initializers unless they are defining occurrences.

Table 4–6 Form of initializers

Storage	Type	Initializer expression	Default initializer
static	scalar	constant	0, 0.0, or null pointer
static	array[a] or structure	brace-enclosed constants	recursive default for each component
static	union[b]	constant	default for the first component
automatic	scalar	any	none
automatic	array[a, b]	brace-enclosed constant	none
automatic	structure[b]	brace-enclosed constant, or a single non-constant expression of the same structure type	none
automatic	union[b]	constant, or a single non-constant expression of the same union type	none

[a] The array may have an unknown size; the initializer determines the size.
[b] ISO C; older implementations may not permit initializations of these objects.

The "shape" of an initializer—the brace-enclosed lists of initializers—should match the structure of the variable being initialized. The language definition specifies that the initializers for scalar variables may optionally be surrounded by braces, although such braces are logically unnecessary. We recommend that braces be reserved to indicate aggregate initialization. There are special rules for abbreviating initializers for aggregates.

Historical note: C originally had a syntax for initializers in which the = operator was omitted, and some current C compilers accept this syntax for compatibility. Users of these compilers, when they accidentally omit a comma or semicolon in a declaration (e.g., "`int a b;`"), get an obscure error message about an invalid initializer. ISO C does not support this obsolete syntax.

The following sections explain the special requirements for each type of variable.

References automatic and static lifetime 4.2; declarations 4.1; external objects 4.8; static storage class 4.3

4.6.1 Integers

The form of an initializer for an integer variable is

declarator = *expression*

The initializing expression must have a type that would be permitted in a simple assignment to the initialized variable; the usual assignment conversions are applied. If the variable is static or external, the expression must be constant. If the variable is automatic or register, any expression is permitted. The default initializer for a static integer is 0.

Example

In the code fragment below, **Count** is initialized by a constant expression, but **ch** is initialized by the result of a function call.

```
#include <stdio.h>
static int Count = 4*200;

int main(void)
{
    int ch = getchar();
    ...
}
```

References constant expression 7.11; integer types 5.1; static and automatic extent 4.2; usual assignment conversions 6.3.2

4.6.2 Floating-point

The form of an initializer for a floating-point variable is

declarator = *expression*

The initializing expression must have a type that would be permitted in a simple assignment to the initialized variable; the usual assignment conversions are applied. If the variable is static or external, the expression must be constant. If the variable is automatic or register, any expression is permitted.

Example

```
static void process_data(double K)
{
    static double epsilon = 1.0e-6;
    auto float fudge_factor = K*epsilon;
    ...
}
```

ISO C specifically permits floating-point constant expressions in initializers. Some older C compilers have been known to balk at complicated floating-point constant expressions.

The default initialization of static, floating-point variables is 0.0. This value might not be represented on the target computer as an object whose bits are zero. ISO C compilers must initialize the variable to the correct representation for 0.0, but most older C compilers always initialize static storage to zero bits.

References arithmetic types ch. 5; constant expressions 7.11; floating-point constant 2.7.2; floating-point types 5.2; static and automatic extent 4.2; unary minus operator 7.5.3; usual assignment conversions 6.3.2

4.6.3 Pointers

The form of an initialization of a pointer variable is

declarator = *expression*

The initializing expression must have a type that would be permitted in a simple assignment to the initialized variable; the usual assignment conversions are applied. If the variable is static or external, the expression must be constant. If the variable is automatic or register, any expression is permitted.

Constant expressions used as initializers of pointer type *PT* may be formed from the following elements.

1. An integral constant expression with the value 0, or such a value cast to type **void ***. These are null pointer constants, usually referred to by the name **NULL** in the standard library.

   ```
   #define NULL ((void *)0)
   double *dp = NULL;
   ```

2. The name of a static or external function of type "function returning *T*" is converted to a constant of type "pointer to function returning *T*."

   ```
   extern int f();
   static int (*fp)() = f;
   ```

3. The name of a static or external array of type "array of *T*" is converted to a constant of type "pointer to *T*."

   ```
   char ary[100];
   char *cp = ary;
   ```

4. The **&** operator applied to the name of a static or external variable of type *T* yields a constant of type "pointer to *T*."

   ```
   static short s; auto short *sp = &s;
   ```

5. The **&** operator applied to an external or static array of type "array of *T*," subscripted by a constant expression, yields a constant of type "pointer to *T*."

```
float PowersOfPi[10];
float *PiSquared = &PowersOfPi[2];
```

6. An integer constant cast to a pointer type yields a constant of that pointer type, although this is not portable.

```
long *PSW = (long *) 0xFFFFFFF0;
```

Not all compilers accept casts in constant expressions.

7. A string literal yields a constant of type "pointer to **char**" when it appears as the initializer of a variable of pointer type.

```
char *greeting = "Type <cr> to begin ";
```

8. The sum or difference of any expression shown for cases 3 through 7 above and an integer constant expression.

```
static short s;
auto short *sp = &s + 3, *msp = &s - 3;
```

In general, the initializer for a pointer type must evaluate to an integer or to an address plus (or minus) an integer constant. This limitation reflects the capabilities of most linkers.

The default initialization for static pointers is the null pointer. In the (rare) case that null pointers are not represented by an object whose bits are zero, ISO C specifies that the correct null pointer value must be used. Most older C compilers simply initialize static storage to zero bits.

References address operator **&** 7.5.6; array types 5.4; conversions involving pointers 6.2.7; function types 5.8; integer constants 2.7; pointer declarator 4.5; pointer types 5.3; string constants 2.7; usual assignment conversions 6.3.2

4.6.4 Arrays

If I_j is a constant expression that is an allowable initializer for objects of type T, then

$$\{\ I_0,\ I_1,\ \ldots,\ I_{n-1}\ \}$$

is an allowable initializer for type "n-element array of T." The initializer I_j is used to initialize element j the array (zero origin). Multidimensional arrays follow the same pattern, with initializers listed by row. (The last subscript varies most rapidly in C.)

Example

A singly-dimensioned array is initialized by listing its elements:

```
int ary[4] = { 0, 1, 2, 3 };
```

A multiply-dimensioned array is initialized by each subarray:

```
int ary[4][2][3] =
        { { { 0, 1, 2}, { 3, 4, 5} },
          { { 6, 7, 8}, { 9, 10, 11} },
          { {12, 13, 14}, {15, 16, 17} },
          { {18, 19, 20}, {21, 22, 23} } };
```

Arrays of structures (section 4.6.6) may be initialized analogously:

```
struct {int a; float b;} a[3] = { {1, 2.5},
                                  {2, 3.9},
                                  {0, -4.0} };
```

Static and external arrays may always be initialized in this way. ISO C permits the initialization of automatic arrays using constant component expressions, but older compilers are likely to reject any initialization of automatic arrays because the feature was not in the original definition of C. Array initialization has a number of special rules:

1. The number of initializers may be less than the number of array elements, in which case the remaining elements are initialized to their default initialization value. If the number of initializers is greater than the number of elements, it is an error.

Example

The declarations

```
float ary[5] = { 1, 2, 3 };
int mat[3][3] = { {1, 2}, {3} };
```

are the same as

```
int ary[5] = { 1.0, 2.0, 3.0, 0.0, 0.0 };
int mat[3][3] = { {1, 2, 0},
                  {3, 0, 0},
                  {0, 0, 0} };
```

2. The bounds of the array need not be specified, in which case the bounds are derived from the length of the initializer. This is true for both static and automatic initializations.

Example

The declaration

```
int squares[] = { 0, 1, 4, 9 };
```

is the same as

```
int squares[4] = { 0, 1, 4, 9 };
```

3. String literals may be used to initialize variables of type "array of **char**." In this case, the first element of the array is initialized by the first character in the string, and so forth. The string's terminating null character, **'\0'**, will be stored in the array if there is room or if the size of the array is unspecified. The string may optional-

ly be enclosed in braces. It is not an error—but it is very poor style—if the string is too long for a character array of specified size. (It is an error in C++.)

An array whose element type is compatible with **wchar_t** can be initialized by a wide string literal in the same way.

Example

The declarations

```
char x[5]   = "ABCDE";
char str[] = "ABCDE";
wchar_t q[5]  = { L"A" };
```

are the same as

```
char x[5]   = { 'A', 'B', 'C', 'D', 'E' }; /* No '\0'! */
char str[6] = { 'A', 'B', 'C', 'D', 'E', '\0' };
wchar_t q[5]   = { L'A', L'\0', L'\0', L'\0', L'\0' };
```

4. A list of strings can be used to initialize an array of character pointers.

Example

```
char *astr[] = { "John", "Bill", "Susan", "Mary" };
```

References array types 5.4; character constants 2.7; character types 5.1.3; pointer types 5.3; string constants 2.7; wide strings 2.7.4

4.6.5 Enumerations

The form of initializers for variables of enumeration type is

declarator = *expression*

The initializing expression must have a type that would be permitted in a simple assignment to the initialized variable; the usual assignment conversions are applied. If the variable is static or external, the expression must be constant. If the variable is automatic or register, any expression is permitted.

Example

Good programming style suggests that the type of the initializing expression should be the same enumeration type as the variable being initialized. For example:

```
static enum E { a, b, c } x = a;
auto enum E y = x;
```

References cast expressions 7.5.1; constant expressions 7.11; enumeration types 5.5; usual assignment conversions 6.3.2

4.6.6 Structures

If a structure type T has n named components of types T_j, j=1,...,n, and if I_j is an initializer that is allowable for an object of type T_j, then

$$\{ I_1 , I_2 , ..., I_n \}$$

is an allowable initializer for type T. Unnamed bit field components do not participate in initialization. The initializers I_j must always be constant expressions.

Example

```
struct S {int a; char b[5]; double c; };
struct S x = { 1, "abcd", 45.0 };
```

Static and external variables of structure types can be initialized by all C compilers. Automatic and register variables of structure types can be initialized in ISO C, and either of two forms may be used. First, a brace-enclosed list of constant expressions may be used, as for static variables. Second, an initialization of the form

declarator = *expression*

may be used, where *expression* has the same type as the variable being initialized. A few older C compilers are deficient in not allowing the initialization of structures containing bit fields.

As with array initializers, structure initializers have some special abbreviation rules. In particular, if there are fewer initializers than there are structure components, the remaining components are initialized to their default initial values. If there are too many initializers for the structure, it is an error.

Example

Given the structure declaration

```
struct S1 {int a;
           struct S2 {double b;
                      char c; } b;
           int c[4]; };
```

the initialization

```
struct S1 x = { 1, {4.5} };
```

is the same as

```
struct S1 x = { 1, { 4.5, '\0' }, { 0, 0, 0, 0 } };
```

References bit fields 5.6.5; constant expressions 7.11; structure types 5.6

4.6.7 Unions

ISO C allows the initialization of union variables. (Traditional C does not.) The initializer for a static, external, automatic, or register union variable must be a brace-enclosed constant expression that would be allowable as an initializer for an object of the type of the first component of the union. The initializer for an automatic or register union may alternatively be any single expression of the same union type.

Example

These two initializer forms are shown below for the union variables **x** and **y**:

```
enum Greek { alpha, beta, gamma };
union U {
            struct { enum Greek tag; int Size; } I;
            struct { enum Greek tag; float Size; } F;
          };
static union U x = {{ alpha, 42 }};
auto union U y = x;
```

The only remaining C types are function types and **void**. Since variables of these types cannot be declared, the question of initialization is moot.

References static extent 4.2; union types 5.7

4.6.8 Eliding Braces

C permits braces to be dropped from initializer lists under certain circumstances, although it is usually clearer to retain them. The general rules are listed below.

1. If a variable of array or structure type is being initialized, the outermost pair of braces may *not* be dropped.
2. Otherwise, if an initializer list contains the correct number of elements for the object being initialized, the braces may be dropped.

Example

The most common use of these rules is in dropping inner braces when initializing a multidimensional array:

```
int matrix[2][3] = { 1, 2, 3,    4, 5, 6 };
        /* same as: { {1, 2, 3}, {4, 5, 6} } */
```

Many C compilers treat initializer lists casually, permitting too many or too few braces. We advise keeping initializers simple and using braces to make their structure explicit.

4.7 IMPLICIT DECLARATIONS

An external function used in a function call need not have been declared previously. If the compiler sees an identifier *id* followed by a left parenthesis, and if *id* has not been previously declared, then a declaration is implicitly entered in the innermost enclosing scope of the form:

```
extern int id();
```

Some non-ISO implementations may declare the identifier at the top level rather than in the innermost scope. In C++, these implicit declarations are not permitted.

Example

Allowing functions to be declared by default is poor programming style and may lead to errors, particularly those concerning incorrect return types. If a pointer-returning function, such as **malloc** (section 16.1), is allowed to be implicitly declared as

```
extern int malloc();
```

rather than the correct

```
extern char *malloc();    /* returns (void *) in ISO C */
```

then calls to **malloc** will probably not work if the types **int** and **char *** are represented differently. Suppose type **int** occupies two bytes and pointers occupy four bytes. When the compiler sees

```
int *p;
...
p = (int *) malloc(sizeof(int));
```

it generates code to extend what it thought was a two-byte value returned by **malloc** to the four bytes required by the pointer. The effect is that only the low half of the address returned by **malloc** is assigned to **p**, and the program begins to fail when enough storage has been allocated to cause **malloc** to return addresses larger than **0xFFFF**.

4.8 EXTERNAL NAMES

An important issue with external names is ensuring consistency among the declarations of the same external name in several files. For instance, what if two declarations of the same external variable specified different initializations? For this and other reasons, it is useful to distinguish a single *defining declaration* of an external name within a group of files. The other declarations of the same name are then considered *referencing declarations*—that is, they reference the defining declaration.

It is a well-known deficiency in C that defining and referencing occurrences of external variable declarations are difficult to distinguish. In general, compilers use one of four models to determine when a top-level declaration is a defining occurrence.

4.8.1 The Initializer Model

The presence of an initializer on a top-level declaration indicates a defining occurrence; all others are referencing occurrences. There must be a single defining occurrence among all the files in the C program. The presence or absence of **extern** is irrelevant. This is the model adopted by ISO C, with one additional rule discussed in the next section.

4.8.2 The Omitted Storage Class Model

In this scheme, the storage class **extern** must be explicitly included on all referencing declarations, and the storage class must be omitted from the single defining declaration for each external variable. The defining declaration can include an initializer, but it is not required to do so. (It is invalid to have both an initializer and the storage class **extern** in a declaration.) This is the C++ rule.

In ISO C, a top-level declaration without a storage class or initializer is considered to be a *tentative declaration*. That is, it is treated as a referencing declaration, but if no other declaration of the same variable with an initializer appears in the file, the former declaration is considered a defining declaration.

4.8.3 The Common Model

This scheme is so named because it is related to the way multiple references to a FORTRAN **COMMON** block are merged into a single defining occurrence in some FORTRAN implementations. Both defining and referencing external declarations have storage class **extern**, whether explicitly or by default. Among all the declarations for each external name in all the object files linked together to make the program, only one may have an initializer. At link time, all external declarations for the same identifier (in all C object files) are combined and a single defining occurrence is conjured, not necessarily associated with any particular file. If any declaration specified an initializer, that initializer is used to initialize the data object. (If several declarations did, the results are unpredictable.)

This solution is the most painless for the programmer and the most demanding on system software.

4.8.4 Mixed Common Model

This model is a cross between the "omitted storage class" model and the "common" model. It is used in many versions of UNIX.

1. If **extern** is omitted and an initializer is present, a definition for the symbol is emitted. Having two or more such definitions among all the files comprising a program results in an error at link time or before.
2. If **extern** is omitted and there is no initializer, a FORTRAN **COMMON**-style definition is emitted. Any number of these definitions of the same identifier may coexist.
3. If **extern** is present, the declaration is taken to be a reference to a name defined elsewhere. It is invalid for such a declaration to have an initializer.

If no explicit initializer is provided for the external variable, the variable is initialized as if the initializer had been the integer constant 0.

4.8.5 Summary and Recommendations

Table 4–7 shows the interpretation of a top-level declaration according to the model for external references in use. To remain compatible with the most compilers, we recommend

Table 4–7 Interpretation of top-level declarations

	Model				
Top-level declaration	Initializer	Omitted storage class (and C++)	Common	Mixed common	ISO C
`int x;`	Reference	Definition	Definition or reference	Definition or reference	Reference[a]
`int x = 0;`	Definition	Definition	Definition	Definition	Definition
`extern int x;`	Reference	Reference	Definition or reference	Reference	Reference
`extern int x = 0;`	Definition	Reference	Definition	(Invalid)	Definition

[a] If no subsequent defining occurrence appears in the file, this becomes a defining occurrence.

following these rules:

1. Have a single definition point (source file) for each external variable; in the defining declaration, omit the **extern** storage class and include an explicit initializer:

   ```
   int errcnt = 0;
   ```

2. In each source file or header file referencing an external variable defined elsewhere, use the storage class **extern** and do not include an initializer:

   ```
   extern int errcnt;
   ```

Independent of the defining/referencing distinction, an external name should always be declared with the same type in all files making up a program. The C compiler cannot verify that declarations in different files are consistent in this fashion, and the punishment for inconsistency is erroneous behavior at run time. The **lint** program, usually supplied with the C compiler in UNIX systems, can check multiple files for consistent declarations, as can several commercial products for UNIX and MS-DOS.

4.8.6 Unreferenced External Declarations

Although not required by the C language, it is customary to ignore declarations of external variables or functions that are never referenced. For example, if the declaration "**extern double fft();**" appears in a program, but the function **fft** is never used, then no external reference to the name **fft** is passed to the linker. Therefore, the function **fft** will not be loaded with the program, where it would take up space to no purpose.

4.9 C++ COMPATIBILITY

4.9.1 Scopes

In C++, **struct** and **union** definitions are scopes. That is, type declarations occurring within those definitions are not visible outside, whereas they are in ISO C (section 5.6.3). To remain compatible, simply move any type declarations out of the structure. (Some C++ implementations may allow this as an anachronism, when no ambiguity can result.)

Example

In the following code, a structure **t** is defined within a structure **s**, but is referenced outside that structure. This is invalid in C++.

```
struct s {
   struct t {int a; int b;} f1;      /* define t here */
} x1;
struct t x2;             /* use t here; OK in C, not in C++ */
```

References scope 4.2.1; structure components 5.6.3

4.9.2 Tag and Typedef Names

Structure and union tag names should not be used as **typedef** names, except for the same tagged type. In C++, tag names are implicitly declared as **typedef** names as well as tags. (However, they can be hidden by a subsequent variable or function declaration of the same name in the same scope.) This can result in diagnostics, or—in rare cases—simply different behavior.

Example

Here are some examples that result in diagnostics in C or C++.

```
typedef struct n1 {…} n1;           /* OK in both C and C++ */
struct n2 {…}; typedef double n2; /* OK in C, not in C++ */
struct n3 {…}; n3 x;              /* OK in C++, not in C */
```

However, the tag name can be used as a variable or function name without confusion. The following sequence of declarations is acceptable to both C and C++, although it would probably be better to avoid the inevitable confusion:

```
struct n4 {…};
int n4;
struct n4 x;
```

A declaration of a **struct** tag in an inner scope in C++ can hide a variable declaration from an outer scope. This can cause a C program's meaning to change without warning. In the following code, the expression **sizeof(ary)** refers to the size of the array in C, but it refers to the size of the **struct** type in C++.

```
int ary[10];
...
void f(int x)
{
    struct ary { ... };   /* In C++, this hides previous ary */
    ...
    x = sizeof(ary);   /* Different meanings in C and C++! */
}
```

See section 5.13.2 concerning the compatibility of **typedef** redefinitions in C++.

References name spaces 4.2.4; redefining **typedef** names 5.10.2

4.9.3 Storage Class Specifiers on Types

Do not place storage class specifiers in type declarations. They are ignored in C, but invalid in C++. They have no useful purpose, anyway.

Example

```
static struct s {int a; int b;} ;     /* invalid in C++ */
```

References storage classes on types 4.4.2

4.9.4 const Type Qualifier

A top-level declaration that has the type qualifier **const** but no explicit storage class is considered to be **static** in C++ but **extern** in C. To remain compatible, examine top-level **const** declarations and provide an explicit storage class.

Example

The following declaration will have different meanings in C and C++:

```
const int c1 = 10;
```

However, the following declarations will have the same meaning in C and C++:

```
static const int c2 = 11;
extern const int c3 = 12;
```

All **const** declarations—except those referencing externally-defined constants—must have initializers in C++.

References **const** type qualifier 4.4.4

4.9.5 Initializers

When a string literal is used to initialize a fixed-size array of characters (or a wide string literal for an array of **wchar_t**), there must be enough room in the array for the entire string, including the terminating null character.

Example

```
char str[5] = "abcde"; /* valid in C, not in C++ */
char str[6] = "abcde"; /* valid in both C and C++ */
```

4.9.6 Implicit Declarations

Implicit declarations of functions (section 4.7) are not allowed in C++. All functions must be declared before they are used.

References implicit declarations 4.7

4.9.7 Defining and Referencing Declarations

In C++, there are no tentative definitions of top-level variables. What would be considered a tentative definition in C is considered a "real" definition in C++. That is, the sequence of declarations

```
int i;
...
int i;
```

would be valid in ISO C, but would cause a duplicate-definition error in C++.

Example

This rule applies to static variables also, which means that it is not possible to create mutually-recursive, statically initialized variables.

```
struct cell {int val; struct cell *next;};
static struct cell a;     /* tentative declaration */
static struct cell b = {0, &a};
static struct cell a = {1, &b);
```

This isn't a problem for global variables: the first **static** above could be replaced by **extern** and the second and third **static** could be removed. (You can declare mutually-recursive, statically initialized variables in C++, but not in a way that is compatible with C.)

References structure type reference 5.6.1; tentative declaration 4.8.2

4.9.8 Function Linkage

When calling a C function from C++, the function must be declared to have "C" linkage. This is discussed in more detail in Chapter 10.

Example

If in a C++ program you wanted to call a function **f** compiled by a C implementation, you would write the (C++) declaration as:

```
/* This is a C++ program. */
extern "C" int f(void);   /* f is a C, not C++, function */
```

4.10 EXERCISES

1. The definition of a static function **P** is shown below. What will be the value of **P(6)**, if **P** has never been called before? What will **P(6)** be the second time it is called?

```
static int P(int x)
{
    int i = 0;
    i = i+1;
    return i*x;
}
```

2. The following program fragment shows a block containing various declarations of the name **f**. Do any of the declarations conflict? If so, cross out declarations until the program is valid, keeping as many different declarations of **f** as possible.

```
{
    extern double f();
    int f;
    typedef int f;
    struct f {int f,g;};
    union f {int x,y;};
    enum {f,b,s};
    f: ...
}
```

3. The following program fragment declares three variables named **i** with types **int**, **long**, and **float**. On which lines is each of the variables declared and used?

```
 1 int i;
 2 void f(i)
 3     long i;
 4 {
 5     long l = i;
 6     {
 7         float i;
 8         i = 3.4;
 9     }
10     l = i+2;
11 }
12 int *p = &i;
```

4. Write C declarations that express the following English statements. Use prototypes for function declarations.

(a) **P** is an external function that has no parameters and returns no result.
(b) **i** is a local integer variable that will be heavily used and should be optimized for speed.
(c) **LT** is a synonym for type "pointer to character."
(d) **Q** is an external function with two arguments and no result. The first, **i**, is an integer and the second, **cp**, is a string. The string will not be modified.
(e) **R** is an external function whose only argument, **p**, is a pointer to a function that takes a single 32-bit integer argument, **i**, and returns a pointer to a value of type **double**. R returns an integer value.
(f) **STR** is a static, uninitialized character string that should be modifiable and hold up to 10 characters, not including the terminating null character.
(g) **STR2** is a character string initialized to the string literal that is the value of the macro **INIT_STR2**. Once initialized, the string will not be modified.
(h) **IP** is a pointer to an integer, initialized with the address of the variable **i**.

5. The matrix **m** is declared as **int m[3][3];** the first subscript specifies the row number and the second subscript specifies the column number. Write an initializer for **m** that places ones in the first column, twos in the second column, and threes in the third column.

5

Types

A *type* is a set of *values* and a set of *operations* on those values. For example, the values of an integer type consist of integers in some specified range, and the operations on those values consist of addition, subtraction, inequality tests, and so forth. The values of a floating-point type include numbers represented differently from integers, and a set of different operations: floating-point addition, subtraction, inequality tests, and so forth.

We say a variable or expression "has type *T*" when its values are constrained to the domain of *T*. The types of variables are established by the variable's declaration; the types of expressions are given by the definitions of the expression operators.

The C language provides a large number of built-in types, including integers of several kinds, floating-point numbers, pointers, enumerations, arrays, structures, unions, and functions.

It is useful to organize C's types into the categories shown in Table 5–1 on page 110. The *integral types* include all forms of integers, characters, and enumerations. The *arithmetic types* include the integral and floating-point types. The *scalar types* include the arithmetic types, pointer types, and enumerated types. The *function types* are the types "function returning...." *Aggregate types* include arrays and structures. *Union types* are created with the **`union`** specifier. The **`void`** type has no values and no operations.

All of C's types are discussed in this chapter. For each type, we indicate how objects of the type are declared, the range of values of the type, any restrictions on the size or representation of the type, and what operations are defined on values of the type.

References array types 5.4; character types 5.1.3; declarations 4.1; enumerated types 5.5; floating-point types 5.2; function types 5.8; integer types 5.1; pointer types 5.3; structure types 5.6; union types 5.7; void type 5.9

Table 5–1 C types and categories

C Types	Type Categories		
`short`, `int`, `long` (signed and unsigned)	Integral types	Arithmetic types	Scalar types
`char` (signed and unsigned)			
`enum {...}`			
`float`, `double`, `long double`	Floating-point types		
`T *`	Pointer types		
`T [...]`	Array types		Aggregate types
`struct {...}`	Structure types		
`union {...}`	Union types		
`T (...)`	Function types		
`void`	Void type		

5.1 INTEGER TYPES

C provides more integer types and operators than do most programming languages. The variety reflects the different word lengths and kinds of arithmetic operators found on most computers, thus allowing a close correspondence between C programs and the underlying hardware. Integer types in C are used to represent:

1. signed or unsigned integer values, for which the usual arithmetic and relational operations are provided
2. bit vectors, with the operations NOT, AND, OR, XOR, and left and right shifts
3. boolean values, for which zero is considered "false" and all nonzero values are considered "true," with the integer 1 being the canonical "true" value
4. characters, which are represented by their integer encoding on the computer

Enumeration types are *integral*, or integer-like, types.They are considered in section 5.5.

ISO C requires implementations to use a binary encoding of integers; this is a recognition that many low-level C operations are not describable in any portable fashion on computers with non-binary representations.

It is convenient to divide the integer types into three classes: signed types, unsigned types, and characters. Each of these classes has a set of type specifiers that can be used to declare objects of the type.

integer-type-specifier :
    signed-type-specifier
    unsigned-type-specifier
    character-type-specifier

5.1.1 Signed Integer Types

C provides the programmer with three sizes of signed integer types, denoted by the type specifiers **short**, **int**, and **long** in nondecreasing order of size. Each type can be named in several equivalent ways; in the syntax below, the equivalent names are shown for each of the three types.

> *signed-type-specifier* :
> **short** *or* **short int** *or* **signed short** *or* **signed short int**
> **int** *or* **signed int** *or* **signed**
> **long** *or* **long int** *or* **signed long** *or* **signed long int**

The keyword **signed** is new in ISO C, and can be omitted for compatibility with other C implementations. The only time the presence of **signed** might affect the meaning of a program is in conjunction with type **char** and with bit fields in structures; in that case a distinction can be made between a signed integer and a "plain integer," i.e., one written without **signed**.

The C language does not specify the range of integers that the integral types will represent, except to say that type **int** may not be smaller than **short** and **long** may not be smaller than **int**. Many implementations represent characters in 8 bits, type **short** in 16 bits, and type **long** in 32 bits, with type **int** using either 16 or 32 bits depending on the implementation ISO C requires implementations to use at least these widths.

The precise range of values representable by a signed integer type depends not only on the number of bits used in the representation but also on the encoding technique. By far the most common binary encoding technique for integers is called *two's-complement notation*, in which a signed integer represented with n bits will have a range from -2^{n-1} through $2^{n-1}-1$ encoded in the following fashion:

1. The high-order (leftmost) bit of the word is the sign bit. If the sign bit is 1, the number is negative; otherwise, the number is positive.
2. Positive numbers follow the normal binary sequence:

   $0 = 000\ldots0000_2$
   $1 = 000\ldots0001_2$
   $2 = 000\ldots0010_2$
   $3 = 000\ldots0011_2$
   $4 = 000\ldots0100_2$
   ...

   In an n-bit word, omitting the sign bit, there are $n-1$ bits for the positive integers, which can represent the integers 0 through $2^{n-1}-1$.
3. To negate an integer, complement all the bits in the word and then add 1 to the result. Thus, to form the integer -1, start with 1 ($00\ldots0001_2$); complement the bits ($11\ldots1110_2$); and add 1 ($11\ldots1111_2 = -1$).
4. The maximum negative value, $10\ldots0000_2$ or -2^{n-1}, has no positive equivalent; negating this value produces the same value.

Other binary integer encoding techniques are *one's-complement notation*, in which negation simply complements all the bits of the word, and *sign magnitude notation*, in which negation involves simply complementing the sign bit. These alternatives have a range from $-(2^{n-1}-1)$ through $2^{n-1}-1$; they have one less negative value and two representations for zero (positive and negative). All three notations represent positive integers identically.

ISO C requires that implementations document the ranges of the integer types in the header file **limits.h**, and also specifies the maximum representable range a C programmer can assume for each integer type in all ISO-conforming implementations. The symbols that must be defined in **limits.h** are shown in Table 5–2. Implementations can

Table 5–2 Values defined in limits.h

Name	Minimum value	Meaning
CHAR_BIT	8	width of **char** type, in bits
SCHAR_MIN	–127	minimum value of **signed char**
SCHAR_MAX	127	maximum value of **signed char**
UCHAR_MAX	255	maximum value of **unsigned char**
SHRT_MIN	–32,767	minimum value of **short int**
SHRT_MAX	32,767	maximum value of **short int**
USHRT_MAX	65,535	maximum value of **unsigned short**
INT_MIN	–32,767	minimum value of **int**
INT_MAX	32,767	maximum value of **int**
UINT_MAX	65,535	maximum value of **unsigned int**
LONG_MIN	–2,147,483,647	minimum value of **long int**
LONG_MAX	2,147,483,647	maximum value of **long int**
ULONG_MAX	4,294,967,295	maximum value of **unsigned long**
CHAR_MIN	**SCHAR_MIN** or 0[a]	minimum value of **char**
CHAR_MAX	**SCHAR_MAX** or **UCHAR_MAX**[b]	maximum value of **char**

[a] If type **char** is signed by default, then **SCHAR_MIN**, else 0.
[b] If type **char** is signed by default, then **SCHAR_MAX**, else **UCHAR_MAX**.

substitute their own values, but they must not be less in absolute magnitude than the values shown, and must have the same sign. Therefore, an ISO-conforming implementation cannot represent type **int** in only 8 bits, nor can a strictly conforming C program depend on, say, the value –32,768 being representable in type **short**. (This is to accommodate computers that use a one's-complement representation of binary integers.) Programmers using non-ISO implementations can create a **limits.h** file for their implementation.

Amendment 1 to ISO C adds the symbols **WCHAR_MAX** and **WCHAR_MIN** for the maximum and minimum values represented in type **wchar_t**. However, these symbols are defined in **wchar.h** header file, not **limits.h**.

Example

Here are some examples of typical declarations of signed integers:

```
short i, j;
long int l;
static signed int k;
```

To keep programs as portable as possible, it is best not to depend on type **int** being able to represent integers outside the range –32,767 to 32,767. Use type **long** if this range is insufficient. It is usually good style to define special integer types with **typedef**, based on the needs of each particular program. For example:

```
/* invdef.h Inventory definitions for the XXX computer. */
typedef short part_number;
typedef int   order_quantity;
typedef long  purchase_order;
```

In addition to making the program more readable, this technique makes it easy to adapt to computers with differing integer sizes by changing the definitions in only one file.

Example

In C, type **int** is used to represent boolean values. The value zero represents "false" and all nonzero values represent "true." Boolean expressions evaluate to 0 if false and 1 if true. For example, **i = (a<b)** assigns to the integer variable **i** the value 1 if **a** is less than **b**, and 0 if **a** is not less than **b**. Likewise, the statement

```
if (i) statement1; /* Do this if i is nonzero */
else statement2;   /* Do this if i is zero */
```

results in ***statement*** $_1$ being executed if **i** is nonzero (true), and ***statement*** $_2$ if **i** is zero.

The use of type **int** to represent boolean values is contrary to Pascal-family programming languages, which define distinct types for boolean. Many C programmers declare their own boolean types to improve readability:

```
typedef int bool;
#define true (1)
#define false (0)
bool b;
...
b = (x < y) && (y < z);
if (b) ...
```

The names **bool**, **true**, and **false** are arbitrary, but have the advantage of being the names used in C++. It is probably more common in current C programs to use **TRUE** and **FALSE** as the boolean constants.

References bit fields in structures 5.6.5; declarations 4.1; integer constants 2.7.1; **signed** type specifier 5.1.1; type conversions ch. 6; **typedef** 5.10

5.1.2 Unsigned Integer Types

For each of the signed integer types there is a corresponding unsigned type that occupies the same amount of storage but has a different integer encoding. The unsigned type is specified by preceding the corresponding signed type specifier with the keyword **`unsigned`** (replacing the keyword **`signed`** if it was present).

unsigned-type-specifier :
  `unsigned short int`$_{opt}$
  `unsigned int`$_{opt}$
  `unsigned long int`$_{opt}$

In each case the keyword **`int`** is optional and does not affect the meaning of the type specifier. Choosing from among the unsigned types involves the same considerations already discussed with respect to the signed integer types.

All unsigned types use straight binary notation, regardless of whether the signed types use two's-complement, one's-complement, or sign magnitude notation; the sign bit is treated as an ordinary data bit. Therefore an n-bit word can represent the integers 0 through 2^n–1. Most computers are easily able to interpret the value in a word using either signed or unsigned notation. For example, when the two's-complement notation is used, the bit pattern $11...1111_2$ (n bits long) can represent either –1 (using the signed notation), or 2^n-1 (using the unsigned notation). The integers from 0 through 2^{n-1}–1 are represented identically in both signed and unsigned notations. The particular ranges of the unsigned types in an ISO C implementation is documented in the header file **`limits.h`**.

Whether an integer is signed or unsigned affects the operations performed on it. All arithmetic operations on unsigned integers behave according to the rules of modular (congruence) arithmetic modulo 2^n. So, for example, adding 1 to the largest value of an unsigned type is guaranteed to produce 0. Overflow is not possible.

Expressions that mix signed and unsigned integers are forced to use unsigned operations. Section 6.3.4 discusses the conversions performed, and Chapter 7 discusses the effect of each operator when its arguments are unsigned.

Example

These conversions can be surprising. For example, because unsigned integers are always nonnegative, you would expect that the following test would always be true:

```
unsigned int u;
...
if (u > -1) ...
```

However, it is always false! The (signed) –1 is converted to an unsigned integer before the comparison, yielding the largest unsigned integer, and the value of **`u`** cannot be greater than that integer.

The original definition of C provided only a single unsigned type, **`unsigned`**. Most non-ISO C implementations now provide the full range of unsigned types.

References integer conversions 6.2.3; constants 2.7; **`limits.h`** 5.1.1; signed types 5.1.1

5.1.3 Character Types

The character type in C is an integral type—that is, values of the type are integers and can be used in integer expressions:

character-type-specifier :
  char
  signed char
  unsigned char

There are three varieties of character types: signed, unsigned and plain. Each occupies the same amount of storage but may represent different values. The signed and unsigned representations used are the same as used for the signed and unsigned integer types. The plain character type corresponds to the absence of both **signed** and **unsigned** in the type specifier. The **signed** keyword is new in ISO C, so in C implementations not recognizing the keyword, there are only two varieties of character types: unsigned and plain. An array of characters is C's notion of a "string."

Example

Typical declarations involving characters are shown below:

```
static char greeting[7];          /* a 7-character string */
char *prompt;                     /* a pointer to a character */
char padding_character = '\0';   /* a single character */
```

The representation of the character types depends upon the nature of the character and string processing facilities on the target computer. The character type has some special characteristics that set it apart from the normal signed and unsigned types. For example, the plain **char** type may be signed, unsigned, or a mixture of both. For reasons of efficiency, C compilers are free to treat type **char** in one of three ways:

1. Type **char** may be a signed integral type, equivalent to **signed char**.
2. Type **char** may be an unsigned integral type, equivalent to **unsigned char**.
3. Type **char** may be a "pseudo-unsigned" integral type—that is, it can contain only nonnegative values but it is treated as if it were a signed type when performing the usual unary conversions.

Example

If a true unsigned character type is needed, the type **unsigned char** can be specified. If a true signed type is needed, the type **signed char** can be specified. If type **char** uses an 8-bit, two's-complement representation, and given the declarations

```
unsigned char uc = -1;
signed char sc = -1;
char c = -1;
int i=uc, j=sc, k=c;
```

then **i** must have the value 255 and **j** must have the value –1 in all ISO C implementations. However, it is implementation-defined whether **k** has the value 255 or –1. If a C implementation does not recognize the keyword **signed**, or does not permit **unsigned char**, you are stuck with the ambiguous plain characters.

The signedness of characters is an important issue because the standard I/O library routines, which normally return characters from files, return a negative value when the end of the file is reached. (The negative value, often –1, is specified by the macro **EOF** in the standard header files.) The programmer should always treat these functions as returning values of type **int**, since type **char** may be unsigned.

Example

The following program is intended to copy characters from the standard input stream to the standard output stream until an end-of-file indication is returned from **getchar**. The first three definitions are typically supplied in the standard header file **stdio.h**:

```
extern int getchar(void);
extern void putchar(int);
#define EOF (-1) /* Could be any negative value */

void copy_characters(void)
{
    char ch; /* Incorrect! */
    while ((ch = getchar()) != EOF)
        putchar(ch);
}
```

However, this function will not work when **char** is unsigned or pseudo unsigned. To see this, assume the **char** type is represented in 8 bits and the **int** type in 16 bits, and that two's-complement arithmetic is used. Then, when **getchar** returns –1, the assignment **ch = getchar()** assigns the value 255 (the low-order 8 bits of –1) to **ch**. The loop test is then **255!=-1**, and if type **char** is pseudo unsigned, this (signed) comparison will evaluate to "true." If type **char** is unsigned, the usual conversions will cause –1 to be converted to an unsigned integer, yielding the (unsigned) comparison **255!=65535**, which still evaluates to "true." Thus, the loop never terminates. Changing the declaration of **ch** to "**int ch;**" makes everything work fine.

Example

To improve readability, you can define a "pseudo-character" type to use in these cases. For example, the following rewriting of **copy_characters** uses a new type, **character**, for characters that are represented with type **int**:

```
typedef int character;
...
void copy_characters(void)
{
    character ch;
    while ((ch = getchar() ) != EOF)
        putchar(ch);
}
```

A second area of vagueness about characters is their size. In the above example, we assumed they occupied 8 bits, and this assumption is almost always valid (although it is still unclear if their values range from 0 to 255 or from –128 to 127). However, a few computers may use 9 bits or even 7 bits. Programmers should be cautious. ISO C requires that implementations document the range of their character types in the header file **limits.h**.

References bit fields 5.6.5; character constants 2.7.3; character set 2.1; **EOF** 15.1; **getchar** 15.6; integer types 5.1; integer conversions 6.2.3; **limits.h** 5.1.1

5.2 FLOATING-POINT TYPES

C's floating-point numbers (somctimes called "real" numbers) come in two sizes: single and double precision, or **float** and **double**:

floating-type-specifier :
    float
    double
    long double (ISO C)

The type specifier **long double** is new in ISO C. The type specifier **long float** is permitted in older implementations as a synonym for **double**, but it was never popular and has been eliminated in ISO C.

Example

Here are some typical declarations of objects of floating-point types:

```
double d;
static double pi;
float coefficients[10];
long double epsilon;
```

The use of **float**, **double**, and **long double** is analogous to the use of **short**, **int**, and **long**. Prior to ISO C, all implementations were required to convert all values of type **float** to type **double** before any operations were performed (see section 6.3.4), so using type **float** was not necessarily more efficient than using type **double**. In ISO C, operations can now be performed using type **float**.

C does not dictate the sizes to be used for the floating-point types, or even that they be different. The programmer can assume that the values representable in type **float** are a subset of those in type **double**, which in turn are a subset of those in type **long double**. Some C programs have depended on the assumption that the type **double** can accurately represent all values of type **long**—that is, converting an object of type **long** to type **double** and then back to type **long** results in exactly the original **long** value. While this is likely to be true, it is not required.

ISO C requires that the characteristics of the floating-point types be documented in the header file **float.h**; Table 5–3 lists the symbols that must be defined. Symbols whose names begin with **FLT** document type **float**, names beginning with **DBL** refer to type **double**, and names beginning with **LDBL** refer to type **long double**. Also shown are the minimum magnitudes for each symbol—that is, the minimum requirements for range and precision of the floating-point types.

Table 5–3 Values defined in float.h

Name	Minimum	Meaning
FLT_RADIX[a]	2	the value of the radix, b
FLT_ROUNDS[a]	*none*	rounding mode: –1: indeterminable; 0: toward 0; 1: to nearest; 2: toward + infinity; 3: toward – infinity[b]
FLT_EPSILON **DBL_EPSILON** **LDBL_EPSILON**	10^{-5} 10^{-5} 10^{-5}	the minimum x>0.0 such that 1.0+$x \neq x$
FLT_DIG **DBL_DIG** **LDBL_DIG**	6 10 10	the number of decimal digits of precision
FLT_MANT_DIG **DBL_MANT_DIG** **LDBL_MANT_DIG**	*none*	p, the number of base-b digits in the significand
FLT_MIN **DBL_MIN** **LDBL_MIN**	10^{-37} 10^{-37} 10^{-37}	the minimum normalized positive number
FLT_MIN_EXP **DBL_MIN_EXP** **LDBL_MIN_EXP**	*none*	e_{min}, the minimum negative integer x such that b^{x-1} is in the range of normalized floating-point numbers
FLT_MIN_10_EXP **DBL_MIN_10_EXP** **LDBL_MIN_10_EXP**	–37 –37 –37	minimum x such that 10^x is in the range of normalized floating-point numbers
FLT_MAX **DBL_MAX** **LDBL_MAX**	10^{+37} 10^{+37} 10^{+37}	maximum representable finite number
FLT_MAX_EXP **DBL_MAX_EXP** **LDBL_MAX_EXP**	*none*	e_{max}, the maximum integer x such that b^{x-1} is a representable finite floating-point numbers
FLT_MAX_10_EXP **DBL_MAX_10_EXP** **LDBL_MAX_10_EXP**	37 37 37	maximum x such that 10^x is in the range of representable finite floating-point numbers

[a] **FLT_RADIX** and **FLT_ROUNDS** apply to all three floating-point types.
[b] Other values are implementation-defined.

Most of the arithmetic and logical operations may be applied to floating-point operands. These include arithmetic and logical negation; addition, subtraction, multiplication, and division; relational and equality tests; logical AND and OR; assignment; and conversions to and from all the arithmetic types.

Most computer floating-point numbers x—those with sign-magnitude representations and no "hidden" bits—can be written as

$$x = s \times b^e \times \sum_{k=1}^{p} f_k \times b^{-k}, e_{min} \le e \le e_{max}$$

where

s	is the sign (±1)
b	is the base or radix of the representation (typically 2, 8, 10, or 16)
e	is the exponent value
p	is the number of base-b digits in the significand
f_k	are the significand digits, $0 \le f_k < b$

Example

A common floating-point representation used by many microprocessors is given by the *IEEE Standard for Binary Floating-Point Arithmetic* (ISO/IEEE Std 754–1985). The models for 32-bit single and 64-bit double precision floating-point numbers under that standard (adjusted to the ISO C notational conventions) are

$$x_{float} = s \times 2^e \times \sum_{k=1}^{24} f_k \times 2^{-k} \qquad 125 \le e \le +128$$

$$x_{double} = s \times 2^e \times \sum_{k=1}^{53} f_k \times 2^{-k} \qquad -1021 \le e \le +1024$$

The values from **`float.h`** corresponding to these types are shown in Table 5–4 on page 120. Floating-point constants of type **`float`** use the ISO C suffix **`F`** to denote their type.

References floating-point constants 2.7.2; floating-point conversions 6.2.4; floating-point representations 6.1.1

5.3 POINTER TYPES

For any type T, a pointer type "pointer to T" may be formed. Pointer types are referred to as *object pointers* or *function pointers*, depending on whether T is an object type or a function type. A value of pointer type is the address of an object or function of type T. The declaration of pointer types is discussed in section 4.5.2.

Example

```
int *ip;        /* ip: a pointer to an object of type int */
char *cp;       /* cp: a pointer to an object of type char */
int (*fp)();    /* fp: a pointer to a function returning
                       an integer */
```

Table 5–4 IEEE floating-point characteristics

Name	FLT_*name* value	DBL_*name* value
RADIX	2	not applicable
ROUNDS	implementation-defined	not applicable
EPSILON	1.19209290E–07F	2.2204460492503131E–16
DIG	6	15
MANT_DIG	24	53
MIN	1.17549435E–38F	2.2250738585072014E–308
MIN_EXP	–125	–1021
MIN_10_EXP	–37	–307
MAX	3.40282347E+38F	1.7976931348623157E+308
MAX_EXP	128	1024
MAX_10_EXP	38	308

The two most important operators used in conjunction with pointers are the address operator, **&**, which creates pointer values, and the indirection operator, *****, which dereferences pointers to access the object pointed to.

Example

In the following example, the pointer **ip** is assigned the address of variable **i** (**&i**). After that assignment, the expression ***ip** refers to the same object denoted by **i**:

```
int i, j, *ip;
ip = &i;
i = 22;
j = *ip;      /* j now has the value 22 */
*ip = 17;     /* i now has the value 17 */
```

Other operations on pointer types include assignment, addition of integers, subtraction, relational and equality tests, logical AND and OR, addition and subtraction of integers, and conversions to and from integers and other pointer types.

The size of a pointer is implementation-dependent and in some cases varies depending on the type of the object pointed to. For example, data pointers may be shorter or longer than function pointers (section 6.1.5). There is not necessarily any relationship between pointer sizes and the size of any integer type, although it is common to assume that type **long** is at least as large any pointer type.

In ISO C, pointer types may be qualified by the use of the type qualifiers **const** or **volatile**. The qualification of a pointer type (if any) can affect the operations and conversions that are possible with it.

References address operator **&** 7.5.6; arrays and pointers 5.4.1; assignment operators 7.9; cast expressions 7.5.1; conversions of pointers 6.2.7; **if** statement 8.5; indirection operator ***** 7.5.7; pointer declarators 4.5.2; type qualifiers 4.4.3; **volatile** type qualifier 4.4.5

5.3.1 Generic Pointers

The need for a generic data pointer that can be converted to any object pointer type arises frequently in C. In traditional C, it is customary to use type **char *** for this purpose, casting these generic pointers to the proper type before dereferencing them. Further details are given in section 6.2, where pointer conversions are discussed. The problem with this use of **char *** is that the compiler cannot check that programmers always convert the pointer type properly.

ISO C introduces the type **void *** as a "generic pointer." It has the same representation as type **char *** for compatibility with older implementations, but the language treats it differently. Generic pointers cannot be dereferenced with the ***** or subscripting operators. Any pointer to an object or incomplete type (but *not* to a function type) can be converted to type **void *** and back without change. (Type **void *** is considered to be neither an object pointer nor a function pointer.)

Example

Some sample pointer declarations and conversions:

```
void *generic_ptr;
int *int_ptr;
char *char_ptr;
generic_ptr = int_ptr;       /* OK */
int_ptr = generic_ptr;       /* OK */
int_ptr = char_ptr;          /* Invalid in ISO C */
int_ptr = (int *) char_ptr;  /* OK */
```

Generic pointers provide additional flexibility in using function prototypes. When a function has a formal parameter that can accept a pointer of any type, the formal should be declared to be of type **void ***. If the formal is declared with any other pointer type, the actual argument must be of the same type, since different pointer types are not assign compatible in ISO C.

Example

The **strcpy** facility copies character strings and therefore requires arguments of type **char ***:

```
char *strcpy(char *s1, const char *s2);
```

On the other hand, **memcpy** can take a pointer to any type and so uses **void ***:

```
void *memcpy(void *s1, const void *s2, size_t n);
```

References assignment compatibility 6.3.2; **const** type specifier 4.4; **memcpy** facility 14.3; **strcpy** facility 13.3

5.3.2 Null Pointers and Invalid Pointers

C has a special "null pointer" value that explicitly points to no object or function. The null pointer may be written as the integer constant **0**, **0L** (when pointers are larger than type

int), or (in ISO C) as **(void *)0**. The macro **NULL** is defined to be one of these constants in standard header files—**stddef.h** in ISO C and **stdio.h** in most other implementations. The null pointer, like the integer value 0, has the value "false" in boolean expressions, so tests for the null pointer can be abbreviated.

Example

The statement

```
if (ip) i = *ip;
```

is a common shorthand notation for

```
if (ip != NULL) i = *ip;
```

It is good programming style to be sure that all pointers have the value **NULL** when they are not designating a valid object or function.

It is also possible to inadvertently create *invalid pointers*—that is, pointer values that are not null but also do not designate a proper object or function. Invalid pointers can be created by casting arbitrary integer values to pointer types, by deallocating the storage for an object to which a pointer refers (as by using the **free** facility), or by using pointer arithmetic to produce a pointer outside the range of an array. An attempt to dereference an invalid pointer may cause a run-time error.

In conjunction with pointer arithmetic, C does require that the address of an object one past the last object of an array be defined, although such an address can still be invalid to dereference. This requirement makes it easier to use pointer expressions to walk through arrays.

Example

The following loop uses the address just beyond the end of an array, although it never attempts to dereference that address:

```
int array[N]; /* last object address is &array[N-1] */
int *p;
...
for (p = &array[0]; p < &array[N]; p++)
    ...
```

This requirement may restrict implementations for a few target computers that have noncontiguous addressing architectures, reducing by one object the maximum length of an array. On such computers it may be impossible to perform arithmetic on pointers that do not fall within a contiguous area of memory, and only by allocating an array is the programmer guaranteed that the memory is contiguous.

References integer constants 2.7.1; pointer arithmetic 7.6.2; **stddef.h** facility 11.1; **void *** type 5.3.1

5.3.3 Some Cautions with Pointers

Many C programmers assume that all pointer types (actually, all addresses) have a uniform representation. On common byte-addressed computers all pointers are typically simple byte addresses occupying, say, one word. Conversions among pointer and integer types on these computers require no change in representation and no information is lost.

In fact, the C language does not require such nice behavior. Section 6.1 discusses the problems in more detail, but here is a brief summary:

1. Pointers are often not the same size as type **int**, and sometimes not the same size as type **long**. Sometimes their size is a compiler option.
2. Character and **void *** pointers can be larger than other kinds of pointers, or may use a representation that is incompatible with other kinds of pointers.
3. Function pointers and data pointers may have significantly different representations, including different sizes.

The programmer should always use explicit casts when converting between pointer types, and should be especially careful that pointer arguments given to functions have the correct type expected by the function. In ISO C, **void *** can be used as a generic object pointer, but there is no generic function pointer.

References casts 7.5.1; **malloc** function 16.1; pointer conversions 6.2.7

5.4 ARRAY TYPES

If *T* is any C type except **void** or "function returning...," the type "array of *T*" may be declared. Values of this type are sequences of elements of type *T*. All arrays are 0-origin.

Example

The array declared **int A[3];** consists of the elements **A[0]**, **A[1]**, and **A[2]**. In the following code, an array of integers (**ints**) and an array of pointers (**ptrs**) are declared, and each of the pointers in **ptrs** is set equal to the address of the corresponding integer in **ints**:

```
int ints[10], *ptrs[10], i;
for (i = 0; i < 10; i++)
    ptrs[i] = &ints[i];
```

The memory size of an array (in the sense of the **sizeof** operator) is always equal to the length of the array in elements multiplied by the memory size of an element.

An array type of unknown size is called an *incomplete type*. A variable of such a type can be declared, but must later have the type completed by supplying a second declaration that includes the array bounds:

```
extern int a[];     /* a has an incomplete array type */
...
int a[10];          /* the type of a is now complete */
```

An incomplete type can be specified only for a top-level identifier, since these are the only declarations that can be duplicated. Objects of incomplete types cannot be allocated storage, but pointers to them can be created and used. An incomplete array type can also be used as the type of a function parameter, because all array types in parameter declarations are converted to pointer types.

References array declarators 4.5.3; **sizeof** operator 7.5.2; storage units 6.1.1

5.4.1 Arrays and Pointers

In C there is a close correspondence between types "array of *T*" and "pointer to *T*." First, when an array identifier appears in an expression, the type of the identifier is converted from "array of *T*" to "pointer to T," and the value of the identifier is converted to a pointer to the first element of the array. This rule is one of the usual unary conversions. The only exception to this conversion rule is when the array identifier is used as an operand of the **sizeof** operator, in which case **sizeof** returns the size of the entire array, not the size of a pointer to the first array element.

Example

In the second line below, the value **a** is converted to a pointer to the first element of the array:

```
int a[10], *ip;
ip = a;
```

It is exactly as if we had written

```
ip = &a[0];
```

The value of **sizeof(a)** will be **sizeof(int)*10**, not **sizeof(int *)**.

Second, array subscripting is defined in terms of pointer arithmetic. That is, the expression **a[i]** is defined to be the same as ***((a) + (i))**, where **a** is converted to **&a[0]** under the usual unary conversions. This definition of subscripting also means that **a[i]** is the same as **i[a]**, and that any pointer may be subscripted just like an array. It is up to the programmer to ensure that the pointer is pointing into an appropriate array of elements.

Example

If **d** has type **double**, and **dp** is a pointer to a **double** object, then the expression

```
d = dp[4];
```

is defined only if **dp** currently points to an element of a **double** array, and if there are at least four more elements of the array following the one pointed to.

References address operator **&** 7.5.6; addition operator **+** 7.6.2; array declarators 4.5.3; conversions of arrays 6.3.3; indirection operator ***** 7.5.7; pointer types 5.3; **sizeof** operator 5.4.4, 7.5.2; subscripting 7.4.1; usual unary conversions 6.3.3

5.4.2 Multidimensional Arrays

Multidimensional arrays are declared as "arrays of arrays," such as in the declaration

```
int matrix[10][10];
```

which declares **matrix** to be a 10-by-10 element array of **int**. The language places no limit on the number of dimensions an array may have.

Multidimensional array elements are stored in row-major order. That is, those elements that differ only in their last subscript are stored adjacently. The conversions of arrays to pointers happens analogously for multidimensional arrays.

Example

The elements of the array **int t[2][3]** are stored (in increasing addresses) as

```
t[0][0], t[0][1], t[0][2], t[1][0], t[1][1], t[1][2]
```

The expression **t[1][2]** is expanded to ***(*(t+1)+2)**, which is evaluated in this sequence of steps:

1. The expression **t**, a 2-by-3 array, is converted to a pointer to the first 3-element subarray.
2. The expression **t+1** is then a pointer to the second 3-element subarray.
3. The expression ***(t+1)**, the second 3-element subarray of integers, is converted to a pointer to the first integer in that subarray.
4. The expression ***(t+1)+2** is then a pointer to the third integer in the second 3-element subarray.
5. Finally, ***(*(t+1)+2)** is the third integer in the second 3-element subarray; **t[1][2]**.

In general, any expression *A* of type "*i*-by-*j*-by-...-by-*k* array of *T*" is immediately converted to "pointer to *j*-by-...-by-*k* array of *T*."

References addition operator **+** 7.6.2; array declarators 4.5.3; indirection operator ***** 7.5.7; pointer types 5.3; subscripting 7.4.1

5.4.3 Array Bounds

Whenever storage for an array is allocated, the size of the array must be known. However, because subscripts are not normally checked to lie within declared array bounds, it is possible to omit the size (that is, to use an incomplete array type) when declaring an external, singly dimensioned array defined in another module or when declaring a singly dimensioned array that is a formal parameter to a function. (See section 4.5.)

Example

The following function, **sum,** returns the sum of the first **n** elements of an external array, **a**, whose bounds are not specified:

```
extern int a[];

int sum(int n)
{
    int i, s = 0;
    for (i = 0; i < n; i++)
        s += a[i];
    return s;
}
```

The array could also be passed as a parameter, like this:

```
int sum(int a[], int n)
{
    int i, s = 0;
    for (i = 0; i < n; i++)
        s += a[i];
    return s;
}
```

The parameter **a** could be declared as **int *a**, without changing the body of the function. That would more accurately reflect the implementation but less clearly indicate the intent.

When multidimensional arrays are used, it is necessary to specify the bounds of all but the first dimension, so that the proper address arithmetic can be calculated:

```
extern int matrix[][10]; /* ?-by-10 array of int */
```

If such bounds are not specified, the declaration is in error.

References array declarators 4.5.3; defining and referencing declarations 4.8; indirection operator * 7.5.7; omitted array bounds 4.5; pointer types 5.3; subscripting 7.4.1

5.4.4 Operations

The only operation that can be performed directly on an array value is the application of the **sizeof** operator. The array must be bounded. The result of such an operation is the number of storage units occupied by the array. For an *n*-element array of type *T*, the result of the **sizeof** operator is always equal to *n* times the result of **sizeof** applied to the type *T*.

In all other contexts, such as subscripting, the array value is actually treated as a pointer, and so operations on pointers may be applied to the array value.

References array declarators 4.5.3; conversions from array to pointer 6.2.7; pointer types 5.3; **sizeof** operator 7.5.2; subscripting 7.4.1

5.5 ENUMERATED TYPES

Enumerated types are a recent addition to C; similar concepts occur in other languages, including Pascal and Ada. The syntax for declaring enumerated types is shown below:

enumeration-type-specifier :
    enumeration-type-definition
    enumeration-type-reference

enumeration-type-definition :
    enum *enumeration-tag*$_{opt}$ **{** *enumeration-definition-list* **}**

enumeration-type-reference :
    enum *enumeration-tag*

enumeration-tag :
    identifier

enumeration-definition-list :
    enumeration-constant-definition
    enumeration-definition-list **,** *enumeration-constant-definition*

enumeration-constant-definition :
    enumeration-constant
    enumeration-constant = *expression*

enumeration-constant :
    identifier

An enumerated type in C is a set of integer values represented by identifiers called *enumeration constants*. The enumeration constants are specified when the type is defined and have type **int**. Each enumerated type is represented by an implementation-defined integer type and is compatible with that type. Thus, for the purposes of type checking, an enumerated type is just one of the integer types. When the C language permits an integer expression in some context, an enumeration constant or a value of an enumerated type can be used instead. (This is not true in C++; see section 5.13.1.)

Example

The declaration

```
enum fish { trout, carp, halibut } my_fish, your_fish;
```

creates a new enumerated type, **enum fish**, whose values are **trout**, **carp**, and **halibut**. It also declares two variables of the enumerated type, **my_fish** and **your_fish**, which can be assigned values with the assignments

```
my_fish = halibut;
your_fish = trout;
```

Variables or other objects of the enumerated type can be declared in the same declaration containing the enumerated type definition or in a subsequent declaration that mentions the enumerated type with an "enumerated type reference."

Example

For example, the single declaration

```
enum color { red, blue, green, mauve }
    favorite, acceptable, least_favorite;
```

is exactly equivalent to the two declarations

```
enum color { red, blue, green, mauve } favorite;
enum color acceptable, least_favorite;
```

and to the four declarations

```
enum color { red, blue, green, mauve };
enum color favorite;
enum color acceptable;
enum color least_favorite;
```

The enumeration tag, **color**, allows an enumerated type to be referenced after its definition. Although the declaration

```
enum { red, blue, green, mauve }
    favorite, acceptable, least_favorite;
```

defines the same type and declares the same variables, the lack of a tag makes it impossible to introduce more variables of the type in later declarations.

Enumeration tags are in the same overloading class as structure and union tags, and their scope is the same as that of a variable declared at the same location in the source program.

Identifiers defined as enumeration constants are members of the same overloading class as variables, functions, and typedef names. Their scope is the same as that of a variable defined at the same location in the source program.

Example

In the code below, the declaration of **shepherd** as an enumeration constant hides the previous declaration of the integer variable **shepherd**. However, the declaration of the floating-point variable **collie** causes a compilation error, because **collie** is already declared in the same scope as an enumeration constant.

```
int shepherd = 12;
{
    enum dog_breeds {shepherd, collie};
        /* Hides outer declaration of the name "shepherd" */
    float collie;
        /* Invalid redefinition of the name "collie" */
}
```

Enumerated types are implemented by associating integer values with the enumeration constants, so that the assignment and comparison of values of enumerated types can be implemented as integer assignment and comparison. Integer values are associated with enumeration constants in the following way:

1. An explicit integer value may be associated with an enumeration constant by writing

   enumeration-constant = *expression*

   in the type definition. The expression must be a constant expression of integral type, although some compilers may also allow expressions involving previously defined enumeration constants, as in

```
enum boys { Bill  = 10,
            John  = Bill+2,
            Fred  = John+2 };
```

2. The first enumeration constant receives the value 0 if no explicit value is specified.
3. Subsequent enumeration constants without explicit associations receive an integer value one greater than the value associated with the previous enumeration constant.

Any signed integer value representable as type **int** may be associated with an enumeration constant. Positive and negative integers may be chosen at random, and it is even possible to associate the same integer with two different enumeration constants.

Example

Given the declaration

```
enum sizes { small, medium=10, pretty_big, large=20 };
```

the values of **small**, **medium**, **pretty_big**, and **large** will be 0, 10, 11, and 20, respectively. Although the following definition is valid:

```
enum people { john=1, mary=19, bill=-4, sheila=1 };
```

its effect is to make the expression **john == sheila** true, which is not intuitive.

Although the form of an enumerated type definition is suggestive of structure and union types, with strict type checking, in fact enumerated types in ISO C (which is the definition given in this book) act as little more than slightly more readable ways to name integer constants. As a matter of style, we suggest that programmers treat enumerated types as different from integers and not mix them in integer expressions without using casts. In fact, some UNIX C compilers implement a weakly typed form of enumerations in which some conversions between enumerated types and integers are not permitted without casts.

References cast expressions 7.5.1; identifiers 2.5; overloading classes 4.2.4; scope 4.2.1

5.6 STRUCTURE TYPES

The structure types in C are similar to the types known as "records" in other programming languages. They are collections of named *components* (also called "members" or "fields") that can have different types. Structures can be defined to encapsulate related data objects.

structure-type-specifier :
    structure-type-definition
    structure-type-reference

structure-type-definition :
    struct *structure-tag*$_{opt}$ **{** *field-list* **}**

structure-type-reference :
    struct *structure-tag*

structure-tag :
    identifier

field-list :
    component-declaration
    field-list component-declaration

component-declaration :
    type-specifier component-declarator-list **;**

component-declarator-list :
    component-declarator
    component-declarator-list **,** *component-declarator*

component-declarator :
    simple-component
    bit-field

simple-component :
    declarator

bit-field :
    declarator$_{opt}$ **:** *width*

width :
    expression

Example

A programmer who wanted to implement complex numbers might define a structure **complex** to hold the real and imaginary parts as components **real** and **imag**. The first declaration below defines the new type, and the second declares two variables, **x** and **y**, of that type:

```
struct complex {
    double real;
    double imag;
};
struct complex x,y;
```

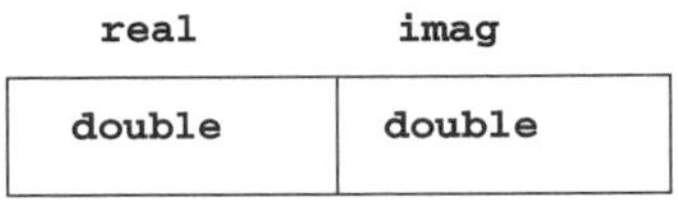

struct complex

A function **new_complex** can be written to create a new object of the type. (Early C compilers did not allow functions to return structures. The code in this example would have to be rewritten for them.) Note that the selection operator (**.**) is used to access the components of the structure:

```
struct complex new_complex(double r, double i)
{
    struct complex new;
    new.real = r;
    new.imag = i;
    return new;
}
```

Operations on the type, such as **complex_multiply**, can also be defined:

```
struct complex complex_multiply( struct complex a,
                                 struct complex b )
{
    struct complex product;
    product.real = a.real * b.real - a.imag * b.imag;
    product.imag = a.real * b.imag + a.imag * b.real;
    return product;
}
```

Example

The single declaration

```
struct complex { double real, imag; } x, y;
```

is equivalent to the two declarations

```
struct complex { double real, imag; };
struct complex x, y;
```

5.6.1 Structure Type References

The use of a type specifier of the syntactic classes *structure-type-definition* or *union-type-definition* (section 5.7) introduces the definition of a new type, different from all others. If present in the definition, the structure tag is associated with the new type and can be used in a subsequent structure type reference.

The scope of the definition (and the type tag, if any) is from the declaration point to the end of the innermost block containing the specifier. The new definition explicitly overrides (hides) any definition of the type tag in an enclosing block.

The use of a type specifier of the syntactic classes *structure-type-reference* or *union-type-reference* (section 5.7) without a preceding definition in the same or enclosing scope is allowed when the size of the structure is not required, including when declaring:

1. pointers to the structure
2. a typedef name as a synonym for the structure

The use of this kind of specifier introduces an "incomplete" definition of the type and type tag in the innermost block containing the use. For this definition to be completed, a *structure-type-definition* or *union-type-definition* must appear later in the same scope.

As a special case, the occurrence of a *structure-type-reference* or *union-type-reference* in a declaration with no declarators hides any definition of the type tag in any enclosing scope and establishes an incomplete type.

Example

Consider the following correct definition of two self-referential structures in an inner block:

```
{
    struct cell;
    struct header { struct cell   *first; ... };
    struct cell   { struct header *head;  ... };
    ...
}
```

The incomplete definition "**struct cell;**" in the first line is necessary to hide any definitions of the tag **cell** in an enclosing scope. The definition of **struct header** in the second line automatically hides any enclosing definitions, and its use of **struct cell** to define a pointer is valid. The definition of **struct cell** on the third line completes the information about **cell**.

An incomplete type declaration also exists within a *structure-type-definition* or *union-type-definition*, from the first mention of the new tag until the definition is complete. This allows a single structure type to include a pointer to itself. (See Figure 5–1 on page 133.)

References declarations 4.1; declarators 4.5; duplicate visibility 4.2.2; scope 4.2.1; selection operator **.** 7.4.2; type equivalence 5.11

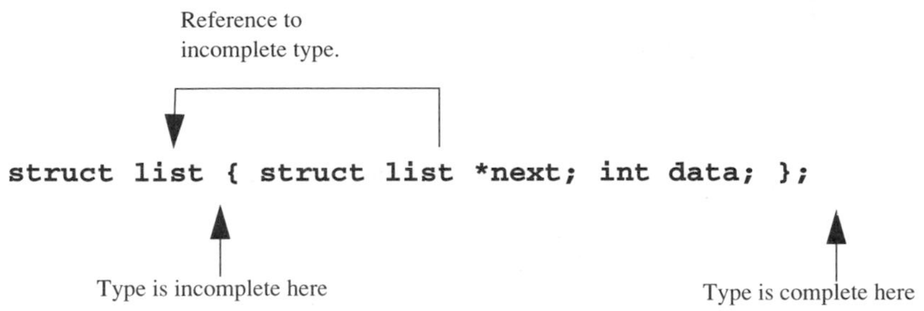

Figure 5–1 Incomplete structure type within a declaration

5.6.2 Operations on Structures

The operations provided for structures may vary from compiler to compiler. All C compilers provide the selection operators `.` and `->` on structures, and newer compilers now allow structures to be assigned, to be passed as parameters to functions, and to be returned from functions. (With older compilers, assignment must be done component by component, and only pointers to structures may be passed to and from functions.)

It is not permitted to compare two structures for equality. An object of a structure type is a sequence of components of other types. Because certain data objects may be constrained by the target computer to lie on certain addressing boundaries, a structure object may contain "holes," storage units that do not belong to any component of the structure. The holes would make equality tests implemented as a wholesale bit-by-bit comparison unreliable, and component-by-component equality tests might be too expensive. (Of course, the programmer may write component-by-component equality functions.)

In any situation where it is permitted to apply the unary address operator & to a structure to obtain a pointer to the structure, it is also permitted to apply the operator to a component of the structure to obtain a pointer to the component. That is, it is possible for a pointer to point into the middle of a structure. An exception to this rule occurs with components defined as bit fields. Components defined as bit fields will in general not lie on machine-addressable boundaries, and therefore it may not be possible to form a pointer to a bit field. The C language therefore forbids such pointers.

References address operator `&` 7.5.6; assignment 7.9; bit fields 5.6.5; equality operator `==` 7.6.5; selection operator `.` and `->` 7.4.2; type equivalence 5.11

5.6.3 Components

A component of a structure may have any type except "function returning..." and **`void`**. Structures may not contain instances of themselves, although they may contain pointers to instances of themselves.

Example

This declaration is invalid:

```
struct S {
    int a;
    struct S next;    /* invalid! */
};
```

But, this one is permitted:

```
struct S {
    int a;
    struct S *next;    /* OK */
};
```

The names of structure components are defined in a special overloading class associated with the structure type. That is, component names within a single structure must be distinct, but they may be the same as component names in other structures and may be the same as variable, function, and type names.

Example

Consider the following sequence of declarations:

```
int x;
struct A { int x; double y; } y;
struct B { int y; double x; } z;
```

The identifier **x** has three nonconflicting declarations: it is an integer variable, an integer component of structure **A**, and a floating-point component of structure **B**. These three declarations are used, respectively, in the expressions

```
x
y.x
z.x
```

If a structure tag is defined in one of the components, then the scope of the tag extends to the end of the block in which the enclosing structure is defined. (If the enclosing structure is defined at the top level, so is the inner tag.)

Example

In the declaration

```
struct S {
    struct T {int a, b; } x;
};
```

The tag **T** is defined from its first occurrence to the end of the scope in which **S** is defined.

Historical note: The original definition of C specified that all components in all structures were allocated out of the same overloading class, and therefore no two structures could have components with the same name. (An exception was made when the components had the same type and the same relative position in the structures!) This interpretation is now anachronistic, but you might see it mentioned in older documentation or actually implemented in some old compilers.

References overloading classes 4.2.4; scope 4.2.1

5.6.4 Structure Component Layout

Most programmers will be unconcerned with how components are packed into structures. However, C does give the programmer some control over the packing. C compilers are constrained to assign components increasing memory addresses in a strict order, with the first component starting at the beginning address of the structure itself.

Example

There is no difference in component layout between the structure

```
struct { int a, b, c; };
```

and the structure

```
struct { int a; int b, c; };
```

Both put **a** first, **b** second, and **c** last in order of increasing addresses, as pictured below

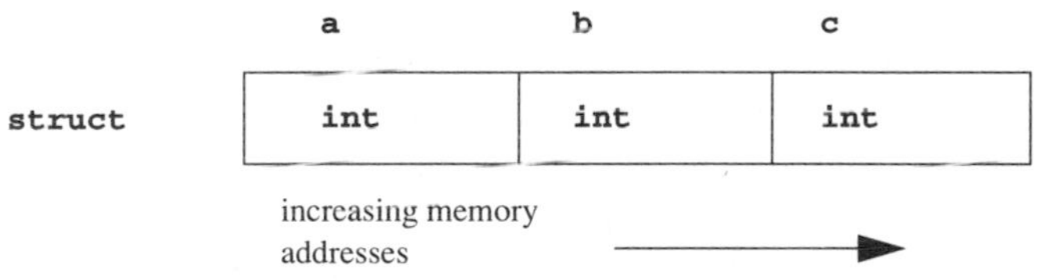

Given two pointers **p** and **q** to components within the same structure, **p < q** will be true if and only if the declaration of the component to which **p** points appears earlier within the structure declaration than the declaration of the component to which **q** points.

Example

```
struct vector3 { int x, y, z; } s;
int *p, *q, *r;
...
p = &s.x;
q = &s.y;
r = &s.z;            /* At this point p < q, q < r, and p < r. */
```

Holes, or padding, may appear between any two consecutive components in the layout of a structure if necessary to allow proper alignment of components in memory. The bit patterns appearing in such holes are unpredictable, and may differ from structure to structure or over time within a single structure.

5.6.5 Bit Fields

C allows the programmer to pack integer components into spaces smaller than the compiler would ordinarily allow. These integer components are called bit fields and are specified by following the component declarator with a colon and a constant integer expression that indicates the width of the field in bits.

Example

The following structure has three components, **a**, **b**, and **c**, occupying four, five, and seven bits, respectively:

```
struct S {
    unsigned a:4;
    unsigned b:5, c:7;
};
```

A bit field of n bits can represent unsigned integers in the range 0 through 2^n-1, and signed integers in the range -2^{n-1} through $2^{n-1}-1$, assuming a two's-complement representation of signed integers. The original definition of C permitted only bit fields of type **unsigned**, but ISO C permits bit fields to be of type **unsigned int**, **signed int**, or just **int**, termed unsigned, signed, and "plain" bit fields. Some C implementations allow bit fields of any integer type, including **char**.

Bit fields are typically used in machine-dependent programs that must force a data structure to correspond to a fixed hardware representation. The precise manner in which components (and especially bit fields) are packed into a structure is implementation-dependent but is predictable for each implementation. The intent is that bit fields should be packed as tightly as possible in a structure, subject to the rules discussed later in this section. The use of bit fields is therefore likely to be nonportable. The programmer should consult the implementation documentation if it is necessary to lay out a structure in memory in some particular fashion, and then verify that the C compiler is indeed packing the components in the way expected.

Example

Here is an example of how bit fields can be used to create a structure that matches a predefined format. Below is the layout of a 32-bit word treated as a virtual address on a hypothetical computer. The word contains fields for the segment number, page number, and offset within a page, plus a "supervisor" bit and an unused bit.

	S		Segment	Page	Offset
field width (bits)	1	1	6	8	16

To duplicate this layout, we first have to know if our computer packs bit fields left to right or right to left—that is, whether it is a "big endian" or a "little endian." (See section 6.1.2.) If packing is right to left, the appropriate structure definition is

```
typedef struct {
    unsigned Offset     : 16;
    unsigned Page       : 8;
    unsigned Segment    : 6;
    unsigned UNUSED     : 1;
    unsigned Supervisor : 1;
} virtual_address;
```

On the other hand, if packing is left to right, the appropriate structure definition is

```
typedef struct {
    unsigned Supervisor : 1;
    unsigned UNUSED     : 1;
    unsigned Segment    : 6;
    unsigned Page       : 8;
    unsigned Offset     : 16;
} virtual_address;
```

The signedness of a plain integer bit field follows the signedness of plain characters. That is, a plain integer bit field may actually be implemented as a signed, unsigned, or pseudo-unsigned type. (See section 5.1.3.) Signed and unsigned bit fields must be implemented to hold signed and unsigned values.

Example

Consider the effect of the following ISO C declarations on a two's-complement computer:

```
struct S { unsigned ubf:3;
           signed   sbf:3;
           int       bf:3; } x = { -1, -1, -1 };
...
int i = x.ubf;
int j = x.sbf;
int k = x.bf;
```

The value of **i** must be 7 and of **j** must be –1, but the value of **k** may be either 7 or –1.

Compilers are free to impose constraints on the maximum size of a bit field and to specify certain addressing boundaries that bit fields cannot cross. These alignment restrictions are usually related to the natural word size of the target computer. When a field is too long for the computer, the compiler will issue an appropriate error message. When a field would cross a word boundary, it may be moved to the next word.

An unnamed bit field may also be included in a structure to provide "padding" between adjacent components. Unnamed bit fields cannot be referenced and their contents at run time are not predictable.

Example

The following structure places component **a** in the first four bits of the structure, followed by two bits of padding, followed by the component **b** in six bits. (Assuming a basic word size of 16 bits, a final four bits will also be unused at the end of the structure. See section 5.6.7.)

```
struct S {
    unsigned a : 4;
    unsigned   : 2;
    unsigned b : 6;
};
```

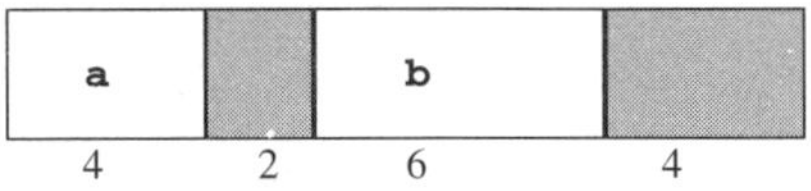

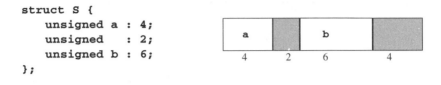

Specifying a length of 0 for an unnamed bit field has a special meaning—it indicates that the following component should begin on the next boundary appropriate to its type. ("Appropriate" is not specified further; in ISO C, it is the next **int**-sized unit.)

Example

In the following structure the component **b** should begin on a natural addressing boundary (for example, 16 bits) following component **a**. The new structure occupies twice as much storage as the old one:

```
struct S {
    unsigned a : 4;
    unsigned   : 0;
    unsigned b : 6;
};
```

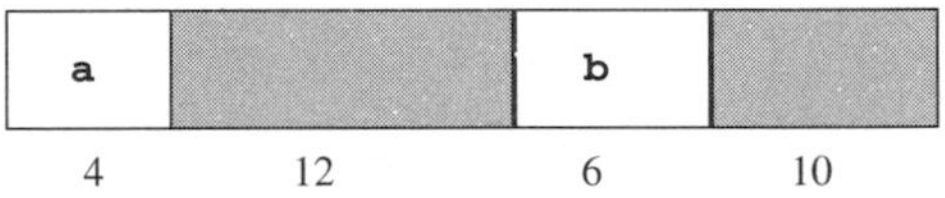

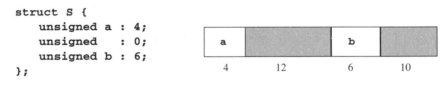

The address operator **&** may not be applied to bit-field components, since many computers cannot address arbitrary-sized fields directly.

References address operator **&** 7.5.6; alignment restrictions 6.1.3; byte order 6.1.2; enumerated types 5.5; signed types 5.1.1; unsigned types 5.1.2

5.6.6 Portability Problems

Depending on packing strategies is dangerous for several reasons. First, computers differ on the alignment constraints on data types. For instance, a 4-byte integer on some computers must begin on a byte boundary that is a multiple of four, whereas on other computers the integer can (and will) be aligned on the nearest byte boundary.

Second, the restrictions on bit-field widths will be different. Some computers have a 16-bit word size, which limits the maximum size of the field and imposes a boundary that fields cannot cross. Other computers have a 32-bit word size, and so forth.

Third, computers differ in the way fields are packed into a word—that is, in their "byte ordering." On the Motorola 68000 family of computers, characters are packed left to right into words, from the most significant bit to the least significant bit. On Intel 80x86 computers, characters are packed right to left, from the least significant bit to the most significant bit. As seen in the **virtual_address** example in the previous section, different structure definitions are needed for computers with different byte ordering.

We know of two situations that seem to justify the use of bit fields:

1. A predefined data structure must be matched exactly so it can be referenced in a C program. (These programs may not be portable anyway.)
2. An array of structured data must be maintained, and its large size requires that its components be packed tightly to conserve memory.

By using the C bitwise operators to perform masking and shifting functions, it is possible to access bit fields in a way that is not sensitive to byte ordering.

Example

Consider the problem of accessing the **Page** field in the **virtual_address** structure (page 136). Since this 8-bit field is located 16 bits from the low-order end of the word, it can be accessed with the following code:

```
unsigned V;     /* formatted as a virtual_address */
int Page
...
Page = (V & 0xFF0000) >> 16;
```

This is equivalent to the more readable structure component access **Page=V.Page**, but the mask-and-shift approach is *not* sensitive to the computer's byte ordering, as is the definition of **virtual_address**. The masking and shifting operations are demonstrated below for **V==0xb393352e** (**Page==0x93**):

```
10110011100100110011010100101110   V
00000000111111110000000000000000   0xFF0000
00000000100100110000000000000000   V & 0xFF0000
00000000000000000000000010010011   (V & 0xFF0000)>>16
```

Similar operations may be used to set the value of a bit field. There may be little difference in the run-time performance of these two access methods.

References alignment restrictions 6.1.3; bitwise operators 7.6.6; byte order 6.1.2; shift operators 7.6.3

5.6.7 Sizes of Structures

The size of an object of a structure type is the amount of storage necessary to represent all components of that type, including any unused padding space between or after the components. The rule is that the structure will be padded out to the size the type would occupy as an element of an array of such types. (For any type *T*, including structures, the size of an *n*-element array of *T* is the same as the size of *T* times *n*.) Another way of saying this is that the structure must terminate on the same alignment boundary on which it started—that is, if the structure must begin on an even byte boundary, it must also end on an even byte boundary. The alignment requirement for a structure type will be at least as stringent as for the component having the most stringent requirements.

Example

On a computer that starts all structures on an address that is a multiple of 4 bytes, the length of the following structure will be a multiple of four (probably exactly four), even though only two characters are actually used:

```
struct S {
    char c1;
    char c2;
};
```

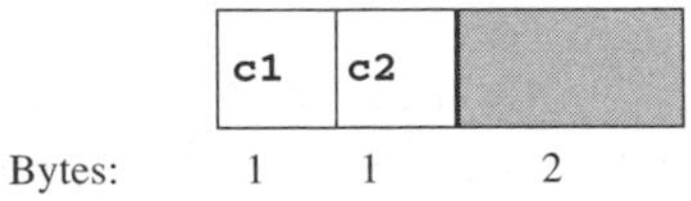

Example

On a computer that requires all objects of type **`double`** to have an address that is a multiple of 8 bytes, the length of the following structure is probably 24 bytes, even though only 18 bytes are declared:

```
struct S {
    double value;
    char name [10];
};
```

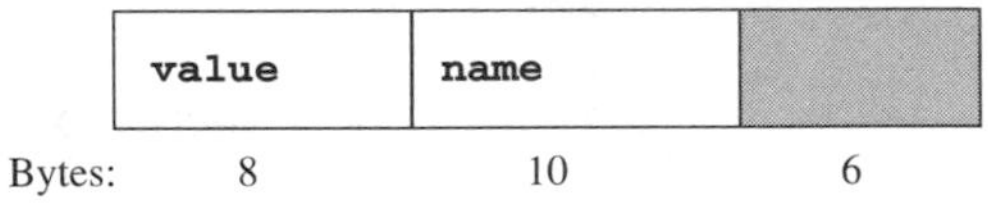

Six extra units of padding are needed at the end to make the size of the structure a multiple of the alignment requirement, eight. If the padding were not used, then in an array of such structures not all of the structures would have the value component aligned properly to a multiple-of-eight address.

Example

Alignment requirements may cause padding to appear in the middle of a structure. If the order of the components in the previous example is reversed, the length remains 24 but the unused space appears between the components, so that the value component may be aligned to an address that is a multiple of 8 bytes relative to the beginning of the structure:

```
struct S {
    char name [10];
    double value;
};
```

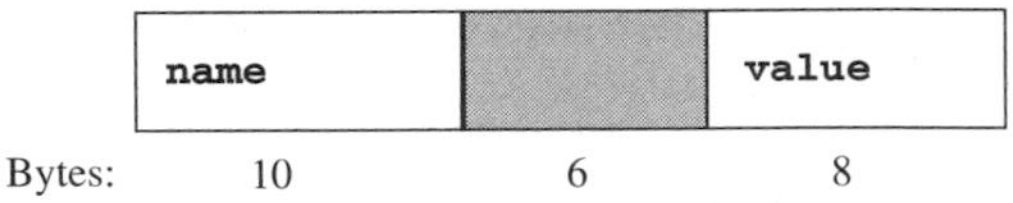

Any object of the structure type will be required to have an address that is a multiple of eight, and so the value component of such an object will always be properly aligned.

5.7 UNION TYPES

The syntax for defining union types is almost identical to that for defining structure types:

union-type-specifier :
  union-type-definition
  union-type-reference

union-type-definition :
  union *union-tag*$_{opt}$ **{** *field-list* **}**

union-type-reference :
  union *union-tag*

union-tag :
  identifier

The syntax for defining components is the same as that used for structures. In traditional C, unions could not contain bit fields, but in ISO C this restriction is removed.

As with structures and enumerations, each union type definition introduces a new union type, different from all others. If present in the definition, the union tag is associated with the new type and can be used in a subsequent union type reference. Forward references and incomplete definitions of union types are permitted with the same rules as structure types.

A component of a union may have any type except "function returning..." and **void**. Also, unions may not contain instances of themselves, although they may contain pointers to instances of themselves. As in structures, the names of union components are defined in a special overload class associated with the union type. That is, component names within a single union must be distinct, but they may be the same as component names in other unions and may be the same as variable, function, and type names.

5.7.1 Union Component Layout

Each component of a union type is allocated storage starting at the beginning of the union. A union can contain only one of its component values at a time. An object of a union type will begin on a storage alignment boundary appropriate for any contained component.

Example

Here is a union with three components, all effectively overlaid in memory:

```
union U {
    double d;
    char c[2];
    int i;
};
```

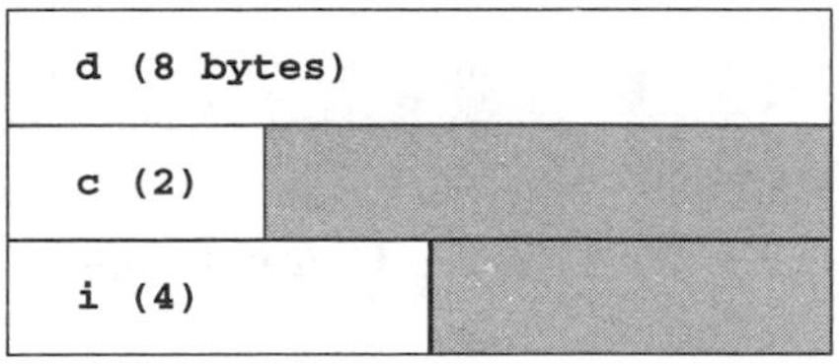

Example

If we have the following union type and object definitions:

```
static union U { ...; int C; ...; } object, *P = &object;
```

then the following two equalities hold:

```
(union U *) & (P->C) == P
&(P->C) == (int *) P
```

Furthermore, these equalities hold no matter what the type of the component C and no matter what other components in the union precede or follow C.

References alignment restrictions 6.1.3

5.7.2 Sizes of Unions

The size of an object of a union type is the amount of storage necessary to represent the largest component of that type, plus any padding that may be needed at the end to raise the length up to an appropriate alignment boundary. The rule is that the union will be padded out to the size the type would occupy as an element of an array of such types. Recall that for any type T, including unions, the size of an n-element array of T is the same as (the size of T)$\cdot n$. Another way of saying this is that the structure must terminate on the same alignment boundary on which it started. That is, if the structure had to begin on an even byte boundary, it must end on an even byte boundary.

Note that the alignment requirement for a union type will be at least as stringent as for the component having the most stringent requirements.

Example

On a computer that requires all objects of type **`double`** to have an address that is a multiple of 8, the length of the following union will be 16, even though the size of the longest component is only 10:

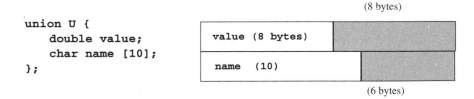

```
union U {
    double value;
    char name [10];
};
```

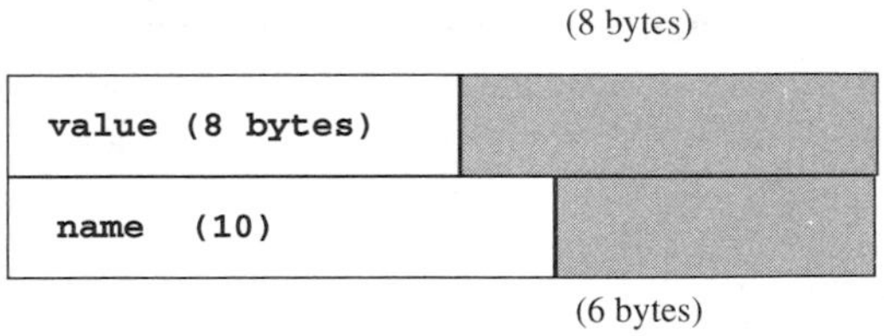

Six extra units of padding are needed to make the size of the union a multiple of the alignment requirement, eight. If the padding were not used, then in an array of such unions not all of the unions would have the **`value`** component aligned properly to a multiple-of-eight address.

5.7.3 Using Union Types

C's union type is somewhat like a "variant record" in other languages. Like structures, unions are defined to have a number of components. Unlike structures, however, a union can hold at most one of its components at a time; the components are conceptually overlaid in the storage allocated for the union. If the union is very large, or if there is a large array of the unions, then the storage savings can be significant.

Example

Suppose we want an object that can be *either* an integer or a floating-point number, depending on the situation. We define union **datum**:

```
union datum {
    int i;
    double d;
};
```

and then define a variable of the union type:

```
union datum u;
```

To store an integer in the union, we write

```
u.i = 15;
```

To store a floating-point number in the union, we assign to the other component

```
u.d = 88.9e4;
```

A component of a union should be referenced only if the last assignment to the union was through the same component. C provides no way to inquire which component of a union was last assigned; the programmer either can remember or can encode explicit data tags to be associated with unions. A data tag is an object associated with a union that holds an indication of which component is currently stored in the union. The data tag and union can be enclosed in a common structure.

Example

We can replace the union

```
union widget { long count; double value; char name[10];} x;
```

with

```
enum widget_tag { count_widget,
                  value_widget,
                  name_widget };

struct WIDGET {
  enum widget_tag tag;
  union { long count;
          double value;
          char name[10]; } data;
} x;

typedef struct WIDGET widget;
```

The size of the **widget** structure is 24 bytes, which is caused by the assumption that objects of type **double** must be aligned on 8-byte boundaries. The layout is shown below:

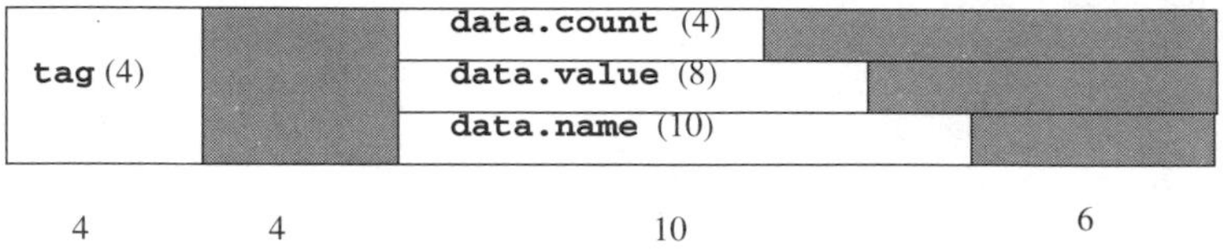

If, as is common, objects of type **double** can be placed on 4-byte boundaries, then **widget**'s length will be only 16 bytes.

To assign an integer to the union, we write

```
x.tag = count_widget;
x.data.count = 10000;
```

To assign a floating-point number, we write

```
x.tag = value_widget;
x.data.value = 3.14159265358979 32384;
```

To assign a string, we can use the **strncpy** library function:

```
x.tag = name_widget;
strncpy(x.data.name, "Millard", 10);
```

Below is a portable function that can discriminate among the possibilities for the union. **print_widget** can be called without regard to which component was last assigned:

```
void print_widget(widget w)
{
    switch(w.tag) {
        case count_widget:
            printf("Count %ld\n", w.data.count); break;
        case value_widget:
            printf("Value %f\n", w.data.value); break;
        case name_widget:
            printf("Name \"%s\"\n", w.data.name); break;
    }
}
```

References cast expression 7.5.1; enumerations 5.5; overloading 4.2.4; scope 4.2.1; **switch** statement 8.7; **strncpy** facility 13.3; structures 5.6; **typedef** 5.10

5.7.4 (Mis)using Union Types

Unions are used in a nonportable fashion any time a union component is referenced when the last assignment to the union was not through the same component. Programmers sometimes do this to "reach under" C's type system and discover something about the computer's underlying data representation (itself a nonportable concept).

Example

To discover how a floating-point number is represented:

1. Create a union with floating-point and integer components of the same size:

`float (4 bytes)`
`int (4 bytes)`

2. Assign a value to the floating-point component.
3. Read the value of the integer component and print it out as, say, a hexadecimal number.

Here is a function that does just this, assuming types **float** and **int** have the same length:

```
void print_rep(float f)
{
    union { float f; int i } f_or_i;
    f_or_i.f = f;
    printf("The representation of %12.7e is %#010x\n",
        f_or_i.f, f_or_i.i );
}
```

When **print_rep(1.0)** is called, the output on our Motorola 68020-based workstation is

```
The representation of 1.0000000e+00 is 0x003f800000
```

Notice that a cast operation cannot be used to discover the underlying representation. The cast operator in C converts its operand to the closest value in the new representation; **(int) 1.0** is 1, not **0x003f800000**.

5.8 FUNCTION TYPES

The type "function returning *T*" is a function type, where *T* may be any type except "array of..." or "function returning...." Said another way, functions may not return arrays or other functions, although they can return pointers to arrays and functions.

Functions may be introduced in only two ways. First, a function definition can create a function object, define its parameters and return value, and supply the body of the function. More information about function definitions is given in section 9.1. Second, a function declaration can introduce a reference to a function object defined elsewhere.

Example

Here is a function definition for **square**:

```
int square(int x)
{
    return x*x;
}
```

If **square** were defined elsewhere, this declaration would introduce the name and allow it to be called.

```
extern int square(int);
```

An external function declaration can refer to a function defined in another C source file or to a function defined later in the same source file (that is, a "forward reference").

Example

Forward references can be used to create mutually-recursive functions, such as **f** and **g**:

```
extern int f(void);
...
int g(void) { ... f(); ...}
int f(void) { ... g(); ...}
```

The same declaration style can also be used for static functions:

```
static int f();
...
static int g() { ... f(); ...}
static int f() { ... g(); ...}
```

Some non-ISO C compilers may not permit this kind of forward reference to static functions. Sometimes they compromise by allowing the first declaration to use the storage specifier **extern**, changing the storage class to **static** when the definition is seen.

Example

```
extern int f(void);   /* not really extern, see below... */
...
static int g(void) { ... f(); ...}
static int f(void) { ... g(); ...}  /* now, make f static */
```

This programming idiom is misleading at best. ISO C requires that the first declaration of a function (in fact, of any identifier) specify whether it will be external or static. This permits one-pass compilation of C programs in those cases in which an implementation must treat static and external functions differently. ISO C does not explicitly disallow the "**extern**-then-**static**" style, but it does not specify its meaning.

The only operation that can be applied to an expression of function type is to convert it to a function pointer or to call it.

Example

In the following declarations, external identifiers **f**, **fp**, and **apf** have types "function returning **int**," "pointer to function returning **int**," and "array of pointers to functions taking a **double** parameter and returning **int**," respectively:

```
extern int f(), (*fp)(), (*apf[])(double);
```

The declaration of **apf** includes an ISO C prototype for the function. These identifiers can be used in function call expressions by writing

```
int i,j,k;
...
i = f(14);
i = (*fp)(j, k);
i = (*apf[j])(k);
```

When a function with no visible prototype is called, certain standard conversions are applied to the actual arguments, but no attempt is made to check the type or number of arguments with the type or number of formal arguments to the function, if known. Arguments to functions with visible prototypes are converted to the indicated parameter type. In the above example, the integer argument **k** to the function designated by ***apf[j]** will be converted to type **double**.

In ISO C and some other implementations, an expression of type "pointer to function" can be used in a function call without an explicit dereferencing; in that case, the call **(*fp)(j,k)** in the example above can be written as **fp(j,k)**.

An expression of type "function returning..." that is not used in a function call, as the argument of the address operator, **&**, or as the argument of the **sizeof** operator is immediately converted to the type "pointer to function returning...." (Not performing the conversion when the function is the argument of **sizeof** ensures that the **sizeof** expression will be invalid and not just result in the size of a pointer.) The only expressions that can yield a value of type "function returning *T*" are the name of such a function and an indirection expression consisting of the unary indirection operator, *****, applied to an expression of type "pointer to function returning...."

Example

The following program assigns the same pointer value to **fp1** and **fp2**:

```
extern int f();
int (*fp1)(), (*fp2)();
fp1 = f;    /* implicit conversion to pointer */
fp2 = &f;   /* explicit manufacture of a pointer */
```

All the information needed to invoke a function is assumed to be encapsulated in an object of type "pointer to function returning...." Although a pointer to a function is often assumed to be the address of the function's code in memory, on some computers a function pcinter actually points to a block of information needed to invoke the function. Such representation issues are normally invisible to the C programmer and need concern only the compiler implementor.

References function argument conversions 6.3.5; function call 7.4.3; function declarator 4.5.4; function definition 9.1; function prototype 9.2; indirection operator ***** 7.5.7; **sizeof** operator 7.5.2; usual unary conversions 6.3.3

5.9 THE VOID TYPE

The type **void** is a recent addition to C. It has no values and no operations and is used mainly as the return type of a function, signifying that the function returns no value:

void-type-specifier :
    void

Example

```
extern void write_line(void);
...
write_line();
```

The **void** type may also be used in a cast expression when it is desired to explicitly discard a value.

Example

```
extern int write_line2(); /* returns error indication */
...
(void) write_line2(...);    /* don't check for error */
```

Casting the return value to **void** indicates clearly that the programmer knows that **write_line2** returns a value but chooses to ignore it.

ISO C introduces the type "**void ***", or pointer to **void**, to represent a "universal" data pointer. Traditionally, C programmers have used **char *** for this purpose.

References casts 7.5.1; discarded expressions 7.13; **void *** 5.3.2

5.10 TYPEDEF NAMES

When a declaration is written whose "storage class" is **typedef**, the type definition facility is invoked.

typedef-name :
    identifier

An identifier enclosed in any declarator of the declaration is defined to be a name for a type (a "**typedef** name"); the type is what would have been given the identifier if the declaration were a normal variable declaration. Once a name has been declared as a type, it may appear anywhere a type specifier is permitted. This allows the use of mnemonic abbreviations for complicated types.

Example

Consider these declarations:

```
typedef int *IP;          /* IP is "pointer to int" */
typedef int (*FP)();      /* FP is "pointer to function
                             returning int" */
typedef int F(int);       /* F is "function with one int
                             parameter, returning int" */

typedef double A5[5];    /* A5 is "5-element array of double" */
typedef int A[];          /* A is "array of int" */
```

After the above declarations, the following declarations are permitted:

```
IP ip;        /* ip is a pointer to an int */
IP fip();     /* fip is a function returning a pointer to int */
FP fp;        /* fp is a pointer to a function returning an int */
F *fp2;       /* fp2 is a pointer to a function taking an
                 int parameter and returning an int */

A5 a5;        /* a5 is a 5-element int array */
A5 a25[2];    /* a25 has type int [5][2]: a 2-element array of
                 5-element arrays of int */
A a;          /* a is an array of int (with unspecified bounds) */
A *ap3[3];    /* ap3 is a 3-element array of pointers to
                 arrays of int (with unspecified bounds) */
```

Example

typedef names should not be mixed with other type specifiers. Some implementations permit the following; ISO C explicitly forbids it:

```
typedef long int bigint;
unsigned bigint x; /* probably invalid */
```

Declarations with the **typedef** storage specifier do not introduce new types; the names are considered to be synonyms for types that could be specified in other ways.

Example

After the declaration

```
typedef struct S { int a; int b; } s1type, s2type;
```

the type specifiers **s1type**, **s2type**, and **struct S** can be used interchangeably to refer to the same type.

Although **typedef** only introduces synonyms for types that can be named in other ways, C implementations may wish to preserve the declared type names internally so that debuggers and other tools can refer to types by the names used by the programmer.

References type compatibility 5.11

5.10.1 Typedef Names for Function Types

A function type may be given a **typedef** name, but functions must not inherit their "function-ness" from **typedef** names. This restricts function **typedef**s somewhat.

Example

DblFunc becomes a synonym for "function returning **double**" with this declaration:

```
typedef double DblFunc();
```

Once declared, **DblFunc** can be used to declare pointers to the function type, arrays of the function type, and so forth, using the normal rules for composing declarators:

```
extern DblFunc *f_ptr, *f_array[];
```

Abiding by the normal rules of type declarations, the programmer must not declare invalid types, such as an array of functions:

```
extern DblFunc f_array[10];    /* Invalid! */
```

However, **DblFunc** cannot be used to declare or define functions. The following definition of **fabs** is rejected because it seems to define a function returning another function:

```
DblFunc fabs(double x)
{
    if (x<0.0) return -x; else return x;
}
```

It is not possible to get around this problem by omitting the parentheses after **fabs**, because that is where the parameter must be listed. The function definition must be written in the usual way, as if **DblFunc** did not exist:

```
double fabs(double x)
{
    if (x<0.0) return -x; else return x;
}
```

In ISO C, **typedef** names can include function prototype information, including parameter names:

```
typedef double DFuncType( double x );
typedef double (*FuncPtr)( int, float );
```

In this example, **DFuncType** is a function type and **FuncPtr** is a function pointer type.

References function declarators 4.5; function definitions 9.1; function prototypes 9.2

5.10.2 Redefining Typedef Names

The language specifies that **typedef** names may be redefined in inner blocks in the same fashion as ordinary identifiers.

Example

```
typedef int T;
T foo;
...
{
    float T;    /* New definition for T */
    T = 1.0;
    ...
}
```

One restriction is that the redeclaration cannot omit the type specifiers on the assumption that the type will default to **int**. Some non-ISO compilers have been known to have problems with redeclarations of **typedef** names, probably because of the pressure **typedef** names put on the C language grammar. We now turn to this problem.

References redefining **typedef** names in C++ 5.13.2; scope of names 4.2.1

5.10.3 Implementation Note

Allowing ordinary identifiers to be type specifiers makes the C grammar context sensitive, and hence not LALR(1). To see this, consider the program line

```
A ( *B ) ;
```

If **A** has been defined as a **typedef** name, then the line is a declaration of a variable **B** to be of type "pointer to **A**." (The parentheses surrounding "***B**" are ignored.) If **A** is not a type name, then the line is a call of the function **A** with the single parameter ***B**. This ambiguity cannot be resolved grammatically.

C compilers based on the parser-generator YACC—such as the Portable C Compiler—handle this problem by feeding information acquired during semantic analysis back to lexical analysis. All C compilers must do **typedef** processing during lexical analysis.

5.11 TYPE COMPATIBILITY

Two types in C are *compatible* if they are either the same type or are "close enough" to be considered the same for many purposes. The notion of compatible types was introduced by ISO C, but for the most part it captures in a more formal way the rules that are used in traditional C. Some additional rules are necessary to handle ISO C features such as function prototypes and type qualifiers. For two types to be compatible, they either must be the same type, or must be pointers, functions, or arrays with certain properties. The specific rules are discussed in the following sections.

Associated with every two compatible types is a *composite type*, which is the common type that arises out of the two compatible types. This is similar to the way in which the usual binary conversions take two integral types and combine them to yield a common result type for some arithmetic operators. The composite type produced by two compatible types is described along with the rules for type compatibility.

References array types 5.4; function prototypes 9.2; function types 5.8; pointer types 5.3; structure types 5.6; type qualifiers 4.4.3; union types 5.7; usual binary conversions 6.3

5.11.1 Identical Types

Two arithmetic types can be compatible only if they are the same type. If a type can be written using different combinations of type specifiers, all the alternate forms are the same type. That is, the types **`short`** and **`short int`** are the same, but the types **`unsigned`**, **`int`**, and **`short`** are all different. The type **`signed int`** is the same as **`int`** (and equivalently for **`short`** and **`long`**), except when they are used as the types of bit fields. The types **`char`**, **`signed char`**, and **`unsigned char`** are always different.

Any two types that are the same are compatible and their composite type is the same type. In ISO C, the presence of any type qualifiers changes the type: type **`const int`** is not the same as—nor is it compatible with—type **`int`**. Names declared as types in **`typedef`** definitions are synonyms for types, not new types.

Example

After these declarations, the types of **`p`** and **`q`** are the same; the types of **`x`** and **`y`** are the same, but neither is the same as the type of **`u`**; the types **`TS`** and **`struct S`** are the same; and the types of **`u`**, **`w`**, and **`y`** are the same.

```
char * p, *q;
struct {int a, b;} x, y;
struct S {int a, b;} u;
typedef struct S TS;
struct S w;
TS y;
```

Example

After these declarations, the type **`my_int`** is the same as type **`int`**, and the type **`my_function`** is the same as the type "**`float *()`**":

```
typedef int my_int;
typedef float *my_function();
```

Example

After these declarations, the variables **`w`**, **`x`**, **`y`**, and **`z`** all have the same type.

```
struct S { int a, b; } x;
typedef struct S t1, t2;
struct S w;
t1 y;
t2 z;
```

References integer types 5.1; pointer types 5.3; structure types 5.6; **`typedef`** names 5.10

5.11.2 Enumeration Compatibility

Each enumerated type definition gives rise to a new integral type. ISO C requires each enumerated type to be compatible with the implementation-defined integer type that represents it. The compatible integer type may be different for different enumerations in the same program. The composite type is the enumerated type. No two different enumerated types defined in the same source file are compatible.

Example

In the following declarations, the types of **E1** and **E2** are not compatible, but the types of **E1** and **E3** are compatible because they are the same type.

```
enum e {a,b} E1;
enum {c,d} E2;
enum e E3;
```

Because enumerated types are generally treated as integer types, values of different enumerated types can be mixed freely regardless of type compatibility.

Example

The effect of the compatibility rule is that ISO C will reject the second function declaration below because the argument type in the prototype does not agree with the first declaration:

```
extern int f( enum {a,b} x);
extern int f( enum {b,c} x);
```

Non-ISO conforming implementations may treat enumerated types as fully compatible with **int** and with each other. Observing ISO C rules provides maximum portability.

References enumerated types 5.5

5.11.3 Array Compatibility

Two (similarly qualified) array types are compatible if their element types are compatible. If both types specify sizes, the sizes must be the same. However, if only one array type specifies a size—or if neither do—the two types are still compatible. The composite type of two compatible array types is the array type with the composite element type. If either original type specifies a size, the composite type has that size also.

Example

```
int a[];            /* compatible with b and c; not d */
int b[5];           /* compatible with a only */
int c[10];          /* compatible with a only */
const int d[10];    /* not compatible with other types */
```

The type of **d** is not compatible with other types because its element type, **const int**, is not compatible with element type **int**. The composite type of the types of **a** and **b** is **int [5]**.

References array types 5.4, type qualifiers 4.4.3

5.11.4 Function Compatibility

For two function types to be compatible, they must specify compatible return types. If both types are specified in traditional (non-prototype) form, that is all that is required. The composite type is a (traditional-form) function type with the composite return type.

For two function types both declared in prototype form to be compatible, the following conditions must hold:

1. The function return types must be compatible.
2. The number of parameters and the use of the ellipsis must agree.
3. The corresponding parameters must have compatible types.

It is not necessary that any parameter names agree. The composite type is a function type whose parameters have the composite parameter type, with the same use of the ellipsis, and with the composite return type.

If only one of the two function types is in prototype form, then for the two types to be compatible the following conditions must hold:

1. The return types must be compatible.
2. The prototype must not include the ellipsis terminator.
3. Each parameter type *T* in the prototype must be compatible with the type resulting from applying the usual argument conversions to *T*.

The composite type is the prototype-form function type with the composite return value.

References function prototypes 9.2; function types 5.8

5.11.5 Structure and Union Compatibility

Each occurrence of a type specifier that is a structure type definition or union type definition introduces a new structure or union type that is neither the same as nor compatible with any other such type in the same source file.

A type specifier that is a structure, union, or enumerated type *reference* is the same type introduced in the corresponding *definition*. The type tag is used to associate the reference with the definition, and in that sense may be thought of as the name of the type.

Example

The types of **x**, **y**, and **u** below are all different, but the types of **u** and **v** are the same:

```
struct { int a; int b; } x;
struct { int a; int b; } y;
struct S { int a; int b; } u;
struct S v;
```

References enumerations 5.5; structures 5.6; unions 5.7

5.11.6 Pointer Compatibility

Two (similarly qualified) pointer types are compatible if they point to compatible types. The composite type for two compatible pointer types is the (similarly qualified) pointer to the composite type.

5.11.7 Compatibility across Source Files

Although structure, union, and enumerated type definitions give rise to new (non-compatible) types, a loophole must be created to allow references across separately compiled source files within the same program.

Example

Suppose a header file contains these declarations:

```
struct S {int a,b;};
extern struct S x;
```

When two source files in a program both import this header file, the intent is that the two files reference the same variable, **x**, which has the single type **struct S**. However, each file theoretically contains a definition of a different structure type that just happens to be named **struct S** in each instance.

Unless two declarations of the same type are compatible, ISO C states that the run-time behavior of the program is undefined, and therefore:

1. Two structures or unions defined in separate source files are compatible if they declare the same members in the same order and each corresponding member has a compatible type (including the width of bit fields).
2. Two enumerations defined in separate source files are compatible if they contain the same enumeration constants (in any order), each with the same value.

In these cases, the composite type is the type in the current source file.

References enumerated types 5.5; structure types 5.6; union types 5.7

5.12 TYPE NAMES AND ABSTRACT DECLARATORS

There are two situations in C programming when it is necessary to write the name of a type without declaring an object of that type: when writing cast expressions and when applying the **sizeof** operator to a type. In these cases, one uses a type name built from an abstract declarator. (Don't confuse "type name" with "**typedef** name.")

type-name :
  declaration-specifiers abstract-declarator$_{opt}$

abstract-declarator :
  pointer
  pointer$_{opt}$ *direct-abstract-declarator*

pointer:
  ***** *type-qualifier-list*$_{opt}$
  ***** *type-qualifier-list*$_{opt}$ *pointer*

type-qualifier-list : (ISO C)
  type-qualifier
  type-qualifier-list type qualifier

direct-abstract-declarator :
  (*abstract-declarator* **)**
  direct-abstract-declarator$_{opt}$ **[** *constant-expression*$_{opt}$ **]**
  direct-abstract-declarator$_{opt}$ **(** *parameter-type-list*$_{opt}$ **)**

An abstract declarator resembles a regular declarator in which the enclosed identifier has been replaced by the empty string. Thus, a type name looks like a declaration from which the enclosed identifier has been omitted. In the syntax, the *declaration-specifiers* must not include storage class specifiers. The *parameter-type-list* is permitted only in ISO C, where it is used for a prototype-form type declaration.

The precedences of the alternatives of the abstract declarator are the same as in the case of normal declarators.

Example

Type name	Translation
`int`	type **`int`**
`float *`	pointer to **`float`**
`char (*)(int)`	pointer to function taking an **`int`** parameter and returning **`char`**
`unsigned *[4]`	array of 4 pointers to **`unsigned`**
`int (*(*)())()`	pointer to function returning pointer to function returning **`int`**

Type names always appear within the parentheses that form part of the syntax of the cast or **`sizeof`** operator. If the type specifier in the type name is a structure, union, or enumerated type *definition*, then ISO C requires an implementation to define a new type with the included type tag (if any) at that point. It is considered bad style to make use of this feature. (It is invalid in C++.)

Example

Assume that **struct S** is not defined when the following two statements are encountered. (A good C implementation should issue a warning on the first line.)

```
i = sizeof( struct S {int a,b;}); /* OK, but strange */
j = sizeof( struct S ); /* OK, struct S is now defined */
```

References casts 7.5.1; function prototypes 9.2; **sizeof** operator 7.5.2

5.13 C++ COMPATIBILITY

5.13.1 Enumeration Types

Do not use enumerated types or enumeration constants as integer types without explicit casts. Unlike C, C++ treats enumerated types as distinct from each other and from integer types, although you can convert between them with casts. (Some C++ implementations allow assignments between integers and enumeration types as an anachronism.)

Example

```
enum e {blue, red, yellow} e_var;
int i_var;
...
i_var = red;             /* valid in C, not in C++ */
e_var = 1;               /* valid in C, not in C++ */
i_var = (int) red;       /* valid in both C and C++ */
e_var = (enum e) 3;      /* valid in both C and C++ */
assert(sizeof(blue) == sizeof(int));
    /* always succeeds in C; may fail in C++ */
```

References enumeration type 5.5

5.13.2 Typedef Names

As in C, **typedef** names can be redeclared as objects in inner scopes. However, in C++ it is not permitted to do so within a structure or union—which are scopes—if the original **typedef** name has been used in the structure or union already. This situation is unlikely to occur in practice.

Example

```
typedef int INT;
struct S {
    INT i;
    double INT; /* OK in C, not C++; everywhere a bad idea*/
}
```

References redefining typedef names 5.10.2

5.13.3 Type Compatibility

C++ does not have C's notion of type compatibility. To do stricter type checking, C++ requires identical types in situations in which C would require only compatible types. In some cases, C++ will issue a diagnostic if the types are not identical. However, because C++ provides "layout compatibility" with C, a C++ program will still work correctly even if it contains undetected occurrences of non-identical but (ISO C) compatible types.

References type compatibility 5.11

5.14 EXERCISES

1. What C type would you choose to represent the following sets of values? Assume your main priority is portability across different compilers and computers, and your secondary priority is to minimize space consumption.
   (a) a 5-digit U. S. Postal Service zip code
   (b) a phone number consisting of a 3-digit area code and a 7-digit local number
   (c) the values 0 and 1
   (d) the values –1, 0, and 1
   (e) either an alphabetic character or the value –1
   (f) the balance in a bank account, in dollars and cents, up to 9,999,999.99
2. Some popular computers support an extended character set that includes the normal ASCII characters as well as additional characters whose values are in the range 128 through 255. Assume that type **char** is represented in 8 bits. The **is_up_arrow** function below is supposed to return "true" if the input character represents the up-arrow key and "false" otherwise. Will this function be portable across different ISO C compilers, assuming that the definition of **UP_ARROW_KEY** has the proper value for the target computer? If not, rewrite it so that it is.

```
#define UP_ARROW_KEY  0x86
...
int is_up_arrow(char c)
{
    return c == UP_ARROW_KEY;
}
```

3. If **vp** has type **void *** and **cp** has type **char ***, which of the following assignment statements are valid in ISO C?
   (a) `vp = cp;`
   (b) `cp = vp;`
   (c) `*vp = *cp;`
   (d) `*cp = *vp;`
4. If **iv** has type **int [3]**, and **im** has type **int [4][5]**, rewrite the following expressions without using the subscript operator.
   (a) `iv[i]`
   (b) `im[i][j]`
5. What integer value is returned by the function **f** below? Is the cast to type **int** in the **return** statement necessary?

```
enum birds {wren, robin=12, blue_jay};
int f()
{
    return (int) blue_jay;
}
```

6. Below is the definition of a structured type and a variable of that type. Write a series of statements that assign a valid value to every component of the structure. If two components of the structure overlap, assign to only one of the overlapping components.

```
struct S {
    int i;
    struct T {
        unsigned s: 1;
        unsigned e: 7;
        unsigned m: 24;
    } F;
    union U {
        double d;
        char a[6];
        int * p;
    } U;
} x;
```

7. Make two sketches of the structure defined in the previous problem, using the same format as in sections 5.6.5 and 5.7.3. Assume that the underlying computer is byte-addressed using 8 bits for type **char**, 32 bits for pointers and type **int**, and 64 bits for type **double**. In the first sketch, assume a big-endian computer with bit fields packed right to left within 32-bit words; in the second, assume a little-endian with bit fields packed right to left within words. In both cases, assume the compiler packs bit fields as tightly as possible.

8. Write a **typedef** definition of the type "function returning pointer to integer." Write a declaration of a variable that holds a pointer to such a function and write an actual function of that type, using the **typedef** definition where possible.

6

Conversions and Representations

Most programming languages are designed to hide from the programmer the details of the language's implementation on a particular computer. For the most part, the C programmer need not be aware of these details, either, although a major attraction of C is that it allows the programmer to go below the abstract language level and expose the underlying representation of programs and data. With this freedom comes a certain amount of risk: some C programmers inadvertently descend below the abstract programming level and build into their programs nonportable assumptions about data representations.

This chapter has three purposes. First, it discusses some characteristics of data and program representations, indicating how the choice of representations can affect a C program.

Second, it discusses in some detail the conversion of values of one type to another, emphasizing the characteristics of C that are portable across implementations.

Finally, it presents the "usual conversion rules" of C, which are the conversions that happen automatically when expressions are evaluated.

6.1 REPRESENTATIONS

This section discusses the representation of programs and data and how the choice of representations can affect C programs and C implementations.

6.1.1 Storage Units and Data Sizes

All data objects in C are represented at run time in the computer's memory in an integral number of abstract *storage units*, or *bytes*. Each storage unit is in turn made up of some fixed number of *bits*, each of which can assume either of two values, denoted 0 and 1.

By definition, the *size* of a data object is the number of storage units (bytes) occupied by that data object. A storage unit is taken to be the amount of storage occupied by one character; the size of an object of type **char** is therefore 1.

Because all data objects of a given type occupy the same amount of storage, we can also refer to the size of a *type* as the number of storage units occupied by an object of that type. The **sizeof** operator may be used to determine the size of a data object or type. We say that a type is "longer" or "larger" than another type if its size is greater. Similarly we say that a type is "shorter" or "smaller" than another type if its size is less. ISO C requires certain minimum sizes for the integer and floating-point types and provides implementation-defined header files **limits.h** and **float.h** that define the sizes.

Example

The following program determines the sizes of the principal C data types:

```
#include <stdio.h>
int main()
{
    printf("\tType sizes:\n");
    printf("char\tshort\tint\tlong\tfloat\tdouble\n");
    printf("%3d\t%3d\t%3d\t%3d\t%3d\t%3d\n",
           sizeof(char), sizeof(short), sizeof(int),
           sizeof(long), sizeof(float), sizeof(double) );
}
```

References character types 5.1.3; **float.h** 5.2; **limits.h** 5.1.1; minimum integer sizes 5.1.1; **sizeof** operator 7.5.2; **stdio.h** standard I/O ch. 15

6.1.2 Byte Ordering

The addressing structure of a computer determines how storage pieces of various sizes are named by pointers. The addressing model most natural for C is one in which each character (byte) in the computer's memory can be individually addressed. Computers using this model are called "byte-addressable" computers. The address of a larger piece of storage—one used to hold an integer or a floating-point number, for example—is typically the same as the address of the first character in the larger unit. (The "first" character is the one with the lowest address.)

Even within this simple model, computers differ in their storage "byte order—that is, they differ in which byte of storage they consider to be the "first" one in a larger piece. In "right-to-left" or "little-endian" architectures, which include the Intel 80x86 and Pentium microprocessors, the address of a 32-bit integer is also the address of the low-order byte of the integer. In "left-to-right" or "big-endian" architectures, which include the Motorola 680x0 microprocessor family, the address of a 32-bit integer is the address of the high-order byte of the integer.

Example

Both the Intel (little-endian) and Motorola (big-endian) architectures are byte-addressed, with 8-bit bytes and 4-byte words which can hold 32-bit integers. The picture below shows a sequence of words on each architecture, with each word containing the 32-bit value **`0x01020304`**. As you can see, the two architectures look the same at this level of detail.

Big-endian, left to right	`01020304`	`01020304`	...
	A	A+4	A+8
Little-endian, right to left	`01020304`	`01020304`	...
	A	A+4	A+8

The situation changes when we look at the contents of individual bytes within a word. On the big-endian, the address of the word is the address of the leftmost (high-order) byte. Since the byte addresses increase left to right, it appears consistent with the way we drew the words above. On the little-endian, however, the address of the word is the address of the rightmost (low-order) byte. You can picture this in two ways: either the addresses in the word increase right to left, or else the bytes are reversed. Both views are shown below.

Big-endian, left to right	`01`	`02`	`03`	`04`	...
	A	A+1	A+2	A+3	A+4
Little-endian, right to left (first view)	`01`	`02`	`03`	`04`	...
	A+3	A+2	A+1	A	A+4
Little-endian, right to left (second view)	`04`	`03`	`02`	`01`	...
	A	A+1	A+2	A+3	A+4

Components of a structure type are allocated in the order of increasing addresses—that is, either left to right or right to left depending on the byte order of the computer. Because bit fields are also packed following the byte order, it is natural to number the bits in a piece of storage following the same convention. Thus, in a left-to-right computer the most significant (leftmost) bit of a 32-bit integer would be bit number 0 and the least significant bit would be bit number 31. In right-to-left computers the least significant (rightmost) bit would be bit 0, and so forth. Programs that assume a particular byte order will not be portable.

Example

Here is a program that determines a computer's byte ordering by using a union in a nonportable fashion. The union has the same size as an object of type **`long`** and is initialized so that the low-order byte of the union contains a 1 and all other bytes contain zeroes. In right-to-left architectures, the character component, **`Char`**, of the union will be overlaid on the low-order byte of the long component, **Long**, whereas in left-to-right architectures **Char** will be overlaid on the high-order byte of **Long**:

```
#include <stdio.h>
union {
    long Long;
    char Char[sizeof(long)];
} u;

int main()
{
    u.Long = 1;
    if (u.Char[0] == 1)
        printf("Addressing is right-to-left\n");
    else if (u.Char[sizeof(long)-1] == 1)
        printf("Addressing is left-to-right\n");
    else printf("Addressing is strange\n");
    return 0;
}
```

6.1.3 Alignment Restrictions

Some computers allow data objects to reside in storage at any address, regardless of the data's type. Others impose *alignment restrictions* on certain data types, requiring that objects of those types occupy only certain addresses. It is not unusual on a byte-addressed computer, for example, to require that 32-bit (4-byte) integers be located on addresses that are a multiple of four. In this case we say that the "alignment modulus" of those integers is four. Failing to obey the alignment restrictions can result either in a run-time error or in unexpected program behavior. Even when there are no alignment restrictions per se, there may be a performance penalty for using data on unaligned addresses, and therefore a C implementation may align data purely for efficiency.

The C programmer is not normally aware of alignment restrictions, because the compiler takes care to place data on the appropriate address boundaries. However, C does give the programmer the ability to violate alignment restrictions by casting pointers to different types.

In general, if the alignment requirement for a type *S* is at least as stringent as that for a type *D* (that is, the alignment modulus for *S* is no smaller than the alignment modulus for *D*), then converting a "pointer to type *S*" to a "pointer to type *D*" is safe. "Safe" here means that the resulting pointer to type *D* will work as expected if used to fetch or store an object of type *D*, and that a subsequent conversion back to the original pointer type will recover the original pointer. A corollary to this is that any data pointer can be converted to type **char *** and back safely. Functions such as **malloc** (section 16.1), which return pointers destined to be cast to various types, always return pointers of type **void *** (**char *** in pre-ISO C), aligned suitably for an object of any type.

If the alignment requirement for a type *S* is less stringent than that for type *D*, then the conversion from a "pointer to type *S*" to a "pointer to type *D*" could result in either of two kinds of unexpected behavior. First, an attempt to use the resulting pointer to fetch or store an object of type *D* may cause an error, halting the program. Second, the hardware or implementation may "adjust" the destination pointer to be valid, usually by forcing it back to the nearest previous valid address. A subsequent conversion back to the original pointer type may not recover the original pointer.

References byte ordering 6.1.2; **malloc** function 16.1; pointer types 5.3

6.1.4 Pointer Sizes

There is no requirement in C that any of the integral types be large enough to represent a pointer, although C programmers often assume that type **long** is large enough, which it is on most computers.

In many C implementations it happens that pointers have the same size as type **int**. Because **int** is also the default type specifier, some programmers are careless with pointer/integer conversions. In particular, they may omit the return type when declaring or defining functions returning pointers, knowing the type will default to **int**, which is "good enough" because of C's standard conversion rules. This has proved to be a frequent source of portability problems.

Although function pointers are usually no larger than the widest data pointers (i.e., **char *** or **void ***), this is not always the case, as discussed in section 6.1.5. Programmers should not use data pointers to hold pointers to functions. Use a function pointer type that specifies the correct return type, such as **double (*)()**. ISO C specifically states that conversions between function and data pointers have undefined behavior. ISO C does *not* guarantee that a function pointer can be safely converted to or from type **void ***.

References function types 5.8; pointer conversions 6.2.7; pointer types 5.3; sizes of types 6.1.1

6.1.5 Effects of Addressing Models

This section describes some ways in which a computer's memory design can impact the C programmer and implementor.

Memory models Some computers are designed in such a way that the choice of a representation for pointers involves a time-space tradeoff that may not be appropriate for all programs. IBM PCs and other computers based on the Intel 80x86 family of microprocessors can make use of both 16-bit and 32-bit addresses. The smaller addresses (those within a single *segment*) are more efficient, but limit the amount of memory that can be referenced. Large programs often require access to multiple segments. (New, "32-bit" compilers use larger pointers and data on the faster processors, thus hiding segmentation.)

To accommodate the needs of different programs, most C compilers for these computers allow the programmer to specify a *memory model*, which establishes the time-space tradeoff used in the program. Table 6–1 on page 166 shows the memory models supported by the Microsoft and Borland C compilers.

There are several points to note here. In all the memory models, code and data are kept in separate memory segments with their own address space. Therefore, it is possible for a data pointer and a function pointer to contain the same value even though one points

Table 6–1 Memory models on IBM PC and compatibles

Memory model name	Data pointer size	Function pointer size	Characteristics
tiny	16 bits	16 bits	code, data, and stack all occupy a single segment
small	16	16	code occupies one 64K-byte segment; data and stack occupy a second 64K-byte segment
medium	16	32	code can occupy many segments; data and stack are limited to one segment
compact	32	16	code and stack are each limited to a single 64K segment; other data can occupy many segments
large	32	32	code and data can both occupy many segments; stack is restricted to one segment
huge (32-bit flat)	32	32	same as large, but single data items can exceed 64K bytes in size

to an object and the other to a function. In the compact and medium memory models, data pointers and function pointers have different sizes. Some care should be used with null pointer constant, **NULL** (section 5.3.2), which is typically defined as a null data pointer. Simple uses of **NULL** in expressions involving function pointers will be properly converted, but passing **NULL** as a function pointer argument may not work correctly in the absence of a prototype.

This problem can be mostly eliminated by the careful use of function prototypes in ISO C, which will cause arguments to be correctly converted. The programmer must use similar care with library functions.

Example

A C programmer unfamiliar with segmented architectures might suppose that a data pointer and function pointer could contain the same value only if both were null pointers, and might incorrectly try to abbreviate a test:

```
char *cp;
int (*fp)();
...
/* See if cp and fp are both null */
if ((int)cp == (int)fp) ...   /* Incorrect!! */
```

Example

In the following example, the behavior of function **f** is undefined when using the compact or medium memory models because the data pointer passed as an argument is not the same size as the function pointer that is expected:

```
extern int f(); /* no parameter information */
...
f(NULL);     /* This is NOT OK! */
...
int f( int (*fp)() ) { ... }
```

Explicit control over pointer sizes An alternative to using a specific memory model for an entire program (or an addition to it) is to specify whether "near" or "far" pointers are to be used for specific functions or data objects. In this way, a programmer can avoid across-the-board performance penalties, although the program will be less portable and probably harder to maintain.

Example

Several C compilers for segmented architectures define new keywords **__near** and **__far** that can be used in declarations of variables and pointers. Syntactically, they can appear where ISO C type qualifiers appear. The keywords are spelled with two leading underscores, which signifies they are implementation-dependent in ISO C. For example:

```
char __near near_char, *cp;
int __far (*fp)(), big_array[30000]
```

The intent is that **far** pointers will occupy 32 bits while **near** pointers will use 16 bits. Functions or data objects declared **far** can be placed in remote segments by the implementation, whereas **near** ones must be grouped in the "root" segment. Programmers using these language extensions must be very careful when passing the pointers to functions not declared with prototypes.

Array addressing Regardless of whether a computer uses a segmented addressing scheme or not, some computers are designed in a way that makes accessing elements of an array more efficient if the array size is small—typically, not bigger than 64K bytes. To use larger arrays, the programmer must supply a special compiler option or must designate the large arrays in some way. In Microsoft C, there are both a "huge" memory model and a **huge** keyword that can be applied to array objects and pointers. Huge pointers are only 32 bits wide, but the compiler understands that subscripting arrays marked "huge" require special (and less efficient) instructions.

Very difficult computers Although C has been implemented efficiently on many computers, a few computers represent data and addresses in forms that are very awkward for C implementations. A major problem can occur when the computer's natural word size is not a multiple of its natural byte size. Suppose—this is a real example—our computer has a 36-bit word and represents characters in 7 bits; each word can hold five characters with one bit remaining unused. All noncharacter data types occupy one or more full words. This memory structure will be very difficult for a C implementor, because C programming relies upon the ability to map any data structure onto an array of characters. That is, to copy an object of type *T* at address *A* it should be sufficient to copy **sizeof(*T*)** characters beginning at *A*. The only alternative for the implementor on this computer would be to represent characters using some nonstandard number of bits (for example, 9 or 36) so that they fit tightly into a word. This representation could have a significant performance penalty.

A similar problem occurs on "word-addressed" computers—such as several kinds of digital signal processors and computers manufactured by Cray Research, Inc.—whose basic addressable storage unit is larger than a single character. On these computers, there may or may not be a special kind of address, a "byte pointer," that can represent characters within a word. Assuming there is such a byte pointer, it may very well be larger than a pointer to objects of noncharacter types, or—as is the case of the Cray computers—may use certain bits in the pointer that are ignored and normally set to zero in other kinds of pointers. A C implementor must decide whether to pay the increased overhead of representing all pointers as byte pointers, whether to use the larger format only for objects of type **`char *`** (and, in ISO C, **`void *`**), or whether to use a full word to represent each character. Having a different size for character pointers will force C programmers to be more careful about pointer conversions.

References array types 5.4; character types 5.1.3; function argument conversions 6.3.5; function prototypes 9.2; pointer types 5.3; storage units 6.1.1

6.2 CONVERSIONS

The C language provides for values of one type to be converted to values of other types under several circumstances:

- A cast expression may be used to explicitly convert a value to another type.
- An operand may be implicitly converted to another type in preparation for performing some arithmetic or logical operation.
- An object of one type may be assigned to a location (lvalue) of another type, causing an implicit type conversion.
- An actual argument to a function may be implicitly converted to another type prior to the function call.
- A return value from a function may be implicitly converted to another type prior to the function return.

There are restrictions as to what types a given object may be converted. Furthermore, the set of conversions that are possible on assignment, for instance, is not the same as the set of conversions that are possible with type casts.

In the following sections we will discuss the set of possible conversions and then discuss which of these conversions are actually performed in each of the circumstances listed above.

6.2.1 Representation Changes

The representation of a data object is the particular pattern of bits in the storage area that holds the object; this pattern distinguishes the value of the object from all other possible values of that type.

A conversion of a value from one type to another may or may not involve a representation change. For instance, whenever the two types have different sizes, a representation change has to be made. When integers are converted to a floating-point representation, a representation change is made even if the integer and floating-point type have the same sizes. However, when a value of type **`int`** is converted to type **`unsigned int`**, a representation change may not be necessary.

Some representation changes are very simple, involving merely discarding of excess bits or padding with extra 0 bits. Other changes may be very complicated, such as conversions between integer and floating-point representations. For each of the conversions discussed in the following sections, we describe the possible representation changes that may be required.

6.2.2 Trivial Conversions

It is always possible to convert a value from a type to another type that is the same as (or compatible with) the first type. See section 5.11 for a discussion of when types are the same or compatible. No representation change needs to occur in this case.

Most implementations will refuse to convert structure or union types to themselves, because no conversions to structure or union types are normally permitted.

6.2.3 Conversions to Integer Types

Arithmetic types and pointer types may be converted to integers.

From integer types The general rule for converting from one integer type to another is that the mathematical value of the result should equal the original mathematical value if that is possible. For example, if an unsigned integer has the value 15 and this value is to be converted to a signed type, the resulting signed value should be 15 also.

If it is not possible to represent the original value of an object of the new type, then there are two cases. If the result type is a signed type, then the conversion is considered to have overflowed and the result value is technically not defined. If the result type is an unsigned type, then the result must be that unique value of the result type that is equal (congruent) mod 2^n to the original value, where n is equal to the number of bits used in the representation of the result type. If signed integers are represented using two's-complement notation, then no change of representation is necessary when converting between signed and unsigned integers of the same size. On the other hand, if signed integers are represented in some other way, such as with one's-complement or sign-magnitude representation, then a change of representation will be necessary.

When an unsigned integer is converted to a signed integer of the same size, the conversion is considered to overflow if the original value is too large to represent exactly in the signed representation (that is, if the high-order bit of the unsigned number is 1). However, many programmers and many programs depend on the conversion being performed quietly and with no change of representation to produce a negative number.

If the destination type is longer than the source type, then the only case in which the source value will not be representable in the result type is when a negative signed value is converted to a longer, unsigned type. In that case, the conversion must necessarily behave as if the source value were first converted to a longer signed type of the same size as the destination type, and then converted to the destination type.

Example

Since the constant expression **-1** has type **int**:

```
((unsigned long) -1) == ((unsigned long) ((long) -1))
```

If the destination type is shorter than the source type, and both the original type and the destination type are unsigned, the conversion can be effected simply by discarding excess high-order bits from the original value. The bit pattern of the result representation will be equal to the *n* low-order bits of the original representation, where *n* is the number of bits in the destination type. This same rule of discarding works for converting signed integers in two's-complement form to a shorter unsigned type. The discarding rule is also one of several acceptable methods for converting signed or unsigned integers to a shorter signed type when signed integers are in two's-complement form. Note that this rule will not preserve the sign of the value in case of overflow, but the action on overflow is not defined in any case. When signed integers are not represented in two's-complement form, the conversions are more complicated. While the C language does not require the two's-complement representation for signed integers, it certainly favors that representation.

From floating-point types The conversion of a floating-point value to an integral value should produce a result that is (if possible) equal in value to the value of the old object. If the floating-point value has a nonzero fractional part, that fraction should be discarded—that is, conversion normally involves truncation of the floating-point value.

The behavior of the conversion is undefined if the floating-point value cannot be represented even approximately in the new type—for example, if its magnitude is much too large, or if a negative floating-point value is converted to an unsigned integer type. The handling of overflow and underflow is left to the discretion of the implementor.

From pointer types When the source value is a pointer, the pointer is treated as if it were an unsigned integer of a size equal to the size of the pointer. Then the unsigned integer is converted to the destination type using the rules listed above. If null pointers are not represented as the value 0, then they must be explicitly converted to 0 when converting the null pointer to an integer.

C programmers have traditionally assumed that pointers could be converted to type **`long`** and back without loss of information. Although this is almost always true, it is not required by the language definition. (It is definitely wrong to assume that type **`int`** is large enough to hold a pointer.) Some computers may have pointer representations that are longer than the largest integer type. Programmers needing a "generic" data pointer type should use **`char *`** in traditional C and **`void *`** in ISO C instead of **`long`**.

References character types 5.1.3; floating-point types 5.2; integer types 5.1; overflow 7.2.2; pointer types 5.3; unsigned types 5.1.2; **`void *`** type 5.3.1

6.2.4 Conversions to Floating-point Types

Only arithmetic types may be converted to floating-point types.

When converting from **`float`** to **`double`** or from **`double`** to **`long double`** the result should have the same value as the original value. This may be viewed as a restriction on the choice of representations for the floating-point types.

When converting from **`double`** to **`float`** or from **`long double`** to **`double`**, such that the original value is within the range of values representable in the new type, the result should be one of the two floating-point values closest to the original value. Whether the original value is rounded up or down is implementation-dependent.

If the original value is outside the range of values representable in the destination type—as when the magnitude of a **`double`** number is too large or too small for the representation of **`float`**—the resulting value is undefined, as is the overflow or underflow behavior of the program.

When converting to floating-point types from integer types, if the integer value is exactly representable in the floating-point type then the result is the equivalent floating-point value. If the integer value is not exactly representable but is within the range of values representable in the floating-point type, then one of the two closest floating-point values should be chosen as the result. If the integer value is outside the range of values representable in the floating-point type, the result is undefined.

References floating types 5.2; integer types 5.1; overflow 7.2.2

6.2.5 Conversions to Structure and Union Types

No conversions between different structure types or union types are permitted.

References structure types 5.6; union types 5.7

6.2.6 Conversions to Enumeration Types

The rules are the same as for conversions to integral types. Some permissible conversions, such as between enumeration and floating-point types, may be symptoms of a poor programming style.

References enumeration types 5.5

6.2.7 Conversions to Pointer Types

In general, pointers and integers may be converted to pointer types. There are special circumstances under which an array or a function will be converted to a pointer.

A null pointer of any type may be converted to any other pointer type, and it will still be recognized as a null pointer. The representation may change in the conversion.

A value of type "pointer to *S*" may be converted to type "pointer to *D*" for any types *S* and *D*. However, the behavior of the resulting pointer may be affected by representation changes or any alignment restrictions in the implementation. In ISO C, object pointers may be converted to function pointers or vice versa only through an intermediate integer.

The integer constant 0 (or **`0L`**) may always be converted to a pointer type. The conversion may or may not involve a representation change, regardless of the relative sizes of **`int`** and the pointer type. The result of such a conversion is a "null pointer" that is different from any valid pointer to a data object. Null pointers of different pointer types may have different internal representations in some implementations.

Integers other than the constant 0 may be converted to pointer type, but the result is nonportable. The intent is that the pointer be considered an unsigned integer (of the same size as the pointer) and the standard integer conversions then be applied to take the source type to the destination type.

An expression of type "array of *T*" is converted to a value of type "pointer to *T*" by substituting a pointer to the first element of the array. This occurs as part of the usual unary conversions (section 6.3.3).

An expression of type "function returning *T*" (i.e., a function designator) is converted to a value of type "pointer to function returning *T*" by substituting a pointer to the function. This occurs as part of the usual unary conversions (section 6.3.3).

References alignment restrictions 6.1.3; array types 5.4; function calls 7.4.3; function designator 7.1; integer types 5.1; pointer types 5.3; **sizeof** operator 7.5.2; usual unary conversions 6.3.3

6.2.8 Conversions to Array and Function Types

No conversions to array or function types are possible.

Example

In particular, it is not permissible to convert between array types or between function types:

```
extern int f();
double d;
d = (( double () )f) ();          /* Invalid! */
d = (double) f();                 /* OK */
d = (*(double (*)()) f)();
            /* Valid, but will have unexpected results */
```

In the last statement, the address of **f** is converted to a pointer to a function returning type **double**; that pointer is then dereferenced and the function called. This is valid, but the resulting value stored in **d** will probably be garbage unless **f** was really defined (contrary to the external declaration above) to return a value of type **double**.

6.2.9 Conversions to the Void Type

Any value may be converted to type **void**. Of course, the result of such a conversion cannot be used for anything. Such a conversion may occur only in a context where an expression value will be discarded, such as in an expression statement.

Example

The most common use of casting an expression to **void** is when ignoring the result of a function call. For example, **printf** is called to write information to the standard output stream. It returns an error indication, but that indication is often ignored. It's not necessary to cast the result to **void**, but does tell the reader that the programmer is ignoring the result on purpose.

```
(void) printf("Goodbye.\n");
```

References discarded expressions 7.13; expression statements 8.2; **void** type 5.9

6.3 THE USUAL CONVERSIONS

6.3.1 The Casting Conversions

Any of the conversions discussed earlier in this chapter may be explicitly performed with a type cast without error. Table 6–2 summarizes the permissible casts. Note that ISO C does not permit a function pointer to be cast directly to an object pointer, or vice versa, although a conversion via a suitable integer type would be possible. This restriction reflects the possibility that object and function pointers could have significantly different representations.

Table 6–2 Permitted casting conversions

Destination (cast) type	Permitted source types
any integer type	(a) any integer type (b) any floating-point type (c) pointer to Q, for any Q
a floating-point type	any arithmetic type
pointer to (object) T, or (**void ***)	(a) any integer type (b) (**void ***) (c) pointer to (object) Q, for any Q (d) pointer to (function) Q, for any Q[a]
pointer to (function) T	(a) any integer type (b) pointer to (function) Q, for any Q (c) pointer to (object) Q, for any Q[a]
structure or union	none; not a permitted cast
array of T, or function returning T	none; not a permitted cast
void	any type

[a] Not permitted in ISO C.

The presence or absence of type qualifiers does not affect the validity of the casting conversions, and some conversions could be used to circumvent the qualifiers. The allowable assignment conversions are more restrictive.

ISO C guarantees that an object pointer converted to **void *** and back to the original type will retain its original value. This is likely to be true for conversions through **char *** in other C implementations.

References assignment conversions 6.3.2; casts 7.5.1; type qualifiers 4.4.3; **void *** 5.3.1

6.3.2 The Assignment Conversions

In a simple assignment expression, the types of the expressions on the left and right sides of the assignment operator should be the same. If they are not, an attempt will be made to convert the value on the right side of the assignment to the type on the left side. The conversions that are valid—a subset of the casting conversions— are listed in Table 6–3. Unless otherwise indicated, the presence of ISO type qualifiers do not affect the validity of the conversion, although a **const**-qualified lvalue cannot be used on the left side of the assignment.

Table 6–3 Allowable assignment conversions

Left side type	Permitted right side types
any arithmetic type	any arithmetic type
a structure or union type[a]	a compatible structure or union type
(**void ***)[b]	(a) the constant 0 (b) pointer to (object) T_1[c] (c) (**void ***)
pointer to (object) T_1[b,c]	(a) the constant 0 (b) pointer to T_2, where T_1 and T_2 are compatible (c) (**void ***)
pointer to (function) F_1[b]	(a) the constant 0 (b) pointer to F_2, where F_1 and F_2 are compatible

[a] Some older C compilers do not support assigning structures or unions.
[b] The referenced type on the left must have all the qualifiers of the referenced type on the right.
[c] T_1 may be an incomplete type if the other pointer has type **void *** (ISO C).

Attempting any other conversion without an explicit cast will be rejected by ISO-conforming implementations, but traditional C compilers almost always permit the assignment of mixed pointer types and often permit any types that would be allowed in a casting conversion.

The rules governing pointer assignment impose conditions on type qualifiers because the assignment could be used to circumvent the qualification.

References assignment operator 7.9.1; casting conversions 6.3.1; compatible types 5.

6.3.3 The Usual Unary Conversions

The usual unary conversions determine whether and how a single operand is converted before an operation is performed. Their purpose is to reduce the large number of arithmetic types to a smaller number that must be handled by the operators. The conversions are applied automatically to operands of the unary **!**, **-**, **~**, and ***** operators, and to each of the operands of the binary **<<** and **>>** operators. These conversions are listed in Table 6–4 for both ISO and traditional C (which differ slightly); an operand of any type not listed in the table is unchanged under these conversions.

The ISO conversions differ from traditional implementations in two ways. First, the promotion from **float** to **double** is no longer mandated in expressions. This allows an implementation to use faster but less precise single-precision operations. Some older implementations include an optional compilation mode that has the same effect.

Table 6–4 Usual unary conversions

Original operand type	ISO C conversion	Traditional conversion
char or **short**	**int**	**int**
unsigned char or **unsigned short**	**int** or **unsigned int**[a]	**unsigned int**
float	**float**	**double**
array of T[b]	pointer to T	pointer to T
function returning T[b]	pointer to function returning T	pointer to function returning T

[a] If type **int** cannot represent all values of the original type without overflow, the converted type will be **unsigned int**.
[b] This conversion is sometimes suppressed; see section 6.2.7 for the exceptions.

The second difference is in the promotion of the shorter integral types. ISO C adopted the "value-preserving" rules used by some C compilers in preference to the "unsigned preserving" rules used by other compilers. The programmer should be cautious of these conversions, since the signedness of the result of the promotion is implementation-dependent and can affect the meaning of the surrounding expression.

Example

If S is a variable of type **unsigned short** in ISO C and its value is 1, then the expression **(-S)** has type **int** and value –1 if **sizeof(short)** is less than **sizeof(int)**, but the same expression has type **unsigned** and a large positive value if **sizeof(short)** is equal to **sizeof(int)** This is because in the first instance **S** is promoted to type **int** prior to the application of the unary minus operator, whereas in the second case **S** is promoted to type **unsigned**.

The usual unary conversions specify that an lvalue of array type is converted to a pointer to the first element of the array, except when:

1. the array is an argument to the **sizeof** or address (**&**) operators
2. a character string literal is used to initialize a character array
3. a wide string literal is used to initialize an array of type **wchar_t**

Example

```
char a[] = "abcd"; /* No conversion */
char *b = "abcd";  /* Array converted to pointer */
int i = sizeof(a); /* No conversion; size of whole array */
b = a + 1;         /* Array converted to pointer. */
```

The usual unary conversions specify that a function designator is converted to a pointer to the function unless the designator is the operand of the **sizeof** or address (**&**) operators. (If it is the operand of **sizeof**, it is also invalid.)

Example

```
extern int f();
int (*fp)();
int i;
fp = f;          /* OK, f is converted to &f */
fp = &f;         /* OK, implicit conversion suppressed */
i = sizeof(fp);  /* OK, result is the size of the pointer */
i = sizeof(f);   /* Invalid */
```

References bitwise negation operator ~ 7.5.5; function calls 7.4.3; function designator 7.1; indirection operator * 7.5.7; initializers 4.6; logical negation operator ! 7.5.4; lvalue 7.1; shift operators << and >> 7.6.3; **sizeof** 7.5.2; unary minus operator - 7.5.3; wide strings 2.7.4

6.3.4 The Usual Binary Conversions

When two values must be operated upon in combination, they are first converted according to the usual binary conversions to a single common type, which is also typically the type of the result. The conversions are applied to the operands of most binary operators and to the second and third operands in a conditional expression.

An operator that performs the usual binary conversions on its two operands first performs the usual unary conversions on each of the operands independently, to widen short values and to convert arrays and functions to pointers. Afterward, if either operand is not of an arithmetic type, no further conversions are performed. Otherwise, the first applicable conversion from Table 6–5 is performed on both operands.

Table 6–5 Usual binary conversions

Type of one operand	Type of the other operand	ISO C conversion	Traditional conversion
`long double`	any	`long double`	not appiicable
`double`	any	`double`	`double`
`float`	any	`float`	`double`
`unsigned long`	any	`unsigned long`	`unsigned long`
`long`	`unsigned`	`long` or `unsigned long`[a]	`unsigned long`
`long`	`int`[b]	`long`	`long`
`unsigned`	`int` or `unsigned`[b]	`unsigned`	`unsigned`
`int`	`int`[b]	`int`	`int`

[a] Type **long** is used if and only if it can represent all values of type **unsigned**.
[b] This is the only remaining possibility for the other operand type.

Example

The ISO rules differ from traditional rules when a **long** operand and an **unsigned** operand come together. Since some non-ISO compilers use the ISO rules, here is a small program that determines which conversion style is in effect:

```
unsigned int UI = -1;
long int LI = 0;
int main()
{
    if (UI < LI) printf("long+unsigned==long\n");
    else printf("long+unsigned==unsigned\n");
    return 0;
}
```

6.3.5 The Function Argument Conversions

When an expression appears as an argument in a function call that is not governed by an ISO C prototype (or when it appears as an argument in the variable part of a prototype argument list), the value of the expression is converted before being passed to the function. The function argument conversions are the same as the usual unary conversions, except that arguments of type **float** are always promoted to type **double**, whereas in ISO C and some other implementations the promotion to **double** is not mandatory in expressions. None of the standard C library routines are prepared to accept arguments of type **float**, because they all expect the automatic conversion to **double** to occur.

References function calls 7.4.3; prototypes 9.2; usual unary conversions 6.3.3

6.3.6 Other Function Conversions

The declared types of the formal parameters of a function, and the type of its return value, are subject to certain adjustments that parallel the function argument conversions. They are discussed in section 9.4.

6.4 C++ COMPATIBILITY

6.4.1 Assignment Conversions

In C++, a cast must be used to convert a pointer of type **void *** to another kind of pointer. You can also use the cast in C, but it is not required in an assignment.

Example

```
char * cp;
void * vp;
...
cp = vp;              /* valid in C, not in C++ */
cp = (char *) vp;     /* valid in both C and C++ */
```

Also, only a pointer to an unqualified (non-**const** and non-**volatile**) object may be converted to a pointer of type **void *** without a cast.

Example

```
char * cp;
const char * ccp;
void * vp;
...
vp = cp;              /* valid in both C and C++ */
vp = ccp;             /* valid in C, not in C++   */
vp = (void *) ccp;    /* valid in both C and C++ */
```

References assignment conversions 6.3.2

6.5 EXERCISES

1. The following table lists pairs of source and destination types to be used in casting conversions. Which of the conversions are allowable in ISO C? Which in traditional C? (For traditional C, replace **void** with **char**.)

	Destination type	*Source type*
(a)	`char`	`int`
(b)	`char *`	`int *`
(c)	`int (*f) ()`	`int *`
(d)	`double *`	`int`
(e)	`void *`	`int (*f)()`
(f)	`int *`	`t *` (where: `typedef int t`)

2. In the table in Exercise 1, which pairs are allowable assignment conversions in ISO C? Which in traditional C? (The destination type is the left-side type; the source type is the right-side type.)

3. What is the resulting type when the usual binary conversions of traditional C are applied to the following pairs of types? In which cases is the result different under ISO C?

   (a) **char** and **unsigned**
   (b) **unsigned** and **long**
   (c) **float** and **double**
   (d) **char** and **long double**
   (e) **int []** and **int ***
   (f) **short ()** and **short ()**

4. Is it allowable to have a C implementation in which type **char** can represent values ranging from –2,147,483,648 through 2,147,483,647? If so, what would be **sizeof(char)** under that implementation? What would be the smallest and largest ranges of type **int**?

5. What relationship must hold between **sizeof(long double)** and **sizeof(int)**?

6. Suppose computers A and B are both byte-addressable and have a word size of 32 bits (four bytes), but computer A is a big-endian and B is a little-endian. The integer 128 is stored in a word of computer A and is then transferred to a word in computer B by moving the first byte of the word in A to the first byte of the word in B, etc. What is the integer value stored in the word of computer B when the transfer is complete? If A were the little-endian and B the big-endian, what would be the result?

7

Expressions

The C language has an unusually rich set of operators that provide access to most of the operations provided by the underlying hardware. This chapter presents the syntax of expressions and describes the function of each operator.

7.1 OBJECTS, LVALUES, AND DESIGNATORS

An *object* is a region of memory that can be examined and stored into. An *lvalue* (pronounced "ell-value") is an expression that refers to an object in such a way that the object may be examined or altered. Only an lvalue expression may be used on the left-hand side of an assignment. An expression that is not an lvalue is sometimes called an *rvalue* (pronounced "are-value") because it can be used only on the right-hand side of an assignment. An lvalue can have an incomplete array type, but not **void**.

As ISO C uses the term, an "lvalue" does not necessarily permit modification of the object it designates. This is true if the lvalue has an array type, an incomplete type, a **const**-qualified type, or if it has a structure or union type one of whose members (recursively applied to nested structures and unions) has a **const**-qualified type. The term *modifiable lvalue* is used to emphasize that the lvalue does permit modification of the designated object.

A *function designator* is a value of function type. It is neither an object nor an lvalue. The name of a function is a function designator, as is the result of dereferencing a function pointer. Functions and objects are often treated differently in C, and we try to be careful to distinguish between "function types" and "object types," "lvalues" and "function designators," and "function pointers" and "object pointers." The phrase "lvalue designating an object" is redundant, but we will use it when appropriate to emphasize the exclusion of function designators.

The C expressions that can be lvalues are listed in Table 7–1, along with any special conditions that must apply for the expression to be an lvalue. No other form of expression can produce an lvalue, and none of the listed expressions can be lvalues if their type is "array of...." Expressions that cannot be lvalues include: array names, functions, enumeration constants, assignment expressions, casts, and function calls.

Table 7–1 Non-array expressions that can be lvalues

Expression	Additional requirements
name	*name* must be a variable
e[*k*]	none
(*e*)	*e* must be an lvalue
e.*name*	*e* must be an lvalue
e->*name*	none
**e*	none

The operators listed in Table 7–2 require certain operands to be lvalues.

Table 7–2 Operators requiring lvalue operands

Operator	Requirement
`&` (unary)	operand must be an lvalue
`++ --`	operand must be an lvalue (postfix and prefix forms)
`= += -= *= /= %=` `<<= >>= &= ^= |=`	left operand must be an lvalue

References address operator 7.5.6; assignment expressions 7.9; cast expression 7.5.1; component selection 7.4.2; decrement expression 7.4.4, 7.5.8; enumerations 5.5; function calls 7.4.3; increment expression 7.4.4, 7.5.8; indirection expression 7.5.7; literals 2.7, 7.3.2; names 7.3.1; subscripting 7.4.1

7.2 EXPRESSIONS AND PRECEDENCE

The grammar for expressions presented in this chapter completely specifies the precedence of operators in C. To summarize the information, Table 7–3 on page 181 contains a concise list of the C operators in order from the highest to the lowest precedence, along with their associativity.

7.2.1 Precedence and Associativity of Operators

Each expression operator in C has a precedence level and a rule of associativity. Where parentheses do not explicitly indicate the grouping of operands with operators, the oper-

Table 7–3 C operators in order of precedence

Tokens	Operator	Class	Precedence	Associates
names, literals	simple tokens	primary	17	n/a
a[*k*]	subscripting	postfix	17	left
f(...)	function call	postfix	17	left
`.`	direct selection	postfix	17	left
`->`	indirect selection	postfix	17	left
`++ --`	increment, decrement	postfix	17	left
`++ --`	increment, decrement	prefix	15	right
`sizeof`	size	unary	15	right
`~`	bitwise not	unary	15	right
`!`	logical not	unary	15	right
`- +`	arithmetic negation, plus	unary	15	right
`&`	address of	unary	15	right
`*`	indirection	unary	15	right
(*type name*)	casts	unary	14	right
`* / %`	multiplicative	binary	13	left
`+ -`	additive	binary	12	left
`<< >>`	left and right shift	binary	11	left
`< > <= >=`	relational	binary	10	left
`== !=`	equality/inequality	binary	9	left
`&`	bitwise and	binary	8	left
`^`	bitwise xor	binary	7	left
`|`	bitwise or	binary	6	left
`&&`	logical and	binary	5	left
`||`	logical or	binary	4	left
`? :`	conditional	ternary	3	right

`= += -= *=`
`/= %= <<= >>=`
`&= ^= |=`
	assignment	binary	2	right

`,`	sequential evaluation	binary	1	left

ands are grouped with the operator having higher precedence. If two operators have the same precedence, the operand is grouped with the left or right operator according whether the operators are left-associative or right-associative. All operators having the same precedence level always have the same associativity.

Example

Here are some examples of the precedence and associativity rules:

Original expression	Equivalent expression	Reason for equivalence
`a*b+c`	`(a*b)+c`	`*` has higher precedence than `+`
`a+=b|=c`	`a+=(b|=c)`	`+=` and `|=` are right-associative
`a-b+c`	`(a-b)+c`	`-` and `+` are left-associative
`sizeof(int)*p`	`(sizeof(int))*p`	`sizeof` has higher precedence than cast
`*p->q`	`*(p->q)`	`->` has higher precedence than `*`

To summarize the associativity rules, all of the binary and ternary operators are left-associative except for the conditional and assignment operators, which are right-associative. The unary and postfix operators are sometimes described as being right-associative, but this is needed only to express the idea that an expression such as `*x++` is interpreted as `*(x++)` rather than as `(*x)++`. We prefer simply to state that the postfix operators have higher precedence than the (prefix) unary operators.

References assignment operators 7.9; binary operators 7.6; concatenation of strings 2.7.4; conditional operator 7.8; postfix operators 7.4.4; unary `+` 7.5.3

7.2.2 Overflow and Other Arithmetic Exceptions

For certain operations in C such as addition and multiplication, it may be that the true mathematical result of the operation cannot be represented as a value of the expected result type (as determined by the usual conversion rules). This condition is called overflow or, in some cases, underflow.

In general, the C language does not specify the consequences of overflow. One possibility is that an incorrect value (of the correct type) is produced. Another possibility is that program execution is terminated. A third possibility is that some sort of machine-dependent trap or exception occurs that may be detected by the program in some implementation-dependent manner.

For certain operations, the C language explicitly specifies that the effects are unpredictable for certain operand values or (more stringently) that a value is always produced but the value is unpredictable for certain operand values. If the right-hand operand of the division operator, `/`, or the remainder operator, `%`, is zero, then the effects are unpredictable. If the right-hand operand of a shift operator, `<<` or `>>`, is too large or negative, then an unpredictable value is produced.

Traditionally, all implementations of C have ignored the question of signed integer overflow, in the sense that the result is whatever value is produced by the machine instruction used to implement the operation. (Many computers that use a two's-complement representation for signed integers handle overflow of addition and subtraction simply by producing the low-order bits of the true two's-complement result. No doubt many existing

C programs depend on this fact, but such code is technically not portable.) Floating-point overflow and underflow are usually handled in whatever convenient way is supported by the machine; if the machine architecture provides more than one way to handle exceptional floating-point conditions, a library function may be provided to give the C programmer access to such options.

For unsigned integers the C language is quite specific on the question of overflow: every operation on unsigned integers always produces a result value that is congruent modulo 2^n to the true mathematical result of the operation (where n is the number of bits used to represent the unsigned result). This amounts to computing the correct n low-order bits of the true result (of the true two's-complement result if the true result is negative, as when subtracting a big unsigned integer from a small one).

Example

As an example, suppose that objects of type unsigned are represented using 16 bits; then subtracting the unsigned value 7 from the unsigned value 4 would produce the unsigned value 65,533 (2^{16}–3) because this value is congruent modulo 2^{16} to the true mathematical result –3.

An important consequence of this rule is that operations on unsigned integers are guaranteed to be completely portable between two implementations *if* those implementations use representations having the same number of bits. It is easy to simulate the unsigned arithmetic of another implementation using some smaller number of bits.

References division operator `/` 7.6.1; floating-point types 5.2; remainder operator `%` 7.6.1; shift operators `<<` and `>>` 7.6.3; signed types 5.1.1; unsigned types 5.1.2

7.3 PRIMARY EXPRESSIONS

There are three kinds of primary expressions: names (identifiers), literal constants, and parenthesized expressions:

primary-expression :
  identifier
  constant
  parenthesized-expression

Function calls, subscript expressions, and component selection expressions were traditionally listed as primary expressions in C, but we have included them in the next section with the postfix expressions.

7.3.1 Names

The value of a name depends on its type. The type of a name is determined by the declaration of that name (if any), as discussed in Chapter 4.

The name of a variable declared to be of arithmetic, pointer, enumeration, structure, or union type evaluates to an object of that type; the name is an lvalue expression. An enumeration constant name evaluates to the associated integer value; it is not an lvalue.

Example

In the example below, the four color names are enumeration constants. The **switch** statement (described in section 8.7) selects one of four statements to execute based on the value of the parameter **color**:

```
typedef enum { red, blue, green } colortype;

colortype next_color(colortype color)
{
    switch (color) {
        case red    : return blue;
        case blue   : return green;
        case green  : return red;
    }
}
```

The name of an array evaluates to that array; it is not an lvalue. In contexts where the result is subject to the usual conversions, the array value is immediately converted to a pointer to the first object in the array. This occurs in all contexts except as the argument to the **sizeof** operator, in which case the size of the array is returned, rather than the size of a pointer:

Example

```
extern void PrintMatrix();
int Matrix[10][10], total_length, row_length;

total_length = sizeof Matrix;
row_length = sizeof Matrix[0];
PrintMatrix(Matrix); /* pointer to first
                        element is passed */
```

The name of a function evaluates to that function; it is not an lvalue. In contexts where the result is subject to the usual conversions, the function value is immediately converted to a pointer to the function. This occurs in all contexts but two: as the argument to the **sizeof** operator, where a function is invalid, and as the function in a function call expression, in which case the function itself is desired, and not a pointer to it.

Example

This example shows a function name used as an argument to another function:

```
extern void PlotFunction(double (*f)(double),
                         double x0, double x1);

double fn(double x) { return x * x - x; }

int main(void)
{   ...
    PlotFunction(fn, 0.01, 100.0); /* fn converts to &fn */
    ...
}
```

It is not possible for a name, as an expression, to refer to a label, **typedef** name, structure component name, union component name, structure tag, union tag, or enumeration tag. Names used for those purposes reside in name spaces separate from the names that can be referred to by a name in an expression. Some of these names may be referred to within expressions by means of special constructs. For example, structure and union component names may be referred to using the **.** or **->** operators, and **typedef** names may be used in casts and as an argument to the **sizeof** operator.

References array types 5.4; casts 7.5.1; enumeration types 5.5; function calls 7.4.3; function types 5.8; lvalue 7.1; name space 4.2; selection operators **.** and **->** 7.4.2; **sizeof** operator 7.5.2; **typedef** names 5.10; usual unary conversions 6.3.3

7.3.2 Literals

A literal (lexical constant) is a numeric constant, and when evaluated as an expression yields that constant as its value. A literal expression is never an lvalue. See section 2.7 for a discussion of literals and their types and values.

7.3.3 Parenthesized Expressions

A parenthesized expression consists of a left parenthesis, any expression, and then a right parenthesis:

parenthesized-expression :
  (*expression* **)**

The type of a parenthesized expression is identical to the type of the enclosed expression; no conversions are performed. The value of a parenthesized expression is the value of the enclosed expression, and will be an lvalue if and only if the enclosed expression is an lvalue. Parentheses do not necessarily force a particular evaluation order. See section 7.12.

The purpose of the parenthesized expression is simply to delimit the enclosed expression for grouping purposes, either to defeat the default precedence of operators or to make code more readable.

Example

```
x1 = (-b + discriminant)/(2.0 * a)
```

References lvalue 7.1

7.4 POSTFIX EXPRESSIONS

There are six kinds of postfix expressions: subscripting expressions, two forms of component selection (direct and indirect), function calls, and postfix increment and decrement expressions.

postfix-expression :
  primary-expression
  subscript-expression
  component-selection-expression
  function-call
  postincrement-expression
  postdecrement-expression

Function calls, subscript expressions, and component selection expressions were traditionally listed as primary expressions, but their syntax is more closely related to the postfix expressions.

7.4.1 Subscripting Expressions

A subscripting expression consists of a postfix expression, a left bracket, an arbitrary expression, and a right bracket. This construction is used for array subscripting, where the postfix expression (commonly an array name) evaluates to a pointer to the beginning of the array and the other expression to an integer offset:

subscript-expression :
  postfix-expression **[** *expression* **]**

In C, the expression e_1**[**e_2**]** is by definition precisely equivalent to the expression ***((**e_1**)+(**e_2**))**. The usual binary conversions are applied to the two operands, and the result is always an lvalue. The indirection (*****) operator must have a pointer as its operand, and the only way that the result of the **+** operator can be a pointer is for one operand to be a pointer and the other an integer, and therefore it follows that for $e_1[e_2]$ one operand must be a pointer and the other an integer. Conventionally, e_1 is the name of an array and e_2 is an integer expression, but e_1 could alternatively be a pointer or the order of the operands could be reversed. A consequence of the definition of subscripting is that arrays use 0-origin indexing.

Multidimensional array references are formed by composing subscripting operators.

Example

```
char buffer[100], *bptr = buffer;
int i = 99;
...
buffer[0]   = '\0';       /* subscripting an array */
bptr[i-1]   = bptr[0];    /* subscripting a pointer */
i[bptr]     = '\0';       /* unconventional subscripting */
```

The first element allocated for the 100-element array **buffer** is referred to as **buffer[0]**, and the last element as **buffer[99]**. The names **buffer** and **bptr** both point to the same place, namely **buffer[0]**, the first element of the **buffer** array, and they can be used in identical ways within subscripting expressions. However, **bptr** is a variable (an lvalue), and thus can be made to point to some other place:

```
bptr = &buffer[6];
```

after which the expression **bptr[-4]** refers to the same place as the expression **buffer[2]**. (This illustrates the fact that negative subscripts make sense in certain circumstances.) An assignment can also make **bptr** point to no place at all:

```
bptr = NULL;    /* Store a null pointer into bptr. */
```

On the other hand, the array name **buffer** is not an lvalue and cannot be modified. Considered as a pointer, it always points to the same fixed place, as if it were declared

```
char * const buffer;
```

Example

The following code stores 1.0 in the diagonal elements of a 10-by-10 array, **matrix**, and stores 0.0 in the other elements:

```
int matrix[10][10];
...
for (i = 0; i < 10; i++)
    for (j = 0; j < 10; j++)
        matrix[i][j] = ((i == j) ? 1.0 : 0.0);
```

It is poor programming style to use a comma expression within the subscripting brackets, because it might mislead a reader familiar with other programming languages to think that it means subscripting of a multidimensional array.

Example

The expression

```
commands[k=n+1, 2*k]
```

might appear to be a reference to an element of a two-dimensional array named **commands** with subscript expressions **k=n+1** and **2*k**, whereas its actual interpretation in C is as a reference to a one-dimensional array named **commands** with subscript **2*k** after **k** has been assigned **n+1**. If a comma expression is really needed (and it is hard for us to think of a plausible example), enclose it in parentheses to indicate that it is something unusual:

```
commands[(k=n+1, 2*k)]
```

It is possible to use pointers and casts to refer to a multidimensional array as if it were a one-dimensional array. This may be desirable for reasons of efficiency. It must be kept in mind that arrays in C are stored in row-major order.

Example

The following code sets up an identity matrix—a matrix whose diagonal elements are 1 and whose other elements are zero. This method is tricky, but fast. It treats the two-dimensional matrix as if it were a one-dimensional vector with the same number of elements, which simplifies subscripting and eliminates the need for nested loops.

```
#define SIZE 10
double matrix[SIZE][SIZE];
int i;
for (i = 0; i < SIZE*SIZE; i++)
    ((double *)matrix)[i] = 0.0;    /* zero all elements */
for (i = 0; i < SIZE*SIZE; i += (SIZE + 1))
    ((double *) matrix)[i] = 1.0;    /* set diagonals to 1 */
```

References addition operator + 7.6.2; array types 5.4; comma expressions 7.10; indirection operator * 7.5.7; integral types 5.1; lvalue 7.1; pointer types 5.3

7.4.2 Component Selection

Component selection operators are used to access fields (components) of structure and union types:

component-selection-expression :
  direct-component-selection
  indirect-component-selection

direct-component-selection :
  postfix-expression **.** *name*

indirect-component-selection :
  postfix-expression **->** *name*

A direct component selection expression consists of a postfix expression, a period (**.**), and a name. The postfix expression must be of a structure or union type, and the name must be the name of a component of that type. The result of the expression is the named member of the structure or union.

The result of the direct component selection expression is an lvalue if the expression before the period is an lvalue and if the selected component is not an array. The first condition is true for all structure and union values except those returned by a function.

Example

```
struct S {int a,b;} x;
extern struct S f();      /* structure-returning function */
int i;
...
x = f();        /* OK */
i = f().a;      /* OK */
f().a = i;      /* Invalid; f() is not an lvalue */
```

(The last assignment, even if valid, would be nonsensical. The function **f** would return a copy of some structure, which would then have one of its components modified—just before the entire copy was discarded at the end of the statement.)

(Some older, non-ISO C implementations do not allow functions to return structures at all. Of those which allow it, a few do not allow a function call to have a selection operator applied to it; they would consider **f().a** to be an error.)

In ISO C, if the expression before the period has a qualified structure or union type, the result has the so-qualified type of the named component.

Example

The assignment below is invalid because **x.a** has type "**const int**", the **const** having been inherited from **x**:

```
const struct {int a,b;} x;
...
x.a = 5;    /* Invalid */
```

An indirect component selection expression consists of a postfix expression, the operator **->**, and a name. The value of the postfix expression must be a pointer to a structure or union type, and the name must be the name of a component of that structure or union type. The result is the named member of the union or structure and is an lvalue unless the member is an array. The expression *e*->*name* is by definition precisely equivalent to the expression (**e*).*name*.

Example

In the following code, both components of structure **Point** are set to 0.0 in a roundabout fashion to demonstrate this equivalence:

```
struct {float x, y; } Point, *Point_Ptr;
...
Point.x = 0.0;          /* Sets x to 0.0 */
Point_Ptr = &Point;
Point_Ptr->y = 0.0;     /* Sets y to 0.0 */
```

In ISO C, if the expression before the **->** operator is a pointer to a qualified structure or union type, the result has the so-qualified type of the named component.

ISO C permits the null pointer to be used on the left of the indirect selection operator. Applying the address operator **&** to the result yields the offset in bytes of a component within the structure.

Example

```
#define OFFSET(type,field)   \
   ((size_t)(char *)&((type *)0)->field)
```

This **OFFSET** macro is similar to the **offsetof** macro that appears in **stddef.h**.

References address operator **&** 7.5.6; indirection operator ***** 7.5.7; lvalue 7.1; **offsetof** macro 11.1; **size_t** 13.1; structure types 5.6; type qualifiers 4.4.3; union types 5.7

7.4.3 Function Calls

A function call consists of a postfix expression (the function expression), a left parenthesis, a possibly empty sequence of expressions (the argument expressions) separated by commas, and then a right parenthesis:

function-call :
  postfix-expression **(** *expression-list*$_{opt}$ **)**

expression-list :
  assignment-expression
  expression-list **,** *assignment-expression*

The type of the function expression, after the usual unary conversions, must be "pointer to function returning *T*" for some type *T*. The result of the function call has type *T* and is never an lvalue. If *T* is **void**, then the function call produces no result and may not be used in a context that requires the call to yield a result. *T* may not be an array type.

In pre-ISO compilers, the function expression is required to have type "function returning *T*," and therefore function pointers have to be explicitly dereferenced. That is, if **fp** is a function pointer, the function to which it points can be called only by writing **(*fp)(...)**. An exception is sometimes made if **fp** is a formal parameter; you can write **fp(...)** in that case.

To perform the function call, the function and argument expressions are first evaluated; the order of evaluation is not specified.

Next, if the function call is governed by an ISO C prototype (section 9.2), then the values of the argument expressions are converted to the types of the corresponding formal parameters as specified in the prototype. If such conversions are not possible, the call is in error. If the function has a variable number of arguments, then the extra arguments are converted according to the usual argument conversions (section 6.3.5) and no further checks on the extra arguments are made.

If the function call is not governed by a prototype, the argument expressions are only converted according to the usual argument conversions and no further checks are required of the compiler. This is because, lacking a prototype, the compiler may not have any information about the formal parameters of external functions.

After the actual arguments have been evaluated and converted, they are copied into the formal parameters of the called function; thus, all arguments are passed by value. Within the called function the names of formal parameters are lvalues, but assigning to a formal parameter changes only the copied value in the formal parameter and has no effect on any actual argument that may happen to be an lvalue.

Example

Consider the following function, **square**, which returns the square of its argument:

```
double square(double y) { y = y*y; return y; }
```

Suppose **x** is a variable of type **double** with value 4.0, and we perform the function call **square(x)**. The function will return the value 16.0, but the value of **x** will remain 4.0. The assignment to **y** within square changes only a copy of the actual argument.

Called functions can change the caller's data only if the data is independently visible to the function (say, in a global variable) or if the caller passes a pointer to the data as an argument to the function. When a pointer is passed, the pointer itself is copied but the object pointed to is not copied. Therefore, changes made indirectly through the pointer can be seen by the caller.

Example

The function **swap** below exchanges the values of two integer objects when pointers to those objects are supplied as parameters:

```
void swap(int *xp, int *yp)
{
    int t = *xp;
    *xp = *yp;
    *yp = t;
}
```

If **a** is an integer array all of whose elements are 0, and **i** is an integer variable with the value 4, then after the call **swap(&a[i],&i)**, **i** will have the value 0 and **a[4]** will have the value 4.

Formal and actual arguments of array types are always converted to pointers by C. Therefore, changes to an array formal parameter in a function will affect the actual argument, although it might not seem obvious that this is so.

Example

Consider the function **f**, below, which has an array parameter:

```
void f(int a[10])
{
    a[4] = 12;   /* changes caller's array */
}
```

If **vec** is an integer array, then calling **f(vec)** will set **vec[4]** to 12. The dimension **10** in the array parameter has no significance; **a** could have been declared **int a[]**.

If a function whose return type is not **void** is called in a context where the value of the function would be discarded, a compiler could issue a warning to that effect. However, it is common for non-**void** functions like **printf** to have their return values discarded, and so many programmers think that such warnings are a nuisance.

Example

The intent to discard the result of the function call may be made explicit by using a cast, as in this call to **strcat**:

```
(void) strcat(word, suffix);
```

Comma expressions may be arguments to functions if they are enclosed in parentheses so that their parts are not interpreted as separate arguments.

Example

We can't think of a plausible reason for doing this, but here is an implausible example:

```
int main()
{
    int i, j;
    f( (i=1, i), (j=1, j)); /* valid, but strange */
    ...
}
```

References agreement of argument and parameters 9.6; comma operator 7.10; discarded expressions 7.13; function types 5.8; function prototypes 9.2; indirection operator `*` 7.5.7; lvalue 7.1; pointer types 5.3; `printf` 15.11; `strcat` 13.1; usual argument conversions 6.3.5; `void` type 5.9

7.4.4 Postfix Increment and Decrement Operators

The postfix operators `++` and `--` are respectively used to increment and decrement their operands while producing the original value as a result. They are side-effect-producing operators:

postincrement-expression :
  postfix-expression `++`

postdecrement-expression :
  postfix-expression `--`

The operand of both operators must be a modifiable lvalue and may be of any scalar type. The constant 1 is added to the operand in the case of `++` or subtracted from the operand in the case of `--`, modifying the operand. The result is the old value of the operand, before it was incremented or decremented. The result is not an lvalue. The usual binary conversions are performed on the operand and the constant 1 before the addition or subtraction is performed, and the usual assignment conversions are performed when storing the modified value back into the operand. The type of the result is that of the lvalue operand before conversion.

Example

If `i` and `j` are integer variables, the statement `i=j--;` may be rewritten as the two statements

```
i = j;
j = j-1;
```

These operations may produce unpredictable effects if overflow occurs and the operand is a signed integer or floating-point number. The result of incrementing the largest representable value of an unsigned type is 0, and the result of decrementing the value 0 of an unsigned integer type is the largest representable value of that type.

If the operand is a pointer, say of type "pointer to *T*" for some type *T*, the effect of `++` is to move the pointer forward beyond the object pointed to, as if to move the pointer to the next element within an array of objects of type *T*. [On a byte-addressed computer, this means advancing the pointer by **sizeof(*T*)** bytes.] Similarly, the effect of **--** is to move the pointer backward as if to the previous element within an array of objects of type *T*. In both cases the value of the expression is the pointer before modification.

Example

It is very common to use the postfix increment operator when scanning the elements of an array or string, as in this example of counting the number of characters in a string:

```
int strlen(const char *cp)
{
    int count = 0;
    while (*cp++) count++;
    return count;
}
```

References addition 7.6.2; array types 5.4; assignment conversions 6.3.2; floating-point types 5.2; integer types 5.1; lvalue 7.1; overflow 7.2.2; pointer types 5.3; scalar types ch. 5; signed types 5.1.1; subtraction 7.6.2; unsigned types 5.1.2; usual binary conversions 6.3.4

7.5 UNARY EXPRESSIONS

There are several kinds of unary expressions, discussed in the following sections.

cast-expression :
  unary-expression
  (*type-name* **)** *cast-expression*

unary-expression :
  postfix-expression
  sizeof-expression
  unary-minus-expression
  unary-plus-expression
  logical-negation-expression
  bitwise-negation-expression
  address-expression
  indirection-expression
  preincrement-expression
  predecrement-expression

The unary operators have precedence lower than the postfix expressions but higher than all binary and ternary operators. For example, the expression ***x++** is interpreted as ***(x++)**, not as **(*x)++**.

References binary expressions 7.6; postfix expressions 7.4; precedence 7.2.1; unary plus operator 7.5.3

7.5.1 Casts

A cast expression consists of a left parenthesis, a type name, a right parenthesis, and an operand expression. The syntax is shown above, with that for *unary-expression*.

The cast causes the operand value to be converted to the type named within the parentheses. Any permissible conversion (section 6.3.1) may be invoked by a cast expression. The result is not an lvalue.

Example

```
extern char *alloc();
struct S *p;
p = (struct S *) alloc(sizeof(struct S));
```

Some implementations of C incorrectly ignore certain casts whose only effect is to make a value "narrower" than normal.

Example

Suppose that type **unsigned short** is represented in 16 bits and type **unsigned** is represented in 32 bits. Then the value of the expression

```
(unsigned)(unsigned short)0xFFFFFF
```

ought to be **0xFFFF**, because the cast (**unsigned short**) should cause truncation of the value **0xFFFFFF** to 16 bits, and then the cast (**unsigned**) should widen that value back to 32 bits. Deficient compilers fail to implement this truncation effect and generate code that passes the value **0xFFFFFF** through unchanged. Similarly, for the expression

```
(double)(float)3.14159265358979323 84
```

deficient compilers do not produce code to reduce the precision of the approximation to π to that of a **float**, but pass through the double-precision value unchanged.

For maximum portability using non-ISO compilers, programmers should truncate values by storing them into variables or, in the case of integers, performing explicit masking operations (such as with the binary bitwise AND operator **&**) rather than relying on narrowing casts.

References bitwise AND operator 7.6.6; type conversions ch. 6; type names 5.12

7.5.2 Sizeof Operator

The **sizeof** operator is used to obtain the size of a type or data object:

sizeof-expression :
  sizeof **(** *type-name* **)**
  sizeof *unary-expression*

The **sizeof** expression has two forms: the operator **sizeof** followed by a parenthesized type name, or the operator **sizeof** followed by an operand expression. The result is a constant integer value and is never an lvalue. In ISO C the result of **`sizeof`** has the unsigned integer type **`size_t`** defined in the header file **`stddef.h`**. Traditional C implementations often use **`int`** or **`long`** as the result type. Following the C precedence rules, **`sizeof(long)-2`** is interpreted as **`(sizeof(long))-2`** rather than as **`sizeof((long)(-2))`**.

Applying the **`sizeof`** operator to a parenthesized type name yields the size of an object of the specified type—that is, the amount of memory (measured in storage units) that would be occupied by an object of that type, including any internal or trailing padding. By definition, **`sizeof`** applied to any of the character types yields 1. The type name may not name an incomplete array type (one with no explicit length), a function type, or the type **`void`**.

Applying the **`sizeof`** operator to an expression yields the same result as if it had been applied to the name of the type of the expression. The **`sizeof`** operator does not of itself cause any of the usual conversions to be applied to the expression in determining its type; this allows **`sizeof`** to be used to obtain the total size of an array, without the array name being converted to a pointer. However, if the expression contains operators that do perform usual conversions, then those conversions are considered when determining the type. The operand of **`sizeof`** may not have an incomplete array type or function type, except that if the **`sizeof`** operator is applied to the name of a formal parameter declared to have array or function type, then the value returned is the size of the pointer type obtained by the normal rules for converting formal parameters of those types. In ISO C the operand of **`sizeof`** may not be an lvalue that designates a bit field in a structure or union object, but some non-ISO implementations allow this and return the size of the declared type of the component (ignoring the bit-field designation).

Example

Below are some examples of the application of **`sizeof`**. Assume that objects of type **`short`** occupy 2 bytes and objects of type **`int`** occupy 4 bytes.

Expression	Value
`sizeof(char)`	1
`sizeof(int)`	4
`short s;... sizeof(s)`	2
`short s;... sizeof(s+0)`	4 (result of + has type **`int`**)
`short sa[10];... sizeof(sa)`	20
`extern int ia[]; ... sizeof(ia)`	*invalid* (type is incomplete)

When **`sizeof`** is applied to an expression, the expression is analyzed at compile time to determine its type, but the expression itself is not evaluated. When the argument to **`sizeof`** is a type name, it is possible to declare a type as a side effect.

Example

This means that any side effects that might be produced by execution of the expression will not take place. Thus, execution of the expression **`sizeof(j++)`** will not increment **`j`**.

Example

The effect of

```
sizeof(struct S {int a,b;})
```

is to create a new type in ISO C, although it would seem to be bad style to do so. The type can be referenced later in the source file. (This is invalid in C++.)

References array types 5.4; C++ compatibility 7.15; function types 5.8; **`size_t`** 11.1; storage units 6.1.1; type names 5.12; unsigned types 5.1.2; usual binary conversions 6.3.4; **`void`** type 5.9

7.5.3 Unary Minus and Plus

The unary minus operator computes the arithmetic negation of its operand. The unary plus operator (introduced with ISO C) simply yields the value of its operand:

unary-minus-expression :
  - *cast-expression*

unary-plus-expression : (ISO C)
  + *cast-expression*

The operands to both operators may be of any arithmetic type and the usual unary conversions are performed. The result has the promoted type and is not an lvalue.

The unary minus expression "**-***e*" is a shorthand notation for "**0-(***e***)**"; the two expressions perform the same computation. This computation may produce unpredictable effects if the operand is a signed integer or floating-point number and overflow occurs. For an unsigned integer operand k, the result is always unsigned and equal to 2^n-k, where n is the number of bits used to represent the result. Because the result is unsigned, it can never be negative. This may seem strange, but note, however, that $(-x)+x$ is equal to 0 for any unsigned integer x. (This identity also holds for any signed integer x for which $-x$ is well defined.)

The unary plus expression "**+***e*" is a shorthand notation for "**0+(***e***)**"; the two expressions perform the same computation. The operator was added in ISO C for symmetry with unary minus; it has no other purpose.

References floating-point types 5.2; integer types 5.1; lvalue 7.1; overflow 7.2.2; subtraction operator **-** 7.6.2; unsigned types 5.1.2; usual unary conversions 6.3.3

7.5.4 Logical Negation

The unary operator **!** computes the logical negation of its operand. The operand may be of any scalar type:

logical-negation-expression :
  ! *cast-expression*

The usual unary conversions are performed on the operand. The result of the **!** operator is of type **int**; the result is 1 if the operand is zero (null in the case of pointers, 0.0 in the case of floating-point values) and 0 if the operand is not zero (or null or 0.0). The result is not an lvalue. The expression **!(x)** is identical in meaning to **(x)==0**.

Example

```
#define assert(x,s) if (!(x)) assertion_failure(s)
...
assert(num_cases > 0, "No test cases.");
average = total_points/num_cases;
...
```

The use of the **assert** macro anticipates a problem—division by zero—that might otherwise be difficult to locate. **assertion_failure** is assumed to be a function that accepts a string and reports it as a message to the user. A similar **assert** macro appears in the standard header file **assert.h**.

References **assert** 19.1; equality operator **==** 7.6.5; floating-point types 5.2; integer types 5.1; lvalue 7.1; pointer types 5.3; scalar types ch. 5; usual unary conversions 6.3.3

7.5.5 Bitwise Negation

The unary operator **~** computes the bitwise negation (NOT) of its operand:

bitwise-negation-expression :
  ~ *cast-expression*

The usual unary conversions are performed on the operand, which may be of any integral type. Every bit in the binary representation of **~***e* is the inverse of what it was in the (converted) operand *e*. The result is not an lvalue.

Example

If **i** is a 16-bit integer with the value **0xF0F0** (1111000011110000_2), then **~i** has the value **0x0F0F** (0000111100001111_2).

Because different implementations may use different representations for signed integers, the result of applying the bitwise NOT operator **~** to signed operands may not be portable. We recommend using **~** only on unsigned operands for portable code. For an unsigned operand *e*, **~***e* has the value **UINT_MAX-***e* if the converted type of *e* is **unsigned**, or **ULONG_MAX-***e* if the converted type of *e* is **unsigned long**. The values **UINT_MAX** and **ULONG_MAX** are defined in the ISO C header file **limits.h**.

References integer types 5.1; **limits.h** 5.1.1; lvalue 7.1; signed types 5.1.1; unsigned types 5.1.2; usual unary conversions 6.3.3

7.5.6 Address Operator

The unary operator **&** returns a pointer to its operand:

address-expression :
    & *cast-expression*

The operand of **&** must be either a function designator or an lvalue designating an object. If it is an lvalue, the object cannot be declared with storage class **register** or be a bit field. If the type of the operand for **&** is "*T*," then the type of the result is "pointer to *T*." The usual conversions are *not* applied to the operand of the **&** operator, and its result is never an lvalue.

The address operator applied to a function designator yields a pointer to the function. Since a function designator is converted to a pointer under the usual conversion rules, the **&** operator is seldom needed for functions. In fact, some pre-ISO C implementations may not allow it.

Example

```
extern int f();
int (*fp)();
...
fp = &f;     /* OK; & yields a pointer to f */
fp = f;      /* OK; usual conversions yield a pointer  to f */
```

A function pointer generated by the address operator is valid throughout the execution of the C program. An object pointer generated by the address operator is valid as long as the object's storage remains allocated. If the operand of **&** is an lvalue designating a variable with static extent, the pointer is valid throughout program execution. If the operand designates an automatic variable, the pointer is valid as long as the block containing the declaration of the variable is active.

The effect of the address operator in ISO C differs from its effect in traditional C in one respect. In ISO C, the address operator applied to an lvalue of type "array of *T*" yields a value of type "pointer to array of T," whereas many pre-ISO compilers treat **&a** the same as **a**—that is, as a pointer to the first element of **a**. These two interpretations are inconsistent with each other, but the ISO rule is more consistent with the interpretation of **&**.

Example

In the ISO C program fragment below, all the assignments to **p** are equivalent and all the assignments to **i** are equivalent:

```
    int a[10], *p, i;
...
    p = &a[0];  p = a;   p = *&a;
    i = a[0];   i = *a;  i = **&a;
```

References array type 5.4; function designator 7.1; function type 5.8; lvalue 7.1; pointer type 5.3; **register** storage class 4.3

7.5.7 Indirection

The unary operator `*` performs indirection through a pointer. The `&` and `*` operators are each the inverse of the other: if `x` is a variable, the expression `*&x` is the same as `x`.

indirection-expression :
    `*` *cast-expression*

The operand must be a pointer; if its type is "pointer to *T*," for some possibly qualified type *T*, then the type of the result is simply "*T*" (with the same qualifications). If the pointer points to an object, then the result is an lvalue referring to the object. If the pointer points to a function, then the result is a function designator.

Example

```
int i,*p;
const int *pc;
...
p   = &i;     /* p now points to variable i */
*p  = 10;     /* sets value of i to 10 */
pc  = &i;     /* pc now points to i, too */
*pc = 10;     /* invalid, *pc has type 'const int' */
```

The usual unary conversions are performed on the operand to the indirection operator. The only relevant conversions are from arrays and function designators to pointers. Therefore, if `f` is a function designator, the expressions `*&f` and `*f` are equivalent; in the latter case `f` is converted to `&f` by the usual conversions.

The effect of applying the `*` operator to invalid or null pointers is undefined. In some implementations dereferencing the null pointer will cause the program to terminate; in others, it is as if the null pointer designated a block of memory with unpredictable contents.

References array types 5.4; function designators 7.1; function types 5.8; lvalue 7.1; pointer types 5.3; usual unary conversions 6.3.3

7.5.8 Prefix Increment and Decrement Operators

The unary operators `++` and `--` are respectively used to increment and decrement their operands while producing the modified values of the operands as a result. These are side-effect-producing operations. (There are also postfix forms of these operators.)

preincrement-expression :
    `++` *unary-expression*

predecrement-expression :
    `--` *unary-expression*

The operands of both operators must be modifiable lvalues and may be of any scalar type. The constant 1 is added to the operand in the case of ++ and subtracted from the operand in the case of `--`. In both cases the result is stored back in the lvalue and the result is the new value of the operand. The result is not an lvalue. The usual binary conversions are performed on the operand and the constant 1 before the addition or subtraction is performed, and the usual assignment conversions are performed when storing the new value. The type of the result is that of the lvalue operand before conversion.

If the operand is a pointer, say of type "pointer to *T*" for some type *T*, then the effect of `++` is to move the pointer forward beyond the object pointed to, as if to move the pointer to the next object within an array of objects of type *T*. [On a byte-addressed computer, this means advancing the pointer by **`sizeof`**(*T*) bytes.] The effect of `--` is to move the pointer back to the previous element within an array of objects of type *T*.

Example

The **`strrev`** function below copies into its second argument a reversed copy of its first argument:

```
int strrev(const char *s1, char *s2)
{
    char *p = s1;
    while (*p++); /* Locate end of first string. */
    --p;          /* Overshot: back up to the null. */
    /* Now copy the characters in reverse order. */
    while (p > s1)
        *s2++ = *--p;
    *s2 = '\0';  /* Terminate the result string. */
}
```

These operations may produce unpredictable effects if overflow occurs and the operand is a signed integer or floating-point number. The result of incrementing the largest representable value of an unsigned type is 0. The result of decrementing the value 0 of an unsigned integer type is the largest representable value of that type.

The expression `++`*e* is identical in meaning to *e*`+=1`, and `--`*e* is identical to *e*`-=1`. When the value produced by the increment and decrement operators is not used, the prefix and postfix forms have the same effect. That is, the statement *e*`++;` is identical to `++`*e*`;`, and *e*`--;` is identical to `--`*e*`;`.

References addition 7.6.2; array types 5.4; assignment conversions 6.3.2; compound assignment 7.9.2; expression statements 8.2; floating-point types 5.2; integer types 5.1; lvalue 7.1; overflow 7.2.2; pointer types 5.3; postfix increment and decrement expressions 7.4.4; scalar types ch. 5; signed types 5.1.1; subtraction 7.6.2; unsigned types 5.1.2; usual binary conversions 6.3.4

7.6 BINARY OPERATOR EXPRESSIONS

A binary operator expression consists of two expressions separated by a binary operator. The kinds of binary expressions and their operand types are listed in order of decreasing precedence in Table 7–4. All the operators are left-associative.

Table 7–4 Binary operator expressions

Expression kind	Operators	Operands	Result
multiplicative-expression	`* /`	arithmetic	arithmetic
	`%`	integer	integer
additive-expression	`+`	arithmetic	arithmetic
		pointer **+** integer or integer **+** pointer	pointer
	`-`	arithmetic	arithmetic
		pointer – integer	pointer
		pointer – pointer	integer
shift expression	`<< >>`	integer	integer
relational-expression	`< <= >= >`	arithmetic or pointer	0 or 1
equality-expression	`== !=`	arithmetic or pointer	0 or 1
bitwise-and-expression	`&`	integer	integer
bitwise-xor-expression	`^`	integer	integer
bitwise-or-expression	`|`	integer	integer

For each of the binary operators described in this section, both operands are fully evaluated (but in no particular order) before the operation is performed.

References order of evaluation 7.12; precedence 7.2.1

7.6.1 Multiplicative Operators

The three multiplicative operators, `*` (multiplication), `/` (division), and `%` (remainder), have the same precedence and are left-associative:

multiplicative-expression :
    cast-expression
    multiplicative-expression mult-op cast-expression

mult-op **: one of**
    `* / %`

References precedence 7.2.1

Multiplication The binary operator `*` indicates multiplication. Each operand may be of any arithmetic type. The usual binary conversions are performed on the operands, and the type of the result is that of the converted operands. The result is not an lvalue. For integral operands, integer multiplication is performed; for floating-point operands, floating-point multiplication is performed.

The multiplication operator may produce unpredictable effects if overflow occurs and the operands (after conversion) are signed integers or floating-point numbers. If the operands are unsigned integers, the result is congruent mod 2^n to the true mathematical result of the operation (where n is the number of bits used to represent the unsigned result).

References arithmetic types ch. 5; floating types 5.2; integer types 5.1; lvalue 7.1; order of evaluation 7.12; overflow 7.2.2; signed types 5.1.1; unsigned types 5.1.2; usual binary conversions 6.3.4

Division The binary operator `/` indicates division. Each operand may be of any arithmetic type. The usual binary conversions are performed on the operands, and the type of the result is that of the converted operands. The result is not an lvalue.

For floating-point operands, floating-point division is performed. For integral operands, if the mathematical quotient of the operands is not an exact integer, then the result will be one of the two integers closest to the mathematical quotient of the operands. Of those two integers, the one closer to 0 must be chosen if both operands are positive (that is, division of positive integers is truncating division). Note that this completely specifies the behavior of division for unsigned operands. If either operand is negative, then the choice is left to the discretion of the implementor. For maximum portability, programs should therefore avoid depending on the behavior of the division operator when applied to negative integral operands.

The division operator may produce unpredictable effects if overflow occurs and the operands (after conversion) are signed integers or floating-point numbers. Note that overflow can occur for signed integers represented in two's-complement form if the most negative representable integer is divided by –1; the mathematical result is a positive integer that cannot be represented. Overflow cannot occur if the operands are unsigned integers.

The consequences of division by zero—integer or floating-point—are undefined.

References arithmetic types ch. 5; floating types 5.2; integer types 5.1; lvalue 7.1; overflow 7.2.2; signed types 5.1.1; unsigned types 5.1.2; usual binary conversions 6.3.4

Remainder The binary operator `%` computes the remainder when the first operand is divided by the second. Each operand may be of any integral type. The usual binary conversions are performed on the operands, and the type of the result is that of the converted operands. The result is not an lvalue. The library functions **`div`**, **`ldiv`**, and **`fmod`** also compute remainders of integers and floating-point values.

It is always true that **`(a/b)*b + a%b`** is equal to **`a`** if **`b`** is not 0, so the behavior of the remainder operation is coupled to that of integer division. When both operands are positive, the remainder operation will always be equivalent to the mathematical "mod" operation. Note that this completely specifies the behavior of the remainder operation for unsigned operands. If either operand is negative, the behavior will be machine-dependent in a manner corresponding to the machine dependence of integer division. For maximum portability, programs should therefore avoid depending on the behavior of the remainder operator when applied to negative integral operands.

Example

The **gcd** function below computes the greatest common divisor by Euclid's algorithm. The result is the largest integer that evenly divides **x** and **y**:

```
unsigned gcd(unsigned x, unsigned y)
{
    while ( y != 0 ) {
        unsigned temp = y;
        y = x % y;
        x = temp;
    }
    return x;
}
```

The remainder operator may produce unpredictable effects if performing division on the two operands would produce overflow. Note that overflow can occur for signed integers represented in two's-complement form if the most negative representable integer is divided by –1; the mathematical result of the division is a positive integer that cannot be represented, and therefore the results are unpredictable, even though the remainder itself (zero) is representable. Overflow cannot occur if the operands are unsigned integers.

The effect of taking a remainder with a second operand of zero is undefined.

References **div**, **ldiv** 17.1; **fmod** 17.3; integer types 5.1; lvalue 7.1; overflow 7.2.2; signed types 5.1.1; unsigned types 5.1.2; usual binary conversions 6.3.4

7.6.2 Additive Operators

The two additive operators, **+** (addition) and **-** (subtraction), have the same precedence and are left-associative:

additive-expression :
  multiplicative-expression
  additive-expression add-op multiplicative-expression

add-op : one *of*
  + -

Addition The binary operator **+** indicates addition. The usual binary conversions are performed on the operands. The operands may both be arithmetic, or one may be an object pointer and the other an integer. No other operand types are allowed. The result is not an lvalue.

When the operands are arithmetic, the type of the result is that of the converted operands. For integral operands, integer addition is performed; for floating-point operands, floating-point addition is performed.

When adding a pointer *p* and an integer *k*, it is assumed that the object that *p* points to lies within an array of such objects or is one object beyond the last object in the array, and the result is a pointer to that object within (or just after) the presumed array that lies *k* objects away from the one *p* points to. For example, *p*+1 points to the object just after the one *p* points to, and *p*+(–1) points to the object just before. If the pointers *p* or *p*+*k* do not lie within (or just after) the array, then the behavior is undefined. It is invalid for *p* to be a function pointer or to have type **void ***.

Example

Suppose we are on a computer that is byte-addressable and on which the type **int** is allocated 4 bytes. Let **a** be an array of 10 integers that begins at address **0x100000**. Let **ip** be a pointer to an integer, and assign to it the address of the first element of array **a**. Finally, let **i** be an integer variable currently holding the value 6. We now have the following situation:

```
int *ip, i, a[10];
ip = &a[0];
i = 6;
```

What is the value of **ip+i**? Because integers are 4 bytes long, the expression **ip+i** becomes **0x100000+4*6**, or **0x100018**. (24_{10} is 18_{16}.)

The addition operator may produce unpredictable effects if overflow occurs and the operands (after conversion) are signed integers or floating-point numbers, or if either operand is a pointer. If the operands are both unsigned integers, then the result is congruent mod 2^n to the true mathematical result of the operation (where *n* is the number of bits used to represent the unsigned result).

References array types 5.4; floating-point types 5.2; integer types 5.1; lvalue 7.1; order of evaluation 7.12; overflow 7.2.2; pointer representations 5.3.2; pointer types 5.3; scalar types ch. 5; signed types 5.1.1; unsigned types 5.1.2; usual binary conversions 6.3.4

Subtraction The binary operator **-** indicates subtraction. The usual binary conversions are performed on the operands. The operands may both be arithmetic or may both be pointers to compatible object types (ignoring any type qualifiers), or the left operand may a pointer and the other an integer. No other operand types are permitted. The result is not an lvalue.

If the operands are both arithmetic, the type of the result is that of the converted operands. For integral operands, integer subtraction is performed; for floating-point operands, floating-point subtraction is performed.

Example

The result of subtracting one unsigned integer from another is always unsigned and therefore cannot be negative. However, unsigned numbers always obey such identities as

```
(a+(b-a)) == b
```

and

```
(a-(a-b)) == b
```

Subtraction of an integer from a pointer is analogous to addition of an integer to a pointer. When subtracting an integer *k* from a pointer *p*, it is assumed that the object that *p* points to lies within an array of such objects or is one object past the last object, and the result is a pointer to that object within (or just after) the presumed array that lies –*k* objects away from the one *p* points to. For example, *p*–1 points to the object just before the one *p* points to, and *p*–(–1) points to the object just after. If the pointers *p* or *p*–*k* do not lie within (or just after) the array, then the behavior is undefined. It is invalid for *p* to be a function pointer or to have type **`void *`**.

Given two pointers *p* and *q* of the same type, the difference *p*–*q* is an integer *k* such that adding *k* to *q* yields *p*. The type of the difference may be either **`int`** or **`long`**, depending on the implementation. (In ISO C the type of the difference is the signed integer type **`ptrdiff_t`**, defined in **`stddef.h`**.) The result is well defined and portable only if the two pointers point to objects in the same array or point to one past the last object of the array. The difference *k* is the difference in the subscripts of the two objects pointed to. If the pointers *p* or *p*–*q* lie outside the array, the behavior is undefined. It is invalid for either *p* or *q* to be a function pointer or to have type **`void *`**.

The subtraction operator may produce unpredictable effects if overflow occurs and the operands (after conversion) are signed integers or floating-point numbers, or if either operand is a pointer. If the operands are both unsigned integers, the result is congruent mod 2^n to the true mathematical result of the operation (where *n* is the number of bits used to represent the unsigned result).

References array types 5.4; floating-point types 5.2; integer types 5.1; lvalue 7.1; overflow 7.2.2; pointer representations 5.3.2; pointer types 5.3; **`ptrdiff_t`** 11.1; scalar types ch. 5; signed types 5.1.1; type compatibility 5.11; type qualifiers 4.4.3; unsigned types 5.1.2; usual binary conversions 6.3.4

7.6.3 Shift Operators

The binary operator **`<<`** indicates shifting to the left and the binary operator **`>>`** indicates shifting to the right. Both have the same precedence and are left-associative:

shift-expression :
  additive-expression
  shift-expression shift-op additive-expression

shift-op : one of
  `<<` **`>>`**

Each operand must be of integral type. The usual unary conversions are performed separately on each operand (the usual binary conversions are not used), and the type of the result is that of the converted left operand. The result is not an lvalue.

The first operand is a quantity to be shifted, and the second operand specifies the number of bit positions by which the first operand is to be shifted. The direction of the shift operation is controlled by the operator used. The operator **`<<`** shifts the value of the left operand to the left; excess bits shifted off to the left are discarded, and 0-bits are shifted in from the right. The operator **`>>`** shifts the value of the left operand to the right; excess bits shifted off to the right are discarded. The bits shifted in from the left for **>>** depend on the type of the converted left operand: if it is unsigned (or signed and nonnegative), then 0-bits are shifted in from the left; but if it is signed, then at the implementor's option either 0-bits or copies of the leftmost bit of the left operand are shifted in from the left. Therefore, applying the shift operator **>>** to signed operands is not portable.

The result value of the shift operators is undefined if the value of the right operand is negative, so specifying a negative shift distance does not (necessarily) cause **<<** to shift to the right or **>>** to shift to the left. The result value is also undefined if the value of the right operand is greater than or equal to the width (in bit positions) of the value of the converted left operand. Note, however, that the right operand may be 0, in which case no shift occurs and the result value is identical to the value of the converted left operand.

The two shift operators have the same precedence and are left-associative.

Example

One can exploit the precedence and associativity of the operators to write expressions that are visually pleasing but semantically confusing:

```
b << 4 >> 8
```

If **b** is a 16-bit quantity, this expression extracts the middle 8 bits. As always, it is better to use parentheses when there is any possibility of confusion:

```
(b << 4) >> 8
```

Example

Here is how unsigned shift operations may be used to compute the greatest common divisor of two integers by the binary algorithm. This method is more complicated than the Euclidean algorithm, but it may be faster because in some implementations of C the remainder operation is slow, especially for unsigned operands.

```
unsigned binary_gcd(unsigned x, unsigned y)
{
    unsigned temp;
    unsigned common_power_of_two = 0;
    if (x == 0) return y; /* Special cases */
    if (y == 0) return x;

    /* Find the largest power of two
       that divides both x and y. */
    while (((x | y) & 1) == 0) {
        x = x >> 1; /* or: "x >>= 1;" */
        y = y >> 1;
        ++common_power_of_two;
    }

    while ((x & 1) == 0) x = x >> 1;
```

```
        while (y) {
            /* x is odd and y is nonzero here. */
            while ((y & 1) == 0) y = y >> 1;
            /* x and y are odd here. */
            temp = y;
            if (x > y) y = x - y;
            else y = y - x;
            x = temp;
            /* Now x has the old value of y, which is odd.
               y is even, because it is the difference of two odd
               numbers; therefore it will be right-shifted
               at least once on the next iteration. */
        }
        return (x << common_power_of_two);
    }
```

References integer types 5.1; lvalue 7.1; precedence 7.2.1; signed types 5.1.1; unsigned types 5.1.2; usual unary conversions 6.3.3

7.6.4 Relational Operators

The binary operators **<**, **<=**, **>**, and **>=** are used to compare their operands:

relational-expression :
 shift-expression
 relational-expression relational-op shift-expression

relational-op : one of
 < <= > >=

The usual binary conversions are performed on the operands. The operands may both be of arithmetic types, or may both be pointers to compatible types, or may both be pointers to compatible incomplete types. The presence of any type qualifiers on the pointer types does not affect the comparison. The result is always of type **int** and has the value 0 or 1. The result is not an lvalue.

The operator **<** tests for the relationship "is less than"; the operator **<=** tests "is less than or equal to"; the operator **>** tests "is greater than"; and the operator **>=** tests "is greater than or equal to." The result is 1 if the stated relationship holds for the particular operand values and 0 if the stated relationship does not hold.

For integral operands, integer comparison is performed (signed or unsigned as appropriate). For floating-point operands, floating-point comparison is performed. For pointer operands, the result depends on the relative locations within the address space of the two objects pointed to; the result is defined only if the objects pointed to lie within the same array or structure, in which case "greater than" means "having a higher index" for arrays or "declared later in the list of components" for structures. As a special case for arrays, the pointer to the object one beyond the end of the array is well defined and compares greater than all pointers to objects strictly within the array. All pointers to members of the same union argument compare equal.

Example

You can write an expression such as `3<x<7`. This does not have the meaning it has in usual mathematical notation, however; by left-associativity it is interpreted as `(3<x)<7`. Because the result of `(3<x)` is 0 or 1, either of which is less than 7, the result of `3<x<7` is always 1. You can express the meaning of the usual mathematical notation by using a logical AND operator, as in `3<x && x<7`.

Example

You should exercise care when using relational operators on mixed types. A particularly confusing case is this expression:

```
-1 < (unsigned) 0
```

One might think that this expression would always produce 1 (true), because –1 is less than 0. However, the usual binary conversions cause the value –1 to be converted to a (large) unsigned value before the comparison, and such an unsigned value cannot be less than 0. Therefore, the expression always produces 0 (false).

Some older implementations permit relational comparisons between pointers and integers, which is disallowed by the language. The implementations may treat the comparisons as signed or unsigned.

References arithmetic types ch. 5; array types 5.4; bitwise AND operator `&` 7.6.6; compatible types 5.11; floating-point types 5.2; incomplete types 5.4, 5.6.1; integer types 5.1; logical AND operator `&&` 7.7; lvalue 7.1; pointer types 5.3; precedence 7.2.1; signed types 5.1.1; type qualifiers 4.4.3; unsigned types 5.1.2; usual binary conversions 6.3.4

7.6.5 Equality Operators

The binary operators `==` and `!=` are used to compare their operands for equality:

equality-expression :
  relational-expression
  equality-expression equality-op relational-expression

equality-op : one of
  `==` `!=`

Several kinds of operands are permitted:

1. Both operands may be arithmetic types.
2. Both operands may be pointers to compatible types, or both may be `void *` types.
3. One operand may be a pointer to an object or to an incomplete type and the other may have type `void *`. The first operand will be converted to the `void *` type.
4. One of the operands may be a pointer and the other a null pointer constant (the integer constant 0).

In the case of pointer operands, the presence or absence of type qualifiers on the type pointed to does not affect whether the comparison is allowed or the result of the comparison. The usual binary conversions are performed on the arithmetic operands. The result is always of type **`int`** and has the value 0 or 1. The result is not an lvalue.

For integral operands, integer comparison is performed. For floating-point operands, floating-point comparison is performed. Pointer operands compare equal if and only if one of the following conditions is met:

1. Both pointers point to the same object or function.
2. Both pointers are null pointers.
3. Both pointers point one past the last element of the same array object.

The operator **`==`** tests for the relationship "is equal to"; **`!=`** tests "is not equal to." The result is 1 if the stated relationship holds for the particular operand values and 0 if the stated relationship does not hold.

Structures or unions cannot be compared for equality, even though assignment of these types is allowed. The gaps in structures and unions caused by alignment restrictions could contain arbitrary values, and compensating for this would impose an unacceptable overhead on the equality comparison or on all operations that modified structure and union types.

The binary equality operators both have the same precedence (but lower precedence than **`<`**, **`<=`**, **`>`**, and **`>=`**) and are left-associative.

Example

The expression **`x==y==7`** does not have the meaning it has in usual mathematical notation. By left-associativity it is interpreted as **`(x==y)==7`**. Because the result of **`(x==y)`** is 0 or 1, neither of which is equal to 7, the result of **`x==y==7`** is always 0. You can express the meaning of the usual mathematical notation by using a logical AND operator, as in

```
x==y && y==7
```

Example

There is a bitwise XOR operator as well as bitwise AND and OR operators, but there is no logical XOR operator to go along with the logical AND and OR operators. The **`!=`** operator serves the purpose of a logical XOR operator: One may write **`a<b != c<d`** for an expression that yields 1 if exactly one of **`a<b`** and **`c<d`** yields 1, and 0 otherwise. If either of the operands might have a value other than 0 or 1, then the unary **`!`** operator can be applied to both operands: **`!x != !y`** yields 1 if exactly one of **`x`** and **`y`** is nonzero, and yields 0 otherwise. In a similar manner, **`==`** serves as a logical equivalence (EQV) operator.

Example

A common C programming error is to write the **`=`** operator (assignment) where the **`==`** operator (comparison) was intended. Several other programming languages use **`=`** for equality comparison. As a matter of style, if it is necessary to use an assignment expression in a context that will test the value of the expression against zero, it is best to write "**`!= 0`**" explicitly to make the intent clear. For example, it is unclear whether the following loop is correct or whether it contains a typographical error:

```
while (x = next_item()) {
/* Should this be "x==next_item()" ?? */
    ...
}
```

If the original form was correct, then the intent can be made clear in this manner:

```
while ((x = next_item()) != 0) {
    ...
}
```

References alignment restrictions 5.6.4, 6.1.3; bitwise operators 7.6.6; compatible types 5.11; logical operators 7.5.4, 7.7; lvalue 7.1; null pointer 5.3.2; pointer types 5.3; precedence 7.2.1; assignment operator **=** 7.9.1; type qualifiers 4.4.3; usual binary conversions 6.3.4; **void *** 5.3.1

7.6.6 Bitwise Operators

The binary operators **&**, **^**, and **|** designate the bitwise AND, XOR, and OR functions. Individually, they are left-associative; together, their different precedences determine the expression evaluation order. Their operands must be integral and are subject to the usual binary conversions. The type of the result is that of the converted operands; the result is not an lvalue:

bitwise-or-expression :
    bitwise-xor-expression
    bitwise-or-expression **|** *bitwise-xor-expression*

bitwise-xor-expression :
    bitwise-and-expression
    bitwise-xor-expression **^** *bitwise-and-expression*

bitwise-and-expression :
    equality-expression
    bitwise-and-expression **&** *equality-expression*

Each bit of the result of these operators is equal to a boolean function of the two corresponding bits of the two (converted) operands:

- The **&** (AND) function yields a 1-bit if both arguments are 1-bits, and otherwise a 0-bit.
- The **^** (XOR) function yields a 1-bit if one argument is a 1-bit and the other is a 0-bit, and yields a 0-bit if both arguments are 1-bits or both are 0-bits.
- The **|** (OR) function yields a 1-bit if either argument is a 1-bit, and otherwise a 0-bit.

This behavior is summarized below:

a	**b**	**a&b**	**a^b**	**a|b**
0	0	0	0	0
0	1	0	1	1
1	0	0	1	1
1	1	1	0	1

Each of the bitwise operators is commutative and associative, and the compiler is permitted to rearrange an expression containing the operators subject to the restrictions discussed in section 7.12.

For portable code we recommend using the bitwise operators only on unsigned operands. Signed operands will cause no problems among the majority of computers that use the two's-complement representation for signed integers, but they may cause failures on other computers.

Programmers should be careful not to accidentally use the bitwise operators **&** and **|** in place of the logical AND and OR operators, **&&** and **||**. The bitwise operators give the same result as the corresponding logical operators only if the arguments have no side effects and are known to be boolean (0 or 1). Also, the bitwise operators always evaluate both their operands, whereas the logical operators do not evaluate their right-hand operand if the value of the left operand is sufficient to determine the final result of the expression.

Example

If **a** is 2 and **b** is 4, then **a&b** is 0 (false) whereas **a&&b** is 1 (true).

7.6.7 Set of Integers Example

Figures 7–1 through 7–6 show the use, declaration, and definition, respectively, of a "set of integers" package. It uses the bitwise operators to implement sets as bit vectors. The example includes a sample program (**testset.c**), the test program's output, the package header file (**set.h**), and the implementation of the functions in the package (**set.c**).

References integer types 5.1; logical operators **&&** and **||** 7.7; lvalue 7.1; order of evaluation 7.12; relational operators 7.6.4; signed types 5.1.1; unsigned types 5.1.2; usual binary conversions 6.3.4

```
#include "set.h"
void main()
{
    print_k_of_n(0, 4);
    print_k_of_n(1, 4);
    print_k_of_n(2, 4);
    print_k_of_n(3, 4);
    print_k_of_n(4, 4);
    print_k_of_n(3, 5);
    print_k_of_n(3, 6);
}
```

Figure 7–1 Sample usage of the SET package: file **testset.c**

```
All the size-0 subsets of {0, 1, 2, 3}:
{}
The total number of such subsets is 1.

All the size-1 subsets of {0, 1, 2, 3}:
{0}  {1}  {2}  {3}
The total number of such subsets is 4.

All the size-2 subsets of {0, 1, 2, 3}:
{0, 1}  {0, 2}  {1, 2}  {0, 3}  {1, 3}  {2, 3}
The total number of such subsets is 6.

All the size-3 subsets of {0, 1, 2, 3}:
{0, 1, 2}  {0, 1, 3}  {0, 2, 3}  {1, 2, 3}
The total number of such subsets is 4.

All the size-4 subsets of {0, 1, 2, 3}:
{0, 1, 2, 3}
The total number of such subsets is 1.

All the size-3 subsets of {0, 1, 2, 3, 4}:
{0, 1, 2}  {0, 1, 3}  {0, 2, 3}  {1, 2, 3}
{0, 1, 4}  {0, 2, 4}  {1, 2, 4}  {0, 3, 4}
{1, 3, 4}  {2, 3, 4}
The total number of such subsets is 10.

All the size-3 subsets of {0, 1, 2, 3, 4, 5}:
{0, 1, 2}  {0, 1, 3}  {0, 2, 3}  {1, 2, 3}
{0, 1, 4}  {0, 2, 4}  {1, 2, 4}  {0, 3, 4}
{1, 3, 4}  {2, 3, 4}  {0, 1, 5}  {0, 2, 5}
{1, 2, 5}  {0, 3, 5}  {1, 3, 5}  {2, 3, 5}
{0, 4, 5}  {1, 4, 5}  {2, 4, 5}  {3, 4, 5}

The total number of such subsets is 20.
```

Figure 7–2 The SET package: output from file **testset.c**

```
/* set.h: A set package, suitable for sets of small integers in the range 0 to N-1, where N is
the number of bits in an unsigned int type. Each integer is represented by a bit position; bit i is
1 if and only if i is in the set. The low-order bit is bit 0. */

/* The PARMS macro is used to express parameter lists in function declarations in a way that
is compatible with both ISO C and Traditional C. */

#ifdef __STDC__
#define PARMS(x) x
#else
#define PARMS(x) ()
#endif

/* Type SET is used to represent sets. */

typedef unsigned SET;

/* SET_BITS: Maximum bits per set (implementation dependent). */

#define SET_BITS 32

/* check(i): true if i can be a set element. */

#define check (i)                 ((unsigned) (i)) < SET_BITS)

/* emptyset: a set with no elements. */

#define emptyset                  ((SET) 0)

/* add(s,i): add a single integer to a set. */

#define add(set,i)                ((set) | singleset (i))

/* singleset(i): return a set with one element in it. */

#define singleset(i)              ((SET) 1) << (i))

/* intersect: return intersection of two sets. */

#define intersect(set1,set2) ((set1) & (set2))

/* union: retun the union of two sets. */

#define union(set1,set2)          ((set1) | (set2))

/* setdiff: return a set of those elements in set1 or set2, but not both. */

#define setdiff(set1,set2)        ((set1) ^ (set2))

/*  element: true if i is in set. */

#define element(i,set)            (singleset((i)) & (set))
```

Figure 7–3 The SET package: file **set.h** (beginning)

/* **forallelements**: perform the following statement once for every element of the set **s**, with the variable **j** set to that element. To print all the elements in set **s**, just write

```
int j;
forallelements(j, s)
   printf("%d ", j);
```

*/

```
#define forallelements(j,s) \
   for ((j)=0; (j)<SET_BITS; ++(j)) if (element((j),(s)))
```

/* **first_set_of_n_elements(n)**: Produce a set of size **n** whose elements are the integers from 0 through **n**–1. This exploits the properties of unsigned subtractions. */

```
#define first_set_of_n_elements(n)(SET)((1<<(n))-1)
```

/* **next_set_of_n_elements(s)**: Given a set of **n** elements, produce a new set of **n** elements. If you start with the result **of first_set_of_n_elements(k)**, and then at each step apply **next_set_of_n_elements** to the previous result, and keep going until a set is obtained containing **m** as a member, you will have obtained set representing all possible ways of choosing **k** things from **m** things. */

```
extern SET next_set_of_n_elements PARMS((SET x));
```

/* **printset(s)**: print a set in the form "{1, 2, 3, 4}". */

```
extern void printset PARMS((SET z));
```

/* **cardinality(s)**: return the number of elements in **s**. */

```
extern int cardinality PARMS((SET x));
```

/* **print_k_of_n(k,n)**: Print all the sets of size **k** having elements less than **n**. Try to print as many as will fit on each line of the output. Also print the total number of such sets; it should equal **n**!/(**k**!(**n**–**k**)!) where **n**! = 1*2*...*n. */

```
extern void print_k_of_n PARMS((int k, int n));
```

Figure 7–4 The SET package: file **set.h** (end)

```
#include <stdio.h>
#include "set.h"

int cardinality(x)
    SET x;
{
```

/* The following loop is faster than just using **forallelements**—the body is executed once for every 1-bit in the set **x**. Each iteration, the smallest remaining element is removed and counted. The expression **(x & -x)** is a set containing only the smallest element in **x**. */

```
        int count = 0;
        while (x != emptyset) {
            x ^= (x & -x);
            ++count;
        }
        return count;
}

SET next_set_of_n_elements(x)
    SET x;
{
```

/* This code exploits many unusual properties of unsigned arithmetic. As an illustration:

```
if x                 == 001011001111000, then
smallest             == 000000000001000
ripple               == 001011010000000
new_smallest         == 000000010000000
ones                 == 000000000000111
the returned value   == 001011010000111
```

The overall idea is that you find the rightmost contiguous group of 1-bits. Of that group, you slide the leftmost 1-bit to the left one place, and slide all the others back to the extreme right. (This code was adapted from HAKMEM.) */

```
        SET smallest, ripple, new_smallest, ones;
        if (x == emptyset) return x;
        smallest     = (x & -x);
        ripple       = x + smallest;
        new_smallest = (ripple & -ripple);
        ones         = ((new_smallest / smallest) >> 1) - 1;
        return (ripple | ones);
}
```

Figure 7–5 The SET package: file **set.c** (beginning)

```
void printset(z)
    SET z;
{
    int first = 1;
    int e;
    forallelements(e, z) {
        if (first) printf("{");
        else printf(", ");
        printf("%d", e);
        first = 0;
    }
    if (first) printf("{"); /* Take care of emptyset */
    printf("}");            /* Trailing punctuation */
}


#define LINE_WIDTH 54

void print_k_of_n(k, n)
    int k, n;
{
    int count = 0;
    int printed_set_width = k * ((n > 10) ? 4 : 3) + 3;
    int sets_per_line = LINE_WIDTH / printed_set_width;
    SET z = first_set_of_n_elements(k);
    printf("\nAll the size-%d subsets of ", k);
    printset (first_set_of_n_elements(n));
    printf(":\n");
    do {      /* Enumerate all the sets. */
        printset(z);
        if ((++count) % sets_per_line) printf (" ");
        else printf("\n");
        z = next_set_of_n_elements(z);
    }while ((z != emptyset) && !element(n, z));
    if ((count) % sets_per_line) printf ("\n");
    printf("The total number of such subsets is %d.\n",
        count);
}
```

Figure 7–6 The SET package: file **set.c** (end)

7.7 LOGICAL OPERATOR EXPRESSIONS

A logical operator expression consists of two expressions separated by one of the logical operators **&&** or **||**. These operators are sometimes called "conditional AND" and "conditional OR" in other languages because their second operand is not evaluated if the value of the first operand provides sufficient information to determine the value of the expression:

logical-or-expression :
　　logical-and-expression
　　logical-or-expression **||** *logical-and-expression*

logical-and-expression :
　　bitwise-or-expression
　　logical-and-expression **&&** *bitwise-or-expression*

The logical operators accept operands of any scalar type. There is no connection between the types of the two operands—each is independently subject to the usual unary conversions. The result, of type **int**, has the value 0 or 1 and is not an lvalue.

AND The left operand of **&&** is fully evaluated first. If the left operand is equal to zero (in the sense of the **==** operator), then the right operand is not evaluated and the result value is 0. If the left operand is not equal to zero, then the right operand is evaluated. The result value is 0 if the right operand is equal to zero, and is 1 otherwise.

OR The left operand of **||** is fully evaluated first. If the value of the left operand is not equal to zero (in the sense of the **!=** operator), then the right operand is not evaluated and the result value is 1. If the left operand is equal to zero, then the right operand is evaluated. The result value is 1 if the right operand is not equal to zero, and is 0 otherwise.

Example

The assignment **r = a && b** is equivalent to

```
if (a == 0) r = 0;
else {
    if (b == 0) r = 0;
    else r = 1;
}
```

The assignment **r = a || b** is equivalent to

```
if (a != 0) r = 1;
else {
    if (b != 0) r = 1;
    else r = 0;
}
```

Example

Here are some examples of the logical operators:

<table>
<tr><th>a</th><th>b</th><th>a&&b</th><th>Is b evaluated?</th><th>a || b</th><th>Is b evaluated?</th></tr>
<tr><td>1</td><td>0</td><td>0</td><td>yes</td><td>1</td><td>no</td></tr>
<tr><td>0</td><td>34.5</td><td>0</td><td>no</td><td>1</td><td>yes</td></tr>
<tr><td>1</td><td>"Hello\n"</td><td>1</td><td>yes</td><td>1</td><td>no</td></tr>
<tr><td>'\0'</td><td>0</td><td>0</td><td>no</td><td>0</td><td>yes</td></tr>
<tr><td>&x</td><td>y=2</td><td>1</td><td>yes</td><td>1</td><td>no</td></tr>
</table>

Both of the logical operators are described as being syntactically left-associative, though this doesn't matter much to the programmer because the operators happen to be fully associative semantically and no other operators have the same levels of precedence. The operator **&&** has higher precedence than **||**, although it often makes programs more readable to use parentheses liberally around logical expressions.

Example

The expression

```
a<b || b<c && c<d || d<e
```

is the same as (and is more clearly written as):

```
a<b || (b<c && c<d) || d<e
```

References bitwise operators **&** and **|** 7.6.6; equality operators **==** and **!=** 7.6.5; lvalue 7.1; pointer types 5.3; precedence 7.2.1; scalar types ch. 5; usual unary conversions 6.3.3

7.8 CONDITIONAL EXPRESSIONS

The **?** and **:** operators introduce a conditional expression, which has lower precedence than the binary expressions and differs from them in being right-associative:

conditional-expression :
    logical-or-expression
    logical-or-expression **?** *expression* **:** *conditional-expression*

A conditional expression consists of three subexpressions, with the first and second operands separated by a question mark and the second and third operands separated by a colon. The first operand must be of a scalar type. The second and third operands can be of various types and they are subject to the usual unary conversions—if they are evaluated at all. The type of the result depends on the types of the second and third operands. In traditional C, the second and third operands can have the types given in Table 7–5, with the indicated result type for the entire conditional expression. ISO C is more complicated; the permissible operand types and the result type are shown in Table 7–6.

Table 7–5 Conditional expression operands (traditional)

One operand type	The other operand type	Result type
arithmetic	arithmetic	type after usual binary conversions
structure or union[a]	the same structure or union	the structure or union type
pointer	the same pointer type, or 0	the pointer type

[a] These operand types may not be permitted in some compilers.

Table 7–6 Conditional expression operands (ISO C)

One operand type	The other operand type	Result type
arithmetic	arithmetic	type after usual binary conversions
structure or union	compatible structure or union	the structure or union type
void	**void**	**void**
pointer to qualified or unqualified version of type T_1	pointer to qualified or unqualified version of type T_2, if types T_1 and T_2 are compatible	composite pointer type[a]
pointer to type T[b]	qualified or unqualified **void ***	**void ***[a]
any pointer type	null pointer constant	the pointer type[a]

[a] The type pointed to by the result has all the qualifiers of the types pointed to by both operands.
[b] T must be an object or incomplete type.

The execution of the conditional expression proceeds as follows:

1. The first operand is fully evaluated and tested against zero.
2. If the first operand is not equal to zero, then the second operand is evaluated and its value, converted to the result type, becomes the value of the conditional expression. The third operand is not evaluated.
3. If the first operand is equal to zero, then the third operand is evaluated and its value, converted to the result type, becomes the value of the conditional expression. The second operand is not evaluated.

Conditional expressions are right-associative with respect to their first and third operands.

Example

The expression **r=a?b:c** is equivalent to

```
if (a != 0) r = b;
else r = c;
```

The expression

```
a ? b : c ? d : e ? f : g
```

is interpreted as

```
a ? b : (c ? d : (e ? f : g))
```

Example

In this example, the nesting of conditional expressions seems useful—the **`signum`** function, which returns 1, –1, or 0 depending on whether its argument is positive, negative, or zero:

```
int signum(int x){ return (x > 0) ? 1 : (x < 0) ? -1 : 0; }
```

Anything more complicated than this is probably better done with one or more **`if`** statements. As a matter of style, it is a good idea to enclose the first operand of a conditional expression in parentheses, but this is not required.

References arithmetic types ch. 5; array types 5.4; floating-point types 5.2; integer types 5.1; lvalue 7.1; pointer types 5.3; precedence 7.2.1; scalar types ch. 5; signed types 5.1.1; structure types 5.6; union types 5.7; unsigned types 5.1.2; usual binary conversions 6.3.4; usual unary conversions 6.3.3; **`void`** type 5.9

7.9 ASSIGNMENT EXPRESSIONS

Assignment expressions consist of two expressions separated by an assignment operator; they are right-associative. The operator = is called the simple assignment operator; all the others are compound assignment operators:

assignment-expression :
conditional-expression
unary-expression assignment-op assignment-expression

assignment-op : one of

```
=    +=    -=    *=    /=    %=
<<=  >>=   &=    ^=    |=
```

Assignment operators are all of the same level of precedence and are right-associative (all other operators in C that take two operands are left-associative).

Example

For example, the expression **`x*=y=z`** is treated as **`x*=(y=z)`**, not as **`(x*=y)=z`**; similarly, the expression **`x=y*=z`** is treated as **`x=(y*=z)`**, not as **`(x=y)*=z`**.

The right-associativity of assignment operators allows multiple assignment expressions to have the "obvious" interpretation. That is, the expression **`a=b=d+7`** is interpreted as **`a=(b=(d+7)`**, and therefore assigns the value of **`d+7`** to **`b`** and then to **`a`**.

Every assignment operator requires a modifiable lvalue as its left operand and modifies that lvalue by storing a new value into it. The operators are distinguished by how they compute the new value. The result of an assignment expression is never an lvalue.

References modifiable lvalue 7.1; precedence 7.2.1

7.9.1 Simple Assignment

The single equal sign, **=**, indicates simple assignment. The value of the right operand is converted to the type of the left operand and is stored into that operand. The permitted operand types are given in Table 7–7.

Table 7–7 Assignment operands

Left operand type	Right operand type
arithmetic	arithmetic
structure or union	compatible structure or union
pointer to T	pointer to T', where T and T' are compatible
void *	pointer to T[a]
pointer to T[a]	**void ***
any pointer	null pointer constant

[a] In ISO C, T must be an object or incomplete type.

The original definition of C did not permit the assignment of structures and unions. A few older compilers may still have this restriction.

In ISO C, there are additional restrictions on the operands having to do with type qualifiers. First, the left operand can never have a **const**-qualified type. In addition:

1. If the operands are arithmetic, they can be qualified or unqualified.
2. If the operands are structures or unions, they must be qualified or unqualified versions of compatible types. This means, for example, that their members must be identically qualified.
3. If the operands are both object or function pointers, they must be qualified or unqualified versions of pointers to compatible types, and the type pointed to by the left operand must have all the qualifiers of the type pointed to by the right operand. This prevents a **const int *** pointer from being assigned to an **int *** pointer, after which the constant integer could be modified.
4. If one operand is a qualified or unqualified version of **void ***, the other must be a pointer to an object or incomplete type. The type pointed to by the left operand must have all the qualifiers of the type pointed to by the right operand. The reason is the same as for the previous case.

The type of the result of the assignment operator is equal to the (unconverted and unqualified) type of the left operand. The result is the value stored into the left operand. The result is not an lvalue. When the two operands are of arithmetic types, the usual assignment conversions are used to convert the right operand to the type of the left operand before assignment.

The simple assignment operator cannot be used to copy the entire contents of one array into another. The name of an array is not an lvalue and so cannot appear on the left-hand side of an assignment. Also, the name of an array appearing on the right-hand side of an assignment is converted (by the usual conversions) to be a pointer to the first element, and so the assignment would copy the pointer, not the contents of the array.

Example

The = operator can be used to copy the address of an array into a pointer variable:

```
int a[20], *p;
...
p = a;
```

In this example, **a** is an array of integers and **p** is of type "pointer to integer." The assignment causes **p** to point to (the first element of) the array **a**.

It is possible to get the effect of copying an entire array by embedding the array within a structure or union, because simple assignment can copy an entire structure or union:

```
struct matrix {double contents[10][10]; };
struct matrix a, b;
...
{
    /* Clear the diagonal elements. */
    for (j = 0; j < 10; j++)
        b.contents[j][j] = 0;
    /* Copy whole 10x10 array from b to a. */
    a = b;
}
```

The implementation of the simple assignment operator assumes that the right-hand value and the left-hand object do not overlap in memory (unless they exactly overlap, as in the assignment **x=x**). If overlap does occur, the behavior of the assignment is undefined.

References arithmetic types 5.1–2; array types 5.4; usual assignment conversions 6.3.2; lvalue 7.1; null pointer 5.3.2; pointer types 5.3; structure types 5.6; type compatibility 5.11; union types 5.7

7.9.2 Compound Assignment

The compound assignment operators may be informally understood by taking the expression "*a op*= *b*" to be equivalent to "*a* = *a op b*," with the proviso that the expression *a* is evaluated only once. The permitted types of the operands depend on the operator being used. The possibilities are listed in Table 7–8.

More precisely, the left and right operands of *op*= are evaluated, and the left operand must be a modifiable lvalue. The operation indicated by the operator *op* is then applied to the two operand values, including any "usual conversions" performed by the operator. The resulting value is then stored into the object designated by the left operand, after performing the usual assignment conversions.

For the compound assignment operators, as for the simple assignment operator, the type of the result is equal to the (unconverted) type of the left operand. The result is the value stored into the left operand, and is not an lvalue.

Table 7–8 Operand types for compound assignment expressions

Assignment operator	Left operand	Right operand
`*= /=`	arithmetic	arithmetic
`%=`	integer	integer
`+= -=`	arithmetic	arithmetic
`+= -=`	pointer	integer
`<<= >>=`	integer	integer
`&=`	integer	integer
`^=`	integer	integer
`|=`	integer	integer

In the earliest versions of C, the compound assignment operators were written in the reverse form, with the equal sign preceding the operation. This led to syntactic ambiguities; **`x=-1`** could be interpreted as either **`x=(-1)`** or **`x=-(1)`**. The newer form eliminates these difficulties. Some non-ISO C compilers continue to support the older forms for the sake of compatibility, and will mistake **`x=-1`** as **`x=-(1)`** unless a blank appears between the equal and minus signs.

References arithmetic types ch. 5; assignment conversions 6.3.2; floating-point types 5.2; integer types 5.1; pointer types 5.3; signed types 5.1.1; unsigned types 5.1.2; usual binary conversions 6.3.4; usual unary conversions 6.3.3

7.10 SEQUENTIAL EXPRESSIONS

A comma expression consists of two expressions separated by a comma. The comma operator is described here as being syntactically left-associative, though this doesn't matter much to the programmer, because the operator happens to be fully associative semantically. Note that the *comma-expression* is at the top of the C expression syntax tree:

comma-expression :
    assignment-expression
    comma-expression **,** *assignment-expression*

expression :
    comma-expression

The left operand of the comma operator is fully evaluated first. It need not produce any value; if it does produce a value, that value is discarded. The right operand is then evaluated. The type and value of the result of the comma expression are equal to the type and value of the right operand, after the usual unary conversions. The result is not an lvalue. Thus, the statement "**`r=(a,b,...,c);`**" (notice that the parentheses are required) is equivalent to "**`a;b;... r=c;`**". The difference is that the comma operator may be used in expression contexts, such as in loop control expressions.

Example

In the **for** statement the comma operator allows several assignment expressions to be combined into a single expression for the purpose of initializing or stepping several variables in a single loop:

```
for( x=0, y=N; x<N && y>0; x++, y--) ...
```

The comma operator is associative, and one may write a single expression consisting of any number of expressions separated by commas; the subexpressions will be evaluated in order, and the value of the last one will become the value of the entire expression.

Example

The overuse of the comma operator can be confusing, and in certain places it conflicts with other uses of the comma. For example, the expression

```
f(a, b=5,2*b, c)
```

is always treated as a call to the function **f** with four arguments. Any comma expressions in the argument list must be surrounded by parentheses:

```
f(a, (b=5,2*b), c)
```

Other contexts where the comma operator may not be used without parentheses include field-length expressions in structure and union declarator lists, enumeration value expressions in enumeration declarator lists, and initialization expressions in declarations and initializers. The comma is also used as a separator in preprocessor macro calls.

While the comma operator guarantees that its operands will be evaluated in left-to-right order, other uses of the comma character do not make this guarantee. For example, the argument expressions in a function invocation need not be evaluated left to right.

References discarded expressions 7.13; enumeration types 5.5; **for** statement 8.6.3; function calls 7.4.3; initializers 4.6; lvalue 7.1; macro calls 3.3; structure types 5.6; union types 5.7

7.11 CONSTANT EXPRESSIONS

In several contexts the C language permits an expression to be written that must evaluate to a constant at compile time. Each context imposes slightly different restrictions on what forms of expression are permitted. There are three classes of constant expressions:

1. *preprocessor constant expressions*, which are used as the tested value in the **#if** preprocessor control statement
2. *integral constant expressions*, which are used for array bounds, the length of a bit field in a structure, explicit enumerator values, and the values in **case** labels in **switch** statements
3. *initializer constant expressions*, which are used as the initializers for static and external variables, or for automatic variables of aggregate types

No constant expression may contain assignment, increment, decrement, function call, or comma expressions unless they are contained within the operand of a **sizeof** operator. Otherwise any literal or operator can appear, subject to the additional restrictions discussed in the following sections for each expression class. These restrictions are imposed by ISO; other compilers may have somewhat looser requirements in individual cases.

7.11.1 Preprocessor Constant Expressions

Preprocessor constant expressions must be evaluated at compile time, and are subject to some relatively strict constraints. Such expressions must have integral type, and can involve only integer constants, character constants, and the special **defined** operator. All arithmetic is to be done using types **long** or **unsigned long**, as appropriate to the signedness of the operands, which frees the preprocessor from having to deal with several sizes of integer types.

Preprocessor expressions must not perform any environmental inquiries. Casts are not permitted, nor is the **sizeof** operator. That is, the expressions remain insulated from implementation details on the target computer.

Example

This code incorrectly attempts to see if type **int** on the target computer is larger than 16 bits:

```
#if 1<<16
/* Target integer has more than 16 bits (NOT!)*/
...
#endif
```

In fact, the code may only be testing the representation of type **long** on the *host* computer.

The preprocessor must recognize escape sequences in character constants, but is allowed to use either the source or target character sets in converting character constants to integers. This means that the expressions **'\n'** or **'z'-'a'** might have different values in a preprocessor expression than they would appearing in, say, an **if** statement. Programmers using cross-compilers in which the host and target character sets are different should beware of this license.

After macro expansion, if the preprocessor constant expression contains any remaining identifiers they are each replaced by the constant 0. This is probably a bad rule, because the presence of such identifiers is almost certainly a programming error. A better way to test whether a name is defined in the preprocessor is to use the **defined** operator or the **#ifdef** and **#ifndef** commands.

Compilers are free to accept additional forms of preprocessor constant expressions, but programs making use of these extensions are not portable.

References cast expressions 7.5.1; character constants 2.7.3; character sets 2.1; **defined** operator 3.5.5; enumeration constants 5.5; escape characters 2.7.5; **#ifdef** and **#ifndef** 3.5.3; **sizeof** operator 7.5.2

7.11.2 Integral Constant Expressions

An integral constant expression is used for array bounds, the length of a bit field in a structure, explicit enumerator values, and the values in **case** labels in **switch** statements. An integral constant expression must have an integral type and can include integer constants, character constants, and enumeration constants. The **sizeof** operator can be used and can have any operand. Cast expressions may be used, but only to convert arithmetic types to integer types (unless they are part of the operand to **sizeof**). A floating-point constant is permitted only if it is the immediate operand of a cast or is part of the operand of **sizeof**.

Constant expressions not appearing in preprocessor commands should be evaluated as they would be on the target computer, including the values of character constants.

Compilers are free to accept additional forms of integral constant expressions, including more general floating-point expressions that are converted to an integer type, but programs making use of these extensions are not portable. Some pre-ISO compilers do not permit casts of any kind in constant expressions. Programmers concerned with portability to these compilers might be wise to avoid casts in constant expressions.

References bit fields 5.6.5; cast expressions 7.5.1; enumeration types 5.5; floating-point constants 2.7.2; **sizeof** operator 7.5.2; switch statement 8.7

7.11.3 Initializer Constant Expressions

The constant expression in an initializer can include arithmetic constant expressions and address constant expressions.

Arithmetic constant expressions include the integral constant expressions, but can also include floating-point constants generally (not just those cast to integers or in **sizeof**), and casts to any arithmetic type (including the floating-point types). If a floating-point expression is evaluated at compile time in a constant expression, the implementation may use a representation that provides more precision or a greater range than the target environment. Therefore, the value of a floating-point expression may be slightly different at compile time than it would be if evaluated during program execution. This rule reflects the difficulty of exactly simulating a foreign floating-point implementation. Other than this case, the expressions should be evaluated just as they would be on the target computer.

An *address constant expression* can be the null pointer constant [for example, **(void *)0**] or the address of a static or external object or function, or the address of a static or external object plus or minus an integer constant expression. In forming addresses, the address (**&**), indirection (*****), subscript (**[]**), and the component selection operators (**.** and **->**) may be used, but no attempt must be made to access the value of any object. Casts to pointer types may also be used.

Compilers are free to accept additional forms of initializer constant expressions, such as more complicated addressing expressions involving several addresses, but programs making use of these extensions are not portable.

ISO C states that an implementation is free to perform initializations at run time, and so could avoid floating-point arithmetic. However, it might be difficult to do this initialization before executing any code that accesses the initialized variable.

Example

Examples of address constant expressions are shown below in the initializers for **p** and **pf**:

```
static int a[10];
static struct { float f1, f2 } s;
extern int f();
int i = 3;
...
int *p[] = { &i, a, &a[0],
             (char *)&a[0]+sizeof(a),
             &s.f2 }}
int (*pf)() = &f;
```

References address operator **&** 7.5.6; array types 5.4; initializers 4.6; **sizeof** operator 7.5.2; structure types 5.6

7.12 ORDER OF EVALUATION

In general, the compiler can rearrange the order in which an expression is evaluated. The rearrangement may consist of evaluating only the arguments of a function call, or the two operands of a binary operator, in some particular order other than the obvious left-to-right order. The binary operators **+**, *****, **&**, **^**, and **|** are assumed to be completely associative and commutative, and a compiler is permitted to exploit this assumption. The compiler is free, for example, to evaluate **(a+b)+(c+d)** as if it were written **(a+d)+(b+c)** (assuming all variables have the same arithmetic type).

The assumption of commutativity and associativity is always true for **&**, **^**, and **|** on unsigned operands. It may not be true for **&**, **^**, and **|** on signed operands, because of potential problems with certain signed representations. It may not be true for ***** and **+**, because of the possibility that the order indicated by the expression as written might avoid overflow but another order might not. Nevertheless, the compiler is allowed to exploit the assumption. Any rearrangement of expressions involving these operators must not alter the implicit type conversions of the operands.

Example

To control the order of evaluations, the programmer can use assignments to temporary variables. However, a good optimizing compiler might even rearrange computations such as this:

```
int temp1, temp2;
...
/* Compute q=(a+b)+(c+d), exactly that way. */
temp1 = a+b;
temp2 = c+d;
q = temp1 + temp2;
```

Example

In the example below, the two expressions are not equivalent and the compiler is not free to substitute one for the other, despite the fact that one is obtained from the other "merely by rearranging the additions":

```
(1.0 + -3) + (unsigned) 1; /* Result is -1.0 */
1.0 + (-3 + (unsigned) 1); /* Result is large */
```

The first assignment is straightforward and produces the expected result. The second produces a large result, because the usual binary conversions cause the signed value –3 to be converted to a large unsigned value 2^n-3, where n is the number of bits used to represent an unsigned integer. This is then added to the unsigned value 1, the result converted to floating-point representation and added to 1.0, resulting in the value 2^n-3 in a floating-point representation. Now, this result may or may not be what the programmer intended, but the compiler must not confuse the issue further by capriciously rearranging the additions.

According to the language definition, the compiler has equal freedom to rearrange floating-point expressions. However, the order in which a floating-point expression is evaluated can have a significant impact on the accuracy of the result, depending on the particular values of the operands. Since the compiler cannot predict the operand values, numerical analysts prefer that compilers always evaluate floating-point expressions exactly as written. That way, the programmer can control the order of evaluation.

When evaluating the actual arguments in a function call, the order in which the arguments and the function expression are evaluated is not specified; but the program should behave as if it chose one argument, evaluated it fully, then chose another argument, evaluated it fully, and so on, until all arguments were evaluated. (A similar restriction holds for each operand to a binary expression operator.)

Example

In this example, the variable **x** is an array of pointers to characters and is to be regarded as an array of strings. The variable **p** is a pointer to a pointer to a character and is to be regarded as a pointer to a string. The purpose of the **if** statement is to determine whether the string pointed to by **p** (call it **s1**) and the next string after that one (call it **s2**) are equal (and, in passing, to step the pointer **p** beyond those two strings in the array).

```
char *x[10], **p=x;
...
if ( strcmp(*p++, *p++) == 0 ) printf("Same.");
```

It is, of course, bad programming style to have two side effects on the same variable in the same expression, because the order of the side effects is not defined; but this all-too-clever programmer has reasoned that the order of the side effects doesn't matter, because the two strings in question may be given to **strcmp** in either order.

7.12.1 Sequence Points

In ISO C, if a single object is modified more than once between successive sequence points, the result is undefined. A *sequence point* is a point in the program's execution sequence at which all previous side effects of execution are to have taken place and at which no subsequent side effects will have occurred. Sequence points occur:

- at the end of a full expression—that is, an initializer, an expression statement, the expression in a **return** statement, and the control expressions in a conditional, iterative, or **switch** statement (including each expression in a **for** statement)
- after the first operand of a **&&**, **||**, **?:**, or comma operator
- after the evaluation of the arguments and function expression in a function call

According to this rule, the value of the expression **++i*++i** is undefined, as is the **strcmp** example above.

References addition operator **+** 7.6.2; binary operators 7.6; bitwise AND operator **&** 7.6.6; bitwise OR operator **|** 7.6.8; bitwise XOR operator **^** 7.6.7; comma operator 7.10; conditional expression **?:** 7.8; conditional statement 8.5; expression statement 8.2; function calls 7.4.3; initializers 4.6; iterative statements 8.6; logical and **&&** and or **||** 7.7; multiplication operator ***** 7.6.1; **return** statement 8.9; **strcmp** function 13.2; usual binary conversions 6.3.4

7.13 DISCARDED VALUES

There are three contexts in which an expression can appear but its value is not used:

1. an expression statement
2. the first operand of a comma expression
3. the initialization and increment expressions in a **for** statement

In these contexts we say that the expression's value is discarded.

When the value of an expression without side effects is discarded, the compiler may presume that a programming error has been made and issue a warning. Side-effect-producing operations include assignment and function calls. The compiler may also issue a warning message if the main operator of a discarded expression has no side effect.

Example

```
extern void f();
f(x);       /* These expressions do not */
i++;        /* justify any warning about */
a = b;      /* discarded values.   */
```

These statements, though valid, may elicit warning messages:

```
extern int g();
g(x);             /* The result of g is discarded. */
x + 7;            /* Addition has no defined side effects. */
x + (a *= 2);     /* The result of the last operation to be
                     performed, "+", is discarded. */
```

The programmer can avoid warnings about discarded values by using a cast to type **void** to indicate that the value is purposely being discarded:

```
extern int g();
(void) g(x);      /* Returned value is purposely discarded */
(void)(x + 7);    /* This is pretty silly, but presumably
                     the programmer has a purpose. */
```

C compilers typically do not issue warnings when the value of a function call is discarded, because traditionally functions that returned no result had to be declared of type "function returning **int**." Although ISO C gives compilers more information, vendors try to be compatible with old code.

If a compiler determines that the main operator of a discarded expression has no side effect, it may choose not to generate code for that operator (whereupon its operands become discarded values and may be recursively subjected to the same treatment).

References assignments 7.9; casts 7.5.1; comma operator 7.10; **for** statement 8.6.3; function calls 7.4.3; expressions statements 8.2; **void** type 5.9

7.14 OPTIMIZATION OF MEMORY ACCESSES

As a general rule, a compiler is free to generate any code equivalent in computational behavior to the program as written. The compiler is explicitly granted certain freedoms to rearrange code, as described in section 7.12. It may also generate no code for an expression when the expression has no side effects and its value is discarded, as described in section 7.13.

Example

Some compilers may also reorganize the code in such a way that it does not always refer to memory as many times, or in the same order, as specified in the program. For example, if a certain array element is referred to more than once, the compiler may cleverly arrange to fetch it only once to gain speed; in effect, it might rewrite this code:

```
int x,a[10];
...
x = a[j] * a[j] * a[j];    /* Cube the table entry. */
```

causing it to be executed as if it had been written like this:

```
int x,a[10];
register int temp;
...
temp = a[j];
x = temp * temp * temp;   /* Cube the table entry. */
```

For most applications, including nearly all portable applications, such optimization techniques are a very good thing, because the speed of a program may be improved by a factor of two or better without altering its effective computational behavior. However, this may be a problem when writing interrupt handlers and certain other machine-dependent programs in C. In this case, the programmer should use the ISO C type qualifier **volatile** to control some memory accesses.

References **volatile** 4.4.5

7.15 C++ COMPATIBILITY

7.15.1 Changes in sizeof Expressions

In C++, it is invalid to declare types in expressions, such as casts or **sizeof**. Also, the values of some **sizeof** expressions can be different in C and C++, for reasons of scoping changes and the type of character literals.

Example

```
i = sizeof(struct S { ... }); /* OK in C, not in C++ */
```

Example

The value of **sizeof(T)** could be different in some cases in which **T** is redefined.

The value of **sizeof('a')** will be **sizeof(int)** in C, but it will be **sizeof(char)** in C++.

The value of **sizeof(e)**, for an enumeration constant **e**, will be **sizeof(int)** in C, but it may be different in C++.

References character literals 2.8.5; enumeration types 5.13.1; scoping differences 4.9.2; **sizeof** 7.5.2

7.16 EXERCISES

1. Which of the following expressions are valid in traditional C? For the ones that are valid, what type does the expression have? Assume that **f** is of type **float**, **i** is of type **int**, **cp** is of type **char ***, and **ip** is of type **int ***.

   (a) **cp+0x23** (f) **f==0**
   (b) **i+f** (g) **!ip**
   (c) **++f** (h) **cp && cp**
   (d) **ip[i]** (i) **f%2**
   (e) **cp?i:f** (j) **f+=i**

2. Assume **p1** and **p2** have type **char ***. Rewrite the following two statements without using the increment or decrement operators.

   (a) ***++p1=*++p2;**
   (b) ***p1--=*p2--;**

3. A "bit mask" is an integer consisting of a specified sequence of binary zeroes and ones. Write macros that produce the following bit masks. If the macro arguments are constants, the result should also be a constant. You can assume a two's-complement representation for integers but

your macros should not depend on how many bits are in an integer or whether the computer is a big-endian or little-endian.

(a) **`low_zeroes(n)`**, a word in which the low-order *n* bits are zeroes and all other bits are ones.

(b) **`low_ones(n)`**, a word whose low-order *n* bits are ones and all other bits are zeroes.

(c) **`mid_zeroes(width,offset)`**, a word whose low-order *offset* bits are ones, whose next higher *width* bits are zeroes, and all other bits are ones.

(d) **`mid_ones(width,offset)`**, a word whose low-order *offset* bits are zeroes, whose next higher *width* bits are ones, and all other bits are zeroes

4. Is **`j++==++j`** a valid expression? What about **`j++&&++j`**? If **`j`** begins with the value 0, what is the result of each of the expressions?

5. The following table lists pairs of types of the left- and right-hand sides of a simple assignment expression. Which of the combinations are allowable in ISO C?

	Left-side type	Right-side type
(a)	**`short`**	**`signed short`**
(b)	**`char *`**	**`const char *`**
(c)	**`int (*)[5]`**	**`int (*)[]`**
(d)	**`short`**	**`const short`**
(e)	**`int (*)()`**	**`signed (*)(int x, float d)`**
(f)	**`int *`**	**`t *`** (where: **`typedef int t`**)

6. If the variable **`x`** has the type **`struct{int f;}`** and the variable **`y`** has a separately defined type **`struct{int f;}`**, is **`x=y`** valid in ISO C?

8

Statements

The C language provides the usual assortment of statements found in most algebraic programming languages, including conditional statements, loops, and the ubiquitous "goto." We describe each in turn after some general comments about syntax:

statement :
  expression-statement
  labeled-statement
  compound-statement
  conditional-statement
  iterative-statement
  switch-statement
  break-statement
  continue-statement
  return-statement
  goto-statement
  null-statement

conditional-statement :
  if-statement
  if-else-statement

iterative-statement :
  do-statement
  while-statement
  for-statement

8.1 GENERAL SYNTACTIC RULES FOR STATEMENTS

Although C statements will be familiar to programmers used to ALGOL-like languages, there are a few syntactic differences that often cause confusion and errors.

As in Pascal or Ada, semicolons typically appear between consecutive statements in C. However, in C the semicolon is not a statement separator, but rather simply a part of the syntax of certain statements. The only C statement that does not require a terminating semicolon is the compound statement (or block), which is delimited by braces (**{}**) instead of the more usual **begin** and **end** keywords:

```
a = b;
{ b = c; d = e; }
x = y;
```

Another rule for C statements is that "control" expressions appearing in conditional and iterative statements must be enclosed in parentheses. There is no special keyword following control expressions, such as "then," "loop," or "do"; the remainder of the statement immediately follows the expression:

```
if (a<b) x=y;
while (n<10) n++;
```

Finally, the assignment statement in other languages is an assignment *expression* in C. It can appear as part of more complicated expressions, or can be followed by a semicolon allowing it to stand by itself:

```
if ((x=y)>3) a=b;
```

References assignment expression 7.9; compound statement 8.4; conditional statements 8.5; iterative statements 8.6

8.2 EXPRESSION STATEMENTS

Any expression can be treated as a statement by writing the expression followed by a semicolon:

expression-statement :
    expression **;**

The statement is executed by evaluating the expression and then discarding the resulting value, if any.

An expression statement is useful only if evaluation of the expression involves a side effect, such as assigning a value to a variable or performing input or output. Usually the expression is an assignment, an increment or decrement operation, or a function call.

Example

```
speed = distance / time;  /* assign a quotient */
++event_count;            /* Add 1 to event_count.*/
printf("Again?");         /* Call the function printf.*/
pattern &= mask;          /* Remove bits from pattern */
(x<y) ? ++x : ++y;        /* Increment smaller of x and y */
```

The last statement, though valid, might be written more clearly with an **if** statement:

```
if (x < y) ++x;
else ++y;
```

The compiler is not obligated to evaluate an expression, or a portion of an expression, that has no side effects and whose result is discarded. (See section 7.13.)

References assignment expressions 7.9; discarded expressions 7.13; expressions ch. 7; function call 7.4.3; increment expressions 7.5.8, 7.4.4

8.3 LABELED STATEMENTS

A label can be used to mark any statement so that control may be transferred to the statement by a **goto** or **switch** statement. There are three kinds of labels. A named label may appear on any statement and is used in conjunction with the **goto** statement. A **case** label or **default** label may appear only on a statement within the body of a **switch** statement:

labeled-statement :
  label : *statement*

label :
  named-label
  case-label
  default-label

A label cannot appear by itself but must always be attached to a statement. If it is desired to place a label by itself, for example at the end of a compound statement, it may be attached to a null statement.

Named labels are discussed further in the description of the **goto** statement. The **case** and **default** labels are discussed with the **switch** statement.

References **goto** statement 8.10; null statement 8.11; **switch** statement 8.7

8.4 COMPOUND STATEMENTS

A compound statement—also called a block—consists of zero or more declarations followed by zero or more statements, all enclosed in braces:

> *compound-statement* :
> **{** *declaration-list*$_{opt}$ *statement-list*$_{opt}$ **}**
>
> *declaration-list* :
> *declaration*
> *declaration-list declaration*
>
> *statement-list* :
> *statement*
> *statement-list statement*

A compound statement may appear anywhere a statement does. When the compound statement has no declarations, it just represents a group of statements. When the compound statement has declarations, it brings into existence a new scope. If there are declarations, they must come before any statements.

A compound statement is normally executed by first processing all the declarations one at a time, in sequence, and then executing all the statements one at a time, in sequence. Execution ceases when the last statement has been executed or when control is transferred out of the compound statement through execution of a **goto**, **return**, **continue**, or **break** statement.

It is also possible to jump to a labeled statement within a compound statement by using a **goto** or **switch** statement outside the compound statement. When that happens, storage is allocated for any **auto** or **register** variables declared in the compound statement, but no initialization expressions for those variables are evaluated and no initialization occurs. Execution then begins at the statement to which control was transferred and continues in sequence until the last statement has been executed or until control is transferred out of the compound statement through execution of a **goto**, **return**, **continue**, or **break** statement.

An unlabeled compound statement used as the body of a **switch** statement cannot be executed normally, but only through transfer of control to labeled statements within it. Therefore, initializations of **auto** and **register** variables in such a compound statement never occur and their presence is *a priori* an error.

Example

```
switch (i) {
          int sum = 0;      /* ERROR! sum is NOT set to 0 */
case 1:   return sum;
default:  return sum+1;
}
```

References **auto** storage class 4.3; **break** and **continue** statements 8.8; declarations ch. 4; **goto** statement 8.10; **register** storage class 4.3; **return** statement 8.9; scope 4.2.1

8.4.1 Declarations within Compound Statements

Each identifier declared at the beginning of a compound statement has a scope that extends from its declaration point to the end of the block. It is visible throughout that scope except when hidden by a declaration of the same identifier in an inner block.

An identifier declared at the beginning of a compound statement without a storage class specifier is assumed to have storage class **extern** if the identifier has a function type, and is assumed to have storage class **auto** in all other cases. It is invalid for an identifier of function type to have any storage class except **extern** when it is declared at the beginning of a block.

If a variable or function is declared in a compound statement with storage class **extern**, then no storage is allocated and no initialization expression is permitted. The declaration refers to an external variable or function defined elsewhere, either in the same source file or a different source file.

If a variable is declared in a compound statement with storage class **auto** or **register**, then it is effectively reallocated every time the compound statement is entered and deallocated when the compound statement is exited. If there is an initialization expression for the variable, then the expression is reevaluated and the variable reinitialized every time the compound statement is entered normally. (The initialization expression is not evaluated and the variable is not initialized when control is passed to a statement with in the compound statement via a **goto** or **switch** statement from outside.) If there is no initialization expression for the variable, then the value of the variable is initially undefined every time the compound statement is executed; the value of the variable does not carry over from one execution of the compound statement to the next.

If a variable is declared in a compound statement with storage class **static**, then it is effectively allocated once, prior to program execution, just like any other static variable. If there is an initialization expression for the variable, then the expression is evaluated only once, prior to program execution, and the variable retains its value from one execution of the compound statement to the next.

References **auto** storage class 4.3; **extern** storage class 4.3; **goto** statement 8.10; initial values 4.2.8; initializers 4.6; **register** storage class 4.3; scope 4.2.1; **static** storage class 4.3; **switch** statement 8.7; visibility 4.2.2

8.4.2 Use of Compound Statements

Compound statements without declarations are particularly useful as parts of other control statements, so that more than one statement can be executed conditionally or in a loop.

With declarations, compound statements can also introduce additional variables with reduced visibility. This often helps to make a program clearer by restricting the area over which a variable—for example, a loop variable—is accessible.

Example

This compound statement is used simply to group a set of statements:

```
if (error_seen) {
    ++error_count;
    print_error_message();
}
```

This compound statement includes a declaration:

```
if (first_time) {
    /* Clear the array. */
    int i;
    for (i = 0; i < 10; i++) a[i] = 0;
    first_time = 0;    /* Reset first-time flag. */
}
```

C permits unrestricted jumps into compound statements, but this is bad programming style. In fact, none of the languages Ada, ALGOL 60, Modula-2, Pascal, or PL/I permit jumps into blocks. (Neither does C++.) The particular danger in C is not having initializations occur.

Example

The following code fragment is unlikely to work if the statement labeled **L:** is the target of a jump from outside the compound statement, because the variable `sum` will not be initialized. Furthermore, it is not possible to tell if any such jump does occur without examining the entire body of the enclosing function:

```
{
        extern int a[100];
        int i, sum = 0;
        ...
    L:
        for (i = 0; i < 100; i++)
            sum += a[i];
        ...
}
```

References declarations ch. 4; **goto** statement 8.10; labeled statement 8.3

8.5 CONDITIONAL STATEMENTS

There are two forms of conditional statement: with or without an **else** clause. Note that C, unlike other programming languages such as Pascal, does not use the keyword "then" as part of the syntax of its **if** statement:

conditional-statement :
  if-statement
  if-else-statement

if-statement :
    if (*expression*) *statement*

if-else-statement :
    if (*expression*) *statement* **else** *statement*

For each form of **if** statement the expression within parentheses is first evaluated. If this value is nonzero (section 8.1), then the statement immediately following the parentheses is executed. If the value of the control expression is zero and there is an **else** clause, then the statement following the keyword **else** is executed instead; but if the value of the control expression is zero and there is no **else** clause, then execution continues immediately with the statement following the conditional statement.

References control expression 8.1

8.5.1 Multiway Conditional Statements

A multiway decision can be expressed as a cascaded series of **if-else** statements, where each **if** statement but the last has another **if** statement in its **else** clause. Such a series looks like this:

```
if (expression1)
    statement1
else if (expression2)
    statement2
else if (expression3)
    statement3
...
else
    statementn
```

Example

Here is a three-way decision: the function **signum** returns –1 if its argument is less than zero, 1 if its argument is greater than zero, and otherwise 0:

```
int signum(int x)
{
    if (x > 0) return 1;
    else if (x < 0) return -1;
    else return 0;
}
```

Compare this with the version of **signum** that uses conditional expressions shown in section 7.8.

The **switch** statement handles the specific kind of multiway decision where the value of an expression is to be compared against a fixed set of constants.

References **switch** statement 8.7

8.5.2 The Dangling-Else Problem

An ambiguity arises because a conditional statement may contain another conditional statement. In some situations it may not be apparent to which of several conditional statements an **else** might belong. The ambiguity is resolved in an arbitrary but customary way: an **else** part is always assumed to belong to the innermost **if** statement possible.

Example

To illustrate the ambiguity, the following example is indented in a misleading fashion:

```
if ((k >= 0) && (k < TABLE_SIZE))
    if (table[k] >= 0)
        printf("Entry %d is %d\n", k, table[k]);
else printf("Error: index %d out of range.\n",k);
```

A casual reader might assume that the **else** part was intended to be an alternative to the outer **if** statement. That is, the error message should be printed when the test

```
(k >= 0) && (k < TABLE_SIZE)
```

is false. However, if we change the wording of the last error message to

```
else printf("Error: entry %d is negative.\n", k);
```

then it might appear that the programmer intended the **else** part to be executed when the test **table[k]>=0** is false. The second interpretation of the code fragment above will work as intended, while the first will not. The first interpretation can be made to work by introducing a compound statement:

```
if (k >= 0 && k < TABLE_SIZE) {
    if (table[k] >= 0)
        printf("Entry %d is %d\n", k, table[k]);
}
else printf("Error: index %d out of range.\n", k);
```

To reduce confusion, the second interpretation could also use a compound statement:

```
if (k >= 0 && k < TABLE_SIZE) {
    if (table[k] >= 0)
        printf("Entry %d is %d\n", k, table[k]);
    else printf("Error: entry %d is negative.\n",k);
}
```

Confusion can be eliminated entirely if braces are always used to surround statements controlled by an **if** statement. However, this conservative rule can clutter a program with unnecessary braces. It seems to us that a good stylistic compromise between confusion and clutter is to use braces with an **if** statement whenever the statement controlled by the **if** is anything but an expression or null statement.

References compound statement 8.4; expression statement 8.2; null statement 8.11

8.6 ITERATIVE STATEMENTS

Three kinds of iterative statements are provided in C:

iterative-statement :
  while-statement
  do-statement
  for-statement

The **while** statement tests an exit condition before each execution of a statement. The **do** statement tests an exit condition after each execution of a statement. The **for** statement provides a special syntax that is convenient for initializing and updating one or more control variables as well as testing an exit condition. The statement embedded within an iteration statement is somctimes called the body of the iterative statement.

8.6.1 While Statement

Unlike other programming languages such as Pascal, C does not use the keyword "do" as part of the syntax of its **while** statement:

while-statement ;
  while (***expression*)** *statement*

The **while** statement is executed by first evaluating the control expression. If the result is true (not zero), then the statement is executed. The entire process is then repeated, alternately evaluating the expression and then, if the value is true, executing the statement. The value of the expression can change from time to time because of side effects in the statement or in the expression itself.

The execution of the **while** statement is complete when the control expression evaluates to false (zero), or when control is transferred out of the body of the **while** statement by a **return**, **goto**, or **break** statement. Also, the **continue** statement can modify the execution of a **while** statement.

Example

The following function uses a **while** loop to raise an integer **base** to the power specified by the nonnegative integer **exponent** (with no checking for overflow). The method used is that of repeated squaring of the base and decoding of the exponent in binary notation to determine when to multiply the base into the result.

To see why this works, note that the **while** loop maintains the invariant condition that the correct answer is **result** times **base** raised to the **exponent** power. When eventually **exponent** is 0, this condition degenerates to stating that **result** has the correct value.

```
int pow(int base, int exponent)
{
    int result = 1;
    while (exponent > 0) {
        if ( exponent % 2 ) result *= base;
        base *= base;
        exponent /= 2;
    }
    return result;
}
```

Example

A **while** loop may usefully have a null statement for its body:

```
while ( *char_pointer++ );
```

In this code, a character pointer is advanced along by the **++** operator until a null character is found, and it is left pointing to the character after the null. This is a compact idiom for locating the end of a string. (Notice that the test expression is interpreted as ***(char_pointer++)**, not as **(*char_pointer)++**, which would increment the character pointed to by **char_pointer**.)

Example

Another common idiom uses two pointers to copy a character string:

```
while ( *dest_pointer++ = *source_pointer++ );
```

Characters are copied until the terminating null character is found (and also copied). Of course, in writing this the programmer should have reason to believe that the destination area will be large enough to contain all the characters to be copied.

References **break** and **continue** statements 8.8; control expression 8.1; **goto** statement 8.10; null statement 8.11; **return** statement 8.9

8.6.2 Do Statement

The **do** statement differs from the **while** statement in that the **do** statement always executes the body at least once, whereas the **while** statement may never execute its body:

do-statement :
    do *statement* **while** **(** *expression* **)** **;**

The **do** statement is executed by first executing the embedded statement. Then the control expression is evaluated; if the value is true (not zero), then the entire process is repeated, alternately executing the statement, evaluating the control expression, and then, if the value is true, repeating the process.

The execution of the **do** statement is complete when the control expression evaluates to zero or when control is transferred out of the body of the **do** statement by a

return, **goto**, or **break** statement. Also, the **continue** statement can modify the execution of a **do** statement.

The C **do** statement is similar in function to the "repeat-until" statement in Pascal. The C **do** statement is unusual in that it terminates execution when the control expression is false, whereas a Pascal repeat-until statement terminates if its control expression is true. C is more consistent in this regard: all iteration constructs in C (**while**, **do**, and **for**) terminate when the control expression is false.

Example

This program fragment reads and processes characters, halting after a newline character has been processed:

```
int ch;
do
    process( ch = getchar());
while (ch != '\n');
```

The same effect could have been obtained by moving the computations into the control expression of a **while** statement, but the intent would be less clear:

```
int ch;
while( ch = getchar(ch),
       process(ch),
       ch != '\n' )  /*empty*/ ;
```

Example

It is possible to write a **do** statement whose body is a null statement:

```
do ; while (expression );
```

However, it is more common to write this loop using a **while** statement:

```
while ( expression );
```

References **break** and **continue** statements 8.8; control expression 8.1; **goto** statement 8.10; null statement 8.11; **return** statement 8.9; **while** statement 8.6.1

8.6.3 For Statement

C's **for** statement is considerably more general than the "increment and test" statements found in most other languages. After explaining the execution of the **for** statement, we give several examples of how it can be used:

for-statement :
    for *for-expressions statement*

for-expressions :
    ($expression_{opt}$ **;** $expression_{opt}$ **;** $expression_{opt}$ **)**

A **for** statement consists of the keyword **for**, followed by three expressions separated by semicolons and enclosed in parentheses, followed by a statement. Each of the three expressions within the parentheses is optional and may be omitted, but the two semicolons separating them and the parentheses surrounding them are mandatory.

Typically, the first expression is used to initialize a loop variable, the second tests whether the loop should continue or terminate, and the third updates the loop variable (for example, by incrementing it). However, in principle the expressions may be used to perform any computation that is useful within the framework of the **for** control structure. The **for** statement is executed as follows:

1. If present, the first expression is evaluated and the value is discarded.
2. If present, the second expression is evaluated like a control expression. If the result is zero, then execution of the **for** statement is complete. Otherwise (if the value is not zero or if the second expression was omitted), proceed to step 3.
3. The body of the **for** statement is executed.
4. If present, the third expression is evaluated and the value is discarded.
5. Return to step 2.

The execution of a **for** statement is terminated when the second (control) expression evaluates to zero or when control is transferred outside the **for** statement by a **return**, **goto**, or **break** statement. The execution of a **continue** statement within the body of the **for** statement has the effect of causing a jump to step 4 above.

Example

Stated another way, a **for** loop of the form

```
for (expression1; expression2; expression3) statement
```

is similar (except for the action of the **continue** statement) to

```
expression1;
while (expression2) {
    statement
    expression3;
}
```

where if ***expression***$_1$ or ***expression***$_3$ is not present in the **for** statement, then it is simply omitted in the expansion also, and if ***expression***$_2$ is not present in the **for** statement, then the constant **1** is used for it in the expansion (and so the **while** loop never terminates due to the control expression becoming zero).

References **break** and **continue** statements 8.8; control expression 8.1; discarded expressions 7.13; **goto** statement 8.10; **return** statement 8.9; **while** statement 8.6.1

8.6.4 Using the For Statement

Example

Typically, the first expression in a **for** statement is used to initialize a variable, the second expression to test the variable in some way, and the third to modify the variable toward some goal. For example, to print the integers from 0 to 9 and their squares, one might write

```
for (j = 0; j < 10; j++)
    printf("%d %d\n", j, j*j);
```

Here the first expression initializes **j**; the second expression tests whether it has reached 10 yet (if it has, the loop is terminated); and the third expression increments **j**.

Example

There are two common ways in C to write a loop that "never terminates" (sometimes known as a "do forever" loop):

for (;;) *statement*

while (1) *statement*

The loops can still be terminated by a **break**, **goto**, or **return** statement within the body.

Example

The **pow** function used above to illustrate the **while** statement can be rewritten using a **for** statement:

```
int pow(int base, int exponent)
{
    int result = 1;
    for (; exponent > 0; exponent /= 2) {
        if ( exponent % 2 )
            result *= base;
        base *= base;
    }
    return result;
}
```

This form stresses the fact that the loop is controlled by the variable **exponent** as it progresses toward 0 by repeated divisions by 2. Note that the loop variable **exponent** still had to be declared outside the **for** statement. The **for** statement itself does not include the declaration of any variables. A common programming error is to forget to declare a variable such as **i** or **j** used in a **for** statement, only to discover that some other variable named **i** or **j** elsewhere in the program is inadvertently modified by the loop.

Example

Here is a simple sorting routine that uses the insertion sort algorithm.

```
void insertsort(int v[], int n)
{
    register int i, j, temp;
    for (i = 1; i < n; i++) {
        temp = v[i];
        for (j = i-1; j >= 0 && v[j] > temp; j--)
            v[j+1] = v[j];
        v[j+1] = temp;
    }
}
```

The outer **for** loop counts **i** up from 1 (inclusive) to **n** (exclusive). At each step, elements **v[0]** through **v[i-1]** have already been sorted, and elements **v[i]** through **v[n-1]** remain to be sorted. The inner loop counts **j** down from **i-1**, moving elements of the array up one at a time, until the right place to insert **v[i]** has been found. (That is why this is called "insertion sort.") This algorithm is not a good method for very large, unordered arrays, because in the worst case the time to perform the sort is proportional to $\mathbf{n}^2$ (i.e., it is $\mathbf{O}(\mathbf{n}^2)$).

Example

The insertion sort can be improved from $\mathbf{O}(\mathbf{n}^2)$ to $\mathbf{O}(\mathbf{n}^{1.25})$ by simply wrapping a third loop around the first two and introducing **gap** in a few places where **insertsort** used the constant 1. The following sort function, using the shell sort algorithm, is similar to one called **shell** that appeared as an example in Kernighan and Ritchie's *The C Programming Language*, but we have modified it here in three ways, two of them suggested by Knuth and Sedgewick (see the Preface), to make it faster:

```
void shellsort(register int v[], int n)
{
    register int gap, i, j, temp;
    gap = 1;
    do (gap = 3*gap + 1); while (gap <= n);
    for (gap /= 3; gap > 0; gap /= 3)
        for (i = gap; i < n; i++) {
            temp = v[i];
            for (j=i-gap; (j>=0)&&(v[j]>temp); j-=gap)
                v[j+gap] = v[j];
            v[j+gap] = temp;
        }
}
```

The improvements are: (1) In the original **shell** function, the value of **gap** started at **n/2** and was divided by two each time through the outer loop. In this version, **gap** is initialized by finding the smallest number in the series (1, 4, 13, 40, 121, ...) that is not greater than **n**, and **gap** is divided by three each time through the outer loop. This makes the sort run 20–30% faster. (This choice of the initial value of **gap** has been shown to be superior to using **n** as the initial value.) (2) The assignments in the inner loop were reduced from three to one. (3) The **register** and **void** storage classes were added. In some implementations, **register** declarations can improve performance dramatically (40% in one case).

Example

The **for** statement need not be used only for counting over integer values. Here is an example of scanning down a linked chain of structures, where the loop variable is a pointer:

```
struct intlist {
    struct intlist *link;
    int data;
};

void print_duplicates(struct intlist *p)
{
    for (; p; p = p->link) {
        struct intlist *q;
        for (q = p->link; q; q = q->link)
            if (q->data == p->data) {
                printf("Duplicate data %d", p->data);
                break;
            }
    }
}
```

The structure **intlist** is used to implement a linked list of records, each record containing some data. Given such a linked list, the function **print_duplicates** prints the data for every redundant record in the list. The first **for** statement uses the formal parameter **p** as its loop variable—it scans down the given list. The loop terminates when a null pointer is encountered. For every record, all the records following it are examined by the inner **for** statement, which scans a pointer **q** along the list in the same fashion.

References pointer types 5.3; **register** storage class 4.3; selection operator **->** 7.4.2; structure types 5.6; **void** type 5.9

8.6.5 Multiple Control Variables

Sometimes it is convenient to have more than one variable controlling a **for** loop. In this connection the comma operator is especially useful, because it can be used to group several assignment expressions into a single expression.

Example

The following function reverses a linked list by modifying the links.

```
struct intlist { struct intlist *link; int data; };

struct intlist *reverse(struct intlist *p)
{
    struct intlist *here, *previous, *next;
    for (here = p, previous = NULL ;
          here != NULL ;
          next = here->link, here->link = previous,
            previous = here, here = next) /*empty*/ ;
    return previous;
}
```

Example

The function **string_equal** below accepts two strings and returns 1 if they are equal and 0 otherwise.

```
int string_equal(const char *s1, const char *s2)
{
    char *p1, *p2;
    for (p1=s1, p2=s2; *p1 && *p2; p1++, p2++)
        if (*p1 != *p2) return 0;
    return *p1 == *p2;
}
```

The **for** statement is used to scan two pointer variables in parallel down the two strings. The expression **p1++, p2++** causes each of the two pointers to be advanced to the next character. If the strings are found to differ at some position, the return statement is used to terminate execution of the entire function and return 0. If a null character is found in either string, as determined by the expression ***p1 && *p2**, then the loop is terminated normally, whereupon the second **return** statement determines whether or not both strings ended with a null character in the same place. (The function would still work correctly if the expression ***p1** were used instead of ***p1 && *p2**. It would also be a bit faster, though not as pleasantly symmetrical.)

References **break** and **continue** statements 8.8; comma operator 7.10; pointer types 5.3; selection operator **->** 7.4.2; structure types 5.6

8.7 SWITCH STATEMENTS

The **switch** statement is a multiway branch based on the value of a control expression. In use, it is similar to the "case" statement in Pascal or Ada, but it is implemented more like the FORTRAN "computed goto" statement:

switch-statement :
  switch **(** *expression* **)** *statement*

case-label :
  case *constant-expression*

default-label :
  default

The control expression that follows the keyword **switch** must have an integral type and is subject to the usual unary conversions. The expression following the keyword **case** must be an integral constant expression (section 7.11.2). The statement embedded within a **switch** statement is sometimes called the body of the **switch** statement; it is usually a compound statement but need not be.

A **case** label or **default** label is said to belong to the innermost **switch** statement that contains it. Any statement within the body of a **switch** statement—or the body itself—may be labeled with a **case** label or a **default** label. In fact, the same statement may be labeled with several **case** labels and a **default** label. A **case** label or

default label is not permitted to appear other than within the body of a **switch** statement, and no two **case** labels belonging to the same **switch** statement may have constant expressions with the same value. At most one **default** label may belong to any one **switch** statement. A **switch** statement is executed as follows:

1. The control expression is evaluated.
2. If the value of the control expression is equal to that of the constant expression in some **case** label belonging to the **switch** statement, then program control is transferred to the point indicated by that **case** label as if by a **goto** statement.
3. If the value of the control expression is not equal to any **case** label, but there is a **default** label that belongs to the **switch** statement, then program control is transferred to the point indicated by that **default** label.
4. If the value of the control expression is not equal to any **case** label and there is no **default** label, no statement of the body of the **switch** statement is executed; program control is transferred to whatever follows the **switch** statement.

When comparing the control expression and the **case** expressions, the **case** expressions are converted to the type of the control expression (after the usual unary conversions).

When control is transferred to a **case** or **default** label, execution continues through successive statements, ignoring any additional **case** or **default** labels that are encountered, until the end of the **switch** statement is reached or until control is transferred out of the **switch** statement by a **goto**, **return**, **break**, or **continue** statement.

Although ISO C allows the control expression to be of any integer type, some older compilers do not permit it to be of type **long** or **unsigned long**. ISO C also permits an implementation to limit the number of separate **case** labels in a **switch** statement to 257—that is, more than enough to handle all values of a typical (8-bit) **char** type.

References **break** and **continue** statements 8.8; constant expressions 7.11; **goto** statement 8.10; integer types 5.1; labeled statement 8.3; **return** statement 8.9

8.7.1 Use of Switch Statements

Normally, the body of a **switch** statement is a compound statement whose inner, top-level statements have **case** and/or **default** labels. It should be noted that **case** and **default** labels do not themselves alter the flow of program control; execution proceeds unimpeded by such labels. The **break** statement can be used within the body of a **switch** statement to terminate its execution.

Example

```
switch (x) {
    case 1: printf("*");
    case 2: printf("**");
    case 3: printf("***");
    case 4: printf("****");
}
```

In the **switch** statement above, if the value of **x** is 2, then nine asterisks will be printed. The reason for this is that the **switch** statement transfers control to the **case** label with the expression 2. The call to **printf** with argument **"**"** is executed; next the call to **printf** with argument **"***"** is executed; and finally the call to **printf** with argument **"****"** is executed. If it is desired to terminate execution of the **switch** body after a single call to **printf** in each case, then the **break** statement should be used:

```
switch (x) {
    case 1: printf("*");
            break;
    case 2: printf("**");
            break;
    case 3: printf("***");
            break;
    case 4: printf("****");
            break;
}
```

While the last **break** statement in this example is logically unnecessary, it is a good thing to put in as a matter of style. It will help to prevent program errors in the event that a fifth **case** is later added to the **switch** statement.

We recommend sticking to this simple rule of style for **switch** statements: the body should always be a compound statement, and all labels belonging to the **switch** statement should appear on top-level statements within that compound statement. (The same stylistic guidelines apply as for **goto** statements.) Furthermore, every **case** (or **default**) label but the first should be preceded by one of two things: either a **break** statement that terminates the code for the previous **case** or a comment noting that the previous code is intended to drop in.

While this is considered good style, the language definition itself does not require that the body be a compound statement, or that **case** and **default** labels appear only at the "top level" of the compound statement, or that **case** and **default** labels appear in any particular order or on different statements.

Example

In the code fragment below, the comment tells the reader that the lack of a **break** statement after case **fatal** is intentional.

```
...
case fatal:
    printf("Fatal ");
    /* Drops through. */
case error:
    printf("Error");
    ++error_count;
    break;
...
```

Example

Here is an example of how good intentions can lead to chaos. The intent was to implement this simple program fragment as efficiently as possible:

```
if (prime(x)) process_prime(x);
else process_composite(x);
```

The function **prime** returns 1 if its argument is a prime number and 0 if the argument is a composite number. Program measurements indicated that most of the calls to **prime** were being made with small integers, so to avoid the overhead of calls to **prime** the code was changed to use a **switch** statement to handle the small integers, leaving the **default** label to handle larger numbers. By steadily compressing the code, the following was produced:

```
switch (x)
    default:
    if (prime(x))
        case 2: case 3: case 5: case 7:
            process_prime(x);
    else
        case 4: case 6: case 8: case 9: case 10:
            process_composite(x);
```

This is, frankly, the most bizarre **switch** statement we have ever seen that still has pretenses to being purposeful.

8.8 BREAK AND CONTINUE STATEMENTS

The **break** and **continue** statements are used to alter the flow of control inside loops and—in the case of **break**—in **switch** statements. It is stylistically better to use these statements than to use the **goto** statement to accomplish the same purpose:

break-statement :
  break;

continue-statement :
  continue;

Execution of a **break** statement causes execution of the smallest enclosing **while**, **do**, **for**, or **switch** statement to be terminated. Program control is immediately transferred to the point just beyond the terminated statement. It is an error for a **break** statement to appear where there is no enclosing iterative or **switch** statement.

A **continue** statement terminates the execution of the *body* of the smallest enclosing **while**, **do**, or **for** statement. Program control is immediately transferred to the end of the body, and the execution of the affected iterative statement continues from that point with a reevaluation of the loop test (or the increment expression, in the case of the **for** statement). It is an error for a **continue** statement to appear where there is no enclosing iterative statement.

The **continue** statement, unlike the **break** statement, has no interaction whatever with **switch** statements. A **continue** statement may appear within a **switch** statement, but it will affect only the smallest enclosing iterative statement, not the **switch** statement.

Example

The **break** and **continue** statements can be explained in terms of the **goto** statement. Consider the statements affected by a **break** or **continue** statement:

```
while ( expression ) statement
do statement while ( expression );
for (expression1; expression2; expression3) statement
switch ( expression ) statement
```

Imagine that all such statements were to be rewritten in this manner:

```
{ while (expression) {statement C:;} B:;}
{ do {statement C:;} while (expression); B:;}
{ for (expression1; expression2; expression3) {statement C:;} B:;}
{ switch (expression) statement B:; }
```

where in each case **B** and **C** are labels that appear nowhere else in the enclosing function. Then any occurrence of a **break** statement within the body of any of these statements is equivalent to "**goto B;**" and any occurrence of a **continue** statement within the body of any of these statements (except **switch**, where it is not permitted) is equivalent to "**goto C;**". This assumes that the loop bodies do not contain yet another loop containing the **break** or **continue**.

Example

The **break** statement is frequently used in two very important contexts: to terminate the processing of a particular **case** within a **switch** statement, and to terminate a loop prematurely. The first use is illustrated in conjunction with **switch** in section 8.7. The second use is illustrated by this example of filling an array with input characters, stopping when the array is full or when the input is exhausted.:

```
#include <stdio.h>
static char array[100];
int i, c;
...
for (i = 0; i < 100; i++) {
    c = getchar();
    if (c == EOF) break;    /* Quit if end-of-file. */
    array[i] = c;
}
/* Now i is the actual number of characters read. */
```

Note how **break** is used to handle the abnormal case. It is generally better style to handle the normal case in the loop test itself.

Example

Here is an example of the use of a **break** statement within a "do forever" loop. The idea is to find the smallest element in the array **a** (whose length is **N**) as efficiently as possible. It is assumed that the array may be modified temporarily:

```
int temp = a[0];
register int smallest = a[0];
register int *ptr = &a[N];   /* just beyond end of a */
...
for (;;) {
    while (*--ptr > smallest) ;
    if (ptr == &a[0]) break;
    a[0] = smallest = *ptr;
}
a[0] = temp;
```

The point is that most of the work is done by a very tight **while** loop, which scans the pointer **ptr** backward through the array, skipping elements that are larger than the smallest one found so far. (If the elements are in a random order, then once a reasonably small element has been found, most elements will be larger than that and so will be skipped.) The **while** loop cannot fall off the front of the array, because the smallest element so far is also stored in the first array element. When the **while** loop is done, if the scan has reached the front of the array, then the **break** statement terminates the outer loop. Otherwise **smallest** and **a[0]** are updated and the **while** loop is entered again.

Example

Compare the code above with a simpler, more obvious approach:

```
register int smallest = a[0];
register int j;
...
for (j = 1; j < n; ++j)
    if (a[j] < smallest) smallest = a[j];
```

This version is certainly easier to understand. However, on every iteration of the loop an explicit check (**j<n**) must be made for falling off the end of the array, as opposed to the implicit check made by the more clever code. Under certain circumstances where efficiency is paramount, the more complicated code may be justified; otherwise, the simpler, clearer loop should be used.

References **do** statement 8.6.2; **for** statement 8.6.3; **goto** statement 8.10; **switch** statement 8.7; **while** statement 8.6.1

8.9 RETURN STATEMENTS

A **return** statement is used to terminate the current function, perhaps returning a value:

return-statement :
  return *expression*$_{opt}$ **;**

Execution of a **return** statement causes execution of the current function to be terminated; program control is transferred to the caller of the function at the point immediately following the call.

If no expression appears in the **return** statement, then no value is returned from the function; this is always permitted, even if the function has a declared return type other than **void**. If the function is called from a context requiring a value, then the program's behavior is undefined. If program control reaches the end of a function body without encountering a **return** statement, then the effect is as if a **return** statement with no expression were executed.

If an expression appears in the **return** statement, then it is converted as if by assignment to the return type of the function in which the statement appears. The **return** statement is invalid if the conversion is not possible, or if the function was declared with return type **void**. The rules governing the agreement of the actual value returned with the declared return value in the function definition are discussed in section 9.8.

Example

Many programmers put parentheses around the expression in a **return** statement, although this is not necessary. It is probably a habit developed after putting parentheses around the expressions following **switch**, **if**, **while**, etc.

```
int twice(int x) { return (2*x); }
```

References discarded values 7.13; function call 7.4.3; function definition 9.1

8.10 GOTO STATEMENTS

A **goto** statement may be used to transfer control to any statement within a function:

goto-statement :
  goto *identifier* **;**

named-label :
  identifier

The identifier following the keyword **goto** must be the same as a named label on some statement within the current function. Execution of the **goto** statement causes an immediate transfer of program control to the point in the function indicated by the label; the statement labeled by the indicated name is executed next.

References labeled statement 8.3

8.10.1 Using the goto Statement

C permits a **goto** statement to transfer control to any other statement within a function, but certain kinds of branching can result in confusing programs, and the branching may hinder compiler optimizations.

The following rules should result in a more clear use of the **goto**:

1. Do not branch into the "then" or "else" arm of an **if** statement from outside the **if** statement.
2. Do not branch from the "then" arm to the "else" arm or back.
3. Do not branch into the body of a **switch** or iteration statement from outside the statement.
4. Do not branch into a compound statement from outside the statement.

Such branches should be avoided not only when using the **goto** statement, but also when placing **case** and **default** labels in a **switch** statement (which, in effect, executes a **goto** statement to get to the appropriate **case** label). Branching into the middle of a compound statement from outside it can be especially confusing, because such a branch bypasses the initialization of any variables declared at the top of the compound statement.

It is good programming style to use the **break**, **continue**, and **return** statements in preference to **goto** whenever possible.

Finally, the programmer wanting to produce a C program that executes as rapidly as possible should remember that the presence of any label—whether explicit, named labels or implicit labels required by **break** and **continue**—may inhibit compiler optimizations and therefore may slow down the C program.

References **break** and **continue** statements 8.8; control expression 8.1; **if** statement 8.5; labeled statement 8.3; **return** statement 8.9; **switch** statement 8.7

8.11 NULL STATEMENTS

The null statement consists simply of a semicolon:

null-statement :
 ;

The null statement is useful primarily in two situations. In the first case, a null body is used as the body of an iterative statement (**while**, **do**, or **for**). The second case is where a label is desired just before the right brace that terminates a compound statement. A label cannot simply precede the right brace, but must always be attached to a statement.

Example

The following loop needs no body because the control expression does all the work:

```
char *p;
...
while ( *p++ ); /* find the end of the string */
```

Example

The label **L** is placed on a null statement:

```
if (e) {
    ...
    goto L;     /* terminate this arm of the 'if' */
    ...
    L:;}
else ...
```

References **do** statement 8.6.2; **for** statement 8.6.2; labeled statement 8.3; **while** statement 8.6.1

8.12 C++ COMPATIBILITY

8.12.1 Compound Statements

C++ does not allow jumping into a compound statement in a way that would skip declarations with initializers.

Example

```
goto L;    /* Valid but unwise in C; invalid in C++ */
{
    int i = 10;
L:
    ...
}
```

References jumping into compound statements 8.4.2

8.13 EXERCISES

1. Rewrite the following statements without using **for**, **while**, or **do** statements.
   (a) `for(n=A;n<B;n++) sum+=n;`
   (b) `while(a<b) a++;`
   (c) `do sum+=*p; while (++p < q);`
2. What is the value of **j** at the end of the following program fragment?

```
{   int j=1;
    goto L;
    {
        static int i = 3;
    L:
        j = i;
    }
}
```

3. What is the value of **sum** after the following program fragment is executed?

```
int i,sum = 0;
for(i=0;i<10;i++) {
    switch(i) {
    case 0: case 1: case 3: case 5: sum++;
    default: continue;
    case 4: break;
    }
    break;
}
```

9

Functions

This chapter discusses the use of functions, and the details of declaring and defining functions, specifying formal parameters and return types, and calling functions. Some information on functions appears previously in this book: function declarators are described in section 4.5.4 and function types and declarations are discussed in section 5.8.

The description of functions has become more complicated since the original definition of C. ISO C introduced a new (better) way of declaring functions using function *prototypes* that specify more information about a function's parameters. The operation of a function call when a prototype has appeared is different from its operation without a prototype. Although the prototype and non-prototype forms are individually easy to understand, there are complicated rules for deciding what should happen when these two forms are mixed for the same function. (In C++, prototypes must be used.)

The presence of a function prototype is determined by the syntax of a function declarator (section 4.5.4). Briefly, in traditional C and when a prototype is *not* used:

1. Function arguments undergo automatic promotions (the usual argument conversions) before a call.
2. No checking of the type or number of arguments occurs.
3. Any function can potentially take a variable number of arguments.

In contrast to this, when the ISO C prototypes *are* used:

1. Function arguments are converted, as if by assignment, to the declared types of the formal parameters.
2. The number and types of the arguments must match the declared types, or else the program is in error.
3. Functions taking a variable number of arguments are designated explicitly, and the unspecified arguments undergo the usual argument conversions

Whether or not to use prototypes in C programs is a tricky portability issue. To remain compatible with non-ISO implementations, you must avoid them. To remain compatible with C++, you must use them. You could write both forms, using conditional compilation directives to decide which to include, but that is awkward, too. The following sections discuss both prototype-form and non-prototype-form function declarations, and discuss some portability options.

9.1 FUNCTION DEFINITIONS

A function definition introduces a new function and provides the following information:

1. the type of the value returned by the function, if any
2. the type and number of the formal parameters
3. the visibility of the function outside the file in which it is defined
4. the code that is to be executed when the function is called

The syntax for a function definition is shown below. Function definitions can appear only at the top level of a C source file, or *translation unit*.

translation-unit :
  top-level-declaration
  translation-unit top-level-declaration

top-level-declaration :
  declaration
  function-definition

function-definition :
  function-specifier compound-statement

function-specifier :
  declaration-specifiers$_{opt}$ *declarator declaration-list*$_{opt}$

declaration-list :
  declaration
  declaration-list declaration

The syntax for other top-level declarations was discussed in Chapter 4. Unlike other top-level declarations, a function definition need not include any storage class specifiers, type specifiers, or type qualifiers; there is no syntactic ambiguity in that case, and the single type specifier **int** will be assumed.

Within a *function-specifier*, the declarator must contain a *function-declarator* that specifies the function identifier immediately before the left parenthesis. The syntax of a function declarator was shown in section 4.5.4 and is repeated below for convenience:

function-declarator :
  direct-declarator **(** *parameter-type-list* **)** (ISO C)
  direct-declarator **(** *identifier-list*$_{opt}$ **)**

parameter-type-list :
  parameter-list
  parameter-list **, ...**

parameter-list :
  parameter-declaration
  parameter-list **,** *parameter-declaration*

parameter-declaration :
  declaration-specifiers declarator
  declaration-specifiers abstract-declarator$_{opt}$

identifier-list :
  identifier
  identifier-list **,** *identifier*

If the function declarator that names the defined function includes a *parameter-type list*, the function definition is said to be in prototype form; otherwise it is in non-prototype, or traditional, form. In prototype form the parameter names and types are listed in the declarator. In traditional form, the parameter names are listed in the declarator and the types are specified (in any order) in the *declaration-list*$_{opt}$ following the declarator. If any parameter is not declared, its type defaults to **int**.

Example

```
int f(int i, int j) { ... }          /* prototype form */
int f(i,j) int i,j; { ... }          /* traditional form */
int f(i,j) int j; int i; { ... } /* traditional form */
```

There are several constraints on the form of the *function-specifier*. The identifier declared in a function definition must have a function type, as indicated by the declarator portion of the definition. That is, the declarator must contain a *function-declarator* that specifies the function identifier immediately before the left parenthesis. It is not allowed for the identifier to inherit its "functionness" from a typedef name.

The function return type cannot be an array or function type.

The declarator must specify the function's parameter names. If the declarator is in prototype form, the *parameter-declarations* must include a *declarator* as opposed to an *abstract-declarator*. If the declarator is not in prototype form, it must include *identifier-list* unless the function takes no arguments. To avoid an ambiguity between an identifier list and a parameter type list, it is invalid to have a parameter name that is the same as a visible **typedef** name. (This restriction is usually not present in older compilers.)

The only storage class specifier allowed in a parameter declaration is **register**.

The *declaration-list*$_{opt}$ is permitted only with non-prototype definitions and can include only declarations of parameter identifiers. Some pre-ISO compilers will permit additional declarations, but the meaning of such declarations is problematic and they are better placed in the function body.

Example

To illustrate these rules, the following are valid function definitions:

Definition	Explanation
`void f() {...}`	**f** is a function taking no parameters and returning no value (traditional form)
`int g(x, y) int x, y; {...}`	**g** is a function taking two integer parameters and returning an integer result (traditional)
`int h(int x, int y) {...}`	h is a function taking two integer parameters and returning an integer result (prototype form)
`int (*f(int x))[] {...}`	**f** is a function taking an integer parameter and returning a pointer to an array of integers (prototype form)

The following are not valid function definitions for the reasons given. Assume the typedef name **T** was declared as "**typedef int T();**".

Definition	Explanation
`int (*q)() {...}`	**q** is a pointer, not a function
`T r {...}`	**r** cannot inherit "functionness" from a **typedef** name
`T s() {...}`	declares **s** as a function returning a function
`void t(int, double) {...}`	**t**'s parameter names do not appear in the declarator
`void u(int x, y) int y; {...}`	parameter declarations are only partially in prototype form

The only storage class specifiers that may appear in a function definition are **extern** and **static**. **extern** signifies that the function can be referenced from other files—that is, the function name is exported to the linker. The specifier **static** signifies that the function cannot be referenced from other files—that is, the name is *not* exported to the linker. If no storage class appears in a function definition, **extern** is assumed. In any case, the function is always visible from the definition point to the end of the file. In particular, it is visible within the body of the function itself.

References declarators 4.5; **extern** storage class 4.3; function declarations 5.8; initialized declaration 4.1; **static** storage class 4.3; type specifiers 4.4

9.2 FUNCTION PROTOTYPES

A function prototype is a function declaration written in the prototype syntax (the *parameter-type-list*), or a function definition written in that syntax. Like a traditional function declaration, a function prototype declares the return type of a function. Unlike a traditional function declaration, a function prototype also declares the number and type of the function's formal parameters.

There are three basic kinds of prototypes depending on whether a function has no parameters, a fixed number of parameters, or a variable number of parameters:

1. A function that has no parameters must have a parameter type list consisting of the single type specifier **void**.

Example

```
extern int random_generator(void);
static void do_nothing(void) { }
```

2. A function that has a fixed number of parameters indicates the types of those parameters in the parameter type list. If the prototype appears in a function declaration, parameter names may be included or not, as desired. (We think they help in documenting the function.) Parameter names must appear in function definitions.

Example

```
double square(double x) { return x*x; }
extern char *strncpy(char *, const char *, size_t);
```

3. A function that has a variable number of parameters or parameters of varying types indicates the types of any fixed parameters as above and follows them by the notation "**, ...**" (which is composed of four tokens: a comma and three periods). There must be at least one fixed parameter, or else the parameter list cannot be referenced using the standard library facilities from **stdarg.h** (section 11.4):

Example

This is a declaration for a function which has a variable number of parameters:

```
extern int fprintf( FILE *file, const char *format, ...);
```

Example

Prototypes may be used in any function declarator, including those used to form more complicated types. The ISO C declaration of **signal** (section 19.6) is

```
void (*signal(int sig, void (*func)(int sig)))(int sig);
```

This declares **signal** to be a function that takes two arguments: **sig**, an integer, and **func**, a pointer to a **void** function of a single integer argument, **sig**. The function **signal** returns a pointer of the same type as its second parameter, i.e., a pointer to a **void** function taking a single integer argument. A clearer way to write the declaration of **signal** is

```
typedef void sig_handler(int sig);
sig_handler *signal(int sig, sig_handler *func);
```

However, when actually defining a signal handler function, the **sig_handler** typedef name cannot be used by the rules for function definitions. Instead, the type must be repeated:

```
void new_signal_handler(int sig) {...}
```

It is possible to use prototypes for some declarators and not for others in the same declaration. If we were to declare **signal2** as

```
typedef void sig_handler2();   /* not a prototype */
sig_handler2 *signal2(int sig, sig_handler2 *func);
```

then the second argument of the **signal2** function would not be in prototype form, although **signal2** itself still has the prototype form.

References function declarator 4.5.4; function declarations 5.8; function definitions 9.1; **void** type 5.9

9.2.1 When Is a Prototype Present?

In order to predict how a function call will be performed, it is important that the programmer know whether or not the function (or function type) being called is governed by a prototype. A function call is governed by a prototype when:

1. a declaration for the function (or type) is visible, and the declaration is in prototype form, or
2. the function definition is visible and that definition is in prototype form.

Note that the visibility of *any* prototype for the function is all that is required; there may be other non-prototype declarations or definitions visible.

If there are two or more prototype declarations of the same function or function type, or a prototype declaration and a prototype definition, then in all the prototypes:

1. the function return types must be compatible,
2. the number of parameters and the use of the ellipsis must agree, and
3. the corresponding parameters must have compatible types.

These are just the rules for compatibility of function types. If these conditions are met, the function is governed by the common prototype. If the conditions are not met, the compiler will reject the program. The names of the formal parameters, if present in the two prototypes, need not agree, but it is always good style to be sure they do.

References compatible types 5.11

9.2.2 Mixing Prototype and Non-Prototype Declarations

Although mixing prototype declarations and non-prototype declarations for the same function is not recommended, ISO C does specify conditions under which the two kinds of declarations are compatible.

The behavior of a function call is undefined if the call supplies arguments that do not "match" the function definition. In traditional C, the programmer assumes all responsibility for making sure the call matches the definition; the language helps by converting arguments and parameters to a smaller and perhaps more manageable set of types. In ISO C, through the use of prototype declarations, the compiler can check at the call site that the arguments match the prototype.

Depending on where function declarations appear, it is possible that some function calls will be governed by prototype declarations, some by traditional declarations, and some by the actual function definition. The calls and definition may be in a single source file or many files. Whenever some calls are not governed by a prototype, the programmer must assume the additional responsibility in being sure that the arguments in those calls match the function definition.

When prototype and non-prototype declarations appear, ISO C sets forth compatibility rules that are necessary (but may not be sufficient) to ensure that the calls are compatible. If these rules are not satisfied, and the declarations appear in the same source file, the compiler will reject the C program. If the declarations appear in different source files, the compiler cannot warn the programmer that executing the program is likely to have unpredictable results.

The compatibility rules can be summarized by saying that the prototype declaration must specify explicitly the argument types that would be passed to a non-prototype function under the implicit argument conversion rules. There are two sets of rules: some "looser" rules that apply when the non-prototype form is a function (or type) declaration (i.e., with no parameter information specified), and a "tighter" set that applies when the non-prototype form is an actual function definition (possibly with parameters).

A function type declared in prototype form is compatible with a function type declaration whose argument list is empty (i.e., which is not a prototype) if:

1. the return types are compatible (in the sense of section 5.11),
2. the prototype does not include the ellipsis terminator, and
3. each parameter type T in the prototype is compatible with the type resulting from applying the usual argument conversions to T.

Example

In general, there are many different prototypes that are individually compatible with a non-prototype declaration. For example, suppose the non-prototype declaration

```
extern int f();
```

appeared somewhere in a C program. Here are some compatible and incompatible prototype declarations.

Prototype	Compatible with **int f()**?	Reason
`extern double f(void);`	no	the parameter list is OK, but the return types are not compatible
`extern int f(int, float);`	no	**float** changes to **double** under the usual argument conversions; the two types are not compatible
`extern int f(double x);`	yes	parameter type does not change upon conversion
`extern int f(int i, ...);`	no	the prototype must not contain ellipses
`extern int f(float *);`	yes	the argument is a pointer that is not converted

Calls under control of two declarations will match if the calls not governed by the prototype in fact supply arguments that, after the usual argument conversions, match the prototype. A function type declared in prototype form is compatible with a non-prototype function definition if:

1. the return types are compatible,
2. the prototype does not include the ellipsis terminator,
3. the number of parameters in the prototype and the function definition is the same, and
4. the type of the *i*th parameter in the prototype is compatible with the type resulting from applying the usual argument conversions to the *i*th parameter in the definition.

These conditions are more stringent and actually check that the prototype matches the parameter specifications in the definition. In general, there is only one prototype that matches a non-prototype function definition; this prototype is sometimes referred to as the function's *Miranda prototype*, since it is "appointed" to a function definition that otherwise would not have one.

In ISO C, functions taking a variable number of arguments must be governed by prototypes. This means that any pre-ISO declarations of functions that take a variable number of arguments (e.g., **printf**) must be rewritten with a prototype before they are used by an ISO C implementation.

Example

For example, suppose the following (non-prototype) definition appeared in a C program:

```
int f(x,y)
    float x;
    int y;
{...}
```

Here are some compatible and incompatible prototype declarations for this definition.

Prototype	Compatible?	Reason
`extern double f(double x, int y);`	no	the parameter list is OK, but the return types are not compatible
`extern int f(float, int);`	no	the first parameter must have type **`double`**
`extern int f(float, int, ...);`	no	the prototype must not contain ellipses
`extern int f(double a, int b);`	yes	this is the only compatible prototype; the parameter names do not matter

References compatible types 5.11; **`printf`** 15.11

9.2.3 Using Prototypes Wisely

Argument checking with prototypes is not foolproof. In a C program divided into many source files, the compiler cannot check that all calls to a function are governed by a prototype, that all the prototypes for the same function are compatible, or that all the prototypes match the function definition.

However, if the programmer follows some simple rules, the loopholes can be eliminated for all practical purposes:

1. Every external function should have a single prototype declaration in a header file. By having a single prototype, the possibility of incompatible prototypes for the same function is eliminated.
2. Every source file that has in it a call to the function should include the header file with the prototype. This ensures that all calls to the function will be governed by the same prototype and allows the compiler to check the arguments at the call sites.
3. The source file containing the definition of the function should also include the header file. This allows the compiler to check that the prototype and the declaration match, and, by transitivity, that all calls match the definition.

It is not necessary that the function definition be in prototype form.

The use of static functions should follow similar rules. Be sure a prototype-form declaration of the static function appears before any calls to the function and before the function's definition.

9.2.4 Prototypes and Calling Conventions

This section will be primarily useful to compiler implementors, although it may give other programmers some insight into the rules for function prototypes. One advantage to function prototypes is that they can permit a compiler to generate more efficient calling sequences for some functions.

Example

For example, under traditional C rules, even if a function were defined to take a parameter of type **`float`**, the compiler had no choice but convert arguments to type **`double`**, call the function, and then convert the arguments back to **`float`**. In ISO C, if the compiler sees a function call governed by the prototype

```
extern int f(float);
```

then the compiler is free to *not* convert the argument to type **`double`**, assuming it makes the corresponding assumption on the other side when it implements the definition of **`f`**:

```
int f(float x) {…}
```

The subtle point here is that the compiler does not have to remain compatible with calls that are not governed by a prototype in this case, because no non-prototype declarations (or definition) of **`f`** could possibly be compatible with the indicated prototype. Hence, ISO C does not define what should happen if a call to **`f`** is made without the prototype visible. The compiler is free to pass the argument in a register even if the non-prototype convention is to pass all arguments on a stack.

On the other hand, if a prototype declaration *could* be a Miranda prototype for a function declared or defined in the traditional way, then the compiler must use a compatible calling convention.

Example

A call to a function **`g`** governed by either of the following declarations would have to be implemented in a compatible way:

```
extern short g();
extern short g(int,double);    /* Could be g's Miranda */
```

Stated another way, if a compiler for ISO C sees the function call

```
process( a, b, c, d );
```

where no prototype is visible and where the types of the actual arguments are

```
short a;
struct {int a,b;} b;
float *c;
float d;
```

then the function call must be implemented the same as if this prototype were in effect:

```
int process(int, struct {int a,b;}, float *, double);
```

This rule does not actually establish a prototype that might affect later calls. Should a second call on **process** appear later in the program or in another source file, at which time the arguments to **process** are three values of type **double**, then that second call must be implemented as if the prototype were

```
int process( double, double, double );
```

even though the two calls will probably be incompatible at execution time.

To summarize the rules, a compiler is allowed to *depend* upon *all* calls to a function being governed by a prototype only if it sees a call of the function that is governed by a prototype and that prototype

1. includes an argument type that is not compatible with the usual argument conversions (**char**, **short**, their unsigned variants, or **float**), or
2. includes ellipses, indicating a variable argument list.

Since the conversions of **char** and **short** to **int** have minimal cost on most computers, the first rule is useful mainly with arguments of type **float**.

The second rule indicates that the compiler's standard calling convention need not support variable argument lists, as it must in traditional C. For example, an ISO compiler could elect in its standard convention to use registers for the first four (fixed) argument words to any function, with the remainder of the arguments passed on the stack. This convention would probably not be appropriate in traditional C, because some functions taking variable arguments depend on all the arguments being passed contiguously on the stack. Any traditional C functions that take a variable number of arguments (e.g., **printf**) must be rewritten to have a prototype before they are compiled by an ISO C implementation.

The storage class **register** is ignored when it appears in a prototype declaration. This means that **register** cannot be used to alter the calling convention of the function; it can only be used as a hint within the function body.

9.2.5 Compatibility with ISO and Traditional C

By writing function declarations using non-prototype syntax, you can remain compatible with both traditional and ISO C implementations. However, you will give up the additional type checking when using an ISO C compiler. One way around this problem is to define a macro **PARMS**:

```
#ifdef __STDC__
#define PARMS(x) x
#else
#define PARMS(x) ()
#endif
```

Then, instead of the prototype declaration

```
extern int f(int a, double b, char c);
```

write this declaration (note the doubled parentheses):

```
extern int f PARMS((int a, double b, char c));
```

When compiled by a traditional implementation, the preprocessor expands this line to

```
extern int f ();
```

But, an ISO C implementation expands it to:

```
extern int f (int a, double b, long c);
```

The **PARMS** macro does not work correctly in function definitions, so you must write the corresponding function definitions using the traditional syntax, which is also accepted by ISO C:

```
int f(a, b, c)
   int a; double b; long c;
{
   ...
}
```

A traditional definition in ISO C does not cause a problem as long as a prototype declaration for the function appears earlier in the source file. This is shown in the "set of integers" example beginning on page 212.

9.3 FORMAL PARAMETER DECLARATIONS

In function definitions, formal parameters are declared either in the prototype syntax allowed in ISO C or in the traditional syntax.

The only storage class specifier that may be present in a parameter declaration is **register**, which is a hint to the compiler that the parameter will be used heavily and might better be stored in a register after the function has begun executing. The normal restrictions as to what types of parameters may be marked register apply (see section 4.3).

In ISO C, formal parameters have the same scope as identifiers declared at the top level of the function body, and therefore they cannot be hidden or redeclared by declarations in the body. Some current C implementations allow such a redeclaration, which is almost invariably a programming error.

Example

In the following function definition, the declaration **double x;** would be an error if compiled by an ISO-conforming compiler. However, some non-ISO compilers permit it, and thereby make the parameter **x** inaccessible within the function body.

```
int f(x)
    int x;
{
    double x;  /* hides parameter!? */
    ...
}
```

In ISO C, a parameter may be declared to be of any type except **void**. However, if a parameter is declared to have a type "function returning *T*" it is implicitly rewritten to have type "pointer to function returning *T*," and if a parameter is declared to have type "array of *T*" it is rewritten to have type "pointer to *T*." (The array type in the parameter declaration can be incomplete.) This adjustment is made regardless of whether a prototype or traditional definition is used. The programmer need not be aware of this change of parameter types in most cases, since the parameters can be used within the function as if they had the declared type.

Example

Suppose the function **FUNC** were defined as

```
void FUNC(int f(void), int (*g)(void), int h[], int *j)
{
    int i;
    i = f();    /* OK */
    i = g();    /* OK */
    i = h[3];   /* OK */
    i = j[3];   /* OK */
    ...
}
```

Suppose moreover that the following call were made to FUNC:

```
extern int a(void), b[20];
...
FUNC( a, a, b, b );
```

Then within **FUNC** the expression **f** would be equivalent to **g**, and **h** would be equivalent to **j**.

In most pre-ISO implementations, parameters with array types are similarly converted, but some implementations reject declarations of parameters of type "function returning *T*," requiring instead that they be explicitly declared as "pointer to function returning *T*." For compatibility with these implementations, the programmer should declare the pointers explicitly.

A formal parameter is treated just like a local variable of the specified (or rewritten) type into which is copied the value of the corresponding argument passed to the function. The parameter can be assigned to, but the assignment only changes the local argument value, not the argument in the calling function. Parameter names declared to have function or array types are lvalues due to the rewriting rules, even though identifiers with those types are not normally lvalues.

It is permissible in pre-ISO implementations to include **typedef**, structure, union, or enumeration type declarations in the parameter declaration section.

Example

```
int process_record(r)
    struct { int a; int b; } *r;
{
    ...
}
```

It is generally bad programming style to do this. If the declarations involve the parameters, the declarations should be moved outside the function where the caller can also use them. If the declarations do not involve the parameters, they should be moved into the function body.

References enumeration types 5.5; function declarator 4.5.4; function prototype 9.2; incomplete types 5.4; register storage class 4.3; storage class specifiers 4.3; structure types 5.6; **typedef** 5.10; union types 5.7; **void** type 5.9

9.4 ADJUSTMENTS TO PARAMETER TYPES

In traditional C—and in ISO C when a prototype is not present—certain conversions (promotions) of the values of function arguments must be made. These conversions, which are designed to simplify and regularize function arguments, are called the usual argument conversions and are listed in section 6.3.5. Expecting these argument conversions by the caller, C functions arrange for the promoted argument values to be converted to the declared parameter types before the function body is executed. For example, if a function **F** were declared to take a parameter, **x**, of type **short**, and a call to **F** specified a value of type **short**, then the call would be implemented as if the following sequence of events occurred:

1. The caller widens the argument of type **short** to become a value of type **int**.
2. The value of type **int** is passed to **F**.
3. **F** narrows the **int** value to type **short**.
4. **F** stores the value of type **short** in the parameter **x**.

Fortunately, the conversions that occur have very little, if any, overhead—at least for integers. The argument types affected by the conversions include **char**, **short**, **unsigned char**, **unsigned short**, and **float**.

In ISO C, when a function call is governed by a prototype, arguments are first converted to the type of the corresponding formal parameter. The C implementation is then permitted to perform the usual argument conversions before passing the argument, but it need not do so. Those arguments corresponding to the variable argument list specified by "**, ...**" in the function prototype always undergo the usual argument conversions.

Example

Programmers should be aware that some pre-ISO compilers fail to perform the required narrowing operations upon entry to a function. Consider the following function, which has a parameter of type **char**:

```
int pass_through(c)
    char c;
{
    return c;
}
```

Some compilers will implement this function as if it were defined with an **int** parameter:

```
int pass_through(c)
    int c;
{
    return c;
}
```

A consequence of this incorrect implementation is that the argument value is not narrowed to type **char**. That is, **pass_through(0x1001)** would return the value **0x1001** instead of **1**. The correct implementation of the function would resemble this:

```
int pass_through(anonymous)
    int anonymous;
{
    char c = anonymous;
    return c;
}
```

References array types 5.4; floating-point types 5.2; function argument conversions 6.3.5; function definition 9.1; function prototypes 9.2; function types 5.8; integer types 5.1; lvalue 7.1; pointer types 5.3

9.5 PARAMETER-PASSING CONVENTIONS

C provides only call-by-value parameter passing. This means that the values of the actual parameters are conceptually copied into a storage area local to the called function. It is possible to use a formal parameter name as the left side of an assignment, for instance, but in that case only the local copy of the parameter is altered. If the programmer wants the called function to alter its actual parameters, the addresses of the parameters must be passed explicitly.

Example

Function **swap** below will not work correctly, because **x** and **y** are passed by value:

```
void swap(x, y)
/* swap: exchange the values of x and y */
/* Incorrect version! */
    int x, y;
{
    int temp;
    temp = x; x = y; y = temp;
}
...
swap(a, b); /* Fails to swap a and b. */
```

A correct implementation of the function requires that addresses of the arguments be passed:

```
void swap(x, y)
/* swap - exchange the values of *x and *y */
/* correct version */
    int *x, *y;
{
    int temp;
    temp = *x; *x = *y; *y = temp;
}
...
swap(&a, &b); /* Swaps contents of a and b. */
```

The local storage area for parameters is usually implemented on a pushdown stack. However, the order of pushing parameters on the stack is not specified by the language, nor does the language prevent the compiler from passing parameters in registers. It is valid to apply the address operator **&** to a formal parameter name (unless it was declared with storage class **register**), thereby implying that the parameter in question would have to be in addressable storage when the address was taken. (Note that the address of a formal parameter is the address of the copy of the actual parameter, not the address of the actual parameter itself.)

When writing functions that take a variable number of arguments, programmers should use the **varargs** or **stdarg** facilities in the standard library for maximum portability.

References address operator **&** 7.5.6; function prototype 9.2; **register** storage class 4.3; **varargs** facility 11.4

9.6 AGREEMENT OF PARAMETERS

Most modern programming languages such as Pascal and Ada check the agreement of formal and actual parameters to functions—that is, both the number of arguments and the types of the individual arguments must agree. This checking is also performed in ISO C when a function is declared with a prototype.

Example

In the example below, the call to the function **sqrt** is not governed by a prototype; therefore, the C compiler is not required to warn the programmer that the actual parameter to **sqrt** is of type **long**, whereas the formal parameter is declared to have type **double**. (In fact, if the call and definition were in different source files, then the compiler would be unable to do so.) The function will simply return an incorrect value:

```
double sqrt( x )      /* not a prototype */
    double x;
{
    ...
}

long hypotenuse(x,y)
    long x,y;
{
    return sqrt(x*x + y*y);
}
```

When a call is governed by a prototype in ISO C, the actual arguments are converted to the corresponding formal parameter type. Only if this conversion is impossible, or if the number of arguments does not agree with the number of formal parameters, will the C compiler reject the program.

Example

By adding a prototype to the definition of **sqrt** above, the example will work correctly: the **long** argument will be converted to **double** without the programmer's knowledge:

```
double sqrt( double x )    /* prototype */
{
    ...
}

long hypotenuse(x,y)
    long x,y;
{
    return sqrt(x*x + y*y);
}
```

As a matter of good programming style, we recommend using explicit casts to convert arguments to the expected parameter type unless that conversion is just duplicating the usual argument conversions. That is, we would write the return statement in the example above like this:

```
return  sqrt( (double) (x*x + y*y) );
```

Some C functions, such as **fprintf**, are written to take arguments that vary in number and type. In traditional C, the **varargs** library facility has evolved to provide a fairly reliable way of writing such functions, although the usage is not portable, since different implementations have slightly different forms of **varargs**. In ISO C a similar library mechanism, **stdarg**, was created to provide portability and reliability. Functions using **stdarg** must be declared with a prototype that uses the ellipses notation, "**, ...**", before any call, thus giving the compiler an opportunity to prepare a suitable calling mechanism.

References conversion of actual parameters 9.4; function argument conversions 6.3.5; function prototypes 9.2; **fprintf** 15.11

9.7 FUNCTION RETURN TYPES

A function may be defined to return a value of any type except "array of *T*" or "function returning *T*." These two cases must be handled by returning pointers to the array or function. There is no automatic rewriting of the return type, as there is for formal parameters.

The value returned by the function is specified by an expression in the **return** statement that causes the function to terminate. The rules governing the expression are discussed in section 9.8.

The value returned by a function is not an lvalue (the return is "by value"), and therefore a function call cannot appear as the outermost expression on the left side of an assignment operator.

Example

```
f() = x;     /* Invalid */
*f() = x;     /* OK if f returns a pointer of suitable type
*/
f().a = x;   /* Invalid--not an lvalue (section 7.4.2) */
```

References array types 5.4; function calls 7.4.3; function parameters 9.4; function types 5.8; lvalue 7.1; pointer types 5.3; **void** type 5.9

9.8 AGREEMENT OF RETURN TYPES

If a function has a declared return type *T* that is not **void**, then the type of any expression appearing in a **return** statement must be convertible to type *T* by assignment, and that conversion in fact happens on return in both ISO and traditional C.

Example

In a function with declared return type **int**, the statement

```
return 23.1;
```

is equivalent to

```
return (int) 23.1;
```

which is the same as

```
return 23;
```

If a function has a declared return type of **void**, it is an error to supply an expression in any **return** statement in the function. It is also an error to call the function in a context that requires a value. With older compilers that do not implement **void**, it is the custom to omit the type specifier on those functions that return no value:

```
process_something()      /* probably returns nothing */
{
    ...
}
```

It is also possible to define your own **void** type to improve readability (section 4.4.1).

Whether a function has a **void** or nonvoid return type, ISO and traditional C permit a **return** statement with no expression—that is, simply "**return;**". This rule is to provide backward compatibility with compilers that do not implement **void**. When a function has a non-**void** return type, and a **return** statement with no arguments is executed, then the value actually returned is unpredictable. It is therefore unwise to call the function in a context that requires a value. (It is invalid in C++.) We recommend that this form of **return** be used only when the function is declared to have return type **void**.

References adjustments to formal parameters 9.4; default type specifiers 4.4.1; lvalue 7.1; **return** statement 8.9; **void** type 5.9

9.9 MAIN PROGRAMS

By convention all C programs must define a single external function named **main**. That function will become the entry point of the program—that is, the first function executed when the program is started. Information about parameters usually supplied to **main**, and about its return value, is given in section 20.1.

References **main** 20.1

9.10 C++ COMPATIBILITY

9.10.1 Prototypes

To be compatible with C++, all functions must be declared with prototypes. In fact, the non-prototype form has a different meaning in C++—an empty parameter list signifies a function that takes no parameters in C++, whereas it signifies a function that takes an unknown number of parameters in C.

Example

```
int f();       /* Means int f(void) in C++, int f(...) in C */
int g(void); /* Means the same in both C and C++ */
...
x = f(2);      /* valid in C, not in C++ */
```

9.10.2 Type Declarations in Parameter and Return Types

Do not place type declarations in parameter lists or return type declarations; they are invalid in C++.

Example

```
struct s { ... } f1(int i); /* OK in C, not in C++ */
void f2(enum e{...} x);     /* OK in C, not in C++ */
```

9.10.3 Agreement of Return Types

In C++, you must return a value of appropriate type from a function that has a non-**void** return type. In ISO C, not returning a value is permitted for backward compatibility.

Example

```
int f(void)
{
    ...
    return ; /* Valid but unpredictable in C;
                invalid in C++ */
}
```

References agreement of return types 9.8

9.11 EXERCISES

1. Which of the following declarations serve as ISO C prototypes?
   (a) `short f(void);`
   (b) `int f();`
   (c) `double f(...);`
   (d) `int f(i,j);`
   (e) `int *f(float);`
   (f) `int f(i) int i; {...}`
2. Declarations and definitions of functions are shown below. Which pairs are compatible in ISO C?

	Declaration	*Definition*
(a)	`extern int f(short x);`	`int f(x) short x; {...}`
(b)	`extern int f();`	`int f(short x) {...}`
(c)	`extern f(short x);`	`int f(short int y) {...}`
(d)	`extern void f(int x);`	`void f(int x,...) {...}`
(e)	`extern f();`	`int f(x,y) short x,y; {...}`
(f)	`extern f();`	`f(void) {...}`

3. Declarations and invocations of functions are shown below. In each case, indicate whether the invocation is valid in ISO C and, if so, what conversions will be applied to each actual parameter. Assume **`s`** has type **`short`** and **`ld`** has type **`long double`**.

	Declaration	*Invocation*
(a)	`extern int f(int *x);`	`f(&s)`
(b)	`extern int f();`	`f(s,ld)`
(c)	`extern f(short x);`	`f(ld)`
(d)	`extern void f(short,...);`	`f(s,s,ld)`
(e)	`int f(x) short x; {...}`	`f(s)`
(f)	`int f(x) short x; {...};`	`f(ld)`

4. In the following program fragment, is the invocation of **`P`** governed by a prototype? Why?

```
extern void P(void);
...
int Q()
{
    extern P();
    P();
    ...
}
```

5. If the declared return type of a function is **`short`**, which of the following types of expressions appearing in a **`return`** statement would be allowable and would produce a predictable value at the call site?

(a) **`int`**
(b) **`long double`**
(c) **`void`** (e.g., the invocation of a function returning **`void`**)
(d) **`char *`**

PART 2
The C Libraries

10

Introduction to the Libraries

Many facilities that are used in C programs are part of the "standard libraries" that are written for use by C programs. These facilities include operations on characters and strings, input and output operations, mathematical functions, date and time conversions, and dynamic storage allocation.

Each of these facilities belongs to a particular library. The correct way to use a facility is to have a preprocessor **#include** command that references the proper library declarations. For example, in order to use the trigonometric function **cos** in a program, the C programmer should put the command

```
#include <math.h>
```

at the start of the program, thus declaring **cos** for subsequent use. Unfortunately, implementations of traditional C do not declare all the facilities in standard header files; some must be declared explicitly by the programmer.

The word *facility* has been used in order to evade the question of whether an operation is implemented as a function or a macro. We will often refer to the operations as "functions," but the implementor is usually free to provide an equivalent macro. A facility implemented as a macro should evaluate every argument expression exactly once, just as a function would. In some cases the implementation choice is important: if an operation is defined as a macro, it can be removed with **#undef**; if it is a function, the function's address can be passed to another function.

ISO C is the first description of C to explicitly include a large standard library that is independent of the host operating system. Older implementations of C provide different sets of facilities, although the libraries originally provided with UNIX have been a model for many implementations. In the following chapters, we will describe not only the facilities included in ISO C, but also the facilities in common use that duplicate facilities in ISO C and other facilities in common use that are fairly portable across many systems.

10.1 ISO C FACILITIES

The ISO C language includes a portable run-time library that includes most of the features commonly used in traditional C. Tables 10–1 through 10–3 list the library facilities in ISO C and give the section numbers of discussions in subsequent chapters.

Amendment 1 to ISO C defines three additional libraries, **iso646.h**, **wchar.h** and **wctype.h**.

Library facilities and header files in ISO C are special in many ways, mostly to protect the integrity of implementations:

1. Library names are in principle reserved. Programmers may not define external objects whose names duplicate the names of the standard library. All names beginning with an underscore are also reserved to implementations.
2. Library header files or file names may be "built in" to the implementation, although they still must be included for their names to become visible. That is, **stdio.h** might not actually correspond to a **#include** file named "**stdio.h**."
3. Programmers may include library header files in any order, any number of times. (This may not be true in traditional C implementations.)

Example

The last requirement is a convenience for programmers, but may force an implementation to use some careful mechanisms to avoid duplicate declarations, such as this:

```
/* Header stddef.h */
#ifndef _STDDEF                    /* Don't try to redeclare */
#define _STDDEF 1
typedef int ptrdiff_t;
...
#endif
```

ISO C requires that most "function-like" library facilities really be implemented as functions, so that the programmer can pass their address, say, to another function. However, to allow for more efficiency, the header files may hide the function name with an equivalent macro.

Example

Here is a hypothetical declaration of a function **nonzero** that returns 1 if its argument is nonzero and otherwise returns 0:

```
extern int nonzero( int x );         /* Functional form */
#define nonzero(x) ((int)(x)?1:0)    /* Macro form */
```

Note that the cast to **int** is necessary in the macro to simulate the action of a function call in the scope of a prototype. A programmer requiring the functional form would have to include an explicit **#undef** command to hide any macros:

```
#ifdef nonzero
#undef nonzero
#endif
```

The library functions are mostly written to take arguments whose types are unchanged under the usual argument conversions. This allows them to be called without the help of a prototype for compatibility with older implementations. Compatibility cannot be guaranteed for functions like **`fprintf`** and **`fscanf`**, which take a variable number of arguments, because ISO C requires such functions to be called in the scope of a prototype.

References **`fprintf`** 15.11; **`fscanf`** 15.8; function prototypes 9.2; **`#undef`** 3.3.5

10.2 C++ COMPATIBILITY

The C++ language includes the ISO C runtime library, but adds a number of C++-specific libraries. None of the additional libraries have names ending in "**`.h`**," so they are unlikely to conflict with your C libraries.

C++ uses a different convention for calling its functions, which means that, in general, it is not possible to call a C++ function from a C program. However, C++ does provide a way to call C functions from C++. There are two requirements on the declarations of the C functions:

1. The function declarations must use ISO C prototypes. C++ requires prototypes.
2. The external C declarations must be explicitly labeled as having C linkage by including the string **`"C"`** after the storage class **`extern`** in the C++ declaration.

Example

If you were calling a C function from another C function, it would be declared as, for example

```
extern int f(void);
```

However, if called from a C++ program, the declaration would have to be

```
extern "C" int f(void);
```

If a group of C functions were to be declared in C++, you can apply the linkage specification to all of them:

```
extern "C" {
    double sqrt(double x);
    int f(void);
    ...
}
```

When writing a header file for a library that might be called from C or C++, you must choose whether to specify the C linkage within the header file, or whether you will require C++ programs to supply the linkage declaration in the file that includes the header.

Example

Suppose a header file **library.h** is to be called from C or C++ programs. The first possibility is to include the **extern "C"** declarations inside the header file, conditional on the **__cplusplus** macro, which indicates that this is a C++ program.

```
/* File library.h */
#ifdef __cplusplus
extern "C" {
#endif
...
/* C declarations */
...
#ifdef __cplusplus
}
#endif
```

The second alternative is to write the header file using normal C declarations and simply require that C++ users wrap the linkage declaration around the **#include** command:

```
extern "C" {
#include "library.h"
}
```

The second alternative in the above example must be used when calling libraries that were written before C++ became a consideration. There is no harm in nesting the **extern "C" {}** declarations.

References **__cplusplus** macro 3.9.1

10.3 LIBRARY DESCRIPTIONS

The facilities are divided into groups according to their general purpose. Each facility is described by giving the appropriate header file (if there is one), a typical function or macro declaration of the facility, and a longer prose description. The declarations are given in two forms: the ISO C form and the traditional C form. For example, here is the declaration of the **perror** facility:

ISO C facilities	Traditional and alternate facilities
`#include <stdio.h>`	`#include <stdio.h>`
`void perror(const char *s)`	`void perror(char *s)`

Both ISO and traditional declarations are written in ISO C prototype notation for readability, although traditional C implementations would not permit that style of declaration. In some cases the ISO and traditional forms differ only subtly; in other cases, facilities may be present in ISO C and not in traditional C, or vice versa. The accompanying descriptions should help to clarify the situation. The grouping of facilities in ISO C does not always follow the divisions used in this book. The facilities are summarized in the following tables:

- Table 10–1, "ISO C library facilities (Integer and floating-point sizes)" on page 287
- Table 10–2, "ISO C library facilities (Basic support)" on page 288
- Table 10–3, "ISO C library facilities (Characters and strings)" on page 289
- Table 10–4, "ISO C library facilities (Mathematics)" on page 290
- Table 10–5, "ISO C library facilities (Input/output)" on page 290

Table 10–1 ISO C library facilities (Integer and floating-point sizes)

Floating-point specifications (**float.h**)		
DBL_EPSILON (5.2)	**FLT_EPSILON** (5.2)	**LDBL_EPSILON** (5.2)
DBL_DIG (5.2)	**FLT_DIG** (5.2)	**LDBL_DIG** (5.2)
DBL_MANT_DIG (5.2)	**FLT_MANT_DIG** (5.2)	**LDBL_MANT_DIG** (5.2)
DBL_MAX (5.2)	**FLT_MAX** (5.2)	**LDBL_MAX** (5.2)
DBL_MAX_EXP (5.2)	**FLT_MAX_EXP** (5.2)	**LDBL_MAX_EXP** (5.2)
DBL_MAX_10_EXP (5.2)	**FLT_MAX_10_EXP** (5.2)	**LDBL_MAX_10_EXP** (5.2)
DBL_MIN (5.2)	**FLT_MIN** (5.2)	**LDBL_MIN** (5.2)
DBL_MIN_EXP (5.2)	**FLT_MIN_EXP** (5.2)	**LDBL_MIN_EXP** (5.2)
DBL_MIN_10_EXP (5.2)	**FLT_MIN_10_EXP** (5.2)	**LDBL_MIN_10_EXP** (5.2)
	FLT_RADIX (5.2)	
	FLT_ROUNDS (5.2)	
Integer specifications (**limits.h**)		
CHAR_BIT (5.1.1)	**LONG_MAX** (5.1.1)	**SHRT_MIN** (5.1.1)
CHAR_MAX (5.1.1)	**LONG_MIN** (5.1.1)	**UCHAR_MAX** (5.1.1)
CHAR_MIN (5.1.1)	**SCHAR_MAX** (5.1.1)	**UINT_MAX** (5.1.1)
INT_MAX (5.1.1)	**SCHAR_MIN** (5.1.1)	**ULONG_MAX** (5.1.1)
INT_MIN (5.1.1)	**SHRT_MAX** (5.1.1)	**USHRT_MAX** (5.1.1)

Table 10–2 ISO C library facilities (Basic support)

Common definitions (stddef.h, wchar.h)		
NULL (11.1)	ptrdiff_t (11.1)	wchar_t (11.1)
offsetof (11.1)	size_t (11.1)	
Built-in facilities		
__DATE__ (11.3)	__LINE__ (11.3)	__TIME__ (11.3)
__FILE__ (11.3)	__STDC__ (11.3)	
Errors (errno.h)		
EDOM (11.2)	ERANGE (11.2)	errno (11.2)
Alternative spellings (iso646.h) (ISO C Amendment 1)		
and (11.9)	compl (11.9)	or_eq (11.9)
and_eq (11.9)	not (11.9)	xor (11.9)
bitand (11.9)	not_eq (11.9)	xor_eq (11.9)
bitor (11.9)	or (11.9)	
Variable arguments (stdarg.h)		
va_list (11.4)	va_arg (11.4)	va_end (11.4)
va_start (11.4)		
General utilities (stdlib.h)		
EXIT_FAILURE (19.3)	strtol (13.8)	system (19.2)
EXIT_SUCCESS (19.3)	strtoul (13.8)	bsearch (20.5)
MB_CUR_MAX (11.7)	rand (17.7)	qsort (20.6)
NULL (11.1)	srand (17.7)	abs (17.1)
RAND_MAX (17.7)	calloc (16.1)	div (17.1)
div_t (17.1)	free (16.2)	labs (17.1)
ldiv_t (17.1)	malloc (16.1)	ldiv (17.1)
size_t (11.1)	realloc (16.3)	mblen (11.7)
wchar_t (11.1)	abort (19.3)	mbtowc (11.7)
atof (13.9)	atexit (19.5)	wctomb (11.7)
atoi (13.9)	exit (19.3)	mbstowcs (11.8)
atol (13.9)	getenv (20.4)	wcstombs (11.8)
strtod (13.8)		
Non-local jumps (setjmp.h)		
jmpbuf (19.4)	setjmp (19.4)	longjmp (19.4)
Signal handling (signal.h)		
sig_atomic_t (19.6)	SIGABRT (19.6)	SIGSEGV (19.6)
SIG_DFL (19.6)	SIGFPE (19.6)	SIGTERM (19.6)
SIG_ERR (19.6)	SIGILL (19.6)	signal (19.6)
SIG_IGN (19.6)	SIGINT (19.6)	raise (19.6)
Diagnostics (assert.h)		
assert (19.1)	NDEBUG (19.1)	
Localization (locale.h) (ISO C)		
LC_ALL (11.5)	LC_NUMERIC (11.5)	localeconv (11.6)
LC_COLLATE (11.5)	LC_TIME (11.5)	NULL (11.1)
LC_CTYPE (11.5)	struct lconv (11.6)	setlocale (11.5)
LC_MONETARY (11.5)		

Table 10–3 ISO C library facilities (Characters and strings)

Character handling (**ctype.h**)

isalnum (12.1)	**islower** (12.5)	**isupper** (12.5)
isalpha (12.1)	**isprint** (12.4)	**isxdigit** (12.3)
iscntrl (12.1)	**ispunct** (12.4)	**tolower** (12.9)
isdigit (12.3)	**isspace** (12.6)	**toupper** (12.9)
isgraph (12.4)		

Wide character handling (**wctype.h**) (ISO C Amendment 1)

iswalnum (12.1)	**iswprint** (12.4)	**towupper** (12.9)
iswalpha (12.1)	**iswpunct** (12.4)	**WEOF** (11.1)
iswcntrl (12.1)	**iswspace** (12.6)	**wint_t** (11.1)
iswctype (12.10)	**iswupper** (12.5)	**wctrans** (12.11)
iswdigit (12.3)	**iswxdigit** (12.3)	**wctrans_t** (12.11)
iswgraph (12.4)	**towctrans** (12.11)	**wctype** (12.10)
iswlower (12.5)	**towlower** (12.9)	**wctype_t** (12.10)

String handling (**string.h**)

NULL (11.1)	**strerror** (11.2)	**strstr** (13.7)
size_t (11.1)	**strlen** (13.4)	**strtok** (13.7)
strchr (13.5)	**strncat** (13.1)	**strxfrm** (13.10)
strcpy (13.3)	**strncmp** (13.2)	**memchr** (14.1)
strcat (13.1)	**strncpy** (13.3)	**memcmp** (14.2)
strcmp (13.2)	**strpbrk** (13.6)	**memcpy** (14.3)
strcoll (13.10)	**strrchr** (13.5)	**memmove** (14.3)
strcspn (13.6)	**strspn** (13.6)	**memset** (14.4)

Extended multibyte/wide-character conversion (**wchar.h**) (ISO C Amendment 1)

btowc (11.7)	**wcrtomb** (11.7)	**wcstod** (13.8)
mbrlen (11.7)	**mbsinit** (11.8)	**wcstol** (13.8)
mbrtowc (11.7)	**mbsrtowcs** (11.8)	**wcstoul** (13.8)
mbstate_t (11.1)	**wcsrtombs** (11.8)	**wctob** (11.7)

Wide string handling (**wchar.h**) (ISO C Amendment 1)

wcscat (13.1)	**wcsncat** (13.1)	**wcsxfrm** (13.10)
wcschr (13.5)	**wcsncmp** (13.2)	**wmemchr** (14.1)
wcscmp (13.2)	**wcsncpy** (13.3)	**wmemcmp** (14.2)
wcscoll (13.10)	**wcspbrk** (13.6)	**wmemcpy** (14.3)
wcscpy (13.3)	**wcsrchr** (13.5)	**wmemmove** (14.3)
wcscspn (13.6)	**wcsspn** (13.6)	**wmemset** (14.4)
wcserror (11.2)	**wcsstr** (13.7)	
wcslen (13.4)	**wcstok** (13.7)	

Table 10–4 ISO C library facilities (Mathematics)

Mathematics (**math.h**)

HUGE_VAL (17)	**cosh** (17.10)	**modf** (17.5)
acos (17.9)	**sinh** (17.10)	**pow** (17.6)
asin (17.9)	**tanh** (17.10)	**sqrt** (17.6)
atan (17.9)	**exp** (17.4)	**ceil** (17.3)
atan2 (17.9)	**frexp** (17.5)	**fabs** (17.2)
cos (17.8)	**ldexp** (17.5)	**floor** (17.3)
sin (17.8)	**log** (17.4)	**fmod** (17.3)
tan (17.8)	**log10** (17.4)	

Table 10–5 ISO C library facilities (Input/output)

Input/output (**stdio.h**)

_IOFBF (15.3)	**rename** (15.15)	**fputc** (15.9)
_IOLBF (15.3)	**tmpfile** (15.16)	**fputs** (15.10)
_IONBF (15.3)	**tmpnam** (15.14)	**getc** (15.6)
BUFSIZ (15.3)	**fclose** (15.2)	**getchar** (15.6)
EOF (15.1)	**fflush** (15.2)	**gets** (15.7)
FILE (15)	**fopen** (15.2)	**putc** (15.9)
FILENAME_MAX (15.2)	**freopen** (15.2)	**putchar** (15.9)
FOPEN_MAX (15.2)	**setbuf** (15.3)	**puts** (15.10)
fpos_t (15.5)	**setvbuf** (15.3)	**ungetc** (15.6)
L_tmpnam (15.14)	**fprintf** (15.11)	**fread** (15.13)
NULL (11.1)	**fscanf** (15.8)	**fwrite** (15.13)
SEEK_CUR (15.5)	**printf** (15.11)	**fgetpos** (15.5)
SEEK_END (15.5)	**scanf** (15.8)	**fseek** (15.5)
SEEK_SET (15.5)	**sprintf** (15.11)	**fsetpos** (15.5)
size_t (11.1)	**sscanf** (15.8)	**ftell** (15.5)
stderr (15.4)	**vfprintf** (15.12)	**rewind** (15.5)
stdin (15.4)	**vprintf** (15.12)	**clearerr** (15.14)
stdout (15.4)	**vsprintf** (15.12)	**feof** (15.14)
TMP_MAX (15.16)	**fgetc** (15.6)	**ferror** (15.14)
remove (15.15)	**fgets** (15.7)	**perror** (11.2)

Wide character input/output (**wchar.h**) (ISO C Amendment 1)

fwprintf (15.11)	**vfwprintf** (15.12)	**fputws** (15.10)
fwscanf (15.8)	**vwprintf** (15.12)	**getwc** (15.6)
wprintf (15.11)	**vwsprintf** (15.12)	**getwchar** (15.6)
wscanf (15.8)	**fgetwc** (15.6)	**putwc** (15.9)
swprintf (15.11)	**fgetws** (15.7)	**putwchar** (15.9)
swscanf (15.8)	**fputwc** (15.9)	**ungetwc** (15.6)

Date and time (**time.h**)

CLOCKS_PER_SEC (18.1)	**clock** (18.1)	**gmtime** (18.4)
NULL (11.1)	**difftime** (18.5)	**localtime** (18.4)
clock_t (18.1)	**mktime** (18.4)	**strftime** (18.6)
time_t (18.2)	**time** (18.2)	**wcsftime** (18.6)
size_t (11.1)	**asctime** (18.3)	
struct tm (18.4)	**ctime** (18.3)	

11

Standard Language Additions

The facilities of this section are closely tied to the C language. They provide some standard definitions and parameterization that help make C programs more portable.

Table 11–1 Chapter summary

Name	Section	Name	Section	Name	Section
`btowc`	11.7	`mbstate_t`	11.1	`stdarg`	11.4
`__DATE__`	11.3	`NULL`	11.1	`strerror`	11.2
`errno`	11.2	`offsetof`	11.1	`__TIME__`	11.3
`__FILE__`	11.3	`perror`	11.2	token respelling	11.9
`__LINE__`	11.3	`ptrdiff_t`	11.1	`vararg`	11.4
`localeconv`	11.6	`setlocale`	11.5	`wctob`	11.7
`mblen`[a]	11.7	`size_t`	11.1	`wctomb`[a]	11.7
`mbtowc`[a]	11.7	`__STDC__`	11.3	`wchar_t`	11.1
`mbstowcs`[a]	11.8	`__STDC_VERSION__`	11.3	`wint_t`	11.1
				`wcstombs`[a]	11.8

[a] A restartable version of this facility is described in the same section.

11.1 NULL, ptrdiff_t, size_t, offsetof, wchar_t, mbstate_t

ISO C facilities	Traditional and alternate facilities
#include <stddef.h>	**#include <stdio.h>**
#define NULL ...	**#define NULL 0**
typedef ... **ptrdiff_t;** **typedef** ... **size_t;** **typedef** ... **wchar_t;**	
#define offsetof(*type*, *member-designator* **)**...	
#include <wchar.h> **typedef** ... **wint_t;** **typedef** ... **mbstate_t;**	
#define WEOF ...	

The value of the macro **NULL** is the traditional null pointer constant. Many implementations define it to be simply the integer constant 0. In ISO C the macro is defined in many header files for convenience. In traditional C **NULL** is often found in **stdio.h**.

Type **ptrdiff_t** is an implementation-defined signed integral type that is the type of the result of subtracting two pointers; most implementations use **long** for this type.

Type **size_t** is the unsigned integral type of the result of the **sizeof** operator—probably **unsigned long**; pre-ISO implementations often use the (signed) type **int** for this purpose.

The macro **offsetof** expands to an integral constant expression (of type **size_t**) that is the offset in bytes of member *member-designator* within structure type *type*. If the member is a bit field, the result is unpredictable. If **offsetof** is not defined (in a non-ISO implementation), it is often possible to define it as follows:

```
#define offsetof(type,memb) ((size_t)&((type *)0)->memb)
```

If the implementation does not permit the use of the null pointer constant in this fashion, it may be possible to compute the offset by using a predefined, non-null pointer and subtracting the member's address from the structure's base address.

Example

At the end of the following program fragment the value of **diff** will be 1 and the values of **size** and **offset** will be equal. [For a byte-addressed computer on which **sizeof(int)** is 4, **size** and **offset** will both be equal to 4.]

```
#include <stdlib.h>
#include <stddef.h>
struct s {int a; int b; } x;
size_t size, offset;
ptrdiff_t diff;
...
```

```
diff = &x.b - &x.a;
size = sizeof(x.a);
offset = offsetof(struct s,b);
```

Type **wchar_t** (the "wide character" type) is an integral type that can represent all distinct values for any extended character set in the supported locales.

Amendment 1 to ISO C provides some related extended character support in header file **wchar.h**. Type **wint_t** is also an integral type that can hold all the values of **wchar_t** and, in addition, at least one additional value that is not a member of the extended character set. That constant value is denoted **WEOF**. Type **mbstate_t** is a non-array object type that can represent the state of a conversion between sequences of multibyte characters and wide strings.

References conversion of integers to pointers 6.2.7; null pointers 5.3.2; pointer types 5.3; **sizeof** operator 7.5.2; subtraction of pointers 7.6.2; wide characters 2.7.3

11.2 errno, strerror, perror

ISO C facilities	Traditional and alternate facilities

`#include <errno.h>`
`extern int errno;`
or `#define errno ...`
`#define EDOM ...`
`#define ERANGE ...`
	`#include <errno.h>`
	`extern int errno;`
	`#define EDOM ...`
	`#define ERANGE ...`

`#include <stdio.h>` `void perror(const char *s)`	`#include <stdio.h>` `void perror(char * s)`

`#include <string.h>`
`char *strerror(int errnum)`
	`#include <stdio.h>`
	`extern int sys_nerr;`
	`extern char *sys_errlist[];`

The external variable **errno** is used to hold implementation-defined error codes from library routines, traditionally defined in the header file **errno.h**. All error codes are positive integers, and library routines should never clear **errno**.

Example

The typical way of using **errno** is to clear it before calling a library function and check it afterward:

```
errno = 0;
x = sqrt(y);
if (errno) {
    printf("?sqrt failed, code %d\n", errno);
    x = 0;
}
```

In ISO C **errno** need not be a variable; it can be a macro that expands to any modifiable lvalue.

Example

It would be possible to define **errno** this way:

```
extern int *_errno_func();
#define errno (*_errno_func())
```

The function **strerror** returns a pointer to an error message string whose contents are implementation-defined; the string is not modifiable and may be overwritten by a subsequent call to the **strerror** function.

The function **perror** prints the following sequence on the standard error output stream: the argument string **s**, a colon, a space, a short message concerning the error whose error code is currently in **errno**, and a newline. In ISO C, if **s** is the null pointer or points to a null character, then only the error message is printed; the prefix string, colon, and space are not printed.

Example

The previous **sqrt** example could be rewritten to use **perror** in this way:

```
#include <math.h>
#include <errno.h>
...
errno = 0;
x = sqrt(y);
if (errno) {
    perror("sqrt failed");
    x = 0;
}
```

If the call to **sqrt** failed, the output might be:

```
sqrt failed: domain error
```

The error messages corresponding to values of **errno** may also be stored in a vector of string pointers, **sys_errlist**, which can be indexed by the value in **errno**. The variable **sys_nerr** contains the maximum integer that can be used to index **sys_errlist**; this should be checked to ensure that **errno** does not contain a nonstandard error number.

C implementations generally define a standard list of error codes that can be stored in **errno**. Traditional implementations define them in a central place, such as the header file **errno.h**; others may define them in the individual library header files. Two standard error codes are

EDOM	An argument was not in the domain accepted by a mathematical function. An example of this is giving a negative argument to the **log** function.
ERANGE	The result of a mathematical function is out of range; the function

has a well-defined mathematical result but cannot be represented because of the limitations of the floating-point format. An example of this is trying to use the **pow** function to raise a large number to a very large power.

Amendment 1 to ISO C adds:

EILSEQ An encoding error was encountered when translating a multibyte character sequence. This error is ultimately detected by **mbrtowc** or **wcrtomb**, which are in turn called by other wide character functions.

References encoding error 2.1.5; **mbrtowc** 11.7; **wcrtomb** 11.7

11.3 __DATE__, __FILE__, __STDC__, etc.

ISO C facilities	Traditional and alternate facilities
`#define __DATE__ ...`	`#define __FILE__ ...`
`#define __FILE__ ...`	`#define __LINE__ ...`
`#define __LINE__ ...`	
`#define __TIME__ ...`	
`#define __STDC__ ...`	
`#define __STDC_VERSION__ ...`	

These identifiers are special macros built into implementations of ISO C; some existing implementations also define them, especially **__FILE__** and **__LINE__**. These macros cannot be redefined or undefined, and no header file is needed to define them. The values of **__DATE__** and **__TIME__** should remain constant throughout the translation unit.

__DATE__ is a string constant representing the date of translation of the source file in the form **"Mmm dd yyyy"**, e.g., **"Jan 1 1990"**. **__FILE__** is a string constant representing the name of the source file. **__LINE__** is a decimal integer constant representing the current line number in the source file. **__TIME__** is a string constant representing the time of day at which translation occurred in the form **"hh:mm:ss"**, e.g., **"14:02:30"**.

__STDC__ is defined (with a nonzero value) only by implementations that conform to ISO C.

Example

The following code fragment checks for ISO C conformance before using **__DATE__** and **__TIME__**.

```
printf("This file was named %s\n", __FILE__);
#ifdef __STDC__
printf("It was compiled on %s at %s\n", __DATE__, __TIME__);
#endif
```

The macro **__STDC_VERSION__** is defined in Amendment 1 of ISO C to expand to the decimal constant **199409L**. It may be used to determine compliance with the Amendment.

Example

This code fragment shows how **__STDC__** and **__STD_VERSION__** can be used to determine the variation of the C language being compiled.

```
#ifdef __STDC__
   /* ISO C compliant; maybe Amendment 1 compliant */
#if defined(__STDC_VERSION__) &&
      __STDC_VERSION__ == 199409L
   /* ISO C compliant and AM1 compliant */
#else
   /* ISO C compliant, but not Amendment 1 compliant */
#endif
#else
   /* Not ISO C compliant */
#endif
```

11.4 varargs, stdarg

ISO C facilities	Traditional and alternate facilities
#include <stdarg.h>	**#include <varargs.h>** **#define va_alist ...** **#define va_dcl ...**
typedef ... va_list;	**typedef ... va_list;**
void va_start(**va_list ap,** *type LastFixedParm***);**	**void va_start(** **va_list ap);**
type **va_arg(va_list ap,** *type***);**	*type* **va_arg(va_list ap,** *type***);**
void va_end(va_list ap);	**void va_end(va_list ap);**

The **varargs** (or **stdarg**) facility gives programmers a portable way to access variable argument lists, as is needed in functions such as **fprintf** (implicitly) and **vfprintf** (explicitly).

C originally placed no restrictions on the way arguments were passed to functions, and programmers consequently made nonportable assumptions based on the behavior of one computer system. Eventually the **varargs** facility arose under UNIX to promote portability, and ISO C adopts a similar facility under the name **stdarg**. The usage of **stdarg** differs from **varargs** because ISO C allows a fixed number of parameters to precede the variable part of an argument list, whereas previous implementations force the entire argument list to be treated as variable.

The meanings of the defined macros, functions, and types are listed below. This facility is very stylized, making very few assumptions about the implementation:

va_alist This macro replaces the parameter list in the definition of a function taking a variable number of arguments; not used in ISO C.

va_dcl In traditional C, this macro replaces the parameter declarations in the function definition. It should not be followed by a semicolon, to allow for it to be empty. The macro is not used in ISO C.

va_list This type is used to declare a local state variable, uniformly called **ap** in this exposition, which is used to traverse the parameters.

va_start This macro initializes the state variable **ap**, and must be called before any calls to **va_arg** or **va_end**. In traditional C, **va_start** sets the internal pointer in **ap** to point to the first argument passed to the function; in ISO C, **va_start** takes an additional parameter—the last fixed parameter name—and sets the internal pointer in **ap** to point to the first variable argument passed to the function.

va_arg This macro returns the value of the next parameter in the argument list and advances the internal argument pointer (in **ap**) to the next argument (if any). The type of the next argument (after the usual argument conversions) must be specified (as *type*) so that **va_arg** can compute its size on the stack. The first call to **va_arg** after calling **va_start** will return the value of the first variable parameter.

va_end This function or macro should be called after all the arguments have been read with **va_arg**. It performs any necessary cleanup operations on **ap** and **va_alist**.

Example

We show how to write a variable-arguments function in both traditional C and ISO C. The function, **printargs**, takes a variable number of arguments of different types and prints their values on the standard output. The first argument to **printargs** is an array of integers that indicates the number and types of the following arguments. The array is terminated by a zero element. The declaration of printargs and the values of the integer type specifiers are kept in file **printargs.h**:

```
/* file printargs.h */
#define INTARG 1     /* codes used in argtypep[] */
#define DBLARG 2
...

#ifdef __STDC__
  #include <stdarg.h>
  void printargs( int *argtypep, ...)
#else
  #include <varargs.h>
  printargs( va_alist )
#endif
```

Here is a simple test program for **printargs**. It is valid in both traditional and ISO C:

```
#include "printargs.h
int arg_types[] = { INTARG, DBLARG, INTARG, DBLARG, 0 };
int main()
{
    printargs( &arg_types[0], 1, 2.0, 3, 4.0 );
    return 0;
}
```

The traditional C implementation of **printargs** is shown below:

```
#include <stdio.h>
#include "printargs.h"
printargs( va_alist )     /* Traditional C */
    va_dcl
{   va_list ap; int argtype, *argtypep;
    va_start(ap);

    argtypep = va_arg(ap, int *);
    while ( (argtype = *argtypep++) != 0 ) {
        switch (argtype) {
        case INTARG:
            printf("int: %d\n", va_arg(ap, int) );
            break;
        case DBLARG:
            printf("double: %f\n", va_arg(ap, double) );
            break;
        /* ... */
        }
    }
    va_end(ap);
}
```

The corresponding definition of **printargs** in ISO C is shown below. The the only differences are in the function argument list and in the call to **va_start**.

```
#include <stdio.h>
#include "printargs.h"
void printargs( int *argtypep, ...)     /* ISO C */
{   va_list ap; int argtype;
    va_start(ap, argtypep);

    while ( (argtype = *argtypep++) != 0 ) {
        switch (argtype) {
        case INTARG:
            printf("int: %d\n", va_arg(ap, int) );
            break;
```

```
            case DBLARG:
                printf("double: %f\n", va_arg(ap, double) );
                break;
            /* ... */
            }
        } /*while*/
        va_end(ap);
    }
```

11.5 setlocale

ISO C facilities

```
#include <locale.h>
#define LC_ALL ...
#define LC_COLLATE ...
#define LC_CTYPE ...
#define LC_MONETARY ...
#define LC_NUMERIC ...
#define LC_TIME ...
char *setlocale(
     int category,
     const char *locale);
```

ISO C was designed for an international community whose members have different alphabets and different conventions for formatting numbers, monetary quantities, dates, and time. The language standard allows implementations to adjust the behavior of the run-time library accordingly, while still permitting reasonable portability across national boundaries.

The set of conventions for nationality, culture, and language is termed the *locale*. The locale affects such things as the format of decimal and monetary quantities, the alphabet and collation sequence (as for the character-handling facilities in Chapter 14), and the format of date and time values. The "current locale" can be changed at run time by choosing from an implementation-defined set of locales. The ISO C standard defines only the "C" locale, which specifies a minimal environment consistent with the original definition of C.

The **setlocale** function is used to change locale-specific features of the run-time library. The first argument, **category**, is a code that specifies the behavior to be changed. The permitted values for **category** include the values of the macros in Table 11–2, possibly augmented by additional implementation-defined categories spelled beginning with the letters **LC_**.

The second argument, **locale**, is an implementation-defined string that names the locale whose conventions are to be used for the behavior designated by **category**. The only predefined values for **locale** are **"C"** for the standard C locale, and the empty string, **""**, which by convention means an implementation-defined native locale. The run-time library always uses the C locale until it is explicitly changed with **setlocale**.

Table 11–2 Predefined setlocale categories

Name	Behavior affected
LC_ALL	all behavior
LC_COLLATE	behavior of **strcoll** and **strxfrm** facilities
LC_CTYPE	character handling functions (Chapter 14)
LC_MONETARY	monetary information returned by **localeconv**
LC_NUMERIC	decimal-point and non-monetary information returned by **localeconv**
LC_TIME	behavior of **strftime** facility

If the **locale** argument to **setlocale** is a null pointer, the function does not change the locale but instead returns a pointer to a string that is the name of the current locale for the indicated category. This name is such that if **setlocale** were to be later called using the same value for **category** and the returned string as the value for **locale**, the effect would be to change the behavior to the one that was in effect when **setlocale** was called with the null **locale**. For example, a programmer who was about to change locale-specific behavior might first call **setlocale** with arguments **LC_AL** and **NULL** to get a value for the current locale that could later be used to restore the previous locale-specific behavior. The string returned must not be altered, and may be overwritten by subsequent calls to **setlocale**.

If the **locale** argument to **setlocale** is not null, **setlocale** changes the current locale and returns a string that names the new locale. A null pointer is returned if **setlocale** cannot honor the request for any reason. The string returned must not be altered, and may be overwritten by subsequent calls to **setlocale**.

Example

The function **original_locale** below returns a description of the current locale so that it can be later restored if necessary. There is no fixed maximum length for the string returned by **setlocale**, so space for it must be dynamically allocated.

```
#include <locale.h>
#include <string.h>
#include <stdlib.h>

char *original_locale(void)
{
    char *temp, *copy;
    temp = setlocale(LC_ALL, NULL);
    if (temp == NULL) return NULL;   /* setlocale() failed */
    copy = (char *)malloc(strlen(temp)+1);
    if (copy == NULL) return NULL;   /* malloc() failed */
    strcpy(copy,temp);
    return copy;
}
```

The following code uses **original_locale** to change and then restore the locale:

```
#include <locale.h>
extern char *original_locale(void);
char *saved_locale;
...
saved_locale = original_locale();
setlocale(LC_ALL,"");           /* Change to native locale */
setlocale(LC_ALL,saved_locale);/* Restore former locale   */
```

References **malloc** 16.1; **localeconv** 11.6; **strcoll** 13.10; **strcpy** 13.3; **strftime** 18.6; **strlen** 13.4; **strxfrm** 13.10

11.6 localeconv

ISO C facilities

```
#include <locale.h>
struct lconv {...};
struct lconv *localeconv(void);
```

The **localeconv** function is used to obtain information about the conventions for formatting numeric and monetary quantities in the current locale. This allows a programmer to implement application-specific conversion and formatting routines with some portability across locales, and avoids the necessity of adding locale-specific conversion facilities to ISO C. The **localeconv** function returns a pointer to an object of type **struct lconv**, whose components must include at least those in Table 11–3. The returned structure must not be altered by the programmer, and it may be overwritten by a subsequent call to **localeconv**. In **struct lconv**, string components whose value is the empty string and character components whose value is **CHAR_MAX** should be interpreted as "don't know."

Example

The following function uses **localeconv** to print a floating-point number with the correct decimal point character:

```
#include <locale.h>
#include <stdio.h>
...
void P(int int_part, int fract_part, int fract_digits)
{
    struct lconv *lconv;
    char *pt;
    lconv = localeconv();
    if (!(pt = lconv->decimal_point))
        pt = ".";
    printf("%d%s%0*d\n",
        int_part, pt, fract_digits, fract_part);
}
```

Other contents of **struct lconv** are listed in Table 11–3 and discussed below.

Table 11–3 lconv structure components

Type	Name	Use	Value in C locale
char *	**decimal_point**	Decimal point character (non-monetary)	"."
char *	**thousands_sep**	Non-monetary digit group separator character(s)	""
char *	**grouping**	Non-monetary digit groupings (see below)	""
char *	**int_curr_symbol**	The three-character international currency symbol, plus the character used to separate the international symbol from the monetary quantity	""
char *	**currency_symbol**	The local currency symbol for the current locale	""
char *	**mon_decimal_point**	Decimal point character (monetary)	""
char *	**mon_thousands_sep**	Monetary digit group separator character(s)	""
char *	**mon_grouping**	Monetary digit groupings (see below)	""
char *	**positive_sign**	Sign character(s) for nonnegative monetary quantities	""
char *	**negative_sign**	Sign character(s) for negative monetary quantities	""
char	**int_frac_digits**	Digits shown to the right of the decimal point for international monetary formats	**CHAR_MAX**
char	**frac_digits**	Digits shown to the right of the decimal point for other than international monetary formats	**CHAR_MAX**
char	**p_cs_precedes**	1 if currency_symbol precedes non-negative monetary values; 0 if it follows	**CHAR_MAX**
char	**p_sep_by_space**	1 if currency_symbol is separated from nonnegative monetary values by a space; else 0	**CHAR_MAX**
char	**n_cs_precedes**	Like **p_cs_precedes**, for negative values	**CHAR_MAX**
char	**n_sep_by_space**	Like **p_sep_by_space**, for negative values	**CHAR_MAX**
char	**p_sign_posn**	The positioning of **positive_sign** for a nonnegative monetary quantity (plus its **currency_symbol**)	**CHAR_MAX**
char	**n_sign_posn**	The positioning of **negative_sign** for a negative monetary quantity (plus its **currency_symbol**)	**CHAR_MAX**

Digit groupings The **grouping** and **mon_grouping** components of **struct lconv** are sequences of integer values of type **char**. Although they are described as strings, the string is just a way to encode a sequence of small integers. Each integer in the sequence specifies the number of digits in a group. The first integer corresponds to the first group to the left of the decimal point; the second integer corresponds to the next group moving leftward, etc. The integer 0 (the null character at the end of the string) means that the previous digit group is to be repeated; the integer **CHAR_MAX** means that no further grouping is to be performed. The conventional grouping by thousands would be specified by **"\3"**—three digits in the first group, repeated for subsequent groups—and the string **"\1\2\3\127"** would group **1234567890** as **1234 567 89 0** (**CHAR_MAX** is assumed to be 127).

Sign positions The **p_sign_posn** and **n_sign_posn** components of **struct lconv** determine where **positive_sign** and **negative_sign** (respectively) are placed. The possible values and their meaning are

0	Parentheses surround the number (including currency_symbol).
1	The sign string precedes the number (including currency_symbol).
2	The sign string follows the number (including currency_symbol).
3	The sign string immediately precedes the currency_symbol.
4	The sign string immediately follows the currency_symbol.

Complete examples of monetary formatting are shown in Table 11–4 and Table 11–5,

Table 11–4 Examples of formatted monetary quantities

	Format		
Country	Positive	Negative	International
Italy	`L.1.234`	`-L.1.234`	`ITL.1.234`
Netherlands	`F 1.234,56`	`F -1.234,56`	`NLG 1.234,56`
Norway	`kr1.234,56`	`kr1.234,56-`	`NOK 1.234,56`
Switzerland	`SFrs.1,234.56`	`SFrs.1,234.56C`	`CHF 1,234.56`

which were taken from the ISO C standard. Table 11–4 shows typical monetary formatting in four countries. Table 11–5 shows the values of the components of **struct lconv** that would specify the formatting illustrated in Table 11–4.

11.7 mblen, mbtowc, wctomb, etc.

The ISO C language has been extended to handle locale-specific character sets ("extended character sets") that are too large for each character to be represented within a single object of type **char** (e.g., an 8-bit byte). For such character sets, ISO C provides both an internal and an external representation scheme. Internally, an extended character code is

Table 11–5 Examples of `lconv` structure contents

Component	Italy	Nether-lands	Norway	Switzer-land
`int_curr_symbol`	`"ITL."`	`"NLG "`	`"NOK "`	`"CHF "`
`currency_symbol`	`"L."`	`"F"`	`"kr"`	`"SFrs."`
`mon_decimal_point`	`""`	`","`	`","`	`"."`
`mon_thousands_sep`	`"."`	`"."`	`"."`	`","`
`mon_grouping`	`"\3"`	`"\3"`	`"\3"`	`"\3"`
`positive_sign`	`""`	`""`	`""`	`""`
`negative_sign`	`"-"`	`"-"`	`"-"`	`"C"`
`int_frac_digits`	0	2	2	2
`frac_digits`	0	2	2	2
`p_cs_precedes`	1	1	1	1
`p_sep_by_space`	0	1	0	0
`n_cs_precedes`	1	1	1	1
`n_sep_by_space`	0	1	0	0
`p_sign_posn`	1	1	1	1
`n_sign_posn`	1	4	2	2

ISO C facilities

```
#include <stdlib.h>
typedef … wchar_t;
#define MB_CUR_MAX …
int mblen(const char *s, size_t n);
int mbtowc(wchar_t *pwc, const char *s, size_t n);
int wctomb(char *s, wchar_t wchar);
```

```
#include <wchar.h>
wint_t btowc(int c);
int wctob(wint_t c);
int mbsinit(const mbstate_t *ps);
size_t mbrlen(const char *s, size_t n, mbstate_t *ps);
size_t mbrtowc(wchar_t *pwc, const char *s, size_t n,
    mbstate_t *ps);
size_t wcrtomb(char *s, wchar_t wc, mbstate_t *ps);
```

assumed to fit in a wide character, an object of the implementation-defined integral type **`wchar_t`**. Strings of extended characters—wide strings—can be represented as objects of type **`wchar_t[]`**. Externally, a single wide character is assumed to encodable as a sequence of normal characters—a multibyte character corresponding to the wide character.

The original facilities for extended characters in ISO C were enhanced in Amendment 1 by the addition of new functions, types, and macros. The original functions were **`mblen`**, **`mbtowc`**, and **`wctomb`**. The new Amendment 1 functions are **`mbrlen`**, **`btowc`**,

wctob, **mbrtowc**, and **wcrtomb**. The new functions are more flexible and their behavior is more completely specified.

11.7.1 Encodings and Conversion States

This section discusses some characteristics of conversions between multibyte characters and wide characters. The terminology here will apply to many of the functions in this chapter.

No particular representation for wide or multibyte characters is mandated or excluded, but the single null character, `'\0'`, must act as a terminator in both normal and multibyte character sequences. Multibyte encodings are in general state-dependent, employing sequences of shift characters to alter the meaning of subsequent characters.

The original ISO C functions in this chapter retain internal conversion state information from the multibyte character they last processed. The new functions in Amendment 1 provide an explicit type, **mbstate_t**, to hold the conversion state, which allows several strings to be processed in parallel. However, if the new state argument is null, each function uses its own internal state. No other standard library calls are permitted to affect these internal shift states.

The maximum number of bytes used in representing a multibyte character in the current locale is given by the (non-constant) expression **MB_CUR_MAX**. Most functions that take as an argument a pointer **s** to a multibyte character also take an integer **n** that specifies the maximum number of bytes at **s** to consider. There is no reason for **n** to be larger than **MB_CUR_MAX**, but it could be smaller to restrict the conversion.

Given a current conversion state, a pointer **s** to a multibyte character, and a length **n**, there are several possibilities:

1. The first **n** or fewer bytes at **s** could form a *valid multibyte character*, which therefore corresponds to a single wide character **wc**. The conversion state would be updated accordingly. If **wc** happens to be the null wide character, we'll say that **s** *yields* the null wide character.
2. All **n** bytes at **s** could form the beginning of a valid multibyte character, but not be a complete one in themselves. No corresponding wide character can be computed. In this case we'll call **s** an *incomplete multibyte character*. (If **n** is at least **MB_CUR_MAX**, this result might occur if **s** contains redundant shift characters.)
3. The **n** bytes at **s** could form an *invalid multibyte character*. That is, it might be impossible for them to form a valid, or incomplete, multibyte character in the current encoding.

Changing the **LC_CTYPE** category of the locale (section 11.5) may change the character encodings and leave the shift state indeterminate. The value of **MB_CUR_MAX** will include enough space for shift characters.

References **mbstate_t** 11.1

11.7.2 Length Functions

The **mblen** function inspects up to **n** bytes from the string designated by **s** to see if those characters represent a valid multibyte character relative to the current shift state. If so, the number of bytes making up the multibyte character is returned. The value –1 is returned if **s** is invalid or incomplete. If **s** is a null pointer, **mblen** returns a nonzero value if the locale-specific encoding of multibyte characters is state-dependent; as a side effect, such a call resets any internal state to a predefined "initial" condition.

The **mbrlen** function is similar to **mblen**, with the following additional specifications. If **s** is a null pointer, the call is treated as if **s** were **""** and **n** were 1. If **s** is valid and corresponds to the null wide character, then 0 is returned (regardless of how many bytes make up the multibyte character). If **s** is any other valid multibyte character, then the number of bytes making up that character are returned (i.e., the value returned is in the range 1 through **n**). If **s** is an incomplete multibyte character, then –2 (cast to **size_t**) is returned. If **s** is an invalid multibyte character, then –1 (cast to **size_t**) is returned and **errno** is set to **EILSEQ**. The conversion state is updated when the return value is nonnegative; it is undefined when –1 is returned; and it is unchanged when –2 is returned.

11.7.3 Conversions to Wide Characters

The **btowc** function (from Amendment 1) returns the wide character corresponding to the byte **c**, which is treated as a one-byte multibyte character in the initial shift state. If **c** (cast to **unsigned char**) does not correspond to a valid multibyte character, or if **c** is **EOF**, then **btowc** returns **WEOF**.

The **mbtowc** function converts a multibyte character **s** to a wide character according to its internal conversion state. The result is stored in the object designated by **pwc** if **pwc** is not a null pointer. The return value is the number of characters that made up the multibyte character. If **s** is an invalid or incomplete multibyte character, then –1 is returned. If **s** is a null pointer, **mbtowc** returns a nonzero value if the locale-specific encoding of multibyte characters is state-dependent; as a side effect the conversion state is reset to the initial state.

Example

Here is an implementation of **mbstowcs** (section 11.8) using the **mbtowc** function:

```
#include <stdlib.h>
size_t mbstowcs(wchar_t *pwcs, const char *pmbs, size_t n)
{
    size_t i = 0; /* index into output array */
    (void) mbtowc(NULL,NULL,0); /* Initial shift state */
    while (*pmbs && i < n) {
        int len = mbtowc(&pwcs[i++],pmbs,MB_CUR_MAX);
        if (len == -1) return (size_t) -1;
        pmbs += len;    /* to next multibyte character */
    }
    return i;
}
```

The **mbrtowc** function (Amendment 1) is similar to **mbtowc**. If **s** is a null pointer, then the call to **mbrtowc** is equivalent to **mbrtowc(NULL, "", 1, ps)**. (That is, **s** is treated as the empty string and the values of **pwc** and **n** are ignored.) If **s** is a valid character corresponding to the null wide character, then 0 is returned (regardless of how many bytes in s were used). Otherwise, if **s** is a valid multibyte character, the number of bytes used is returned. If **s** is an incomplete multibyte character, then –2 (cast to **size_t**) is returned. Finally, if **s** is an invalid multibyte character, then –1 (cast to **size_t**) is returned. The conversion state specified by **ps** (or the internal conversion state if **ps** is the null pointer) is updated when a valid conversion occurs. The conversion state is unchanged if **s** is incomplete, and is undefined if **s** is invalid.

References **mbstate_t** 11.1; multibyte characters 2.1.5; **size_t** 11.1; **WEOF** 11.1;

11.7.4 Conversions from Wide Characters

The **wctob** function (Amendment 1) returns the single-byte multibyte character corresponding to the wide character **c** in the initial conversion state. If no such single byte exists, **EOF** is returned.

The **wctomb** function converts the wide character **wc** to multibyte representation (according to its current shift state) and stores the result in the character array designed by **s**, which should be at least **MB_CUR_MAX** characters long. The conversion state is updated. A null character is not appended. The number of characters stored at **s** is returned if **wc** is a valid character encoding; otherwise –1 is returned. If **s** is a null pointer, **wctomb** returns a nonzero value if the locale-specific encoding of multibyte characters is state-dependent; as a side effect, such a call resets any internal state to a predefined "initial" condition.

The **wcrtomb** function converts a wide character **wc** to a multibyte character relative to the conversion state designated by **ps**. The multibyte character is stored into the array whose first element is designated by **s** and which must be at least **MB_CUR_MAX** characters long. The conversion state is updated. If **wc** is a null wide character, then a null byte is stored, preceded by any shift sequence needed to restore to the initial conversion state. The function returns the number of characters stored into **s**. If **s** is a null pointer, then **wc** is ignored and the effect of calling **wcrtomb** is simply to restore the initial conversion state and return 1 (as if **L'\0'** had been converted into a hidden buffer). If wc is not a valid wide character, then **EILSEQ** is stored into **errno** and –1 (cast to **size_t**) is returned.

References **EILSEQ** 11.2; **errno** 11.2; multibyte characters 2.1.5; **mbstate_t** 11.1; **size_t** 11.1; **wchar_t** 11.1; **wint_t** 11.1

11.8 mbstowcs, wcstombs, mbsrtowcs, wcsrtombs

ISO C facilities

```
#include <stdlib.h>
size_t mbstowcs(wchar_t *pwcs, const char *s, size_t n);
size_t wcstombs(char *s, const wchar_t *pwcs, size_t n);
```

```
#include <wchar.h>
size_t mbsrtowcs(wchar_t *pwcs, const char **src, size_t n,
    mbstate_t *ps);
size_t wcsrtombs(char *s, const wchar_t **src, size_t n,
    mbstate_t *ps);
```

The functions in this section convert between wide strings and sequences of multibyte characters. The functions **mbstowcs** and **wcstombs** were included in original ISO C; the functions **mbsrtowcs** and **wcsrtombs**, the "restartable" versions, were added in Amendment 1.

11.8.1 Conversions to Wide Strings

The function **mbstowcs** converts a sequence of multibyte characters in the null-terminated string **s** to a corresponding sequence of wide characters, storing the result in the array designated by **pwcs**. The multibyte characters in **s** must begin in the initial shift state and be terminated by a null character. Each multibyte character, up to and including the terminating null character, is converted as if by a call to **mbtowc**. The conversion stops when **n** elements have been stored into the wide character array, when the end of **s** is reached (in which case a null wide character is stored in the output), or when a conversion error occurs (whichever occurs first). The function returns the number of wide characters stored (not including the terminating null wide character, if any), or –1 (cast to **size_t**) if a conversion error occurred.

The **mbsrtowcs** function (from Amendment 1) is similar to **mbstowcs** but somewhat more flexible. The initial conversion state is specified by **ps**, and the input sequence of multibyte characters is specified indirectly by **src**. In normal operation, each multibyte character, up to and including the terminating null character, is converted as if by a call to **mbrtowc**, with the output wide characters being placed in the character array designated by **pwcs**. After the conversion, the pointer designated by **src** is set to the null pointer to indicate that the entire input string was converted, and the number of wide characters stored into **pwcs** (not counting the terminating null wide character) is returned. The conversion state will be updated to be initial shift state—a consequence of converting the null character at the end of the input multibyte string.

The output pointer **pwcs** may be the null pointer, in which case no output wide characters are stored and the length argument **n** is ignored. Such a call to **mbsrtowcs** simply calculates the length of the output wide string required for the conversion.

The conversion of the input multibyte string will stop before the terminating null character is converted if **n** output wide characters have been written to **pwcs** (and **pwcs** is not a null pointer). In this case, the pointer designated by **src** is set to point just after the last-converted multibyte character. The conversion state is updated—it will not necessarily be the initial state—and **n** is returned.

The conversion of the input multibyte string will also stop prematurely if a conversion error occurs. In this case, the pointer designated by **src** is updated to point to the multibyte character whose attempted conversion caused the error. The function returns –1 (cast to **size_t**), **EILSEQ** is stored in **errno**, and the conversion state will be indeterminate.

11.8.2 Conversions from Wide Strings

The function **wcstombs** converts a sequence of wide characters beginning with the value designated by **pwcs** to a sequence of multibyte characters, storing the result into the character array designated by **s**. Each wide character is converted as if by a call to **wctomb**. The sequence of input wide characters must be terminated by a null wide character. The output multibyte character sequence will begin in the initial shift state. The conversion stops when **n** characters have been written to **s**, when the end of **pwcs** is reached (in which case a null character is appended to **s**), or when a conversion error occurs (whichever occurs first). The function returns the number of characters written to **s**, not counting the terminating null character (if any). If a conversion error occurs, the function returns –1 (cast to **size_t**).

The function **wcsrtombs** (from Amendment 1) is similar to **wcstombs** but is somewhat more flexible. The initial conversion state is specified by **ps**, and the input wide string is specified indirectly by **src**. In normal operation, each wide character, up to and including the terminating null wide character, is converted as if by a call to **wcrtomb**, with the output multibyte characters being placed in the character array designated by **s**. After the conversion, the pointer designated by **src** is set to the null pointer to indicate that the entire input string was converted, and the number of bytes stored into **s** (not counting the terminating null character) is returned. The conversion state will be updated to be initial shift state—a consequence of converting the null wide character at the end of the input wide string.

The output pointer **s** may be the null pointer, in which case no output bytes are stored and the length argument **n** is ignored. Such a call to **wcsrtombs** simply calculates the length of the output character array that would be needed for the conversion.

The conversion of the input wide string will stop before the terminating null wide character is converted if **n** output bytes have been written to **s** (and **s** is not a null pointer). In this case, the pointer designated by **src** is set to point just after the last-converted wide character. The conversion state is updated—it will not necessarily be the initial state—and **n** is returned.

The conversion of the input wide string will also stop prematurely if a conversion error occurs. In this case, the pointer designated by **src** is updated to point to the wide character whose attempted conversion caused the error. The function returns –1 (cast to **size_t**), **EILSEQ** is stored in **errno**, and the conversion state will be indeterminate.

Example

The following statements read in a multibyte character string (**mbs**), convert it to a wide character string (**wcs**), and then convert it back to a multibyte character string (**mbs2**). We consider it to be an error if the conversion functions completely fill the destination arrays because then the converted strings will not be null-terminated:

```
#include <stdlib.h>
#include <stdio.h>
#define MAX_WCS 100
#define MAX_MBS (100*MB_CUR_MAX)
wchar_t wcs[MAX_WCS+1];
char mbs[MAX_MBS], mbs2[MAX_MBS];
size_t len_wcs, len_mbs;

/* Read in multibyte string; check for error */
if (!fgets(mbs, MAX_MBS, stdin))
    abort();

/* Convert to wide character string; check for error */
len_wcs = mbstowcs(wcs, mbs, MAX_WCS);
if (len_wcs == MAX_WCS || len_wcs == (size_t)-1)
    abort();

/* Convert back to multibyte string; check for error */
len_mbs = wcstombs(mbs2, wcs, MAX_MBS);
if (len_mbs == MAX_MBS || len_mbs == (size_t)-1)
    abort();
```

References conversion state 2.1.5; multibyte character 2.1.5; wide character 2.1.5;

11.9 ISO Operator Macros

ISO C facilities

```
#include <iso646.h>
#define and      &&
#define and_eq   &=
#define bitand   &
#define bitor    |
#define compl    ~
#define not      !
#define not_eq   !=
#define or       ||
#define or_eq    |=
#define xor      ^
#define xor_eq   ^=
```

Amendment 1 to ISO C adds the header file **iso646.h**, which contains definitions of macros which can be used in place of certain operator tokens. Those tokens could be inconvenient to write in a restricted source character set (such as ISO 646).

Example

Each of the following three **if** statements has the same effect.

```
#include <iso646.h>
...
if (p || *p == 0) *p ^= q;          /* customary */
if (p ??!??! *p == 0) *p ??'= q;    /* ISO C trigraphs */
if (p or *p == 0) *p xor_eq q;      /* ISO C iso646.h*/
```

Amendment 1 also provides for the spelling of punctuator tokens such as **{** and **}** using other characters that are more common in foreign alphabets.

References token respelling 2.4.1; trigraphs 2.1.4;

12

Character Processing

There are two kinds of facilities for handling characters: classification and conversion. Every character classification facility has a name beginning with **is** and returns a value of type **int** that is nonzero (true) if the argument is in the specified class and zero (false) if not. Every character conversion facility has a name beginning with **to** and returns a value of type **int** representing a character or **EOF**. ISO C reserves names beginning with **is** and **to** for more conversion and classification facilities that may be added to the library in the future. The character-related facilities described here are declared by the library header file **ctype.h**.

Table 12–1 Chapter summary

Name	Section	Name	Section	Name	Section
isalnum[a]	12.1	**islower**[a]	12.5	**isxdigit**[a]	12.3
isalpha[a]	12.1	**isodigit**	12.3	**toascii**	12.7
isascii	12.1	**isprint**[a]	12.4	**toint**	12.8
iscntrl[a]	12.1	**ispunct**[a]	12.4	**tolower**[a]	12.9
iscsym	12.2	**isspace**[a]	12.6	**toupper**[a]	12.9
iscsymf	12.2	**isupper**[a]	12.5	**towctrans**	12.11
isdigit[a]	12.3	**iswctype**	12.10	**wctype**	12.10
isgraph[a]	12.4	**iswhite**	12.6	**wctrans[_t]**	12.11

[a] A wide-character version of this facility is described in the same section.

Amendment 1 to ISO C defines a parallel set of classification and conversion facilities that operate on wide characters. These facilities have names beginning with **isw** and **tow**, with the remainder of the name matching the corresponding character-based facility.

The wide character classification facilities accept arguments of **wint_t** and return a truth value of type **int**. The conversion facilities map between values of type **wint_t**. There are also generalized classification functions **wctrans** and **iswctrans**, and generalized conversion functions, **wctrans** and **towctrans**, since extended character sets may have special classifications. These facilities are all defined in the header file **wctype.h**. Amendment 1 reserves names beginning with **is** or **to** and followed by a lowercase letter for future additions to **wctype.h**.

The negative integer **EOF** is a value that is not an encoding of a "real character." (**WEOF** serves the same purpose for wide characters.) For example, **fgetc** (section 15.6) returns **EOF** when at end-of-file, because there is no "real character" to be read. It must be remembered, however, that the type **char** may be signed in some implementations, and so **EOF** is not necessarily distinguishable from a "real character" if nonstandard character values appear. (Standard character values are always nonnegative, even if the type **char** is signed.) All of the facilities described here operate properly on all values representable as type **char** or type **unsigned char**, and also on the value **EOF**, but are undefined for all other integer values, unless the individual description states otherwise. **WEOF** serves the same purpose for **wchar_t** as **EOF** does for char, but **WEOF** does not have to be negative.

The formulation of these facilities in ISO C takes into account the possibility that several locales will be supported, and in general tries to make as few assumptions as possible about character encodings or concepts such as "letter." The traditional C version of these functions is roughly equivalent to the ISO C formulation for the "C" locale, except that any ASCII-dependencies (such as **isascii** and **toascii**) are also removed.

Warning: Some non-ISO implementations of C let the type **char** be signed and also support a type **unsigned char**, yet the character-handling facilities fail to operate properly on all values representable by type **unsigned char**. In some cases the facilities even fail to operate properly on all values representable by type **char**, but handle only "standard" character values and **EOF**.

References **EOF** 11.1; **WEOF** 11.1; wide character 2.1.4; **wchar_t** 11.1; **wint_t** 11.1

12.1 isalnum, isalpha, iscntrl, iswalnum, iswalpha, iswcntrl

ISO C facilities	Traditional and alternate facilities
`#include <ctype.h>`	`#include <ctype.h>`
`int isalnum(int c);`	`int isalnum(char c);`
`int isalpha(int c);`	`int isalpha(char c);`
	`int isascii(int c);`
`int iscntrl(int c);`	`int iscntrl(char c);`
`#include <wctype.h>`	
`int iswalnum(wint_t c);`	
`int iswalpha(wint_t c);`	
`int iswcntrl(wint_t c);`	

The **isalnum** function tests whether **c** is an alphanumeric character—that is, one of the following in the C locale:

```
0 1 2 3 4 5 6 7 8 9
A B C D E F G H I J K L M N O P Q R S T U V W X Y Z
a b c d e f g h i j k l m n o p q r s t u v w x y z
```

This function is by definition equivalent to

```
isalpha(c) || isdigit(c)
```

The **isalpha** function tests whether **c** is an alphabetic character—that is, one of the following for the C locale:

```
A B C D E F G H I J K L M N O P Q R S T U V W X Y Z
a b c d e f g h i j k l m n o p q r s t u v w x y z
```

In any locale, this function is true whenever **islower(c)** or **isupper(c)** is true, and it is false whenever **iscntrl(c)**, **isdigit(c)**, **ispunct(c)**, or **isspace(c)** is true, but otherwise it is implementation-defined.

The function **isascii** tests whether the value of **c** is in the range 0 through 127 (177_8 or $7F_{16}$), the range of the standard 128-character ASCII character set. Unlike most of the character classification functions in traditional C, **isascii** operates properly on any value of type **int**. Because of its non-generality, **isascii** is not supplied in ISO C.

The function **iscntrl** tests whether **c** is a "control character." If the standard 128-character ASCII set is in use, the control characters are those with values 0 through 31 (37_8 or $1F_{16}$), and also 127 (177_8 or $7F_{16}$). The **isprint** function (section 12.4) is the complementary function, at least for standard ASCII implementations.

Example

The function **is_id** below returns **TRUE** if the argument string **s** is a valid C identifier; otherwise it returns **FALSE**. The current locale must be C for this function to work correctly.

```
#include <ctype.h>
int is_id(const char *s)
{
    char ch;
    if ((ch = *s++) == '\0') return FALSE; /*empty string*/
    if (!(isalpha(ch) || ch == '_')) return FALSE;
    while ((ch = *s++) != '\0') {
        if (!(isalnum(ch) || ch == '_')) return FALSE;
    }
    return TRUE;
}
```

12.1.1 Wide-character Facilities

File header **wctype.h** defined in Amendment 1 of ISO C provides three additional functions.

The **iswalnum** function is equivalent to **iswalpha(c) || iswdigit(c)**.

The **iswalpha** function tests whether **c** is a locale-specific set of "alphabetic" wide characters. In any locale, this function is true whenever **iswlower(c)** or **iswupper(c)** is true, and it is false whenever **iswcntrl(c)**, **iswdigit(c)**, **iswpunct(c)**, or **iswspace(c)** is true, but otherwise it is implementation-defined.

The function **iswcntrl** returns a nonzero value if **c** is the code for a locale-specific set of *control wide characters*. A control wide character cannot be a printing wide character, as classified by **iswprint** (section 12.4).

12.2 iscsym, iscsymf

ISO C facilities	Traditional and alternate facilities
	#include <ctype.h> **int iscsym(char c);** **int iscsymf(char c);**

The **iscsym** function tests whether **c** is a character that may appear in a C identifier. **iscsymf** tests if **c** is the code for a character that may additionally appear as the first character of an identifier.

The **iscsymf** function will be true for at least the 52 upper and lowercase letters, and the underscore character. **iscsym** will additionally be true for at least 10 decimal digits. These functions may be true for other characters as well, depending on the implementation. These functions are not found in ISO C.

12.3 isdigit, isodigit, isxdigit, iswdigit, iswxdigit

ISO C facilities	Traditional and alternate facilities
#include <ctype.h> **int isdigit(int c);** **int isxdigit(int c)**	**#include <ctype.h>** **int isdigit(char c);** **int isxdigit(char c);** **int isodigit(char c);**
#include <wctype.h> **int iswdigit(int c);** **int iswxdigit(int c);**	

The **isdigit** function tests whether **c** is one of the 10 decimal digits. The **isodigit** function tests if **c** is the code for one of the 8 octal digits. The **isxdigit** function tests if **c** is one of the 22 hexadecimal digits—that is, one of the following:

```
0 1 2 3 4 5 6 7 8 9 A B C D E F a b c d e f
```

12.3.1 Wide-character Facilities

The **iswdigit** function (ISO C Amendment 1) tests whether **c** corresponds to one of the decimal-digit characters. The **iswxdigit** function tests whether **c** corresponds to one of the hexadecimal-digit characters.

12.4 isgraph, isprint, ispunct, iswgraph, iswprint, iswpunct

ISO C facilities	Traditional and alternate facilities
#include <ctype.h> **int isgraph(int c);** **int ispunct(int c);** **int isprint(char c);**	**#include <ctype.h>** **int isprint(int c);** **int isgraph(char c);** **int ispunct(char c);**
#include <wctype.h> **int iswgraph(wint_t c);** **int iswpunct(wint_t c);** **int iswprint(wint_t c);**	

The **isprint** function tests whether **c** is a *printing character*—that is, any character that is not a control character. A space is always considered to be a printing character. The **isgraph** function tests whether **c** is the code for a "graphic character"—that is, any printing character other than space. The **isprint** and **isgraph** functions differ only in how they handle the space character; **isprint** is the opposite of **iscntrl** in most implementations, but this need not be so for every locale in ISO C.

Example

If the standard 128-character ASCII set is in use, the printing characters are those with codes **040** through **0176**—that is, space plus the following:
32 126

```
! " # $ % & ' ( ) * + , - . /
0 1 2 3 4 5 6 7 8 9 : ; < = > ?
@ A B C D E F G H I J K L M N O P Q R S T U V W X Y Z
[ \ ] ^ _
` a b c d e f g h i j k l m n o p q r s t u v w x y z
{ | } ~
```

The graphic characters are the same, but space is omitted.

The function **ispunct** tests whether **c** is the code for a "punctuation character"—a printing character that is neither a space nor any character for which **isalnum** is true.

Example

If the standard 128-character ASCII character set is in use, the punctuation characters are space plus the following:

```
! " # $ % & ' ( ) * + , - . / : ; < = >
? @ [ \ ] ^ _ ` { | } ~
```

12.4.1 Wide-character Facilities

The **iswprint** function (ISO C Amendment 1) tests whether **c** is a *printing wide character*—that is, a locale-specific wide character that occupies at least one position on a display device and is not a control wide character.

The **iswgraph** function is equivalent to **iswprint(c) && !iswspace(c)**. The function **iswpunct** tests whether **c** is a local-specific wide character for which:

```
iswprint(c) && !(iswalnum(c) || iswspace(c))
```

12.5 islower, isupper, iswlower, iswupper

ISO C facilities	Traditional and alternate facilities
`#include <ctype.h>`	`#include <ctype.h>`
`int islower(int c);`	`int islower(char c);`
`int isupper(int c);`	`int isupper(char c);`
`#include <wctype.h>`	
`int iswlower(wint_t c);`	
`int iswupper(wint_t c);`	

In the C locale, the **islower** function tests whether **c** is one of the 26 lowercase letters, and the **isupper** function tests whether **c** is one of the 26 uppercase letters. In other locales, the functions may return true for other characters as long as they satisfy:

```
!iscntrl(c) && !isdigit(c) && !ispunct(c) && !isspace(c)
```

12.5.1 Wide-character Facilities

The **iswlower** function (ISO C Amendment 1) tests whether **c** corresponds to a lowercase letter, or is another of a local-specific set of wide characters which satisfies:

```
!iswcntrl(c) && !iswdigit(c) &&
!iswpunct(c) && !iswspace(c)
```

The **iswupper** function tests whether **c** corresponds to an uppercase letter, or is another of a locale-specific set of wide characters which satisfies the same logical condition as **iswlower**.

12.6 isspace, iswhite, iswspace

ISO C facilities	Traditional and alternate facilities
#include <ctype.h> **int isspace(int c);**	**#include <ctype.h>** **int isspace(char c);** **int iswhite(char c);**
#include <wctype.h> **int iswspace(wint_t c);**	

The **isspace** function tests whether **c** is the code for a whitespace character. In the C locale, **isspace** returns true for only the tab (**'\t'**), carriage return (**'\r'**), newline (**'\n'**), vertical tab (**'\v'**), form feed (**'\f'**), and space (**' '**) characters. Many other library facilities use **isspace** as the definition of whitespace. Some implementations of C provide not this exact function but a variant called **iswhite**.

12.6.1 Wide-character Facilities

The **iswspace** function (ISO C Amendment 1) tests whether **c** is a locale-specific wide character which satisfies:

```
!iswalnum(c) && !iswgraph(c) && !ispunct(c)
```

12.7 toascii

ISO C facilities	Traditional and alternate facilities
	#include <ctype.h> **int toascii(int c);**

The **toascii** function accepts any integer value and reduces it to the range of valid ASCII characters (codes 0 through 127 [177_8 or $3F_{16}$]) by discarding all but the low-order seven bits of the value. If the argument is already a valid ASCII code, then the result is equal to the argument. This facility is not present in ISO C.

12.8 toint

ISO C facilities	Traditional and alternate facilities
	`#include <ctype.h>` `int toint(char c);`

The **`toint`** function returns the "weight" of a hexadecimal digit: 0 through 9 for the characters **`'0'`** through **`'9'`**, respectively, and 10 through 15 for the letters **`'a'`** through **`'f'`** (or **`'A'`** through **`'F'`**), respectively. The function's behavior if the argument is not a hexadecimal digit is implementation-defined.

Example

This facility is not present in ISO C, but it is easily implemented. This implementation assumes that certain characters are contiguous in the target encoding:

```
int toint( int c )
{
    if (c >= '0' && c <= '9') return c - '0';
    if (c >= 'A' && c <= 'F') return c - 'A' + 10;
    if (c >= 'a' && c <= 'f') return c - 'a' + 10;
    /* c is not a hexadecimal digit */
    return 0;
}
```

12.9 tolower, toupper, towlower, towupper

ISO C facilities	Traditional and alternate facilities

`#include <ctype.h>`
`int tolower(int c);`
`int toupper(int c);`
	`#include <ctype.h>`
	`int tolower(char c);`
	`int toupper(char c);`
	`#define _tolower(c) ...`
	`#define _toupper(c) ...`

`#include <wctype.h>`
`wint_t towlower(wint_t c);`
`wint_t towupper(wint_t c);`	

If **`c`** is an uppercase letter, then **`tolower`** returns the corresponding lowercase letter. If **`c`** is a lowercase letter, then **`toupper`** returns the corresponding uppercase letter. In all other cases, the argument is returned unchanged.

In some locales, there may be uppercase letters without corresponding lowercase letters, or vice versa; in these cases, the functions return their arguments unchanged.

When using non-ISO implementations, you should be wary of the value returned by **`tolower`** when its argument is not an uppercase letter, and of the value returned by

toupper when its argument is not a lowercase letter. Many non-ISO implementations work correctly only when the argument is a letter of the proper case.

Implementations that allow more general arguments to **tolower** and **toupper** may provide faster versions of these—**_tolower** and **_toupper**—which require the more restrictive arguments and which are correspondingly faster.

Example

If the version of **tolower** in your C library is not well behaved for arbitrary arguments, the function **safe_tolower** below acts like **tolower** but is safe for all arguments. It is difficult to write **safe_tolower** as a macro, because the argument is evaluated twice (by **isupper** and by **tolower**):

```
#include <ctype.h>
int safe_tolower(int c)
{
    if (isupper(c)) return tolower(c);
    else return c;
}
```

12.9.1 Wide-character Facilities

The functions **towlower** and **towupper** are defined in Amendment 1 to ISO C.

If **c** is a wide character for which **iswupper(c)** is true, and if **d** is a wide character corresponding to **c** for which **iswlower(d)** is true, then **towlower(c)** returns **d** and **towupper(d)** returns **c**. Otherwise, the two functions return their arguments unchanged.

12.10 wctype_t, wctype, iswctype

ISO C facilities

```
#include <wctype.h>

typedef ... wctype_t;
wctype_t wctype(const char *property);
int iswctype(wint_t c, wctype_t desc);
```

The functions **wctype** and **iswctype** are defined in Amendment 1 to ISO C. They implement an extensible, locale-specific, wide-character classification facility.

The type **wctype_t** must be scalar; it holds values representing locale-specific wide character classifications.

The **wctype** function constructs a value of type **wctype_t** that represents a class of wide characters. The class is specified by the string name **property**, which is specific to the value of the **LC_CTYPE** category of the current locale. All locales must permit **property** to have any of the string names in Table 12–2 on page 322, with the listed meaning.

Table 12–2 Property names for **wctype**

property name	specifies the class for which
"alnum"	**iswalnum(c)** is true
"alpha"	**iswalpha(c)** is true
"cntrl"	**iswcntrl(c)** is true
"digit"	**iswdigit(c)** is true
"graph"	**iswgraph(c)** is true
"lower"	**iswlower(c)** is true
"print"	**iswprint(c)** is true
"punct"	**iswpunct(c)** is true
"space"	**iswspace(c)** is true
"upper"	**iswupper(c)** is true
"xdigit"	**iswxdigit(c)** is true

The **iswctype** function tests if **c** is a member of the class represented by the value **desc**. The setting of the **LC_TYPE** category when **iswctype** is called must be the same as the setting of **LC_TYPE** when the value **desc** was determined by **wctype**.

Example

The expression **iswctype(c, wctype("alnum"))** has the same truth value as **iswalnum(c)**, for any wide character **c** and any locale setting. The same holds for the other property strings and their corresponding classification functions.

References **LC_CTYPE** 11.5; locale 11.5

12.11 *wctrans_t, wctrans*

ISO C facilities

```
#include <wctype.h>

typedef ... wctrans_t;
wctrans_t wctrans(const char *property);
wint_t towctrans(wint_t c, wctrans_t desc);
```

The facilities in this section are defined in Amendment 1 to ISO C. They implement an extensible, locale-specific, wide-character mapping facility.

The type **wctrans_t** must be scalar; it holds values representing locale-specific wide character mappings.

The **wctrans** function constructs a value of type **wctrans_t** that represents a mapping between wide characters. The mapping is specified by the string name **property**, which is specific to the value of the **LC_CTYPE** category of the current locale. All locales must permit **property** to have any of the following string values, with the listed meaning:

property value	specifies the same mapping as performed by
"tolower"	**towlower(c)**
"toupper"	**towupper(c)**

(Note that the property names are different from the function names.)

The **towctrans** function maps **c** to another wide character as specified by the value **desc**. The setting of the **LC_TYPE** category when **towctrans** is called must be the same as the setting of **LC_TYPE** when the value **desc** was determined by **wctrans**.

Example

The expression **towctrans(c, wctrans("tolower"))** has the same value as **towlower(c)**, for any wide character **c** and any locale setting. The same holds for the other property string and its corresponding mapping function.

References **LC_CTYPE** 11.5; locale 11.5

13

String Processing

By convention, strings in C are arrays of characters ending with a null character (`'\0'`). The compiler automatically supplies an extra null character after all string constants, but it is up to the programmer to make sure that strings created in character arrays end with a null character. All of the string-handling facilities described here assume that strings are terminated by a null character.

All the characters in a string, not counting the terminating null character, are together called the contents of the string. An empty string contains no characters and is represented by a pointer to a null character. Note that this is not the same as a null character pointer (**NULL**), which is a pointer that points to no character at all.

Table 13–1 Chapter summary

Name	Section	Name	Section	Name	Section
atof	13.9	**strlen**[a]	13.4	**strspn**[a]	13.6
atoi	13.9	**strncat**[a]	13.1	**strstr**[a]	13.7
atol	13.9	**strncmp**[a]	13.2	**strtod**[a]	13.8
strcat[a]	13.1	**strncpy**[a]	13.3	**strtok**[a]	13.7
strchr[a]	13.5	**strpbrk**[a]	13.6	**strtol**[a]	13.8
strcoll[a]	13.10	**strpos**	13.5	**strtoul**[a]	13.8
strcmp[a]	13.2	**strrchr**[a]	13.5	**strxfrm**[a]	13.10
strcpy[a]	13.3	**strrpbrk**	13.6		
strcspn[a]	13.6	**strrpos**	13.5		

[a] A wide-string version of this function is described in the same section.

When characters are transferred to a destination string, often no test is made for overflow of the destination. It is up to the programmer to make sure that the destination area in memory is large enough to contain the result string, including the terminating null character.

Most of the facilities described here are declared by the library header file **string.h**; some ISO C conversion facilities are provided by **stdlib.h**. In ISO C, string parameters that are not modified are generally declared to have type **const char *** instead of **char ***; integer arguments or return values that represent string lengths have type **size_t** instead of **int**.

Amendment 1 to ISO C adds a set of wide-string functions that parallel the normal string functions. The differences are that the wide-string functions take arguments of type **wchar_t *** instead of **char ***, and the names of the wide-string functions are derived from the string functions by replacing the initial letters **str** with **wcs**. Wide strings are terminated with a wide null character. When comparing wide strings, the integral values of the **wchar_t** elements are compared. The wide characters are not interpreted, and no encoding errors are possible.

Other string facilities are provided by the memory functions (Chapter 14), **sprintf** (section 15.11), and **sscanf** (section 15.8).

References **wchar_t** 11.1; wide character 2.1.4

13.1 strcat. strncat, wcscat, wcsncat

ISO C facilities	Traditional and alternate facilities
#include <string.h> **char *strcat(** **char *dest,** **const char *src);** **char *strncat(** **char *dest,** **const char *src, size_t n);**	**#include <string.h>** **char *strcat(** **char *dest,** **char *src);** **char *strncat(** **char *dest,** **char *src, int n);**
#include <wchr.h> **wchar_t *wcscat(** **wchar_t *dest,** **const wchar_t *src);** **wchar_t *wcsncat(** **wchar_t *dest,** **const wchar_t *src, size_t n);**	

The function **strcat** appends the contents of the string **src** to the end of the string **dest**. The value of **dest** is returned. The null character that terminates **dest** (and perhaps other characters following it in memory) is overwritten with characters from **src** and a new terminating null character. Characters are copied from **src** until a null character is encountered in **src**. The memory area beginning with **dest** is assumed to be large enough to hold both strings.

wcscat is the same as **strcat** except for the types of the arguments and result.

Example

The following statements append three strings to **D**; at the end, **D** contains the string **"All for one."**:

```
#include <string.h>
char D[20];
...
D[0] = '\0';          /* Set string to empty */
strcat(D,"All ");
strcat(D,"for ");
strcat(D,"one.");
```

The **strncat** function appends up to **n** characters from the contents of **src** to the end of **dest**. If the null character that terminates **src** is encountered before **n** characters have been copied, then the null character is copied but no more. If no null character appears among the first **n** characters of **src**, then the first **n** characters are copied and then a null character is supplied to terminate the destination string; that is, **n**+1 characters in all are written. If the value of **n** is zero or negative, then calling **strncat** has no effect. The function always returns **dest**.

wcsncat is like **strncat** except for the types of the arguments and result.

The behavior of all these functions is undefined if the strings overlap in memory.

13.2 strcmp, strncmp, wcscmp, wcsncmp

ISO C facilities	Traditional and alternate facilities

`#include <string.h>`
`int strcmp(`
`  const char *s1, const char *s2);`
`int strncmp(`
`  const char *s1, const char *s2,`
`  size_t n);`
	`#include <string.h>`
	`int strcmp(`
	`  char *s1, char *s2);`
	`int strncmp(`
	`  char *s1, char *s2,`
	`  int n);`

`#include <wchr.h>`
`int wcscmp(`
`  const wchar_t *s1,`
`  const wchar_t *s2);`
`int wcsncmp(`
`  const wchar_t *s1,`
`  const wchar_t *s2, size_t n);`	

The function **strcmp** lexicographically compares the contents of the null-terminated string **s1** with the contents of the null-terminated string **s2**. It returns a value of type

int that is less than zero if **s1** is less than **s2**; equal to zero if **s1** is equal to **s2**; and greater than zero if **s1** is greater than **s2**.

Example

To check only whether two strings are equal, you negate the return value from **strcmp**:

```
if (!strcmp(s1,s2)) printf("Strings are equal\n");
else printf("Strings are not equal\n");
```

Two strings are equal if their contents are identical. String **s1** is lexicographically less than string **s2** under either of two circumstances:

1. The strings are equal up to some character position, and at that first differing character position the character value from **s1** is less than the character value from **s2**.
2. The string **s1** is shorter than the string **s2**, and the contents of **s1** are identical to those of **s2** up to length of **s1**.

wcscmp (Amendment 1) is like **strcmp** except for the types of the arguments.

The function **strncmp** is like **strcmp** except that it compares up to **n** characters of the null-terminated string **s1** with up to **n** characters of the null-terminated string **s2**. In comparing the strings, the entire string is used if it contains fewer than **n** characters, and otherwise the string is treated as if it were **n** characters long. If the value of **n** is zero or negative, then both strings are treated as empty and therefore equal, and zero is returned.

wcsncmp is like **strncmp** except for the types of the arguments.

The function **memcmp** (section 14.2) provides similar functionality to **strcmp**. The **strcoll** function (section 13.10) provides locale-specific comparison facilities.

13.3 *strcpy, strncpy, wcscpy, wcsncpy*

ISO C facilities	Traditional and alternate facilities
#include <string.h> **char *strcpy(** **char *dest, const char *src);** **char *strncpy(** **char *dest, const char *src,** **size_t n);**	**#include <string.h>** **char *strcpy(** **char *dest, char *src);** **char *strncpy(** **char *dest, char *src,** **int n);**
#include <wchar.h> **wchar_t *wcscpy(** **wchar_t *dest,** **const wchar_t *src);** **wchar_t *wcsncpy(** **wchar_t *dest,** **const wchar_t *src, size_t n);**	

The function **strcpy** copies the contents of the string **src** to the string **dest**, overwriting the old contents of **dest**. The entire contents of **src** are copied, plus the terminating null character, even if **src** is longer than **dest**. The argument **dest** is returned.

wcscpy (ISO Amendment 1) is like **strcpy** except for the types of its arguments.

Example

The **strcat** function (section 13.1) can be implemented with the **strcpy** and **strlen** (section 13.4) functions as follows:

```
#include <string.h>
char *strcat(char *dest, const char *src)
{
    char *s = dest + strlen(dest);
    strcpy(s, src);
    return dest;
}
```

The function **strncpy** copies exactly **n** characters to **dest**. It first copies up to **n** characters from **src**. If there are fewer than **n** characters in **src** before the terminating null character, then null characters are written into **dest** as padding until exactly **n** characters have been written. If there are **n** or more characters in **src**, then only **n** characters are copied, and so only a truncated copy of **src** is transferred to **dest**. It follows that the copy in **dest** is terminated with a null by **strncpy** only if the length of **src** (not counting the terminating null) is less than **n**. If the value of **n** is zero or negative, then calling **strncpy** function has no effect. The value of **dst** is always returned.

wcsncpy (Amendment 1) is like **strcpy** except for the types of its arguments.

The functions **memcpy** and **memccpy** (section 14.3) provide similar functionality to **strcpy**. The results of both **strcpy**, **strncpy**, and their wide-string equivalents are unpredictable if the two string arguments overlap in memory. The functions **memmove** and **wcsmove** (section 14.3) are provided in ISO C for cases in which overlap may occur.

13.4 strlen, wcslen

ISO C facilities	Traditional and alternate facilities
`#include <string.h>` `size_t strlen(const char *s);`	`#include <string.h>` `int strlen(char *s);`
`#include <wchar.h>` `size_t wcslen(const wchar_t *s);`	

The function **strlen** returns the number of characters in **s** preceding the terminating null character. An empty string has a null character as its first character and therefore its length is zero. In some implementations of C this function is called **lenstr**.

wcslen (ISO Amendment 1) is like **strlen** except for the type of its argument.

13.5 strchr, strrchr, wcschr, wcsrchr

ISO C facilities	Traditional and alternate facilities

`#include <string.h>`
`char *strchr(`
`  const char *s, int c);`
`char *strrchr(`
`  const char *s, int c);`
	`#include <string.h>`
	`char *strchr(`
	`  char *s, char c);`
	`char *strrchr(`
	`  char *s, char c);`
	`int strpos(char *s, char c);`
	`int strrpos(char *s, char c);`

`#include <wchar.h>`
`wchar_t *wcschr(`
`  const wchar_t *s, wchar_t c);`
`wchar_t *wcsrchr(`
`  const wchar_t *s, wchar_t c);`	

The functions in this section all search for a single character **c** within a null-terminated string **s**. In the ISO C functions, the terminating null character of **s** is considered to be part of the string. That is, if **c** is the null character (0), the functions will return the position of the terminating null character of **s**.

The function **strchr** searches the string **s** for the first occurrence of the character **c**. If the character **c** is found in the string, a pointer to the first occurrence is returned. If the character is not found, a null pointer is returned.

The function **wcschr** (ISO Amendment 1) is like **strchr** except for the types of its arguments and return value.

The function **strrchr** is like **strchr** except that it returns a pointer to the last occurrence of the character **c**. If the character is not found, a null pointer is returned.

The function **wcsrchr** (ISO Amendment 1) is like **strrchr** except for the types of its arguments and return value.

The function **strpos** is like **strchr** except that the position of the first occurrence of **c** is returned, where the first character of **s** is considered to be at position 0. If the character is not found, the value –1 is returned. The function **strrpos** is like **strrchr** except that the position of the last occurrence of **c** is returned. Neither **strpos** nor **strrpos** is provided by ISO C.

These functions consider the terminating null character to be a part of **s** for the purposes of the search, so searching for a null character will always succeed and result in a pointer to (or the position of) the terminating null character.

The functions **memchr** and **wcschr** (section 14.1) provide similar functionality to **strchr** and **wcschr**. In some implementations of C **strchr** and **strrchr** are called **index** and **rindex**, respectively. Some implementations of C provide the function **scnstr**, which is a variant of **strpos**.

Example

The function **how_many** below uses **strchr** to count the number of times a specified non-null character appears in a string. The parameter **s** is repeatedly updated to point to the portion of the string just after the last-found character:

```
int how_many(const char *s, int c)
{
    int n = 0;
    if (c == 0) return 0;
    while(s) {
        s = strchr(s, c);
        if (s) n++, s++;
    }
    return n;
}
```

13.6 strspn, strcspn, strpbrk, strrpbrk, wcsspn, wcscspn, wcspbrk

ISO C facilities	Traditional and alternate facilities
`#include <string.h>`	`#include <string.h>`

`size_t strspn(`
`  const char *s,`
`  const char *set);`
`size_t strcspn(`
`  const char *s,`
`  const char *set);`
`char *strpbrk(`
`  const char *s,`
`  const char *set);`
	`int strspn(`
	`  char *s,`
	`  char *set);`
	`int strcspn(`
	`  char *s,`
	`  char *set);`
	`char *strpbrk(`
	`  char *s,`
	`  char *set);`
	`char *strrpbrk(`
	`  char *s,`
	`  char *set);`

`#include <wchar.h>`	

`size_t wcsspn(`
`  const wchar_t *s,`
`  const wchar_t *set);`
`size_t wcscspn(`
`  const wchar_t *s,`
`  const wchar_t *set);`
`wchar_t *wcspbrk(`
`  const wchar_t *s,`
`  const wchar_t *set);`	

The functions in this section all search a null-terminated string **s** for occurrences of characters specified by whether or not they are included in a second null-terminated string

set. The second argument is regarded as a set of characters; the order of the characters, or whether there are duplications, does not matter.

The function **strspn** searches the string **s** for the first occurrence of a character that is not included in the string **set**, skipping over ("spanning") characters that are in set. The value returned is the length of the longest initial segment of **s** that consists of characters found in **set**. If every character of **s** appears in **set**, then the total length of **s** (not counting the terminating null character) is returned. If **set** is an empty string, then the first character of **s** will not be found in it, and so zero will be returned.

The function **strcspn** is like **strspn** except that it searches **s** for the first occurrence of a character that is included in the string **set**, skipping over characters that are not in **set**.

The function **strpbrk** is like **strcspn** except that it returns a pointer to the first character found from **set** rather than the number of characters skipped over. If no characters from **set** are found, a null pointer is returned.

The function **strrpbrk** is like **strpbrk** except that it returns a pointer to the last character from **set** found within **s**. If no character within **s** occurs in **set**, then a null pointer is returned. This function is not provided by ISO C.

The **wcsspn**, **wcsspn**, and **wcspbrk** functions (ISO C Amendment 1) are the same as their **str** counterparts except for the types of their arguments and result.

In some implementations, **strspn** and **strcspn** are called **notstr** and **instr**.

Example

The function **is_id** determines whether the input string is a valid C identifier. **strspn** is used to see whether all the string's characters are letters, digits, or the underscore character. If so, a final test is made to be sure the first character is not a digit. Compare this solution with the one given in section 12.1:

```
#include <string.h>
#define TRUE (1)
#define FALSE (0)

int is_id(const char *s)
{
    static char *id_chars =
          "abcdefghijklmnopqrstuvwxyz"
          "ABCDEFGHIJKLMNOPQRSTUVWXYZ"
          "0123456789_";
    if (s == NULL) return FALSE;
    if (strspn(s,id_chars) != strlen(s)) return FALSE;
    return isalpha(*s) || *s == '_';
}
```

13.7 *strstr, strtok, wcsstr, wcstok*

ISO C facilities	Traditional and alternate facilities

`#include <string.h>`
 	
`char *strtok(`
`  char *str, const char *set);`
`char *strstr(`
`  const char *src, const char *sub );`
	`#include <string.h>`
	
	`char *strtok(`
	`  char *str,`
	`  char *set);`

`#include <wchar.h>`
 	
`wchar_t *wcstok(`
`  wchar_t *str, const wchar_t *set,`
`  wchar_t **ptr);`
`wchar_t *wcsstr(`
`  const wchar_t *src, const wchar_t *sub );`	

The function **strstr** is new in ISO C. It locates the first occurrence of the string **sub** in the string **src** and returns a pointer to the beginning of the first occurrence. If **sub** does not occur in **src**, a null pointer is returned.

The **wcsstr** function (ISO C Amendment 1) id the same as **strstr** except for the types of its arguments and result.

The function **strtok** may be used to separate a string **str** into tokens separated by characters from the string **set**. A call is made on **strtok** for each token, possibly changing the value of **set** in successive calls. The first call includes the string **str**; subsequent calls pass a null pointer as the first argument, directing **strtok** to continue from the end of the previous token. (The original string **str** must not be modified while **strtok** is being used to find more tokens in the string.)

More precisely, if **str** is not null, then **strtok** first skips over all characters in **str** that are also in **set**. If all the characters of **str** occur in **set**, then **strtok** returns a null pointer, and an internal state pointer is set to a null pointer. Otherwise, the internal state pointer is set to point to the first character of **str** not in **set**, and execution continues as if **str** had been null.

If **str** is null and the internal state pointer is null, then **strtok** returns a null pointer, and the internal state pointer is unchanged. (This handles extra calls to **strtok** after all the tokens have been returned.) If **str** is null but the internal state pointer is not null, then the function searches beginning at the internal state pointer for the first character contained in **set**. If such a character is found, the character is overwritten with **'\0'**, **strtok** returns the value of the internal state pointer, and the internal state pointer is adjusted to point to the character immediately following inserted null character. If no such character is found, **strtok** returns the value of the internal state pointer, and the internal state pointer is set to null.

Library facilities in ISO C are not permitted to alter the internal state of **strtok** in any way that the programmer could detect. That is, the programmer does not have to worry about a library function using **strtok** and thereby interfering with the programmer's own use of the function.

The **wcstok** function (ISO C Amendment 1) is the same as **strtok**, except for the types of its arguments and result. Also, the additional **ptr** parameter indirectly designates a pointer that is used as the "internal state pointer" of **strtok**. That is, the caller of **wcstok** provides a holder for the internal state.

Example

The following program reads lines from the standard input and uses **strtok** to break the lines into "words"—sequences of characters separated by spaces, commas, periods, quotation marks, and/or question marks. The words are printed on the standard output:

```
#include <stdio.h>
#include <string.h>
#define LINELENGTH 80
#define SEPCHARS " .,?\"\n"
int main(void)
{
    char line[LINELENGTH];
    char *word;

    while(TRUE) {
        printf("\nNext line?  (empty line to quit)\n");
        fgets(line,LINELENGTH,stdin);
        if (strlen(line) <= 1) break;    /* exit program */
        printf("That line contains these words:\n");
        word = strtok(line,SEPCHARS);/* find first word */
        while (word != NULL) {
            printf("\"%s\"\n",word);
            word = strtok(NULL,SEPCHARS);/*find next word*/
        }
    }
}
```

Here is a sample execution of the program:

```
Next line?  (empty line to quit)
"My goodness," she said, "Is that right?"
That line contains these words:
"My"
"goodness"
"she"
"said"
"Is"
"that"
"right"

Next line?  (empty line to quit)
```

13.8 strtod, strtol, strtoul, wcstod, wcstol, wcstoul

ISO C facilities	Traditional and alternate facilities
#include <stdlib.h> **double strtod(** **const char *str, char **ptr);** **long strtol(** **const char *str, char **ptr,** **int base);** **unsigned long strtoul(** **const char *str, char **ptr,** **int base);**	 **double strtod(** **char *str,** **char **ptr);** **long strtol(** **char *str,** **char **ptr,** **int base);**
#include <wchar.h> **double wcstod(** **const wchar_t *str, wchar_t **ptr);** **long wcstol(** **const wchar_t *str, wchar_t **ptr,** **int base);** **unsigned long wcstoul(** **const wchar_t *str, wchar_t **ptr,** **int base);**	

The string-to-number conversion functions **strtod** and **strtol** originated in System V UNIX and were adopted by ISO for C. The **strtoul** function was invented by the ISO for completeness. In each case, **str** points to the string to be converted, and **ptr** (if not null) is set by the functions to point to the first character in **str** immediately following the converted part of the string. If **str** begins with whitespace characters (as defined by the **isspace** function), they are skipped. In general, these functions provide more control over conversions than, say, the corresponding facilities of **sscanf**. Note that the functions are defined in the ISO C header **stdlib.h**, not **string.h**.

The functions **wcstod**, **wcstol**, and **wcstoul** (ISO C Amendment 1) are the same as their corresponding **str** functions except for the types of their arguments. Whitespace characters are defined by the **iswspace** function, and the decimal-point wide character is used in place of the period. These wide-string conversion functions can accept implementation-defined input strings in addition to the strings described below.

The function **strtod** expects the number to be converted to consist of

1. an optional plus or minus sign,
2. a sequence of decimal digits possibly containing a single decimal point, and
3. an optional exponent part, consisting of the letter **e** or **E**, an optional sign, and a sequence of decimal digits.

The longest sequence of characters matching this model is converted to a floating-point number of type **double**, which is returned. The model differs from C's own floating-point constant syntax in that an optional **-** or **+** may appear, no decimal point is needed, the decimal point may not be a period (based on locale), and no floating suffix (**f**, **F**, **l**, or **L**) may appear.

If no conversion is possible because the string does not match the expected number model (or is empty), zero is returned, ***ptr** (if **ptr** is not null) is set to the value of **str**, and **errno** is set to **ERANGE**. If the number converted would cause overflow, **HUGE_VAL** (with the correct sign) is returned; if the number converted would cause underflow, zero is returned. In either case, **errno** is set to **ERANGE**. (According to this definition, an invalid number is indistinguishable from one that causes underflow, except perhaps by the value set in ***ptr**. Some non-ISO implementations may set **errno** to **EDOM** when the string does not match the number model.)

The functions **strtol** and **strtoul** convert the initial portion of the argument string to an integer of type **long int** or **unsigned long int**, respectively. The expected format of the number—which changes with the value of **base**, the expected radix—is the same in both cases, including an optional **-** or **+** sign. No integer suffix (**l**, **L**, **u**, or **U**) may appear for either function.

If **base** is zero, the number (after the optional sign) should have the format of a *decimal-constant*, *octal-constant*, or *hexadecimal-constant*. The number's radix is deduced from its format. If the value of **base** is between 2 and 36, inclusive, the number must consist of a nonzero sequence of letters and digits representing an integer in the specified base. The letters **a** through **z** (or **A** through **Z**) represent the values 10 through 36, respectively. Only those letters representing values less than **base** are permitted. As a special case, if **base** is 16 then the number may begin with **0x** or **0X**, which is ignored.

If no conversion can be performed, the functions return zero, ***ptr** (if **ptr** is not null) is set to the value of **str**, and **errno** is set to **ERANGE**. If the number to be converted would cause an overflow, then **strtol** returns **LONG_MAX** or **LONG_MIN** (depending on the sign of the result) and **strtoul** returns **ULONG_MAX** ; **errno** is set to **ERANGE**.

References *decimal-constant* 2.7; **errno** 11.2; *floating-constant* 2.7; *hexadecimal-constant* 2.7; **HUGE_VAL** 19; *integer-constant* 2.7; **isspace** function 12.6; **LONG_MAX**, **LONG_MIN**, **ULONG_MAX** 5.1.1; *octal-constant* 2.7; *type-marker* 2.7

13.9 atof, atoi, atol

ISO C facilities	Traditional and alternate facilities
`#include <stdlib.h>`	
`double atof( const char *str );`	`double atof( char *str );`
`int atoi( const char *str );`	`int atoi( char *str );`
`long atol( const char *str );`	`long atol( char *str );`

These functions, which convert the initial portion of the string **str** to numbers, are found in many UNIX implementations. In ISO C they are present for compatibility, but the functions **strtod**, **strtol**, and **strtoul** are preferred. If **atoi**, **atof**, or **atol** are unable to convert the input string, their behavior is undefined.

Example

Except for their behavior on error, these functions may be defined in terms of the more general ones:

```
#include <stdlib.h>

double atof(char *str) {
   return strtod(str, (char **) NULL);
}

int atoi(char *str) {
   return (int) strtol(str, (char **) NULL, 10);
}

long atol(char * str) {
   return strtol(str, (char **) NULL, 10);
}
```

Note that these functions are defined in the ISO C header **stdlib.h**, not **string.h**.

13.10 strcoll, strxfrm, wcscoll, wcsxfrm

ISO C facilities

```
#include <string.h>

int strcoll(const char *s1, const char *s2);
size_t strxfrm(char *dest, const char *src, size_t len);
```

```
#include <wchar.h>

int wcscoll(const wchar_t *s1, const wchar_t *s2);
size_t wcsxfrm(wchar_t *dest, const wchar_t *src, size_t len);
```

The **strcoll** and **strxfrm** functions provide locale-specific string-sorting facilities. The **strcoll** function compares the strings **s1** and **s2** and returns an integer greater than, equal to, or less than zero depending on whether the string **s1** is greater than, equal to, or less than the string **s2**. The comparison is computed according to the locale-specific collating conventions (**LC_COLLATE** with **setlocale**, section 11.5). In contrast, the **strcmp** and **wcscmp** functions (section 13.2) always compare two strings using the normal collating sequence of the target character set (**char** or **wchar_t**).

The function **wcscoll** (ISO C Amendment 1) is the same as **strcoll** except for the types of its arguments.

The **strxfrm** function transforms (in a way described below) the string **src** into a second string that is stored in the character array **dest**, which is assumed to be at least **len** characters long. The number of characters needed to store the string (excluding the terminating null character) is returned by **strxfrm**. Thus, if the value returned by **strxfrm** is greater than or equal to **len**, or if **src** and **dest** overlap in memory, the final contents of **dest** is undefined. Additionally, if **len** is 0 and **dest** is a null pointer,

strxfrm simply computes and returns the length of the transformed string corresponding to **src**.

The **strxfrm** function transforms strings in such a way that the **strcmp** function can be used on the transformed strings to determine the correct sorting order. That is, if **s1** and **s2** are strings, and **t1** and **t2** are the transformed strings produced by **strxfrm** from **s1** and **s2**, then

- **strcmp(t1,t2) > 0** if **strcoll(s1,s2) > 0**
- **strcmp(t1,t2) == 0** if **strcoll(s1,s2) == 0**
- **strcmp(t1,t2) < 0** if **strcoll(s1,s2) < 0**

The function **wcsxfrm** (ISO Amendment 1) is like **strxfrm** except for the types of its arguments. The **wcscmp** function must be used to compare the transformed wide string.

The functions **strcoll** and **strxfrm** have different performance tradeoffs. The **strcoll** function does not require the programmer to supply extra storage, but it may have to perform string transformations internally each time it is called. Using **strxfrm** may be more efficient when many comparisons must be done on the same set of strings.

Example

The function transform below uses **strxfrm** to create a transformed string corresponding to the argument **s**. Space for the string is dynamically allocated:

```
#include <string.h>
#include <stdlib.h>

char *transform( char *s )
/* Return the result of applying strxfrm to s */
{
    char *dest;       /* Buffer to hold transformed string */
    size_t length;    /* Buffer length required */
    length = strxfrm(NULL,s,0) + 1;
    dest = (char *) malloc(length);
    (void) strxfrm(dest,s,length);
    return dest;
}
```

14

Memory Functions

The facilities in this chapter give the C programmer efficient ways to copy, compare, and set blocks of memory. In ISO C these functions are considered part of the string functions and are declared in the library header file **string.h**. In many other implementations they are declared in their own header file, **memory.h**.

Blocks of memory are designated by a pointer of type **void *** in ISO C and **char *** in traditional C. In ISO C, memory is interpreted as an array of objects of type **unsigned char**; in traditional C, this is not explicitly stated, and either **char** or **unsigned char** might be used. These functions do not treat null characters any differently from other characters.

Amendment 1 to ISO C adds five new functions for manipulating wide character arrays, which are designated by pointers of type **wchar_t ***. These functions are defined in header **wchar.h**, and their names all begin with the letters **wmem**. The ordering of wide characters is simply the ordering of integers in the underlying integer type **wchar_t**. No interpretation of the wide characters is made, so no encoding errors are possible.

References **wchar_t** 11.1; wide character 2.1.4

Table 14–1 Chapter summary

Name	Section	Name	Section	Name	Section
bcmp	14.2	**memccpy**	14.3	**memcpy**[a]	14.3
bcopy	14.3	**memchr**[a]	14.1	**memmove**[a]	14.3
bzero	14.4	**memcmp**[a]	14.2	**memset**[a]	14.4

[a] A wide-character version of this facility is described in the same section.

14.1 memchr, wmemchr

ISO C facilities	Traditional and alternate facilities

`#include <string.h>`
 	
`void *memchr(`
`  const void *ptr,`
`  int val, size_t len );`
	`#include <memory.h>`
	
	`char *memchr(`
	`  char *ptr,`
	`  int val, int len );`

`#include <wchar.h>`
 	
`wchar_t *wmemchr(`
`  const wchar_t *ptr,`
`  wchar_t val, size_t len );`	

The function **memchr** searches for the first occurrence of **val** in the first **len** characters beginning at **ptr**. It returns a pointer to the first character containing **val**, if any, or returns a null pointer if no such character is found. Each character **c** is compared to **val** as if by the expression **(unsigned char) c == (unsigned char) val**. See also **strchr** (section 13.5).

The **wmemchr** function (ISO C Amendment 1) finds the first occurrence of **val** in the **len** wide characters beginning at **ptr**. A pointer to the found wide character is returned. If no match is found, a null pointer is returned.

14.2 memcmp, wmemcmp

ISO C facilities	Traditional and alternate facilities

`#include <string.h>`
 	
`int memcmp(`
`  const void *ptr1,`
`  const void *ptr2,`
`  size_t len );`
	`#include <memory.h>`
	
	`int memcmp(`
	`  char *ptr1,`
	`  char *ptr2,`
	`  int len );`
	`int bcmp(`
	`  char *ptr1,`
	`  char *ptr2,`
	`  int len );`

`#include <wchar.h>`
 	
`int wmemcmp(`
`  const wchar_t *ptr1,`
`  const wchar_t *ptr2,`
`  size_t len );`	

The function **memcmp** compares the first **len** characters beginning at **ptr1** with the first **len** characters beginning at **ptr2**. If the first string of characters is lexicographically less than the second, then **memcmp** returns a negative integer. If the first string of characters is lexicographically greater than the second, then **memcmp** returns a positive integer. Otherwise **memcmp** returns 0.

The function **bcmp** is found in some implementations, but it is not part of ISO C. It also compares two strings of characters, but returns 0 if they are the same and nonzero otherwise. No comparison for less or greater is made. See also **strcmp** (section 13.2).

The **wmemcmp** function (ISO C Amendment 1) performs the same comparison on wide character arrays. The ordering function on wide characters is simply the integer ordering on the underlying integral type **wchar_t**. The value returned is negative, zero, or positive according to whether the wide characters at **ptr1** are less than, equal to, or greater than the sequence of wide characters at **ptr2**.

14.3 memcpy, memccpy, memmove, wmemcpy, wmemmove

ISO C facilities

```
#include <string.h>

void *memcpy(
  void *dest,
  const void *src,
  size_t len );
void * memmove(
  void *dest,
  const void *src,
  size_t len);
```

Traditional and alternate facilities

```
#include <memory.h>

char *memcpy(
  char *dest,
  char *src,
  int len );
char * memccpy(
  char *dest,
  char *src,
  int val,
  int len);
char *bcopy(
  char *src,
  char *dest,
  int len );
```

ISO C facilities (continued)

```
#include <wchar.h>

wchar_t *wmemcpy(
  wchar_t *dest,
  const wchar_t *src,
  size_t len );
wchar_t * wmemmove(
  wchar_t *dest,
  const wchar_t *src,
  size_t len);
```

The functions **memcpy** and **memmove** (ISO C) both copy **len** characters from **src** to **dest** and return the value of **src**. The difference is that **memmove** will work correctly for overlapping memory regions—that is, **memmove** acts as if the source area were first copied to a separate temporary area and then copied back to the destination area. (In fact, no temporary areas are needed to implement **memmove**.) The behavior of **memcpy** is undefined when the source and destination overlap, although some versions of **memcpy** do implement the copy-to-temporary semantics. If both versions are available, the programmer should expect **memcpy** to be faster.

The function **memccpy**, found in some implementations, also copies **len** characters from **src** to **dest**, but it will stop immediately after copying a character whose value is **val**. When all **len** characters are copied, **memccpy** returns a null pointer; otherwise it returns a pointer to the character following the copy of **val** in **dest**.

The function **bcopy** is found in some implementations, but is not part of ISO C. It works like **memcpy**, but the source and destination operands are reversed. See also **strcpy** (section 13.3).

The functions **wmemcpy** and **wmemmove** (ISO C Amendment 1) are analogous to **memcpy** and **memmove**, respectively, but they operate on wide character arrays. They both return **dest**.

14.4 memset, wmemset

ISO C facilities	Traditional and alternate facilities

`#include <string.h>`
`void *memset(`
`  void *ptr,`
`  int val,`
`  size_t len );`
	`#include <memory.h>`
	`char *memset(`
	`  char *ptr,`
	`  int val,`
	`  int len );`
	`void bzero(`
	`  char *ptr,`
	`  int len );`

`#include <wchar.h>`
`wchar_t *wmemset(`
`  wchar_t *ptr,`
`  int val,`
`  size_t len );`	

The function **memset** copies **val** into each of **len** characters beginning at **ptr**. The characters designated by **ptr** are considered to be of type **unsigned char**. The function returns the value of **ptr**.

The more restricted function **bzero** copies 0 into each of **len** characters at **ptr**; it is found in some UNIX implementations but is not part of ISO C.

The function **wmemset** (ISO C Amendment 1) is analogous to **memset**, but it fills an array of wide characters.

15

Input/Output Facilities

C has a very rich and useful set of I/O facilities based on the concept of a stream, which may be a file or some other source or consumer of data, including a terminal or other physical device. The data type **FILE** (defined in **stdio.h** along with the res t of the I/O

Table 15–1 Chapter summary

Name	Sction	Name	Section	Name	Section
clearerr	15.14	**fscanf**[a]	15.8	**rename**	15.15
EOF	15.1	**fseek**	15.5	**rewind**	15.5
fclose	15.2	**fsetpos**	15.5	**scanf**[a]	15.8
feof	15.14	**ftell**	15.5	**setbuf**	15.3
ferror	15.14	**fwide**	15.2	**setvbuf**	15.3
fflush	15.2	**fwrite**	15.13	**sprintf**[a]	15.11
fgetc[a]	15.6	**getc**[a]	15.6	**sscanf**[a]	15.8
fgetpos	15.5	**getchar**[a]	15.6	**stderr**	15.4
fgets[a]	15.7	**gets**[a]	15.7	**stdin**	15.4
FILE	15.1	**mktemp**	15.16	**stdout**	15.4
fopen	15.2	**perror**	11.2	**tmpfile**	15.16
fprintf[a]	15.11	**printf**[a]	15.11	**tmpnam**	15.16
fputc[a]	15.9	**putc**[a]	15.9	**ungetc**	15.6
fputs[a]	15.10	**putchar**[a]	15.9	**vfprintf**[a]	15.12
fread	15.13	**puts**	15.10	**vprintf**[a]	15.12
freopen	15.2	**remove**	15.15	**vsprintf**[a]	15.12

[a] A wide-character version of this facility is described in the same section.

facilities) holds information about a stream. A *file pointer*, an object of type **FILE ***, is created by calling **fopen** and is used as an argument to most of the I/O facilities described in this chapter.

Among the information included in a **FILE** object is the current position within the stream (the *file position*), pointers to any associated buffers, and indications whether an error or end-of-file has occurred. Streams are normally buffered unless they are associated with interactive devices. The programmer has some control over buffering with the **setvbuf** facility, but in general streams can be implemented very efficiently, and the programmer should not have to worry about performance.

There are two general forms of streams: text and binary. A text stream consists of a sequence of characters divided into lines; each line consists of zero or more characters followed by (and including) a newline character, **'\n'**. Text streams are portable when they consist only of complete lines made from characters from the standard character set. The hardware and software components underlying a particular C run-time library implementation may have different representations for text files (especially for the end-of-line indication), but the run-time library must map those representations into the standard one. ISO C requires implementations to support text stream lines of at least 254 characters including the terminating newline.

Binary streams are sequences of data values of type **char**. Because any C data value may be mapped onto an array of values of type **char**, binary streams can transparently record internal data. Implementations do not have to distinguish between text and binary streams if it is more convenient not to.

When a C program begins execution, there are three text streams predefined and open: *standard input* (**stdin**), *standard output* (**stdout**), and *standard error* (**stderr**).

References **fopen** 15.2; **setvbuf** 15.3; standard character set 2.1

Wide-Character Input and Output

Amendment 1 to ISO C adds a wide-character I/O facility to C. The new *wide-character input/output functions* in header file **wchar.h** correspond to older *byte input/output functions*, except the underlying program datatype (and stream element) is the wide character (**wchar_t**) instead of the character (**char**). In fact, the implementation of these wide-character I/O functions may translate the wide characters to and from multibyte sequences held on external media, but this is generally transparent to the programmer.

Instead of creating a new stream type for wide-character I/O, Amendment 1 adds an *orientation* to existing text and binary streams. After a stream is opened and before any input/output operations are performed on it, a stream has no orientation. The stream becomes *wide-oriented* or *byte-oriented* depending on whether the first input/output operation is from a wide-character function or a byte function. Once a stream is oriented, only I/O functions of the same orientation may be used, or else the result is undefined. The **fwide** function (section 15.2) may be used to set and/or test the orientation of a stream.

When the external representation of a file is a sequence of multibyte characters, some rules for multibyte character sequences are relaxed in the files:

1. Multibyte encodings in a file may contain embedded null characters.
2. Files do not need to begin or end in the initial conversion state.

Different files may use different multibyte character encodings of wide characters. The encoding for a file, which is logically part of the internal conversion state, is established by the setting of the **LC_CTYPE** category of the locale when that internal conversion state is first *bound*, not later than after the first wide-character input/output function is called. After the conversion state (and the encoding rule) of a file is bound, the setting of **LC_CTYPE** no longer affects the conversions on the associated stream.

Because the conversion between wide character and multibyte character may have state associated with it, a hidden **mbstate_t** object is associated with every wide-oriented stream. Conversion during input/output conceptually occurs by calling **mbrtowc** or **wcrtomb**, using the hidden conversion state. The **fgetpos** and **fsetpos** functions must record this conversion state with the file position. Conversion during wide-character input/output can fail with an encoding error, in which case **EILSEQ** is stored in **errno**. When multiple encodings of files are permitted, the encoding for a stream will probably be part of the **mbstate_t** object, or at least will be recorded with it.

References conversion state 2.1.5; **EILSEQ** 11.2; **fgetpos** and **fsetpos** 15.5; **mbrtowc** 11.7; **mbstate_t** 11.1; multibyte character 2.1.5; orientation 15.2.2; **wcrtomb** 11.7; wide characters 2.1.5

15.1 FILE, EOF, wchar_t, wint_t, WEOF

ISO C facilities	Traditional and alternate facilities
#include <stdio.h> **typedef … FILE …;** **#define EOF (-*n*)** **#define NULL …** **#define size_t …**	**#include <stdio.h>** **typedef … FILE …;** **#define EOF (-1)** **#define NULL …**
#include <wchar.h> **typedef … wchar_t;** **typedef … wint_t;** **#define WEOF …** **#define WCHAR_MAX …** **#define WCHAR_MIN …** **#define NULL …** **#define size_t …**	

Type **FILE** is used throughout the standard I/O library to represent control information for a stream. It is used for reading from both byte- and wide-character-oriented files.

The value **EOF** is conventionally used as a value that signals *end-of-file*—that is, the exhaustion of input data. It has the value –1 in most traditional implementations, but ISO

C requires only that it be a negative integral constant expression. Because **EOF** is sometimes used to signal other problems, it is best to use the **feof** facility (section 15.14) to determine whether end-of-file has indeed been encountered when **EOF** is returned. The macro **WEOF** (Amendment 1) is used in wide-character I/O for the same purpose as **EOF** in byte I/O; it is a value of type **wint_t** (not necessarily **wchar_t**) and need not be a negative value. **WCHAR_MAX** is the largest value representable by type **wchar_t**, and **WCHAR_MIN** is the smallest.

The type **size_t** and the null pointer constant **NULL** are defined in the header files **stdio.h** and **wchar.h** for convenience. In ISO C they are also defined in **stddef.h**, and it does no harm to use more than one header file.

References **wchar_t** 2.1.5, 11.1; **wint_t** 2.1.5, 11.1

15.2 fopen, fclose, fflush, freopen, fwide

ISO C facilities

```
#include <stdio.h>

FILE *fopen(
  const char *filename,
  const char *mode);
int fclose(
  FILE *stream);
int fflush(
  FILE *stream);
FILE *freopen(
  const char *filename,
  const char *mode,
  FILE *stream);

#define FOPEN_MAX ...
#define FILENAME_MAX ...
```

```
#include <wchar.t>

int fwide(FILE *stream,
  int orient);
```

Traditional and alternate facilities

```
#include <stdio.h>

FILE *fopen(
  char *filename,
  char *mode);
int fclose(
  FILE *stream);
int fflush(
  FILE *stream);
FILE *freopen(
  char *filename,
  char *mode,
  FILE *stream);
```

The function **fopen** takes as arguments a file name and a mode; each is specified as a character string. The file name is used in an implementation-specified manner to open or create a file and associate it with a stream. (The value of the macro **FILENAME_MAX** is the maximum length for a file name, or an "appropriate" length if there is no practical maximum.) A pointer of type **FILE *** is returned to identify the stream for other input/output operations. If any error is detected, **fopen** stores an error code into **errno** and returns a null pointer. The number of streams that may be open simultaneously is not specified; in ISO C it is given by the value of the macro **FOPEN_MAX**, which must be at least eight (including the three predefined streams). Under ISO C Amendment 1, the stream returned by **fopen** has no orientation, and either byte or wide-character input/output (but not both) may be performed on it.

The function **fclose** closes an open stream in an appropriate and orderly fashion, including any necessary emptying of internal data buffers. The function **fclose** returns **EOF** if an error is detected; otherwise, it returns zero.

Example

Here are some functions that open and close normal text files. They handle error conditions and print diagnostics as necessary, and their return values match those of **fopen** and **fclose**:

```
#include <errno.h>
#include <stdio.h>

FILE *open_input(const char *filename)
    /* Open filename for input; return NULL if problem */
{
    FILE *f;
    errno = 0;
    /* Functions below might choke on a NULL filename. */
    if (filename == NULL) filename = "\0";
    f = fopen(filename,"r");    /* "w" for open_output */
    if (f == NULL)
        fprintf(stderr,
                "open_input(\"%s\") failed: %s\n",
                filename, strerror(errno));
    return f;
}

int close_file(FILE *f)
    /* Close file f */
{
    int s  = 0;
    if (f == NULL) return 0; /* Ingore this case */
    errno = 0;
    s = fclose(f);
    if (s == EOF) perror("Close failed");
    return s;
}
```

The function **fflush** empties any buffers associated with the output or update stream argument. The stream remains open. If any error is detected, **fflush** returns **EOF**; otherwise, it returns 0. **fflush** is typically used only in exceptional circumstances; **fclose** and **exit** normally take care of flushing output buffers.

The function **freopen** takes a file name, a mode, and an open stream. It first tries to close **stream** as if by a call to **fclose**, but any error while doing so is ignored. Then, **filename** and **mode** are used to open a new file as if by a call to **fopen**, except that the new stream is associated with **stream** rather than getting a new value of type **FILE ***. The function **freopen** returns **stream** if it is successful; otherwise (if the new open fails) a null pointer is returned. One of the main uses of **freopen** is to reassociate one of the standard input/output streams **stdin**, **stdout**, and **stderr** with another file. Under Amendment 1 to ISO C, **freopen** removes any previous orientation from the steam.

References **EOF** 15.1; **exit** 19.3; **stdin** 15.4

15.2.1 File Modes

The values shown in Table 15–2 are permitted for the mode specification in the functions **fopen** and **freopen**.

Table 15–2 Type specifications for fopen and freopen

Mode[a]	Meaning
"r"	Open an existing file for input.
"w"	Create a new file, or truncate an existing one, for output.
"a"	Create a new file, or append to an existing one, for output.
"r+"	Open an existing file for update (both reading and writing), starting at the beginning of the file.
"w+"	Create a new file, or truncate an existing one, for update.
"a+"	Create a new file, or append to an existing one, for update.

[a] All modes can have the letter **b** appended to them, signifying that the stream is to hold binary rather than character data.

When a file is opened for update (**+** is present in the mode string), the resulting stream may be used for both input and output. However, an output operation may not be followed by an input operation without an intervening call to **fsetpos**, **fseek**, **rewind**, or **fflush**, and an input operation may not be followed by an output operation without an intervening call to **fsetpos**, **fseek**, **rewind**, or **fflush** or an input operation that encounters end-of-file. (These operations empty any internal buffers.)

ISO C allows any of the types listed in Table 15–2 to be followed by the character **b** to indicate a "binary" (as opposed to "text") stream is to be created. (The distinction under UNIX was blurred because both kinds of files are handled the same; other operating systems are not so lucky.) ISO C also allows any of the "update" file types to assume binary mode; the **b** designator may appear before or after the **+** in the stream mode specification.

In ISO C the mode string may contain other characters after the modes listed above. Implementations may use these additions to specify other attributes of streams, e.g.:

```
f = fopen("C:\\work\\dict.txt","r,access=lock");
```

Table 15–3 lists some properties of each of the stream modes.

Table 15–3 Properties of fopen modes

	Mode					
Property	`r`	`w`	`a`	`r+`	`w+`	`a+`
Named file must already exist	yes	no	no	yes	no	no
Existing file's contents are lost	no	yes	no	no	yes	no
Read from stream permitted	yes	no	no	yes	yes	yes
Write to stream permitted	no	yes	yes	yes	yes	yes
Write begins at end of stream	no	no	yes	no	no	yes

15.2.2 File Orientation

The **fwide** function (ISO C Amendment 1) is used to test and/or set the orientation of a stream. The function returns a positive, negative, or zero value according to whether **stream** is wide-oriented, byte-oriented, or has no orientation, respectively, after the call. The **orient** argument determines whether **fwide** will first attempt to set the orientation. If **orient** is 0, no attempt to set the orientation is made, and the return value reflects the orientation at the time of the call. If **orient** is positive, then **fwide** attempts to set wide orientation; if **orient** is negative, then **fwide** attempts to set byte orientation. These attempts can only be successful if the stream previously had no orientation—that is, if it had just been opened by **fopen** or **freopen**. Otherwise, the orientation remains unchanged.

Example

When using wide-oriented streams, it is a good idea to use **fwide** to establish the orientation at the time fopen is called. Here's a function that opens a specified file in a specified mode and sets it to be wide-oriented in a given locale. If successful, the function returns a file pointer; otherwise, it returns **NULL**.

```
FILE *fopen_wide(
    const char *filename, /* file to open */
    const char *mode,     /* mode for open */
    const char *locale)   /* locale for encoding */
{
    FILE *f = fopen(filename, mode);
    if (f != NULL) {
        char *old_locale = setlocale(LC_CTYPE, locale);
        if (old_locale == NULL || fwide(f, 1) <= 0) {
            fclose(f);   /* setlocale or fwide failed */
            f = NULL;
        }
        /* return locale to its original value */
        (void) setlocale(LC_CTYPE, old_locale);
    }
    return f;
}
```

The multibyte encoding used (if any) is determined when the orientation of the stream is established. It will be affected by the **LC_CTYPE** category of the current locale at the time the orientation is established.

15.3 setbuf, setvbuf

ISO C facilities	Traditional and alternate facilities
#include <stdio.h>	**#include <stdio.h>**
int setvbuf(	**int setvbuf(**
FILE *stream,	**FILE *stream,**
char *buf,	**char *buf,**
int bufmode,	**int bufmode,**
size_t size);	**int size);**
void setbuf(	**void setbuf(**
FILE *stream,	**FILE *stream,**
char *buf);	**char *buf);**
#define BUFSIZ ...	**#define BUFSIZ** ...
#define _IOFBF ...	**#define _IOFBF** ...
#define _IOLBF ...	**#define _IOLBF** ...
#define _IONBF ...	**#define _IONBF** ...

These functions allow the programmer to control the buffering strategy for streams in those rare instances in which the default buffering is unsatisfactory. The functions must be called after a stream is opened and before any data are read or written.

The function **setvbuf** is the more general function, adopted from UNIX System V. The first argument is the stream being controlled; the second (if not null) is a character array to use in place of the automatically generated buffer; **bufmode** specifies the type of buffering, and **size** specifies the buffer size. The function returns zero if it is successful and nonzero if the arguments are improper or the request cannot be satisfied.

The macros **_IOFBF**, **_IOLBF**, and **_IONBF** expand to values that can be used for **bufmode**. If **bufmode** is **_IOFBF**, the stream is fully buffered; if **bufmode** is **_IOLBF**, the buffer is flushed when a newline character is written or when the buffer is full; if **bufmode** is **_IONBF**, the stream is unbuffered. If buffering is requested and if **buf** is not a null pointer, then the array specified by **buf** should be **size** bytes long and will be used in place of the automatically generated buffers. The constant **BUFSIZ** is an "appropriate" value for the buffer size.

The function **setbuf** is a simplified form of **setvbuf**. The expression

```
setbuf(stream,buf)
```

is equivalent to the expression

```
((buf==NULL) ?
  (void) setvbuf(stream,NULL,_IONBF,0) :
  (void) setvbuf(stream,buf,_IOFBF,BUFSIZ))
```

References **EOF** 15.1; **fopen** 15.2; **size_t** 11.1

15.4 stdin, stdout, stderr

ISO C facilities	Traditional and alternate facilities
`#include <stdio.h>`	`#include <stdio.h>`

`#define stderr ...`
`#define stdin ...`
`#define stdout ...`
	`#define stderr ...`
	`#define stdin ...`
	`#define stdout ...`

The expressions **stdin**, **stdout**, and **stderr** have type **FILE ***, and their values are established prior to the start of an application program to certain standard text streams. **stdin** points to an input stream that is the "normal input" to the program; **stdout** to an output stream for the "normal output"; and **stderr** to an output stream for error messages and other unexpected output from the program. In an interactive environment, all three streams are typically associated with the terminal used to start the program, and, except **stderr**, are buffered.

These expressions are not usually lvalues, and in any case they should not be altered by assignment. The **freopen** function (section 15.2) may be used to change them.

Example

The expressions **stdin**, **stdout**, and **stderr** are often defined as addresses of static or global stream descriptors:

```
extern FILE iob[FOPEN_MAX];
...
#define stdin  (&iob[0])
#define stdout (&iob[1])
#define stderr (&iob[2])
```

UNIX systems in particular provide convenient ways to associate these standard streams with files or other programs when the application is launched, making them very powerful when used according to certain standard conventions.

Under ISO C Amendment 1, **stdin**, **stdout**, and **stderr** have no orientation when a C program is started. Therefore, those streams can be used for wide-character input/output by calling **fwide** (section 15.2) or using a wide-character input/output function on them.

15.5 fseek, ftell, rewind, fgetpos, fsetpos

ISO C facilities	Traditional and alternate facilities

`#include <stdio.h>`
`int fseek(`
`  FILE *stream,`
`  long int offset,`
`  int wherefrom);`
`long int ftell(FILE *stream);`
`void rewind(FILE *stream);`
`#define SEEK_SET 0`
`#define SEEK_CUR 1`
`#define SEEK_END 2`
`typedef ... fpos_t ...;`
`int fgetpos(`
`  FILE *stream,`
`  fpos_t *pos);`
`int fsetpos(`
`  FILE *stream,`
`  const fpos_t *pos);`
	`#include <stdio.h>`
	`int fseek(`
	`  FILE *stream,`
	`  long int offset,`
	`  int wherefrom);`
	`long int ftell(FILE *stream);`
	`void rewind(FILE *stream);`

The functions in this section allow random access within text and binary streams—typically, streams associated with files.

15.5.1 fseek and ftell

The function **ftell** takes a stream that is open for input or output and returns the position in the stream in the form of a value suitable for the second argument to **fseek**. Using **fseek** on a saved result of **ftell** will result in resetting the position of the stream to the place in the file at which **ftell** had been called.

For binary files, the value returned will be the number of characters preceding the current file position. For text files, the value returned is implementation-defined. The returned value must be usable in **fseek**, and the value **0L** must be a representation—not necessarily the only one—of the beginning of the file.

If **ftell** encounters an error, it returns **-1L** and sets **errno** to an implementation-defined, positive value. Since **-1L** may also be a valid file position, **errno** must be checked to confirm the error. Conditions that can cause **ftell** to fail include an attempt to locate the position in a stream attached to a terminal, or an attempt to report a position that cannot be represented as an object of type **long int**.

The function **fseek** allows random access within the (open) **stream**. The second two arguments specify a file position: **offset** is a signed (long) integer specifying (for binary streams) a number of characters, and **wherefrom** is a "seek code" indicating from what point in the file **offset** should be measured. The stream is positioned as indicated below, and **fseek** returns zero if successful or a nonzero value if an error occurs. (The value of **errno** is not changed.) Any end-of-file indication is cleared and any effect of **ungetc** is undone. ISO C defines the constants **SEEK_SET**, **SEEK_CUR**, and

SEEK_END to represent the values of **wherefrom**; programmers using non-ISO implementations must use the integer values specified or define the macros themselves.

When repositioning a binary file, the new position is given by the following table.

If **wherefrom** is:	Then the new position is:
SEEK_SET or 0	**offset** characters from the beginning of the file
SEEK_CUR or 1	**offset** characters from the current position in the file
SEEK_END or 2	**offset** characters from the end of the file (Negative values specify positions before the end; positive values extend the file with unspecified contents.)

ISO C does not require implementations to "meaningfully" support a **wherefrom** value of **SEEK_END** for binary streams. The following, more limited set of calls is permitted on text streams by ISO C:

A call of the form	Positions (text) stream
fseek(stream,0L,SEEK_SET)	at the beginning of the file
fseek(stream,0L,SEEK_CUR)	at the same location (i.e., the call has no effect)
fseek(stream,0L,SEEK_END)	at the end of the file
fseek(stream,*ftell-pos*,SEEK_SET)	at a position returned by a previous call to **ftell** for **stream**

These limitations recognize that a position within a text file may not map directly onto the file's internal representation. For example, a position may require a record number and an offset within the record. (On the other hand, ISO C requires that implementations support the call **fseek(stream,0L,SEEK_END)** for text files, whereas they do not have to "meaningfully" support it for binary streams.)

Under Amendment 1 of ISO C, file positioning operations performed on wide-oriented streams must satisfy all restrictions applicable to either binary or text files. The **fseek** and **ftell** functions are in general not powerful enough to support wide-oriented streams, even for the simplest positioning operations such as the beginning or end of the stream. The **fgetpos** and **fsetpos** functions described in the next section should be used for wide-oriented streams.

The function **rewind** resets a stream to its beginning. By ISO C definition, the call **rewind(stream)** is equivalent to

```
(void) fseek(stream, 0L, SEEK_SET)
```

15.5.2 fgetpos and fsetpos

The functions **fgetpos** and **fsetpos** are new to ISO C. They were added to handle files that are too large for their positions to be representable within an integer of type **long int** (as in **ftell** and **fseek**).

The **fgetpos** function stores the current file position in the object pointed to by **pos**. It returns zero if successful. If an error is encountered, it returns a nonzero value and stores an implementation-defined, positive value in **errno**.

The **fsetpos** function sets the current file position according to the value in ***pos**, which must be a value returned earlier by **fgetpos** on the same stream. **fsetpos** undoes any effect of **ungetc** or **ungetwc**. It returns zero if successful. If an error is encountered, it returns a nonzero value and stores an implementation-defined, positive value in **errno**.

Under ISO C Amendment 1, the file position object used by **fgetpos** and **fsetpos** will have to include a representation of the hidden conversion state associated with the wide-oriented stream (i.e., a value of type **mbstate_t**). That state, in addition to the position in the file, is needed to interpret the following multibyte characters after a repositioning operation.

In wide-oriented output streams, using **fsetpos** to set the output position and then writing one or more multibyte characters will cause any following multibyte characters in the file to become undefined. This is because the output could partially overwrite an existing multibyte character, or could change the conversion state in such a way that later multibyte characters could not properly interpreted.

References **mbstate_t** 11.1; **ungetc** 15.6

15.6 fgetc, fgetwc, getc, getwc, getchar, getwchar, ungetc, ungetwc

ISO C facilities:

```
#include <stdio.h>

int fgetc(FILE *stream);
int getc(FILE *stream);
int getchar(void);
int ungetc(int c,
    FILE *stream);
```

Traditional and alternate facilities:

```
#include <stdio.h>

int fgetc(FILE *stream);
int getc(FILE *stream);
int getchar(void);
int ungetc(char c,
    FILE *stream);
```

ISO C facilities:

```
#include <stdio.h>
#include <wchar.h>

wint_t fgetwc(FILE *stream);
wint_t getwc(FILE *stream);
wint_t getwchar(void);
wint_t ungetwc(wint_t c,
    FILE *stream);
```

The function **fgetc** takes an input stream as its argument. It reads the next character from the stream and returns it as a value of type **int**. The internal stream position indicator is advanced. Successive calls to **fgetc** will return successive characters from the input stream. If an error occurs or if the stream is at end-of-file, then **fgetc** returns **EOF**. The **feof** and/or **ferror** facilities should be used in this case to determine whether end-of-file has really been reached.

The "function" **getc** is identical to **fgetc**, except that **getc** is usually implemented as a macro for efficiency. The **stream** argument should not have any side effects, because it may be evaluated more than once.

The function **getchar** is equivalent to **getc(stdin)**. Like **getc**, **getchar** is often implemented as a macro.

In ISO C Amendment 1, the functions **fgetwc**, **getwc**, and **getwchar** are analogous to their byte-oriented counterparts—including probable macro implementations—but they read and return the next wide character from the input stream. **WEOF** is returned to indicate error or end-of-file; if the error is an encoding error, **EILSEQ** is stored in **errno**. Reading a wide character involves a conversion from a multibyte character to a wide character; this is performed as if by a call to **mbrtowc** using the stream's internal conversion state.

The function **ungetc** causes the character **c** (converted to **unsigned char**) to be pushed back onto the specified input stream, so that it will be returned by the next call to **fgetc**, **getc**, or **getchar** on that stream. If several characters are pushed, they are returned in the reverse order of their pushing (that is, last character first). **ungetc** returns **c** when the character is successfully pushed back, **EOF** if the attempt fails. A successful file-positioning command on the stream (**fseek**, **fsetpos**, or **rewind**) discards all pushed-back characters. After reading (or discarding) all pushed-back characters, the file position is the same as immediately before the characters were pushed.

One character of pushback is guaranteed, provided the stream is buffered and at least one character has been read from the stream since the last **fseek**, **fopen**, or **freopen** operation on the stream. An attempt to push the value **EOF** back onto the stream as a character has no effect on the stream and returns **EOF**. A call to **fsetpos**, **rewind**, **fseek**, or **freopen** erases all memory of pushed back characters from the stream, without affecting any external storage associated with the stream.

The function **ungetc** is useful for implementing input-scanning operations such as **scanf**. A program can "peek ahead" at the next input character by reading it and then putting it back if it is unsuitable. (However, **scanf** and other library functions are not permitted to preempt the use of **ungetc** by the programmer—that is, the programmer is guaranteed to have at least one character of pushback even after a call to **scanf** or similar function.)

The function **ungetwc** (ISO C Amendement 1) is analogous to **ungetc**.

References **EOF** 15.1; **feof** 15.14; **fseek** 15.5; **fopen** 15.2; **freopen** 15.2; **scanf** 15.8; **stdin** 15.4

15.7 fgets, fgetws, gets

ISO C facilities	Traditional and alternate facilities

`#include <stdio.h>`
 	
`char *fgets(`
`  char *s, int n,`
`  FILE *stream);`
`char *gets(`
`  char *s);`
	`#include <stdio.h>`
	
	`char *fgets(`
	`  char *s, int n,`
	`  FILE *stream);`
	`char *gets(`
	`  char *s);`

`#include <stdio.h>`
`#include <wchar.h>`
 	
`wchar_t *fgetws(`
`  wchar_t *s, int n,`
`  FILE *stream);`	

The function **fgets** takes three arguments: a pointer **s** to the beginning of a character array, a count **n**, and an input stream. Characters are read from the input stream into **s** until: a newline is seen; end-of-file is reached; or **n**–1 characters have been read without encountering end-of-file or a newline character. A terminating null character is then appended to the array after the characters read. If the input is terminated because a newline was seen, the newline character will be stored in the array just before the terminating null character. The argument **s** is returned upon successful completion.

If end-of-file is encountered before any characters have been read from the stream, then **fgets** returns a null pointer and the contents of the array **s** are unchanged. If an error occurs during the input operation, then **fgets** returns a null pointer and the contents of the array **s** are indeterminate. The **feof** facility (section 15.14) should be used to determine whether end-of-file has really been reached when **NULL** is returned.

The function **gets** reads characters from the standard input stream, **stdin**, into the character array **s**. However, unlike **fgets**, when the input is terminated by a newline character **gets** discards the newline and does not put it into **s**. The use of **gets** can be dangerous, because it is always possible for the input length to exceed the storage available in the character array. The function **fgets** is safer, because no more than **n** characters will ever be placed in **s**.

The function **fgetws** (ISO C Amendment 1) is analogous to **fgets**, but it operates on wide-oriented input streams and stores wide characters into **s**, including a null wide character at the end. There is no wide-character function corresponding to **gets**—another hint that **gets** is to be avoided.

References **feof** 15.14; **stdin** 15.4

15.8 *fscanf, fwscanf, scanf, wscanf, sscanf, swscanf*

ISO C facilities	Traditional and alternate facilities

`#include <stdio.h>`
 	
`int fscanf(`
`  FILE *stream,`
`  const char *format, ...);`
`int scanf(`
`  const char *format, ...);`
`int sscanf(`
`  char *s,`
`  const char *format, ...);`
	`#include <stdio.h>`
	
	`int fscanf(`
	`  FILE *stream,`
	`  char *format, ...);`
	`int scanf(`
	`  char *format, ...);`
	`int sscanf(`
	`  char *s,`
	`  char *format, ...);`

`#include <stdio.h>`
`#include <wchar.h>`
 	
`int fwscanf(`
`  FILE *stream,`
`  const wchar_t *format, ...);`
`int wscanf(`
`  const wchar_t *format, ...);`
`int swscanf(`
`  wchar_t *s,`
`  const wchar_t *format, ...);`	

The function **fscanf** parses formatted input text, reading characters from the stream specified as the first argument and converting sequences of characters according to the control string format. Additional arguments may be required, depending on the contents of the control string. Each argument after the control string must be a pointer; converted values read from the input stream are stored into the objects designated to by the pointers.

The functions **scanf** and **sscanf** are like **fscanf**. In the case of **scanf** characters are read from the standard input stream **stdin**. In the case of **sscanf** characters are read from the string **s**. When **sscanf** attempts to read beyond the end of the string **s**, it operates as **fscanf** and **scanf** do when end-of-file is reached.

The input operation may terminate prematurely because the input stream reaches end-of-file or because there is a conflict between the control string and a character read from the input stream. The value returned by these functions is the number of successful assignments performed before termination of the operation for either reason. If the input reaches end-of-file before any conflict or assignment is performed, then the functions return **EOF**. When a conflict occurs, the character causing the conflict remains unread and will be processed by the next input operation.

Amendment 1 to ISO C defines a set of wide-character formatted input functions corresponding to **fscanf**, **scanf**, and **sscanf**. The new **wscanf** "family" of functions use wide-character control strings and expect the input to be a sequence of wide characters. Any conversions from underlying multibyte sequences in the external file are transparent to the programmer. In the descriptions that follow, the byte-oriented functions are described. The behavior of the wide-oriented functions can be derived by subsituting "wide character" for "character" or "byte," unless otherwise noted.

Amendment 1 also extends ISO C's formatting strings, permitting the **l** size specifier to be added to the **s**, **c**, and **[** conversion operations to indicate that the associated argument is a pointer to a wide string or character. See the description of those conversion operations for more information.

15.8.1 Control String

The control string is a picture of the expected form of the input. In ISO C it is a multibyte character sequence beginning and ending in its initial shift state for the **scanf** family, and it is a sequence of wide characters for the **wscanf** family. One may think of these functions as performing a simple matching operation between the control string and the input stream. The contents of the control string may be divided into three categories:

1. *Whitespace characters.* A whitespace character in the control string causes whitespace characters to be read and discarded. The first input character encountered that is not a whitespace character remains as the next character to be read from the input stream. Note that if several consecutive whitespace characters appear in the control string, the effect is the same as if only one had appeared. Thus, any sequence of consecutive whitespace characters in the control string will match any sequence of consecutive whitespace characters, possibly of different length, from the input stream.
2. *Conversion specifications.* A conversion specification begins with a percent sign, **%**; the remainder of the syntax for conversion specifications is described in detail below. The number of characters read from the input stream depends on the conversion operation. As a rule of thumb, a conversion operation processes characters until: (a) end-of-file is reached, (b) a whitespace character or other inappropriate character is encountered, or (c) the number of characters read for the conversion operation equals the specified maximum field width. The processed characters are normally converted (e.g., to a numeric value) and stored in a place designated by a pointer argument following the control string.
3. *Other characters.* Any character other than a whitespace character or a percent sign must match the next character of the input stream. If it does not match, a conflict has occurred; the conversion operation is terminated, and the conflicting input character remains in the input stream to be read by the next input operation on that stream.

There should be exactly the right number of pointer arguments, each of exactly the right type, to satisfy the conversion specifications in the control string. If there are too many arguments, the extra ones are ignored; if there are too few, the results are undefined. If any conversion specification is malformed, the behavior is likewise undefined.

15.8.2 Conversion Specifications

A conversion specification begins with a percent sign, **%**. After the percent sign, the following conversion specification elements should appear in this order:

1. An optional *assignment suppression flag*, written as an asterisk ,*****. If this is present for a conversion operation that normally performs an assignment, then characters are read and processed from the input stream in the usual way for that operation, but no assignment is performed and no pointer argument is consumed.
2. An optional *maximum field width*, expressed as a positive decimal integer.
3. An optional *size specification*, expressed as the character **h**, meaning **short**; or as the character **l** (lowercase letter **L**), meaning **long**, **double**, or **wchar_t**; or as the character **L** meaning **long double**. The conversion operations to which these may be applied are listed in Table 15–4.
4. A required *conversion operation* (or *conversion specifier*), expressed (with one exception) as a single character: **c**, **d**, **e**, **f**, **g**, **i**, **n**, **o**, **p**, **s**, **u**, **x**, **%**, or **[**. The exception is the **[** operation, which causes all following characters up to the next **]** to be part of the conversion specification.

The conversion specifications for **fscanf** are similar in syntax and meaning to those for **fprintf**, but there are certain differences. It is best to regard the control string syntax for **fprintf** and **fscanf** as being only vaguely similar; do not use the documentation for one as a guide to the other.

Example

Here are some of the differences between the conversions in **fscanf** and **fprintf**:

The **[** conversion operation is peculiar to **fscanf**.

fscanf does not admit any precision specification of the kind accepted by **fprintf**, nor any of the flag characters **-**, **+**, *space*, **0**, and **#** that are accepted by **fprintf**.

An explicitly specified field width is a minimum for **fprintf**, but a maximum for **fscanf**.

Whereas **fprintf** allows a field width to be specified by a computed argument, indicated by using an asterisk for the field width, **fscanf** uses the asterisk for another purpose, namely assignment suppression; this is perhaps the most glaring inconsistency of all.

Except as noted, all conversion operations skip over any initial whitespace before conversion. This initial whitespace is not counted toward the maximum field width. None of the conversion operations normally skips over trailing whitespace characters as a matter of course. Trailing whitespace characters (such as the newline that terminates a line of input) will remain unread unless explicitly matched in the control string. (Doing this may be tricky because a whitespace character in the control string will attempt to match many whitespace characters in the input, resulting in an attempt to read beyond a newline.)

It is not possible to determine directly whether matches of literal character in the control string succeed or fail. It is also not possible to determine directly whether conversion operations involving suppressed assignments succeed or fail. The value returned by these functions reflects only the number of successful assignments performed.

The conversion operations are very complicated. A brief summary is presented in Table 15–4 and discussed in detail below.

Table 15–4 Input conversions (scanf, fscanf, sscanf)

Conversion letter	Size specifier	Argument type	Input format
d	none	**int ***	[−|+]dd...d
	h	**short ***	
	l	**long ***	
i[a]	none	**int ***	[−|+][**0**[**x**]]dd...d[b]
	h	**short ***	
	l	**long ***	
u	none	**unsigned ***	[−|+]dd...d
	h	**unsigned short ***	
	l	**unsigned long ***	
o	none	**unsigned ***	[−|+]dd...d[c]
	h	**unsigned short ***	
	l	**unsigned long ***	
x	none	**unsigned ***	[−|+][**0x**]dd...d[d]
	h	**unsigned short ***	
	l	**unsigned long ***	
c	none	**char ***	a fixed-width sequence of characters; must be multibytes if **l** is used
	l[e]	**wchar_t ***	
s	none	**char ***	a sequence of non-whitespace characters; must be multibytes if **l** is used
	l[e]	**wchar_t ***	
p[a]	none	**void ****	a sequence of characters such as output with **%p** in **fprintf**.
n[a]	none	**int ***	none; the number of characters read is stored in the argument
	h	**short ***	
	l	**long ***	
f, **e**, **g**	none	**float ***	any floating-point constant or decimal integer constant, optionally preceded by – or +
	l	**double ***	
	L[a]	**long double ***	
[	none	**char ***	a sequence of characters from a scanning set; must be multibytes if **l** is used
	l[e]	**wchar_t ***	

[a] ISO C addition.
[b] The base of the number is determined by the first digits in the same way as for C constants.
[c] The number is assumed to be octal.
[d] The number is assumed to be hexadecimal regardless of the presence of **0x**.
[e] ISO C Amendment 1 addition.

The d conversion Signed decimal conversion is performed. One argument is consumed; it should be of type **int ***, **short ***, or **long *** depending on the size specification.

The format of the number read is the same as expected for the input to the **strtol** function (**wcstol** for **wscanf**) with the value 10 for the **base** argument—that is, a sequence of decimal digits optionally preceded by **-** or **+**. If the value expressed by the input is too large to be represented as a signed integer of the appropriate size, then the behavior is undefined.

The i conversion Signed integer conversion is performed. One argument is consumed; it should be of type **int *, short ***, or **long *** depending on the size specification.

The format of the number read is the same as expected for the input to the **strtol** function (**wcstol** for **wscanf**) with the value 0 for the **base** argument—that is, a C *integer-constant,* without suffix, and optionally preceded by **-** or **+**, and **0** (octal) or **0x** (hexadecimal) prefixes. If the value expressed by the input is too large to be represented as a signed integer of the appropriate size, then the behavior is undefined.

The u conversion Unsigned decimal conversion is performed. One argument is consumed; it should be of type **unsigned *, unsigned short ***, or **unsigned long *** depending on the size specification.

The format of the number read is the same as expected for the input to the **strtoul** function (**wcstoul** for **wscanf**) with the value 10 for the **base** argument—that is, a sequence of decimal digits optionally preceded by **-** or **+**. If the value expressed by the input is too large to be represented as an unsigned integer of the appropriate size, then the behavior is undefined.

The o conversion Unsigned octal conversion is performed. One argument is consumed; it should be of type **unsigned *, unsigned short ***, or **unsigned long *** depending on the size specification.

The format of the number read is the same as expected for the input to the **strtoul** function (**wcstoul** for **wscanf**) with the value 8 for the **base** argument—that is, a sequence of octal digits optionally preceded by **-** or **+**. If the value expressed by the input is too large to be represented as an unsigned integer of the appropriate size, then the behavior is undefined.

The x conversion Unsigned hexadecimal conversion is performed. One argument is consumed; it should be of type **unsigned *, unsigned short ***, or **unsigned long *** depending on the size specification.

The format of the number read is the same as expected for the input to the **strtoul** function (**wcstoul** for **wscanf**) with the value 16 for the **base** argument—that is, a sequence of hexadecimal digits optionally preceded by **-** or **+**. The operation accepts all of the characters **0123456789abcdefABCDEF** as valid hexadecimal digits. If the value expressed by the input is too large to be represented as an unsigned integer of the appropriate size, then the behavior is undefined.

Some non-ISO C implementations accept the letter **X** as an equivalent conversion operation.

The c conversion One or more characters are read. One pointer argument is consumed; it must be of type **char *** or, if the **l** size specification is present, **wchar_t ***. The **c** conversion operation does not skip over initial whitespace characters. The conversions applied to the input character(s) depend on whether the **l** size specifier is present and on whether **scanf** or **wscanf** is used. The possibilities are listed in Table 15–5.

Table 15–5 Input conversions of the c specifier

Function	Size specifier	Argument type	Input	Conversions
scanf	none	**char ***	character(s)	none; characters are copied
	l	**wchar_t ***	multibyte character(s)	to wide character(s), as if by one or more calls to **mbrtowc**
wscanf	none	**char ***	wide character(s)	to multibyte character(s), as if by one or more calls to **wcrtomb**
	l	**wchar_t ***	wide character(s)	none; wide characters are copied

If no field width is specified, then exactly one character is read unless the input stream is at end-of-file, in which case the conversion operation fails. The character value is assigned to the location indicated by the next pointer argument

If a field width is specified, then the pointer argument is assumed to point to the beginning of an array of characters, and the field width specifies the number of characters to be read; the conversion operation fails if end-of-file is encountered before that many characters have been read. The characters read are stored into successive locations of the array. No extra terminating null is appended to the characters that are read.

The s conversion A string is read. One pointer argument is consumed; it must be of type **char *** or, if the **l** size specification is present (ISO C Amendment 1), **wchar_t ***. The **s** conversion operation always skips initial whitespace characters.

Characters are read until end-of-file is reached, until a whitespace character is seen (in which case that character remains unread), or (if a field width was specified) until the maximum number of characters has been read. If end-of-file is encountered before any non-whitespace character is seen, the conversion operation is considered to have failed. Conversions may be applied to the input characters depending on whether the **l** size specifier is present and on whether **scanf** or **wscanf** is used. See Table 15–6. In the case of the **l** specifier used with **scanf**, the input is terminated by the first whitespace character, *before* the input characters are interpreted as multibyte characters.

Table 15–6 Input conversions of the s specifier

Function	Size specifier	Argument type	Input	Conversion
scanf	none	**char ***	characters	none; characters are copied
	l	**wchar_t ***	multibyte characters	to wide characters, as if by calls to **mbrtowc**
wscanf	none	**char ***	wide characters	to multibyte characters, as if by calls to **wcrtomb**
	l	**wchar_t ***	wide characters	none; wide characters are copied

An extra terminating null is always appended to the stored characters. The **s** conversion operation can be dangerous if no maximum field width is specified, because it is always possible for the input length to exceed the storage available in the character array.

The **s** operation with an explicit field width differs from the **c** operation with an explicit field width. The **c** operation does not skip over whitespace characters, and will read exactly as many characters (or wide characters) as were specified unless end-of-file is encountered. The **s** operation skips over initial whitespace characters, will be terminated by a whitespace character after reading in some number of characters (or wide characters) that are not whitespace, and will append a null character to the stored characters.

The p conversion Pointer conversion is performed. One argument is consumed; it should be of type **void ****. The format of the pointer value read is implementation-specified, but it will usually be the same as the format produced by the **%p** conversion in the **printf** family. The interpretation of the pointer is likewise implementation-defined, but if you write out a pointer and later read it back, all during the same program execution, then the pointer read in will compare equal to the pointer written out. The **p** conversion is new with ISO C.

The n conversion No conversion is performed and no characters are read. Instead, the number of characters processed so far by the current call of the **scanf**-family function is written to the argument, which must be of type **int ***, **short ***, or **long ***, depending on the size specification. The **n** conversion is new with ISO C.

The f, e, and g conversions Signed decimal floating-point conversion is performed. One pointer argument is consumed; it must be of type **float ***, **double ***, or **long double ***, depending on the size specification.

The format of the number read is the same as expected for the input to the **strtod** function (**wcstod** for **wscanf**)—that is, a sequence of decimal digits optionally preceded by – or + and optionally containing a decimal point and signed exponent part. (An integer with no decimal point is acceptable.)

The characters read are interpreted as a floating-point number representation and converted to a floating-point number of the specified size. If no digits are read, or at least no digits are read before the letter **e** or **E** is seen, then the value is zero. If no digits are seen after the letter **e** or **E**, then the exponent part of the decimal representation is assumed to be zero. If the value expressed by the input is too large or too small to be represented as a floating-point number of the appropriate size, then the value **HUGE_VAL** is returned (with the proper sign) and the value **ERANGE** is stored in **errno**. (In implementations that do not conform to ISO C, the return value and setting of **errno** are unpredictable.) If the value expressed by the input is not too large or too small but nevertheless cannot be represented exactly as a floating-point number of the appropriate size, then some form of rounding or truncation occurs.

The **f**, **e**, **E**, and **g** conversion operations are completely identical; any one of them will accept any style of floating-point representation. Some implementations may accept **G** and **E** as floating-point conversion letters.

The % conversion A single percent sign is expected in the input. Because a percent sign is used to indicate the beginning of a conversion specification, it is necessary to write two of them in order to have one matched. No pointer argument is consumed. The assignment suppression flag, field width, and size specification are not relevant to the `%` conversion operation.

The [conversion A string is read and one pointer argument of type **`char *`** or **`wchar_t *`** (if the **`l`** size specifier is present) is consumed. The `[` conversion operation does not skip over initial whitespace characters. The conversion specification indicates exactly what characters may be read as a part of the input field. The `[` must be followed in the control string by more characters, terminated by `]`. All the characters up to the `]` are part of the conversion specification, called the *scanset*. If the character immediately following the `[` is the circumflex `^`, it has a special meaning as a negation flag, and the scanset consists of all characters *not* appearing between `^` and `]`. The characters in the scanset are regarded as a set in the mathematical sense.

Any `[` between the initial `[` and the terminating `]` is treated as any other character. Similarly, any `^` that does not immediately follow the initial `[` is treated as any other character. In ISO C, if `]` immediately follows the initial `[`, then it is in the scanset and the *next* `]` will terminate the conversion specification. If `[` immediately follows the negation flag `^`, then the `]` is *not* in the scanset and the next `]` will terminate the scanset. Non-ISO implementations might not support this special treatment of `]` at the beginning of the conversion specification.

Example

If the conversion is...	Then the scanset is...
`%[abca]`	the three characters **a**, **b**, and **c**
`%[^abca]`	all characters except **a**, **b**, and **c**
`%[[]`	the single character `[`
`%[]]`	the single character `]`
`%[ ,\t]`	the characters space, comma, and horizontal tab

Characters are read until end-of-file is reached, until a character not in the scanset is seen (in which case that character remains unread), or (if a field width was specified) until the maximum number of characters has been read. Then, if the assignment is not suppressed by `*`, the input characters are stored into the object designated by the argument pointer, just as for the **`s`** conversion operation, including any conversions to or from multibyte characters (see Table 15–6 on page 362). Then an extra terminating null character is appended to the stored characters. Size specification is not relevant to the `[` conversion operation.

Like the **`s`** conversion, the `[` conversion operation can be dangerous if no maximum field width is specified, because it is always possible for the input length to exceed the storage available in the character array.

References **`EOF`** 15.1; **`fprintf`** 15.11; **`stdin`** 15.4;

15.9 *fputc, fputwc, putc, putwc, putchar, putwchar*

ISO C facilities	Traditional and alternate facilities

`#include <stdio.h>`
 	
`int fputc(int c, FILE *stream);`
`int putc(int c, FILE *stream);`
`int putchar(int c);`
	`#include <stdio.h>`
	
	`int fputc(char c, FILE *stream);`
	`int putc(char c, FILE *stream);`
	`int putchar(char c);`

`#include <stdio.h>`
`#include <wchar.h>`
 	
`wint_t fputwc(wchar_t c, FILE *stream);`
`wint_t putwc(wchar_t c, FILE *stream);`
`wint_t putwchar(wchar_t c);`	

The function **fputc** takes as arguments a character value and an output stream. It writes the character to the stream at its current position and also returns the character as a value of type **int**. Successive calls to **fputc** will write the given characters successively to the output stream. If an error occurs, **fputc** returns **EOF** instead of the character that was to have been written.

The function **putc** operates like **fputc**, but it is usually implemented as a macro. The argument expressions must not have any side effects, because they may be evaluated more than once.

The function **putchar** writes a character to the standard output stream **stdout**. Like **putc**, **putchar** is usually implemented as a macro and is quite efficient. The call **putchar(c)** is equivalent to **putc(c, stdout)**.

Amendment 1 to ISO C adds the wide-character functions **fputwc**, **putwc**, and **putwchar**, which correspond to the byte-oriented functions. The value **WEOF** is returned on error. If an encoding error occurs, **EILSEQ** is also stored into **errno**.

References **EOF** 15.1; **stdout** 15.4

15.10 *fputs, fputws, puts*

ISO C facilities	Traditional and alternate facilities

`#include <stdio.h>`
 	
`int fputs(`
`  const char *s, FILE *stream);`
`int puts(const char *s);`
	`#include <stdio.h>`
	
	`int fputs(`
	`  char *s, FILE *stream);`
	`int puts(char *s);`

`#include <stdio.h>`
`#include <wchar.h>`
 	
`int fputws(`
`  const wchar_t *s, FILE *stream);`	

The function **fputs** takes as arguments a null-terminated string and an output stream. It writes to the stream all the characters of the string, not including the terminating null character. If an error occurs, **fputs** returns **EOF**; otherwise, it returns some other, nonnegative value.

The function **puts** is like **fputs** except that the characters are always written to the stream **stdout**, and after the characters in **s** are written out, an additional newline character is written (regardless of whether **s** contained a newline character).

Several non-ISO UNIX implementations of **fputs** have an error that causes the return value to be indeterminate if **s** is the empty string. Programmers might be alert for that boundary case.

Amendment 1 to ISO C adds the function **fputws**, which is analogous to **fputs**. The function returns **EOF** (not **WEOF**) on error, and **EILSEQ** is stored in **errno** if the error was an encoding error.

References **EOF** 15.1; **stdout** 15.4

15.11 *fprintf, fwprintf, printf, wprintf, sprintf, swprintf*

ISO C facilities	Traditional and alternate facilities

`#include <stdio.h>`
`int fprintf(`
`  FILE *stream,`
`  const char *format, ... );`
`int printf(`
`  const char *format, ...);`
`int sprintf(`
`  char *s,`
`  const char *format, ...);`
	`#include <stdio.h>`
	`int fprintf(`
	`  FILE *stream,`
	`  char *format, ... );`
	`int printf(`
	`  char *format, ...);`
	`int sprintf(`
	`  char *s,`
	`  char *format, ...);`

`#include <stdio.h>`
`#include <wchar.h>`
`int fwprintf(`
`  FILE *stream,`
`  const wchar_t *format, ... );`
`int wprintf(`
`  const wchar_t *format, ...);`
`int swprintf(`
`  wchar_t *s, size_t n,`
`  const wchar_t *format, ...);`	

The function **fprintf** performs output formatting, sending the output to the stream specified as the first argument. The second argument is a format control string. Additional arguments may be required, depending on the contents of the control string. A series of output characters is generated as directed by the control string; these characters are sent to the specified stream.

The **printf** function is related to **fprintf**, but sends the characters to the standard output stream **stdout**.

The **sprintf** function causes the output characters to be stored into the string buffer **s**. A final null character is output to **s** after all characters specified by the control string have been output. It is the programmer's responsibility to ensure that the **sprintf** destination string area is large enough to contain the output generated by the formatting operation. However, the **swprintf** function (see below), unlike **sprintf**, includes a count of the maximum number of wide characters, including the terminating null character, to be written to the output string **s**.

The value returned by these functions is **EOF** if an error occurred during the output operation; otherwise, the result is some value other than **EOF**. In ISO C and most current implementations the functions return the number of characters sent to the output stream if no error occurs. In the case of **sprintf**, the count does not include the terminating null character. (ISO C allows these functions to return any negative value if an error occurs.)

Amendment 1 to ISO C specifies three wide-character versions of these functions; **fwprintf**, **wprintf**, and **swprintf**. The output of these functions is conceptually a wide string, and they convert their additional arguments to wide strings under control of the conversion operators. We will denote these functions as the **wprintf** family of functions, or just ***wprintf** functions*, to distinguish them from the original byte-oriented ***printf** functions*.

Under Amendment 1 also, the **l** size specifier may be applied to the **c** and **s** conversion operators in both the **printf** and **wprintf** functions.

References **EOF** 15.1; **scanf** 15.8; **stdout** 15.4; wide characters 2.1.4

15.11.1 Output Format

The control string is simply text to be copied verbatim, except that the string may contain conversion specifications. In ISO C, the control string is an (uninterpreted) multibyte character sequence beginning and ending in its initial shift state. In the **wprintf** functions, it is a wide character string.

A conversion specification may call for the processing of some number of additional arguments, resulting in a formatted conversion operation that generates output characters not explicitly contained in the control string. There should be exactly the right number of arguments, each of exactly the right type, to satisfy the conversion specifications in the control string. Extra arguments are ignored, but the result from having too few arguments is unpredictable. If any conversion specification is malformed, then the effects are unpredictable. The conversion specifications for output are similar to those used for input by **fscanf** and related functions; the differences are discussed in section 15.8.2.

The sequence of characters or wide characters output for a conversion specification may be conceptually divided into three elements: the *converted value* proper, which reflects the value of the converted argument; the *prefix*, which, if present, is typically **+**, **-**, or a space; and the *padding*, which is a sequence of spaces or zero digits added if necessary to increase the width of the output sequence to a specified minimum. The prefix always precedes the converted value. Depending on the conversion specification, the padding may precede the prefix, separate the prefix from the converted value, or follow the converted value. Examples are shown in the figure below; the enclosing boxes show the extent of the output governed by the conversion specification.

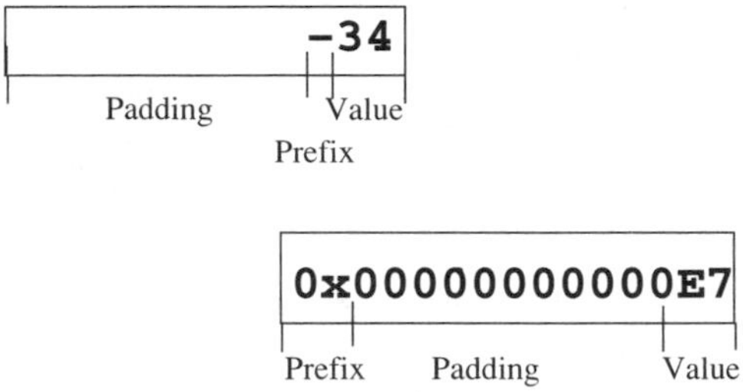

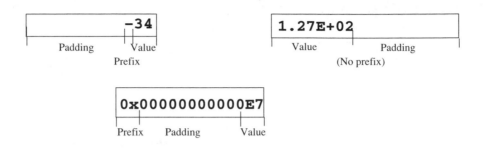

15.11.2 Conversion Specifications

In what follows, the terms "characters," "letters," etc. are to be understood as normal characters or letters (bytes) in the case of the **printf** functions, and wide characters or letters in the case of the **wprintf** functions. For example, in **wprintf**, conversion specifications begin with the wide-character percent sign, **%**.

A conversion specification begins with a percent sign character, **%**, and has the following elements in order:

1. Zero or more *flag characters* (**-**, **+**, **0**, **#**, or space), which modify the meaning of the conversion operation.
2. An optional *minimum field width*, expressed as a decimal integer constant.
3. An optional *precision specification*, expressed as a period optionally followed by a decimal integer.
4. An optional *size specification*, expressed as one of the letters **l**, **L**, or **h**.
5. The *conversion operation*, a single character from the set **c**, **d**, **e**, **E**, **f**, **g**, **G**, **i**, **n**, **o**, **p**, **s**, **u**, **x**, **X**, and **%**.

The conversion letter terminates the specification. The size specification letters **L** and **h**, and the conversion operations **i**, **p**, and **n**, are available in ISO C only. The conversion specification "**%-#012.4hd**" is shown below broken into its constituent elements:

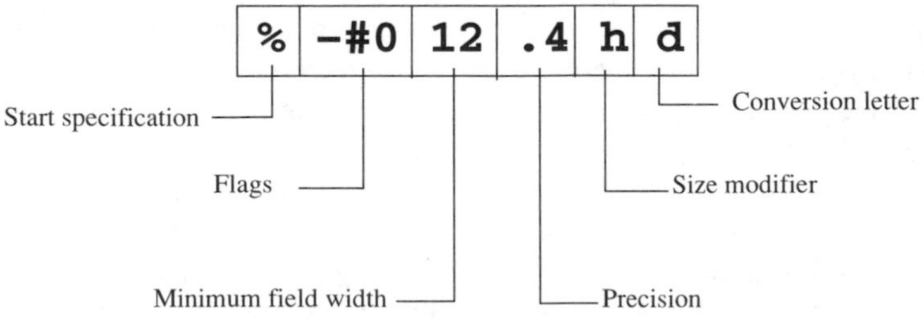

15.11.3 Conversion Flags

The optional flag characters modify the meaning of the main conversion operation:

-	Left-justify the value within the field width.
0	Use 0 for the pad character rather than space.
+	Always produce a sign, either **+** or **-**.
space	Always produce either the sign – or a space.
#	Use a variant of the main conversion operation.

The effects of the flag characters are described in more detail below.

The - flag If a minus-sign flag is present, then the converted value will be left-justified within the field—that is, any padding will be placed to the right of the converted value. If no minus sign is present, then the converted value will be right-justified within the field. This flag is relevant only when an explicit minimum field width is specified and the converted value is smaller than that minimum width; otherwise, the value will fill the field without padding.

The 0 flag If a **0** (zero) flag is present, then **0** will be used as the pad character if padding is to be placed to the left of the converted value. The **0** flag is relevant only when an explicit minimum field width is specified and the converted value is smaller than that minimum width. In integer conversions, this flag is superseded by the precision specification.

If no zero-digit flag is present, then a space will be used as the pad character. Space is always used as the pad character if padding is to be placed to the right of the converted value, even if the **-** flag character is present.

The + flag If a **+** flag is present, then the result of a signed conversion will always begin with a sign—that is, an explicit + will precede a converted positive value. (Negative values are always preceded by – regardless of whether a plus-sign flag is specified.) This flag is relevant only for the conversion operations **d**, **e**, **E**, **f**, **g**, **G**, and **i**.

The space flag If a *space* flag is present and the first character in the converted value resulting from a signed conversion is not a sign (+ or –), then a space will be added before the converted value. The adding of this space on the left is independent of any padding that may be placed to the left or right under control of the **-** flag character. If both the *space* and **+** flags appear in a single conversion specification, the *space* flag is ignored because the **+** flag ensures that the converted value will always begin with a sign. This flag is relevant only for the conversion operations **d**, **e**, **E**, **f**, **g**, **G**, and **i**.

The # flag If a **#** flag is present, then an alternate form of the main conversion operation is used. This flag is relevant only for the conversion operations **e**, **E**, **f**, **g**, **G**, **i**, **o**, **x**, and **X**. The modifications implied by the **#** flag are described in conjunction with the relevant conversion operations.

15.11.4 Minimum Field Width

An optional minimum field width, expressed as an decimal integer constant, may be specified. The constant must be a nonempty sequence of decimal digits that does not begin with a zero digit (which would be taken to be the **0** flag). If the converted value (including prefix) results in fewer characters than the specified field width, then pad characters are used to pad the value to the specified width. If the converted value results in more characters than the specified field width, then the field is expanded to accommodate it without padding.

The field width may also be specified by an asterisk, *****, in which case an argument of type **int** is consumed and specifies the minimum field width. The result of specifying a negative width is unpredictable.

Example

The following two calls to **printf** result in the same output:

```
int width=5, value;
...
printf("%5d", value);
printf("%*d", width, value);
```

15.11.5 Precision

An optional precision specification may be specified, expressed as a period followed by an optional decimal integer. The precision specification is used to control

1. the minimum number of digits to be printed for **d**, **i**, **o**, **u**, **x**, and **X** conversions
2. the number of digits to the right of the decimal point in **e**, **E**, and **f** conversions
3. the number of significant digits in the **g** and **G** conversions
4. the maximum number of characters to be written from a string in the **s** conversion

If the period appears but the integer is missing, then the integer is assumed to be zero, which usually has a different effect from omitting the entire precision specification.

The precision may also be specified by an asterisk following the period, in which case an argument of type **int** is consumed and specifies the precision. If both the field width and the precision are specified with asterisks, then the field width argument precedes the precision argument.

15.11.6 Size Specification

An optional size modifier, one of the letters **l**, **L**, or **h**, may precede some conversion operations. The letter **l** in conjunction with the conversion operations **d**, **i**, **o**, **u**, **x**, and **X**, indicates that the conversion argument has type **long** or **unsigned long**. In conjunction with the **n** conversion, it specifies that the argument has type **long ***. In ISO C Amendment 1, **l** may also be used with **c**, in which case the argument is of type **wint_t**, or with **s**, in which case it specifies that the argument has type **wchar_t ***.

The letter **h** in conjunction with the conversion operations **d**, **i**, **o**, **u**, **x**, and **X**, indicates that the conversion argument has type **short** or **unsigned short**. That is, although the argument would have been converted to **int** or **unsigned** by the argument promotions, it should be converted to **short** or **unsigned short** before conversion. In conjunction with the **n** conversion, the **h** modifier specifies that the argument has type **short ***. The **h** size modifier is available in ISO C but is rare elsewhere.

The letter **L** in conjunction with the conversion operations **e**, **E**, **f**, **F**, **g**, and **G**, indicates that the argument has type **long double**. The **L** size modifier is available in ISO C but is rare elsewhere.

15.11.7 Conversion Operations

The conversion operation is expressed as a single character: **c**, **d**, **e**, **E**, **f**, **g**, **G**, **i**, **n**, **o**, **p**, **s**, **u**, **x**, **X**, or **%**. The specified conversion determines the permitted flag and size specification characters, the expected argument type, and how the output looks. Table 15–7 summarizes the conversion operations. Each operation is then discussed individually.

The d and i conversions Signed decimal conversion is performed. The argument should be of type **int** if no size modifier is used, type **short** if **h** is used, or type **long** if **l** is used. The **i** operator is present in ISO C for compatibility with **fscanf**; it is recognized on output for uniformity, where it is identical to the **d** operator.

The converted value consists of a sequence of decimal digits that represents the absolute value of the argument. This sequence is as short as possible but not shorter than the specified precision. The converted value will have leading zeros if necessary to satisfy the precision specification; these leading zeros are independent of any padding, which might also introduce leading zeros. If the precision is 1 (the default), then the converted value will not have a leading 0 unless the argument is 0, in which case a single 0 is output. If the precision is 0 and the argument is 0, then the converted value is empty (the null string).

The prefix is computed as follows. If the argument is negative, the prefix is a minus sign. If the argument is nonnegative and the **+** flag is specified, then the prefix is a plus sign. If the argument is nonnegative, the *space* flag is specified, and the **+** flag is not specified, then the prefix is a space. Otherwise, the prefix is empty. The **#** flag is not relevant to the **d** and **i** conversions. Table 15–8 shows examples of the **d** conversion.

The u conversion Unsigned decimal conversion is performed. The argument should be of type **unsigned** if no size modifier is used, type **unsigned short** if **h** is used, or type **unsigned long** if **l** is used.

The converted value consists of a sequence of decimal digits that represents the value of the argument. This sequence is as short as possible but not shorter than the specified precision. The converted value will have leading zeros if necessary to satisfy the precision specification; these leading zeros are independent of any padding, which might also introduce leading zeros (see below). If the precision is 1 (the default), then the converted value will not have a leading 0 unless the argument is 0, in which case a single 0 is output. If the precision is 0 and the argument is 0, then the converted value is empty (the null string). The prefix is always empty. The **+**, *space*, and **#** flags are not relevant to the **u** conversion operation. Table 15–9 shows examples of the **u** conversion.

Table 15–7 Output conversion specifications

Conversion	Defined flags - + # 0 *space*	Size modifier	Argument type	Default precision[a]	Output
d, i[b]	- + 0 *space*	*none*	**int**	1	dd...d
		h	**short**		-dd...d
		l	**long**		+dd...d
u	- + 0 *space*	*none*	**unsigned int**	1	dd...d
		h	**unsigned short**		
		l	**unsigned long**		
o	- + # 0 *space*	*none*	**unsigned int**	1	oo...o
		h	**unsigned short**		**0**oo...o
		l	**unsigned long**		
x, X	- + # 0 *space*	*none*	**unsigned int**	1	hh...h
		h	**unsigned short**		**0x**hh...h
		l	**unsigned long**		**0X**hh...h
f	- + # 0 *space*	*none*	**double**	6	d...d.d...d
		L	**long double**		-d...d.d...d
					+d...d.d...d
e, E	- + # 0 *space*	*none*	**double**	6	d.d...de+dd
		L	**long double**		-d.d...d**E**-dd
g, G	- + # 0 *space*	*none*	**double**	6	*like* **e**, **E**,
		L	**long double**		*or* **f**
c	-	*none*	**int**	1	c
		l[c]	**wint_t**		
s	-	*none*	**char ***	∞	cc...c
		l[c]	**wchar_t ***		
p[b]	*impl. defined*	*none*	**void ***	1	*impl. defined*
n[b]		*none*	**int ***	*n/a*	*none*
		h	**short ***		
		l	**long ***		
%		*none*	*none*	*n/a*	**%**

[a] Default precision, if none is specified.
[b] Available in ISO C; may be rare elsewhere. The conversions **i** and **d** are equivalent on output.
[c] ISO C Amendment 1.

The o conversion Unsigned octal conversion is performed. The argument should be of type **unsigned** if no size modifier is used, type **unsigned short** if **h** is used, or type **unsigned long** if **l** is used.

The converted value consists of a sequence of octal digits that represents the value of the argument. This sequence is as short as possible but not shorter than the specified precision. The converted value will have leading zeros if necessary to satisfy the precision specification; these leading zeros are independent of any padding, which might also introduce leading zeros. If the precision is 1 (the default), then the converted value will not have a leading 0 unless the argument is 0, in which case a single 0 is output. If the preci-

Table 15–8 Examples of the d conversion

Sample format	Sample output Value = 45	Sample output Value = –45
`%12d`	`45`	`-45`
`%012d`	`000000000045`	`-00000000045`
`% 012d`	`00000000045`	`-00000000045`
`%+12d`	`+45`	`-45`
`%+012d`	`+00000000045`	`-00000000045`
`%-12d`	`45`	`-45`
`%- 12d`	`45`	`-45`
`%-+12d`	`+45`	`-45`
`%12.4d`	`0045`	`-0045`
`%-12.4d`	`0045`	`-0045`

Table 15–9 Examples of the u conversion

Sample format	Sample output Value = 45	Sample output Value = –45
`%14u`	`45`	`4294967251`
`%014u`	`00000000000045`	`00004294967251`
`%#14u`	`45`	`4294967251`
`%#014u`	`00000000000045`	`00004294967251`
`%-14u`	`45`	`4294967251`
`%-#14u`	`45`	`4294967251`
`%14.4u`	`0045`	`4294967251`
`%-14.4u`	`0045`	`4294967251`

sion is 0 and the argument is 0, then the converted value is empty (the null string). If the **#** flag is present, then the prefix is 0. If the **#** flag is not present, then the prefix is empty. The **+** and *space* flags are not relevant to the **o** conversion operation. Table 15–10 shows examples of the **o** conversion.

Table 15–10 Examples of the o conversion

Sample format	Sample output Value = 45	Sample output Value = –45
`%14o`	`55`	`37777777723`
`%014o`	`00000000000055`	`00037777777723`
`%#14o`	`055`	`037777777723`
`%#014o`	`00000000000055`	`00037777777723`
`%-14o`	`55`	`37777777723`
`%-#14o`	`055`	`037777777723`
`%14.4o`	`0055`	`37777777723`
`%-#14.4o`	`00055`	`037777777723`

The x and X conversions Unsigned hexadecimal conversion is performed. The argument should be of type **`unsigned`** if no size modifier is used, type **`unsigned short`** if **`h`** is used, or type **`unsigned long`** if **`l`** is used.

The converted value consists of a sequence of hexadecimal digits that represents the value of the argument. This sequence is as short as possible but not shorter than the specified precision. The **`x`** operation uses **`0123456789abcdef`** as digits, whereas the **`X`** operation uses **`0123456789ABCDEF`**. The converted value will have leading zeros if necessary to satisfy the precision specification; these leading zeros are independent of any padding, which might also introduce leading zeros (see below). If the precision is 1, then the converted value will not have a leading 0 unless the argument is 0, in which case a single 0 is output. If the precision is 0 and the argument is 0, then the converted value is empty (the null string). If no precision is specified, then a precision of 1 is assumed.

If the **#** flag is present, then the prefix is **`0x`** (for the **`x`** operation) or **`0X`** (for the **`X`** operation). If the **#** flag is not present, then the prefix is empty. The **+** and *space* flags are not relevant. Table 15–11 shows examples of **`x`** and **`X`** conversions.

Table 15–11 Examples of the x and X conversions

Sample format	Sample output Value = 45	Sample output Value = –45
`%12x`	`          2d`	`    ffffffd3`
`%012x`	`00000000002d`	`0000ffffffd3`
`%#12X`	`        0X2D`	`  0XFFFFFFD3`
`%#012X`	`0X000000002D`	`0X00FFFFFFD3`
`%-12x`	`2d`	`ffffffd3`
`%-#12x`	`0x2d`	`0xffffffd3`
`%12.4x`	`        002d`	`    ffffffd3`
`%-#12.4x`	`0x002d`	`ffffffd3`

The c conversion The argument is printed as a character or wide character. One argument is consumed. The **+**, *space*, and **#** flags, and the precision specification, are not relevant to the **`c`** conversion operation. The conversions applied to the argument character depend on whether the **`l`** size specifier is present and on whether **`printf`** or **`wprintf`** is used. The possibilities are listed in Table 15–12. Table 15–13 shows examples of the **`c`** conversion.

The s conversion The argument is printed as a string. One argument is consumed. If the **`l`** size specifier is not present, the argument must be a pointer to an array of any character type. If **`l`** is present, the argument must have type **`wchar_t *`** and designate a sequence of wide characters. The prefix is always empty. The **+**, *space*, and **#** flags are not relevant to the **`s`** conversion.

If no precision specification is given, then the converted value is the sequence of characters in the string argument up to but not including the terminating null character or null wide character. If a precision specification *p* is given, then the converted value is the first *p* characters of the output string, or up to but not including the terminating null character, whichever is shorter. When a precision specification is given, the argument string

Table 15–12 Conversions of the c specifier

Function	Size specifier	Argument type	Conversion
printf	none	**int**	argument is converted to **unsigned char** and copied to the output
	l	**wint_t**	argument is converted to **wchar_t**, converted to a multibyte characters as if by **wcrtomb**[a], and output
wprintf	none	**int**	argument is converted to a wide character as if by **btowc** and copied to the output
	l	**wint_t**	argument is converted to **wchar_t** and copied to the output

[a] The conversion state for the **wcrtomb** function is set to zero before the character is converted.

Table 15–13 Examples of the c conversion

Sample format	Sample output Value = '*'
`%12c`	`           *`
`%012c`	`00000000000*`
`%-12c`	`*`

need not end in a null character as long as it contains enough characters to yield the maximum number of output characters. When writing multibyte characters (**printf**, with **l**), in no case will a partial multibyte character be written, so the actual number of bytes written may be less than *p*.

The conversions that occur on the argument string depend on whether the **l** size specifier is present and on whether the **printf** or **wprintf** functions are used. The possibilities are listed in Table 15–14. Table 15–15 shows examples of the **s** conversion.

Table 15–14 Conversions of the s specifier

Function	Size specifier	Argument type	Conversion
printf	none	**char ***	characters from the argument string are copied to the output
	l	**wchar_t ***	wide characters from the argument string are converted to multibyte characters as if by **wcrtomb**[a]
wprintf	none	**char ***	multibyte characters from the argument string are converted to wide characters as if by **mbrtowc**[a]
	l	**wchar_t ***	wide characters from the argument string are copied to the output

[a] The conversion state for the **wcrtomb** or **mbrtowc** function is set to zero before the first character is converted. Subsequent conversions use the state as modified by the preceding characters.

Table 15–15 Examples of the s conversion

Sample format	Sample output Value = **"zap"**	Sample output Value = **"longish"**
%12s	**zap**	**longish**
%12.5s	**zap**	**longi**
%012s	**000000000zap**	**00000longish**
%-12s	**zap**	**longish**

The p conversion The argument must have type **void ***, and it is printed in an implementation-defined format. For most computers, this will probably be the same as the format produced by the **o**, **x**, or **X** conversions. This conversion operator is found in ISO C but is otherwise not common.

The n conversion The argument must have type **int *** if no size modifier is used, type **long *** if the **l** specifier is used, or type **short *** if the **h** specifier is used. Instead of outputting characters, this conversion operator causes the number of characters output so far to be written into the designated integer. This conversion operator is found in ISO C but is otherwise not common.

The f conversion Signed decimal floating-point conversion is performed. One argument is consumed, which should be of type **double** if no size modifier is used or type **long double** if **L** is used. If an argument of type **float** is supplied, it is converted to type **double** by the usual argument promotions, so it does work to use **%f** to print a number of type **float**.

The converted value consists of a sequence of decimal digits, possibly with an embedded decimal point, that represents the approximate absolute value of the argument. At least one digit appears before the decimal point. The precision specifies the number of digits to appear after the decimal point. If the precision is 0, then no digits appear after the decimal point; moreover, the decimal point itself also does not appear unless the **#** flag is present. If no precision is specified, then a precision of 6 is assumed.

If the floating-point value cannot be represented exactly in the number of digits produced, then the converted value should be the result of rounding the exact floating-point value to the number of decimal places produced. (Some C implementations do not perform correct rounding in all cases.)

The prefix is computed as follows. If the argument is negative, the prefix is a minus sign. If the argument is nonnegative and the **+** flag is specified, then the prefix is a plus sign. If the argument is nonnegative, the *space* flag is specified, and the **+** flag is not specified, then the prefix is a space. Otherwise, the prefix is empty. Table 15–16 shows examples of the **f** conversion.

The e and E conversions Signed decimal floating-point conversion is performed. One argument is consumed, which should be of type **double** if no size specifier is used or type **long double** if **L** is used. An argument of type **float** is permitted, as for the **f** conversion. The **e** conversion is described; the **E** conversion differs only in that the letter **E** appears whenever **e** appears in the **e** conversion.

Table 15–16 Examples of the f conversion

Sample format	Sample output Value = 12.678	Sample output Value = –12.678
`%10.2f`	`12.68`	`-12.68`
`%010.2f`	`000000012.68`	`-00000012.68`
`% 010.2f`	`00000012.68`	`-00000012.68`
`%+10.2f`	`+12.68`	`-12.68`
`%+010.2f`	`+00000012.68`	`-00000012.68`
`%-10.2f`	`12.68`	`-12.68`
`%- 10.2f`	`12.68`	`-12.68`
`%-+10.4f`	`+12.6780`	`-12.6780`

The converted value consists of a decimal digit, then possibly a decimal point and more decimal digits, then the letter **e**, then a plus sign or minus sign, then finally at least two more decimal digits. Unless the value is zero, the part before the letter **e** represents a value between 1.0 and 9.99.... The part after the letter **e** represents an exponent value as a signed decimal integer. The value of the first part, multiplied by 10 raised to the value of the second part, is approximately equal to the absolute value of the argument. The number of exponent digits is the same for all values and is the maximum number needed to represent the range of the implementation's floating-point types. Table 15–17 shows examples of **e** and **E** converrsions.

Table 15–17 Examples of e and E conversions

Sample format	Sample output Value = 12.678	Sample output Value = –12.678
`%10.2e`	`1.27e+01`	`-1.27e+01`
`%010.2e`	`00001.27e+01`	`-0001.27e+01`
`% 010.2e`	`0001.27e+01`	`-0001.27e+01`
`%+10.2E`	`+1.27E+01`	`-1.27E+01`
`%+010.2E`	`+0001.27E+01`	`-0001.27E+01`
`%-10.2e`	`1.27e+01`	`-1.27e+01`
`%- 10.2e`	`1.27e+01`	`-1.27e+01`
`%-+10.2e`	`+1.27e+01`	`-1.27e+01`

The precision specifies the number of digits to appear after the decimal point; if not supplied, then 6 is assumed. If the precision is 0, then no digits appear after the decimal point; moreover, the decimal point itself also does not appear unless the **#** flag is present. If the floating-point value cannot be represented exactly in the number of digits produced, then the converted value is obtained by rounding the exact floating-point value. The prefix is computed as for the **f** conversion.

The g and G conversions Signed decimal floating-point conversion is performed. One argument is consumed, which should be of type **double** if no size specifier is used, or type **long double** if **L** is used. An argument of type **float** is permitted, as for the **f**

conversion. Only the **g** conversion operator is discussed below; the **G** operation is identical except that wherever **g** uses **e** conversion, **G** uses **E** conversion. If the specified precision is less than 1, then a precision of 1 is used. If no precision is specified, then a precision of 6 is assumed.

The **g** conversion begins the same as either the **f** or **e** conversions; which one is selected depends on the value to be converted. The ISO C specification says that the **e** conversion is used only if the exponent resulting from the **e** conversion is less than –4 or greater than or equal to the specified precision. Some other implementations use the **e** conversion if the exponent is less than –3 or strictly greater than the specified precision.

The converted value (whether by **f** or **e**) is then further modified by stripping off trailing zeros to the right of the decimal point. If the result has no digits after the decimal point, then the decimal point also is removed. If the **#** flag is present, this stripping of zeros and the decimal point does not occur.

The prefix is computed as for the **f** and **e** conversions.

The % conversion A single percent sign is printed. Because a percent sign is used to indicate the beginning of a conversion specification, it is necessary to write two of them in order to have one printed. No arguments are consumed and the prefix is empty.

ISO C does not permit any flag characters, minimum width, precision, or size modifiers to be present; the complete conversion specification must be **%%**. However, other C implementations perform padding just as for any other conversion operation; for example, the conversion specification **%05%** prints **0000%** in these implementations. The **+**, *space*, and **#** flags, the precision specification, and the size specifications are never relevant to the **%** conversion operation.

Example

The following two-line program is known as a *quine*, a self-reproducing program. When executed, it will print a copy of itself on the standard output. (The first line of the program is too long to fit on a printed line in this book, so we have split it after **%cmain()** by inserting a backslash and a line break.)

```
char*f="char*f=%c%s%c,q='%c',n='%cn',b='%c%c';%cmain()\
{printf(f,q,f,q,q,b,b,b,n,n);}%c",q='"',n='\n',b='\\';
main(){printf(f,q,f,q,q,b,b,b,n,n);}
```

The following one-line program is almost a quine. (We have split it after **";main()** by inserting a backslash and a line break since it does not fit on a printed line.) We leave it to the reader to discover why it is not exactly a quine.

```
char*f="char*f=%c%s%c;main(){printf(f,34,f,34);}";main()\
{printf(f,34,f,34);}
```

15.12 vfprintf, vfwprintf, vprintf, vwprintf, vsprintf, vswprintf

ISO C facilities	Traditional and alternate facilities

`#include <stdarg.h>`
`#include <stdio.h>`
 	
`int vfprintf(FILE *stream,`
`  const char *format,`
`  va_list arg);`
`int vprintf(`
`  const char *format,`
`  va_list arg);`
`int vsprintf(char *s,`
`  const char *format,`
`  va_list arg);`
	`#include <varargs.h>`
	`#include <stdio.h>`
	
	`int vfprintf(FILE *stream,`
	`  char *format,`
	`  va_list arg);`
	`int vprintf(`
	`  char *format,`
	`  va_list arg);`
	`int vsprintf(char *s,`
	`  char *format,`
	`  va_list arg);`

`#include <stdarg.h>`
`#include <stdio.h>`
`#include <wchar.h>`
 	
`int vfwprintf(FILE *stream,`
`  const wchar_t *format,`
`  va_list arg);`
`int vwprintf(`
`  const wchar_t *format,`
`  va_list arg);`
`int vswprintf(wchar_t *s,`
`  size_t n,`
`  const wchar_t *format,`
`  va_list arg);`	

The functions **vfprintf**, **vprintf**, and **vsprintf** are the same as the functions **fprintf**, **printf**, and **sprintf**, respectively, except that the extra arguments are given as a variable argument list as defined by the **vararg** (or **stdarg**) facility (section 11.4). The argument **arg** must have been initialized by the **va_start** macro, and possibly subsequent **va_arg** calls. These functions are useful when the programmer wants to define his or her own variable-argument functions that use the formatted output facilities. The functions do not invoke the **va_end** facility.

Amendment 1 to ISO C adds the functions **vfwprintf**, **vwprintf**, and **vswprintf**, which are analogous to **fwprintf**, **wprintf**, and **swprintf**, respectively.

Example

Suppose you want to write a general function, **trace**, that prints the name of a function and its arguments. Any function to be traced would begin with a call to **trace** of the form:

```
trace(name,format,parm1,parm2,...,parmN)
```

where **name** is the name of the function being called and **format** is a format string suitable for printing the argument values **parm1**, **parm2**, ..., **parmN**. For example:

```
int f(int x, double y)    /* Trace this function. */
{
    trace("f","x=%d, y=%f", x, y);
    ...
}
```

A possible implementation of **trace** is given below for traditional C:

```
#include <varargs.h>
#include <stdio.h>
void trace(va_alist)
    va_dcl
{
    va_list args;
    char *name;
    char *format;
    va_start(args);
    name = va_arg(args,char *);
    format = va_arg(args,char *);
    fprintf(stderr,"--> entering %s(", name);
    vfprintf(stderr, format, args);
    fprintf(stderr,")\n");
    va_end(args);
}
```

15.13 fread, fwrite

ISO C facilities	Traditional and alternate facilities
`#include <stdio.h>`	`#include <stdio.h>`

`size_t fread(`
`void *ptr,`
`size_t element_size,`
`size_t count,`
`FILE *stream);`
`size_t fwrite(`
`void *ptr,`
`size_t element_size,`
`size_t count,`
`FILE *stream);`
	`int fread(`
	`char *ptr,`
	`unsigned element_size,`
	`int count,`
	`FILE *stream);`
	`int fwrite(`
	`char *ptr,`
	`unsigned element_size,`
	`int count,`
	`FILE *stream);`

The functions **fread** and **fwrite** perform input and output, respectively, to binary files. In both cases, **stream** is the input or output stream and **ptr** is a pointer to an array of **count** elements, each of which is **element_size** characters long.

The function **fread** reads up to **count** elements of the indicated size from the input stream into the specified array. The actual number of items read is returned by **fread**; it may be less than **count** if end-of-file is encountered. If an error is encountered, zero is returned. The **feof** or **ferror** facilities may be used to determine whether an error or an immediate end-of-file caused zero to be returned. If either **count** or **element_size** is zero, no data are transferred and zero is returned.

Example

The following program reads an input file containing objects of a structure type and prints the number of such objects read. The program depends on **exit** closing the input file:

```
/* Count the number of elements
   of type "struct S" in file "in.dat" */
#include <stdio.h>
static char *FileName = "in.dat";
struct S { int a,b; double d; char str[103]; };

int main(void)
{
    struct S buffer;
    int items_read = 0;
    FILE *in_file = fopen(FileName,"r");
    if (in_file == NULL)
    { fprintf(stderr,"?Couldn't open %s\n",FileName);
      exit(1); }

    while (fread((char *) &buffer,
            sizeof(struct S), 1, in_file) == 1)
        items_read++;

    if (ferror(in_file))
        { fprintf(stderr,"?Read error, file %s record %d\n",
            FileName,items_read+1); exit(1); }
    printf("Finished; %d elements read\n",items_read);
    return 0;
}
```

The function **fwrite** writes **count** elements of size **element_size** from the specified array. The actual number of items written is returned by **fwrite**; it will be the same as **count** unless an error occurs.

References **exit** 19.3; **feof**, **ferror** 15.14; **fseek**, **ftell** 15.5

15.14 feof, ferror, clearerr

ISO C facilities	Traditional and alternate facilities
`#include <stdio.h>`	`#include <stdio.h>`

`int feof(FILE *stream);`
`int ferror(FILE *stream);`
`void clearerr(FILE *stream);`
	`int feof(FILE *stream);`
	`int ferror(FILE *stream);`
	`void clearerr(FILE *stream);`

The function **feof** takes as its argument an input stream. If end-of-file has been detected while reading from the input stream, then a nonzero value is returned; otherwise, zero is returned. Note that even if there are no more characters in the stream to be read, **feof** will not signal end-of-file unless and until an attempt is made to read "past" the last character. The function is normally used after an input operation has signaled a failure.

The function **ferror** returns the error status of a stream. If an error has occurred while reading from or writing to the stream, then **ferror** returns a nonzero value; otherwise, zero is returned. Once an error has occurred for a given stream, repeated calls to **ferror** will continue to report an error unless **clearerr** is used to explicitly reset the error indication. Closing the stream, as with **fclose**, will also reset the error indication.

The function **clearerr** resets any error and end-of-file indication on the specified stream; subsequent calls on **ferror** will report that no error has occurred for that stream unless and until another error occurs.

15.15 remove, rename

ISO C facilities	Traditional and alternate facilities
`#include <stdio.h>`	`#include <stdio.h>`

`int rename(`
`   const char *oldname,`
`   const char *newname);`
`int remove(char *filename);`
	`int rename(`
	`   const char *oldname,`
	`   const char *newname);`

The **remove** function removes or deletes the named file; it returns zero if the operation succeeds and a nonzero value if it does not. The string pointed to by **filename** is not altered. Implementations may differ in the details of what "remove" or "delete" actually mean, but it should not be possible for a program to open a file it has deleted. If the file is open or if the file does not exist, then the action of **remove** is implementation-defined. This function is not present in traditional C; instead, a UNIX-specific **unlink** function is commonly provided.

The **rename** function changes the name of **oldname** to **newname**; it returns zero if the operation succeeds and a nonzero value if it does not. The strings pointed to by **oldname** and **newname** are not altered. If **oldname** names an open or nonexistent file, or if **newname** names a file that already exists, then the action of **rename** is implementation-defined.

15.16 tmpfile, tmpnam, mktemp

ISO C facilities	Traditional and alternate facilities
`#include <stdio.h>`	`#include <stdio.h>`
`FILE *tmpfile(void);`	`FILE *tmpfile(void);`
`char *tmpnam(char *buf);`	`char *tmpnam(char *buf);`
`#define L_tmpnam ...`	`#define L_tmpnam ...`
`#define TMP_MAX ...`	`char *mktemp(char *buf);`

The function **tmpfile** creates a new file and opens it using **fopen** mode **"w+b"** (**"w+"** in traditional C). A file pointer for the new file is returned if the operation succeeds, or a null pointer if it fails. The intent is that the new file be used only during the current program's execution. The file is deleted when it is closed or upon program termination. After writing data to the file, the programmer can use the **rewind** function to reposition the file at its beginning for reading.

The function **tmpnam** is used to create new file names that do not conflict with other file names currently in use; the programmer can then open a new file with that name using the full generality of **fopen**. The files so created are not "temporary"; they are not deleted automatically upon program termination. If **buf** is **NULL**, **tmpnam** returns a pointer to the new file name string; the string may be altered by subsequent calls to **tmpnam**. If **buf** is not **NULL** it must point to an array of not less than **L_tmpnam** characters; **tmpnam** will copy the new file name string into that array and return **buf**. If **tmpnam** fails, it returns a null pointer. ISO C defines the value **TMP_MAX** to be the number of successive calls to **tmpnam** that will generate unique names; it must be at least 25.

The function **mktemp** is like **tmpnam** except that **buf** (the "template") must point to a string with six trailing **X** characters, which will be overwritten with other letters or digits to form a unique file name. The value **buf** is returned. Successive calls to **mktemp** should specify different templates to ensure unique names. UNIX implementations often substitute the program's process identification for **XXXXXX**. **mktemp** is not in ISO C.

Example

A common but poor programming practice in C is to write

```
ptr = fopen(mktemp("/tmp/abcXXXXXX"),"w+");
```

This idiom will fail if the string constant is not modifiable. The programmer also loses the ability to reference the file name string. It is better and no less efficient to write

```
char filename[]="/tmp/abcXXXXXX";
ptr = fopen(mktemp(filename),"w+");
```

16

Storage Allocation

The storage allocation facilities provide a simple form of heap memory management that allows a program to repeatedly request allocation of a "fresh" region of memory and perhaps later to deallocate such a region when it is no longer needed. Explicitly deallocated regions are recycled by the storage manager for satisfaction of further allocation requests.

When a region of memory is allocated in response to a request, a pointer to the region is returned to the caller. This pointer will be of type **char *** (**void *** in ISO C) but is guaranteed to be properly aligned for any data type. The caller may then use a cast operator to convert this pointer to another pointer type.

In ISO C the facilities described in this section are declared in the header file **stdlib.h**. In other C implementations there is typically no associated header file, and the programmer must declare the facilities.

Table 16–1 Chapter summary

Name	Section	Name	Section	Name	Section
calloc	16.1	**free**	16.2	**realloc**	16.3
cfree	16.2	**malloc**	16.1	**relalloc**	16.3
clalloc	16.1	**mlalloc**	16.1		

16.1 malloc, calloc, mlalloc, clalloc

ISO C facilities	Traditional and alternate facilities
`#include <stdlib.h>`	
`void *malloc(size_t size);`	`char *malloc(unsigned size);`
`void *calloc(size_t elt_count, size_t elt_size);`	`char *calloc(unsigned elt_count, unsigned elt_size);`
	`char *mlalloc(unsigned long size);`
	`char *clalloc(unsigned long elt_count, unsigned long elt_size);`

The function **malloc** allocates a region of memory large enough to hold an object whose size (as measured by the **sizeof** operator) is **size**. A pointer to the first element of the region is returned. If it is impossible for some reason to perform the requested allocation, a null pointer is returned. If the requested size is 0, the ISO C functions will return either a null pointer or an implementation-defined unique pointer. The allocated memory is not initialized in any way, so the caller cannot depend on its contents.

The function **calloc** allocates a region of memory large enough to hold an array of **elt_count** elements, each of size **elt_size** (typically given by the **sizeof** operator). The region of memory is cleared bitwise to zero, and a pointer to the first element of the region is returned. If it is impossible for some reason to perform the requested allocation, or if **elt_count** or **elt_size** is zero, then the return value is the same as for **malloc**. Note that memory cleared bitwise to zero might not have the same representation as a floating-point zero or as a null pointer.

The traditional function **mlalloc** is just like **malloc**, except that its arguments are of type **unsigned long** rather than **unsigned int**. In some C implementations it is possible to allocate memory regions so large that numbers of type **unsigned int** are not large enough to specify them. This function is not provided in ISO C, because the use of type **size_t** for the parameter of **malloc** avoids the problem. Similarly, the function **clalloc** is just like **calloc**, except for its argument types.

Example

The caller of an allocation routine will typically convert the result pointer to an appropriate pointer type by casting or assignment. Below, we assume that **T** is some object type that we wish to allocate dynamically; it might be a structure, array, or even a character:

```
T *NewObject(void)
{
    T *objptr = (T *) malloc(sizeof(T));
    if (objptr==NULL) printf("NewObject: ran out of memory!\n");
    return objptr;
}
```

The cast is not necessary in ISO C because **malloc** returns a pointer of type **void ***. In traditional C, not using the cast may provoke a warning message from the **lint** type-checking program, for it appears that you are implicitly converting a **char *** pointer to **T ***, which could be considered suspicious.

References assignment conversions 6.3.2

16.2 free, cfree

ISO C facilities	Traditional and alternate facilities
#include <stdlib.h>	
void free(void *ptr);	**void free(char *ptr);** **void cfree(char *ptr);**

The ISO C function **free** deallocates a region of memory previously allocated by **malloc**, **calloc**, or **realloc** (section 16.3). The traditional version of **free** deallocates memory previously allocated by **malloc**, **mlalloc**, **realloc**, or **relalloc** (section 16.3). The traditional C function **cfree** deallocates memory previously allocated by **calloc** or **clalloc**.

The argument to **free** or **cfree** must be a pointer that is the same as a pointer previously returned by one of the allocation functions. If the argument to the ISO C **free** function is a null pointer, then the call has no effect. However, passing a null pointer to a traditional **free** or **cfree** function is known to cause trouble in many non-ISO C implementations.

Once a region of memory has been explicitly freed (or reallocated), it must not be used for any other purpose. The use of any pointer into the region (a "dangling pointer") will have unpredictable effects. Likewise, allocating a region of storage once but freeing it more than once has unpredictable effects.

16.3 realloc, relalloc

ISO C facilities	Traditional and alternate facilities
#include <stdlib.h>	

void *realloc(
  void *ptr,
  size_t size);
	char *realloc(
	  char *ptr,
	  unsigned size);
	char *relalloc(
	  char *ptr,
	  unsigned long size);

The function **realloc** takes a pointer to memory region previously allocated by one of the standard functions and changes its size while preserving its contents. If necessary, the contents are copied to a new memory region. A pointer to the (possibly new) memory region is returned. If the request cannot be satisfied, a null pointer is returned and the old region is not disturbed.

If the first argument to **realloc** is a null pointer, then the function behaves like **malloc** (section 16.1). If **ptr** is not null and size is zero, **realloc** returns a null pointer and the old region is deallocated. If the new size is smaller than the old size, then some of the old contents at the end of the old region will be discarded. If the new size is larger than the old size, then all of the old contents are preserved and new space is added at the end; the new space is not specially initialized in any way, and the caller must assume that it contains garbage information. Whenever **realloc** returns a pointer that is different from its first argument, the programmer should assume that the old region of memory was deallocated and should not be used.

The function **relalloc** behaves like **realloc** except that the **size** argument has type **unsigned long int** instead of **unsigned int**. This function is not present in ISO C, in which the **size** argument to **realloc** has type **size_t**.

Example

Below is shown a typical use of **realloc** to expand the dynamic array designated by the pointer **samples**. (The elements of such an array must be referenced using subscript expressions; any pointers into the array could be invalidated by the call to **realloc**.)

```
#include <stdlib.h>
#define SAMPLE_INCREMENT 100
int sample_limit = 0;       /* Max size of current array */
int sample_count = 0;       /* Number of elements in array */
double *samples = NULL;     /* Will point to array */

int AddSample( double new_sample )
    /* Add an element to the end of the array */
{
    if (sample_count < sample_limit) {
        samples[sample_count++] = new_sample;
    } else {
        /* Allocate a new, larger array. */
        int new_limit = sample_limit + SAMPLE_INCREMENT;
        double *new_array =
            realloc(samples, new_limit * sizeof(double));
        if (new_array == NULL) {
            /* Can't expand; leave samples untouched. */
            fprintf(stderr,"?AddSample: out of memory\n");
        } else {
            samples = new_array;
            sample_limit = new_limit;
            samples[sample_count++] = new_sample;
        }
    }
    return sample_count;
}
```

17

Mathematical Functions

Most of the facilities described in this section are declared by the library header file **math.h**, although in ISO C a few of the more common facilities are in **stdlib.h**. All of the operations on floating-point numbers are defined only for arguments of type **double**, because of the rule that all actual function arguments of type **float** are converted to type **double** before the call is performed. In ISO C this convention is maintained for compatibility.

Two general kinds of errors are possible with the mathematical functions, although older C implementations may not handle them consistently. When an input argument lies outside the domain over which the function is defined, a *domain error* occurs. The variable **errno** (section 11.2) is set to the value **EDOM** and the function returns an implementation-defined value. Zero is the traditional error return value, but some implementations may have better choices, such as special "not a number" values. (System V UNIX has a more elaborate mechanism, **matherr**.)

Table 17–1 Chapter summary

Name	Section	Name	Section	Name	Section
abs	17.1	**fabs**	17.2	**modf**	17.5
acos	17.9	**floor**	17.3	**pow**	17.6
asin	17.9	**fmod**	17.3	**rand**	17.7
atan	17.9	**frexp**	17.5	**sin**	17.8
atan2	17.9	**HUGE_VAL**	17.0	**sinh**	17.10
ceil	17.3	**labs**	17.1	**sqrt**	17.6
cos	17.8	**ldexp**	17.5	**srand**	17.7
cosh	17.10	**ldiv**	17.1	**tan**	17.8
div	17.1	**log**	17.4	**tanh**	17.10
exp	17.4	**log10**	17.4		

If the result of a function is too large in magnitude to be represented as a value of the function's return type, then a *range error* occurs. When this happens, **errno** should be set to the value **ERANGE** and the function should return the largest representable floating-point value with the same sign as the correct result. In ISO C this is the value of the macro **HUGE_VAL**; in UNIX System V it is **HUGE**.

If the result of a function is too small in magnitude to be represented, then the function should return zero; whether **errno** is also set to **ERANGE** is left to the discretion of the implementation.

17.1 abs, labs, div, ldiv

ISO C facilities	Traditional and alternate facilities
`#include <stdlib.h>`	`#include <math.h>`
`int abs(int x);`	`int abs(int x);`
`long labs(long int x);`	`long labs(long x);`
`typedef ... div_t;`	
`typedef ... ldiv_t;`	
`div_t div(int n,int d);`	
`ldiv_t ldiv(long n,long d);`	

The four functions in this section are integer arithmetic functions, defined in **stdlib.h** in ISO C and in **math.h** in traditional C. The functions **abs**, **fabs** (section 17.2), and **labs** all return the absolute value of their arguments. The argument and the result are both of type **int** for **abs**, of type **double** for **fabs**, and of type **long int** for **labs**. The absolute-value functions are so easy to implement that some compilers may treat them as built-in functions; this is permitted in ISO C.

The functions **div** and **ldiv** are found in ISO C but are otherwise not common in C implementations. They compute simultaneously the quotient and remainder of the division of **n** by **d**. The type **div_t** is a structure containing two components, **quot** and **rem** (in any order), both of type **int**. The type **ldiv_t** is also a structure with components **quot** and **rem**, both of type **long int**. The returned quotient **quot** has the same sign as **n/d**, and its magnitude is the largest integer not greater than **abs(n/d)**. The remainder **rem** is such that **quot*d+rem** equals **n**. The behavior of the functions when **d** is zero, or when **n/d** is not representable, is undefined (not necessarily a domain error) to allow for the most efficient implementation.

The **div** and **ldiv** functions are provided because most computers can compute the quotient and remainder at the same time. Therefore, using this function—which could be expanded in-line—will be faster than using **/** and **%** separately.

17.2 fabs

ISO C facilities	Traditional and alternate facilities
`#include <math.h>`	`#include <math.h>`
`double fabs(double x);`	`double fabs(double x);`

The **fabs** function computes the absolute value. In ISO C, it is defined in **math.h** rather than **stdlib.h**, where the other absolute-value functions are defined.

17.3 ceil, floor, fmod

ISO C facilities	Traditional and alternate facilities
`#include <math.h>`	`#include <math.h>`

`double ceil(double x);`
`double floor(double x);`
`double fmod(`
`   double x,`
`   double y);`
	`double ceil(double x);`
	`double floor(double x);`
	`double fmod(`
	`   double x,`
	`   double y);`

The function **ceil** returns the smallest floating-point number not less than **x** whose value is an exact mathematical integer. If the **x** is already an integer, it is returned. Similarly, **floor** returns the largest floating-point number not greater than **x** whose value is an exact mathematical integer.

The function **fmod** returns an approximation to the mathematical value *f* such that *f* has the same sign as **x**, the absolute value of *f* is less than the absolute value of **y**, and there exists an integer *k* such that *k****y+***f* equals **x**. If **y** is zero, an ISO C conforming implementation may generate a domain error or may return 0; in some traditional C implementations, **x** is returned in this case. If the quotient **x/y** cannot be represented, the result is undefined.

The function **fmod** should not be confused with **modf** (section 17.5), a function that extracts the fractional and integer parts of a floating-point number.

17.4 exp, log, log10

ISO C facilities	Traditional and alternate facilities
`#include <math.h>`	`#include <math.h>`
`double exp(double x);`	`double exp(double x);`
`double log(double x);`	`double log(double x);`
`double log10(double x);`	`double log10(double x);`

The function **exp** computes the exponential function of **x**—that is, $e^{\mathbf{x}}$, where e is the base of the natural logarithms. A range error can occur for large arguments.

The function **log** computes the natural logarithm function of **x**. If **x** is negative, a domain error occurs. If **x** is zero or close to zero, a range error may occur (toward minus infinity). Some traditional C implementations treat zero as a domain error, and some implementations name this function **ln**.

The function **log10** computes the base-10 logarithm function. The conditions causing domain and range errors are the same as for the function **log**.

17.5 frexp, ldexp, modf

ISO C facilities	Traditional and alternate facilities
`#include <math.h>`	`#include <math.h>`
`double frexp(`	`double frexp(`
`double x,`	`double x,`
`int *nptr);`	`int *nptr);`
`double ldexp(`	`double ldexp(`
`double x,`	`double x,`
`int n);`	`int n);`
`double modf(`	`double modf(`
`double x,`	`double x,`
`double *nptr);`	`double *nptr);`

The function **frexp** splits a floating-point number into a fraction f and an exponent n, such that either f is 0.0 or $0.5 \leq |f| < 1.0$, and $f * 2^n$ is equal to **x**. The fraction f is returned, and as a side effect the exponent n is stored into the place pointed to by **nptr**. If **x** is zero, then both returned values will be zero.

The function **ldexp** is the inverse of **frexp**; it computes the value $\mathbf{x} * 2^{\mathbf{n}}$. A range error may occur.

The function **modf** splits a floating-point number into a fractional part f and an integer part n, such that $|f| < 1.0$ and $f+n$ is equal to **x**. Both f and n will have the same sign as **x**. The fractional part f is returned, and as a side effect the integer part n is stored as a floating-point number into the object pointed to by **nptr**. The name **modf** is a misnomer; the value it computes is properly called a remainder.

The function **modf** should not be confused with **fmod** (section 17.3), a function that computes the remainder from dividing one floating-point number by another. Some non-ISO UNIX implementations are reported to define **modf** differently; check your local library documentation.

17.6 pow, sqrt

ISO C facilities	Traditional and alternate facilities
`#include <math.h>`	`#include <math.h>`

`double pow(`
`double x,`
`double y);`
`double sqrt(double x);`
	`double pow(`
	`double x,`
	`double y);`
	`double sqrt(double x);`

The function **pow** computes x^y. When **x** is nonzero and **y** is zero, the result is 1.0. When **x** is zero and **y** is positive, the result is zero. Domain errors occur if **x** is negative and **y** is not an exact integer, or if **x** is zero and **y** is nonpositive. Range errors may also occur.

The function **sqrt** computes the nonnegative square root of **x**. A domain error occurs if **x** is negative.

17.7 rand, srand

ISO C facilities	Traditional and alternate facilities
`#include <stdlib.h>`	`#include <math.h>`

`int rand(void);`
`void srand(unsigned seed);`
`#define RAND_MAX ...`
	`int rand(void);`
	`void srand(int seed);`

Successive calls to **rand** return integer values in the range 0 to the largest representable positive value of type **int** (inclusive) that are the successive results of a pseudo-random-number generator. In ISO C the facility is defined in **stdlib.h**, and the upper bound of the range of **rand** is given by **RAND_MAX**, which will be at least 32,767.

The function **srand** may be used to initialize the pseudo-random-number generator that is used to generate successive values for calls to **rand**. After a call to **srand**, successive calls to **rand** will produce a certain series of pseudo-random numbers. If **srand** is called again with the same argument, then after that point successive calls to **rand** will produce the same series of pseudo-random numbers. Successive calls made to **rand** before **srand** is ever called in a user program will produce the same series of pseudo-random numbers that would be produced after **srand** is called with argument 1.

ISO C library facilities must not call **rand** or **srand** in a way that affects the programmer's observed sequence of pseudo-random numbers.

17.8 cos, sin, tan

ISO C facilities	Traditional and alternate facilities
`#include <math.h>`	`#include <math.h>`
`double cos(double x);`	`double cos(double x);`
`double sin(double x);`	`double sin(double x);`
`double tan(double x);`	`double tan(double x);`

The function **cos** computes the trigonometric cosine function of **x**, which is taken to be in radians. No domain or range errors are possible, but the programmer should be aware that the result may have little significance for very large values of **x**.

The functions **sin** and **tan** similarly compute the trigonometric sine and tangent functions, respectively. A range error may occur in the **tan** function if the argument is close to an odd multiple of $\pi/2$. The same caution about large-magnitude arguments applies to **sin** and **tan**.

17.9 acos, asin, atan, atan2

ISO C facilities	Traditional and alternate facilities
`#include <math.h>`	`#include <math.h>`
`double acos(double x);`	`double acos(double x);`
`double asin(double x);`	`double asin(double x);`
`double atan(double x);`	`double atan(double x);`
`double atan2(`	`double atan2(`
`   double y,`	`   double y,`
`   double x);`	`   double x);`

The function **acos** computes the principal value of the trigonometric arc cosine function of **x**. The result is in radians and lies between 0 and π. (The range of these functions is approximate, because of the effect of round-off errors.) A domain error occurs if the argument is less than –1.0 or greater than 1.0.

The function **asin** computes the principal value of the trigonometric arc sine function of **x**. The result is in radians and lies between $-\pi/2$ and $\pi/2$. A domain error occurs if the argument is less than –1.0 or greater than 1.0.

The function **atan** computes the principal value of the arc tangent function of **x**. The result is in radians and lies between $-\pi/2$ and $\pi/2$. No range or domain errors are possible. In some implementations of C this function is called **arctan**.

The function **atan2** computes the principal value of the trigonometric arc tangent function of the value **y/x**. The signs of the two arguments are taken into account to determine quadrant information. Viewed in terms of a Cartesian coordinate system, the result is the angle between the positive x-axis and a line drawn from the origin through the point (**x**, **y**). The result is in radians and lies between $-\pi$ and π. If **x** is zero the result is $\pi/2$ or $-\pi/2$, depending on whether **y** is positive or negative. A domain error occurs if both **x** and **y** are zero.

17.10 cosh, sinh, tanh

ISO C facilities	Traditional and alternate facilities
`#include <math.h>`	`#include <math.h>`
`double cosh(double x);`	`double cosh(double x);`
`double sinh(double x);`	`double sinh(double x);`
`double tanh(double x);`	`double tanh(double x);`

The function **cosh** computes the hyperbolic cosine function of **x**. The function **sinh** computes the hyperbolic sine function of **x**. The function **tanh** computes the hyperbolic tangent function of **x**. A range error can occur if the absolute value of the argument to **sinh** or **cosh** is large.

18

Time and Date Functions

The facilities in this section give the C programmer ways to retrieve and use the (calendar) date and time, and the process time—that is, the amount of processing time used by the running program.

Calendar time may be used to record the date that a program was run or a file was written, or to compute a date in the past or future. Calendar time is represented in two forms: a simple arithmetic value returned by the time function, and a "broken-down," structured form computed from the arithmetic value by the **`gmtime`** and **`localtime`** functions. Locale-specific formatting is provided by the ISO C function **`strftime`**.

Process time is often used to measure how fast a program or a part of a program executes. Process time is represented by an arithmetic value (usually integral) returned by the **`clock`** function.

Table 18–1 Chapter summary

Name	Section	Name	Section	Name	Section
`asctime`	18.3	**`difftime`**	18.5	**`time`**	18.2
`clock`	18.1	**`gmtime`**	18.4	**`time_t`**	18.2
`clock_t`	18.1	**`localtime`**	18.4	**`times`**	18.1
`CLOCKS_PER_SEC`	18.1	**`mktime`**	18.4	**`tm`** **(struct)**	18.4
`ctime`	18.3	**`strftime`**[a]	18.6		

[a] This function has a wide-character equivalent in Amendment 1 to ISO C.

18.1 clock, clock_t, CLOCKS_PER_SEC, times

ISO C facilities	Traditional and alternate facilities
`#include <time.h>`	`#include <sys/types.h>` `#include <sys/times.h>`

`typedef ... clock_t;`
`#define CLOCKS_PER_SEC ...`
`clock_t clock();`
	`long clock(void);`
	`void times(struct tms *);`
	`struct tms {...};`

The **clock** function returns an approximation to the processor time used by the current process. The units in which the time is expressed vary with the implementation; microseconds are customary. Although in traditional C the return type of **clock** is long, the value returned is really of type **unsigned long**; the use of **long** predates the addition of **unsigned long** to the language. Unsigned arithmetic should always be used when computing with process times.

Programmers should be aware of "wrap-around" in the process time. For instance, if type **long** is represented in 32 bits and **clock** returns the time in microseconds, the time returned will "wrap around" to its starting value in about 36 minutes.

The ISO C version of **clock** allows the implementor freedom to use any arithmetic type, **clock_t**, for the process time. The number of time units ("clock ticks") per second is defined by the macro **CLOCKS_PER_SEC**. If the processor time is not available, the value –1 (cast to be of type **clock_t**) will be returned.

Example

Here is how the **clock** function can be used to time an ISO C program:

```
#include <time.h>
clock_t start, finish, duration;
...
start = clock();
process();
finish = clock();
printf("process() took %f seconds to execute\n",
       ((double) (finish - start)) / CLOCKS_PER_SEC );
```

The cast to type **double** allows **clock_t** and **CLOCKS_PER_SEC** to be either floating-point or integral.

The **times** function is found in Berkeley UNIX and in some non-UNIX systems instead of **clock**; it returns a structured value that reports various components of the process time, each typically measured in units of 1/60 of a second.

Example

A rough equivalent to the (ISO C) **clock** function can be written using (non-ISO) **times**:

```
#include <sys/types.h>
#include <sys/times.h>
#define CLOCKS_PER_SEC 60
long clock(void)
{
    struct tms tmsbuf;
    times(&tmsbuf);
    return (tmsbuf.tms_utime + tmsbuf.tms_stime);
}
```

There is a type, **time_t**, used in the above structure; it is a "process time" unit and therefore is not the same as the "calendar time" type **time_t** defined in ISO C.

References **time** 18.2; **time_t** 18.2

18.2 time, time_t

ISO C facilities	Traditional and alternate facilities
`#include <time.h>`	
`typedef ... time_t;`	
`time_t time(time_t *tptr);`	`long time(long *tptr);`

The ISO C function **time** returns the current calendar time encoded in a value of type **time_t**, which can be any arithmetic type. If the parameter **tptr** is not null, the return value is also stored at ***tptr**. If errors are encountered, the value –1 (cast to type **time_t**) is returned

In pre-ISO implementations, type **long** is used in place of **time_t**, but the value returned is logically of type **unsigned long**. When errors occur, **-1L** is returned. In System V UNIX, **errno** is also set to **EFAULT**.

Typically, the value returned by **time** is passed to the function **asctime** or **ctime** to convert it to a readable form, or is passed to **localtime** or **gmtime** to convert it to a form that is more easily processed. Computing the interval between two calendar times can be done by the ISO C function **difftime**; in other implementations the programmer must either work with the broken-down time from **gmtime** or depend on a customary representation of the time as the number of seconds since some arbitrary past date. (January 1, 1970, seems to be popular.)

References **asctime** 18.3; **ctime** 18.3; **difftime** 18.5; **errno** 11.2; **gmtime** 18.4; **localtime** 18.4

18.3 asctime, ctime

ISO C facilities	Traditional and alternate facilities
`#include <time.h>`	`#include <sys/time.h>`
`char *asctime(` `  const struct tm *ts);`	`char *asctime(struct tm *ts);`
`char *ctime(` `  const time_t *timptr);`	`char *ctime(long *timptr);`

The **asctime** and **ctime** functions both return a pointer to a string that is a printable date and time of the form

```
"Sat May 15 17:30:00 1982\n"
```

The **asctime** function takes as its single argument a pointer to a structured calendar time; such a structure is produced by **localtime** or **gmtime** from the arithmetic time that is returned by **time**. The **ctime** function takes a pointer to the value returned by **time**, and therefore **ctime(tp)** is equivalent to **asctime(localtime(tp))**.

In most implementations—including many ISO C-conforming implementations—the functions return a pointer to a static data area, and therefore the returned string should be printed or copied (with **strcpy**) before any subsequent call to either function.

Example

Many programs need to print the current date and time. Here's how to do it using **time** and **ctime**:

```
#include <time.h>
#include <stdio.h>
time_t now;
...
now = time(NULL);
printf("The current date and time is: %s",ctime(&now));
```

References **gmtime** 18.4; **localtime** 18.4; **strcpy** 13.3; **struct tm** 18.4; **time** 18.2

18.4 gmtime, localtime, mktime

ISO C facilities	Traditional and alternate facilities

`#include <time.h>`
`struct tm { ... };`
`struct tm *gmtime(`
`  const time_t *t);`
`struct tm *localtime(`
`  const time_t *t);`
`time_t mktime(`
`  struct tm *tmptr );`
	`#include <sys/time.h>`
	`struct tm { ... };`
	`struct tm *gmtime(`
	`  long *t);`
	`struct tm *localtime(`
	`  long *t);`

The functions **gmtime** and **localtime** convert an arithmetic calendar time returned by **time** to a "broken-down" form of type **struct tm**. The **gmtime** function converts to Greenwich mean time (GMT) while **localtime** converts to local time, taking into account the time zone and possible Daylight Savings Time. The functions return a null pointer if they encounter errors, and are portable across UNIX systems and ISO C. The structure **struct tm** includes the fields listed in Table 18–2. All fields have type **int**.

Table 18–2 Fields in struct tm type

Name	Units	Range
tm_sec	seconds after the minute	0..61[a]
tm_min	minutes after the hour	0..59
tm_hour	hours since midnight	0..23
tm_mday	day of month	1..31
tm_mon	month since January	0..11
tm_year	years since 1900	≥0
tm_wday	day since Sunday	0..6
tm_yday	day since January 1	0..365
tm_isdst	daylight saving time flag	>0 if daylight saving time; 0 if not; <0 if don't know

[a] The range allows up to 2 leap-seconds.

In most implementations—including many ISO-conforming implementations—**gmtime** and **localtime** return a pointer to a single static data area that is overwritten on every call. Therefore, the returned structure should be used or copied before any subsequent call to either function.

The function **mktime** constructs a value of type **time_t** from the broken-down local time specified by the argument **tmptr**. The values of **tmptr->tm_wday** and **tmptr->tm_yday** are ignored by **mktime**. If successful, **mktime** returns the new time value and adjusts the contents of ***tmptr**, setting the **tm_wday** and **tm_yday** components. If the indicated calendar time cannot be represented as a value of **time_t**, then **mktime** returns the value **-1** (cast to **time_t**). Section 18.5 shows an example.

18.5 difftime

ISO C facilities	Traditional and alternate facilities

`#include <time.h>`
`double difftime(`
`time_t t1,`
`time_t t0);`	

The **difftime** function is found only in ISO C. It subtracts calendar time **t0** from calendar time **t1**, returning the difference in seconds as a value of type **double**. Programmers cannot assume that calendar time is encoded in **time_t** as a scalar value (such as a number of microseconds), and so **difftime** must be used rather than simply subtracting two values of type **time_t**.

Example

The following function returns the number of seconds between midnight on April 15, 1990, and the current date and time.

```
#include <time.h>
...
double Secs_Since_Apr_15(void)
{
    struct tm Apr_15_struct = {0}; /* Set all fields to 0 */
    time_t Apr_15_t;
    Apr_15_struct.tm_year = 90;
    Apr_15_struct.tm_mon  = 3;
    Apr_15_struct.tm_mday = 15;
    Apr_15_t = mktime(&Apr_15_struct);
    if (Apr_15_t == (time_t)-1)
        return 0.0; /* error */
    else
        return difftime( time(NULL), Apr_15_t);
}
```

References **time_t** 18.2

18.6 strftime

ISO C facilities	Traditional and alternate facilities

`#include <time.h>`
`size_t strftime(`
`char *s,`
`size_t maxsize,`
`const char *format,`
`const struct tm *timeptr);`	

`#include <wchar.h>`
`size_t wcsftime(`
`wchar_t *s,`
`size_t maxsize,`
`const wchar_t *format,`
`const struct tm *timeptr);`	

Like **sprintf** (section 15.11) **strftime** stores characters into the character array pointed to by the parameter **s** under control of the string **format**. However, **strftime** only formats a single date and time quantity specified by **timeptr** (section 18.4), and the formatting codes in **format** are interpreted differently from **sprintf**. (See Table 18–3.) No more than **maxsize** characters (including the terminating null character) are placed into the array designated by **s**. The actual number of characters stored (not including the terminating null character) is returned. If **maxsize** is not large enough to hold the entire formatted string, zero is returned.

Amendment 1 to ISO C adds the **wcsftime** function for formatting the date and time as a wide string. (The function is analogous to **wsprintf**, section 15.11.)

The formatting is locale-specific. See **setlocale**, section 11.5.

Example

A plausible implementation of **asctime** (section 18.3) using **strftime** is shown below. Since the formatting is locale-specific, the length of the output string (including the terminating null character) is not easily predictable (which is the case for the output from **asctime**:

```
#include <time.h>
#define TIME_SIZE 30  /* hope this is big enough */
char *asctime2( const struct tm *tm )
{
    static char time_buffer[TIME_SIZE];
    size_t len;
    len = strftime( time_buffer, TIME_SIZE,
        "%a %b %d %H:%M:%S %Y\n", tm);
    if (len == 0)
        return NULL;  /* time_buffer is too short */
    else
        return time_buffer;
}
```

Table 18–3 Formatting codes for strftime

Code	Replaced By
`%a`	abbreviated weekday name, e.g., "**Mon**"
`%A`	full weekday name, e.g., "**Monday**"
`%b`	abbreviated month name, e.g., "**Feb**"
`%B`	full month name, e.g., "**February**"
`%c`	locale-specific date and time
`%d`	day of the month as a decimal integer (01–31)
`%H`	the hour (24-hour clock) as a decimal integer (00–23)
`%I`	the hour (12-hour clock) as a decimal integer (01–12)
`%j`	day of the year as a decimal number (001–366)
`%m`	month, as a decimal number (01–12)
`%M`	minute, as a decimal number (00–59)
`%p`	the locale's equivalent of AM/PM designation for 12-hour clock
`%S`	second, as a decimal number (00–61)[a]
`%U`	week number of the year (00–53)[b]
`%w`	weekday as a decimal number (0–6, Sunday=0)
`%W`	week number of the year[c]
`%x`	locale-specific date
`%X`	local-specific time
`%y`	year without century as a decimal number (00–99)
`%Y`	year with century as a decimal number, e.g., 1952
`%z`	time zone name or abbreviation, or none if not known
`%%`	a single `%`

[a] Allows for up to 2 leap-seconds (60 and 61).
[b] Week number 1 has the first Sunday; previous days are week 0.
[c] Week number 1 has the first Monday; previous days are week 0.

19

Control Functions

The facilities in this chapter provide extensions to the standard flow of control in C programs. The functions **signal** and **raise** implement a primitive exception-handling mechanism; **assert** and **exit** provide program-termination capabilities; and **exec** and **system** allow other programs to be started from within a C program.

Table 19–1 Chapter summary

Name	Section	Name	Section	Name	Section
abort	19.3	**gsignal**	19.6	**raise**	19.6
alarm	19.7	**jmp_buf**	19.4	**setjmp**	19.4
assert	19.1	**kill**	19.6	**signal**	19.6
atexit	19.5	**longjmp**	19.4	**sleep**	19.7
exec	19.2	**NDEBUG**	19.1	**ssignal**	19.6
exit	19.3	**psignal**	19.6	**system**	19.2

19.1 assert, NDEBUG

ISO C facilities	Traditional and alternate facilities
`#include <assert.h>`	`include <assert.h>`

`#ifndef NDEBUG`
`void assert(int expression);`
`#else`
`#define assert(x) ((void)0)`
`#endif`
	`#ifndef NDEBUG`
	`void assert(`*scalar* `expression);`
	`#else`
	`#define assert(x) ((void)0)`
	`#endif`

The macro **assert** takes as its single argument a value of any integer type. (Many implementations allow any scalar type.) If that value is 0 and if additionally the macro **NDEBUG** is not defined, then **assert** will print a diagnostic message on the standard output stream and halt the program by calling **abort** (in ISO C) or **exit** (in traditional C). The **assert** facility is always implemented as a macro, and the header file **assert.h** must be included in the source file to use the facility. The diagnostic message will include the text of the argument, the file name (**__FILE__**) and the line number (**__LINE__**).

If the macro **NDEBUG** is defined when the header file **assert.h** is read, the **assert** facility is disabled, usually by defining **assert** to be the empty statement. No diagnostic messages are printed, and the argument to **assert** is not evaluated.

Example

The **assert** facility is typically used during program development to verify that certain conditions are true at run time. It provides reliable documentation to people reading the program and can greatly aid in debugging. When a program is operational, assertions can easily be disabled, after which they have no run-time overhead. In the example below, the assertion is better documentation than the English comment, which can be misinterpreted:

```
#include <assert.h>
int f(int x)
{
    /* x should be between 1 and 10 */     /* !? */
    assert(x>0 && x<10);
    ...
}
```

References **abort** 19.3; **exit** 19.3

19.2 exec, system

ISO C facilities	Traditional and alternate facilities
`#include <stdlib.h>`	
`int system( const char *command);`	`int system( char *command);`
	`execl(char *name, char *argi, ..., NULL );`
	`execlp(char *name, char *argi, ..., NULL );`
	`execle(char *name, char *argi, ..., NULL, char *envp);`
	`execv(char *name, char *argv[] );`
	`execvp(char *name, char *argv[] );`
	`execve(char *name, char *argv[], char *envp[]);`

The function **system** passes its string argument to the operating system's *command processor* for execution in some implementation-defined way. In UNIX systems, the command processor is the shell. The value returned by **system** is implementation-defined but is usually the completion status of the command. In ISO C, **system** may be called with a null argument, in which case 0 is returned if there is no command processor provided in the implementation and a nonzero value is returned if there is.

The various forms of **exec** are not part of ISO C—they are found mainly in UNIX systems. In all cases, they transform the current *process* into a new process by executing the program in file **name**. They differ in how arguments are supplied for the new process:

1. The functions **execl**, **execlp**, and **execle** take a variable number of arguments, the last of which must be a null pointer. By convention, the first argument should be the same as **name**—that is, it should be the name of the program to be executed.

2. The functions **execv**, **execvp**, and **execve** supply a pointer to a null-terminated vector of arguments, such as is provided to function **main**. By convention, **argv[0]** should be the same as **name**—that is, it should be the name of the program to be executed.

3. The functions **execle** and **execve** also pass an explicit "environment" to the new process. The parameter **envp** is a null-terminated vector of string pointers. Each string is of the form **"name=value"**. (In the other versions of **exec**, the environment pointer of the calling process is implicitly passed to the new process.)

4. The functions **execlp** and **execvp** are the same as **execl** and **execv**, respectively, except that the system looks for the file in the set of directories normally containing commands (usually the value of the environment variable **path** or **PATH**).

When the new process is started, the arguments supplied to **exec** are made available to the new process's **main** function (section 20.1).

19.3 exit, abort

ISO C facilities	Traditional and alternate facilities
`#include <stdlib.h>`	
`#define EXIT_FAILURE ...`	
`#define EXIT_SUCCESS ...`	
`void exit(int status);`	`void exit(int status);`
	`void _exit(int status);`
`void abort(void);`	`void abort(void);`

The **exit**, **_exit**, and **abort** functions cause the program to terminate. Control does not normally return to the caller of these functions.

The function **exit** terminates a program normally, with these cleanup actions:

1. (ISO C only) All functions registered with the **atexit** function are called in the reverse order of their registration as many times as they were registered.
2. Open output streams are flushed. All open streams are closed.
3. Files created by the **tmpfile** function are removed.
4. Control is returned to the host environment with a status value.

By convention in many systems, a **status** value of 0 signifies successful program termination, and nonzero values are used to signify various kinds of abnormal termination. In ISO C the value 0 and the value of the macro **EXIT_SUCCESS** will signify successful termination, and the value of the macro **EXIT_FAILURE** will signify unsuccessful termination; the meaning of other values is implementation-defined. Returning an integer value from the function **main** acts like calling **exit** with the same value.

The function **_exit**, provided in some traditional C implementations, differs from **exit** in that cleanup activities are not performed.

The **abort** function causes "abnormal" program termination. Whether or not **abort** causes cleanup actions is implementation-defined. The status value returned to the host system is implementation-defined but must denote "unsuccessful." In ISO C and many traditional implementations the call to **abort** is translated to a special signal (**SIGABRT** in ISO C) that can be caught. If the signal is ignored or if the handler returns, then ISO C implementations will still terminate the program, but other implementations may allow the **abort** function to return to the caller.

References **fflush** 15.2; **atexit** 19.5; **main** function 9.9; **return** statement 8.9; **signal** 19.6; **tmpfile** 15.16

19.4 setjmp, longjmp, jmp_buf

ISO C facilities	Traditional and alternate facilities
`#include <setjmp.h>`	`include <setjmp.h>`

`typedef ... jmp_buf;`
`int setjmp(jmp_buf env);`
`void longjmp(`
`  jmp_buf env,`
`  int status);`
	`typedef ... jmp_buf;`
	`int setjmp(jmp_buf env);`
	`void longjmp(`
	`  jmp_buf env,`
	`  int status);`

The **setjmp** and **longjmp** functions implement a primitive form of nonlocal jumps, which may be used to handle abnormal or exceptional situations. This facility is traditionally considered more portable than **signal** (section 19.6), but the latter has also been incorporated into ISO C.

The macro **setjmp** records its caller's environment in the "jump buffer" **env**, an implementation-defined array, and returns 0 to its caller. (The type **jmp_buf** must be implemented as an array type so that a pointer to **env** is actually passed to **setjmp**.)

The function **longjmp** takes as its arguments a jump buffer previously filled by calling **setjmp** and an integer value, **status**, that is usually nonzero. The effect of calling **longjmp** is to cause the program to return from the call to **setjmp** again, this time returning the value **status**. Some implementations, including ISO C, do not permit **longjmp** to cause 0 to be returned from **setjmp**, and will return 1 from **setjmp** if **longjmp** is called with status 0.

The **setjmp** and **longjmp** functions are notoriously difficult to implement, and the programmer would do well to make minimal assumptions about them. When **setjmp** returns with a nonzero value, the programmer can assume that static variables have their proper value as of the time **longjmp** was called. Automatic variables local to the function containing **setjmp** are guaranteed to have their correct value in ISO C only if they have a **volatile**-qualified type or if their values were not changed between the original call to **setjmp** and the corresponding **longjmp** call. Furthermore, ISO C requires that the call to **setjmp** either be an entire expression statement (possibly cast to **void**), the right-hand side of a simple assignment expression, or be used as the controlling expression of an **if**, **switch**, **do**, **while**, or **for** statement in one of the following forms:

```
(setjmp(...))
(!setjmp(...))
(exp relop setjmp(...))
(setjmp(...) relop exp)
```

where *exp* is an integer constant expression and *relop* is a relational or equality operator. ISO C requires that **longjmp** operate correctly in unnested signal (interrupt) handlers, but in some older implementations a call to **setjmp** or **longjmp** during interrupt processing or signal handling will not operate correctly.

If the jump buffer argument to **longjmp** is not set by **setjmp**, or if the function containing **setjmp** is terminated before the call to **longjmp**, the behavior is undefined.

Example

```
#include <setjmp.h>
jmp_buf ErrorEnv;
...

int guard(void) /* Return 0 if successful; else longjmp code. */
{
    int status = setjmp(ErrorEnv);
    if ( status != 0) return status;   /* error */
    process();
    return 0;
}

int process(void)
{   ...
    if (error_happened) longjmp(ErrorEnv, error_code);
    ...
}
```

The **longjmp** function is to be called when an error is encountered in function **process**. The function **guard** is the "backstop," to which control will be transferred by **longjmp**. The function **process** should be called directly or indirectly from **guard**; this ensures that **longjmp** cannot be called after **guard** returns, and that no attempt is made to depend on the values of local variables in the function containing **longjmp**. (This is a conservative policy.) Note that the return value from **setjmp** must be tested to determine if the return was caused by **longjmp** or not.

19.5 atexit

ISO C facilities	Traditional and alternate facilities
`#include <stdlib.h>`	
`int atexit(void (*func)(void));`	

The **atexit** function is found in ISO C. It "registers" a function so that the function will be called when **exit** is called or when the function **main** returns. The functions are not called when the program terminates abnormally, as with **abort** or **raise**. Implementations must allow at least 32 functions to be registered. The **atexit** function returns zero if the registration succeeds and returns a nonzero value otherwise.

The registered functions are called in the reverse order of their registration, before any standard cleanup actions are performed by **exit**. Each function is called with no arguments and should have return type **void**. A registered function should not attempt to reference any objects with storage class **auto** or **register** (e.g., through a pointer) except those it defines itself. Registering the same function more than once will cause the function to be called once for each registration.

Some C implementations define a related function, **onexit**.

Example

In the following example, the **main** function opens a file and then registers the **cleanup** function that will close the file in case **exit** is called. (In fact, **exit** closes all files, but perhaps the programmer wants to close this one first.)

```
#include <stdlib.h>
#include <stdio.h>
FILE *Open_File;

void cleanup(void) {
    if (Open_File != NULL) fclose(Open_File);
}

int main(void)
{
    int status;
    ...
    Open_File = fopen("out.dat","w");
    status = atexit(cleanup);
    assert(status == 0);
    ...
}
```

References **abort** 19.3; **exit** 19.3; **main** function 9.9; **raise** 19.6; **void** type 5.9

19.6 signal, raise, gsignal, ssignal, psignal

ISO C facilities	Traditional and alternate facilities

`#include <signal.h>`
 	
`#define SIG_IGN ...`
`#define SIG_DFL ...`
`#define SIG_ERR ...`
`#define SIGxxx ...`
`...`
`void (*signal(`
`    int sig,`
`    void (*func)(int)))(int);`
`int raise(int sig);`
`typedef ... sig_atomic_t;`
	`#include <signal.h>`
	
	`#define SIG_IGN ...`
	`#define SIG_DFL ...`
	`#define SIG_ERR ...  /* ISO */`
	`#define SIGxxx ...`
	`...`
	`void (*signal(`
	`    int sig,`
	`    void (*func)(int)))(int);`
	`int raise(int sig)  /* ISO */;`
	`int kill(int pid, intsig);`
	`int (*ssignal(`
	`    int softsig,`
	`    int (*func)(int)))(int);`
	`int gsignal(int softsig);`
	`void psignal(int sig,`
	`    char *prefix);`

Signals are (potentially) asynchronous events that may require special processing by the user program or by the implementation. Signals are named by integer values, and each implementation defines a set of signals in header file **signal.h**, spelled beginning with the letters **SIG**. Signals may be triggered or *raised* by the computer's error-detection mechanisms, by the user program itself via **kill** or **raise**, or by actions external to the program. Software signals used by the functions **ssignal** and **psignal** are user-defined, with values generally in the range 1..15; otherwise they operate like regular signals.

A signal handler for signal **sig** is a user function that is invoked when signal **sig** is "raised." The handler function is expected to perform some useful action and then return, generally causing the program to resume at the point it was interrupted. Handlers may also call **exit** or **longjmp**. Signal handlers are normal C functions taking one argument, the raised signal:

```
void my_handler(int the_signal) { ... }
```

Some non-ISO implementations may pass extra arguments to handlers for certain predefined signals.

The function **signal** is used to associate signal handlers with specific signals. In the normal case **signal** is passed a signal value and a pointer to the signal handler for that signal. If the association is successful, then **signal** returns a pointer to the previous signal handler; otherwise it returns the value –1 (**SIG_ERR** in ISO C) and sets **errno**.

Example

```
void new_handler(int sig) { ... }
void (*old_handler)();
...
/* Set new handler, saving old handler */
old_handler = signal( sig, &new_handler );
if (old_handler==SIG_ERR)
    printf("?Couldn't establish new handler.\n");
...
/* Restore old handler */
if (signal(sig,old_handler)==SIG_ERR)
    printf("?Couldn't put back old handler.\n");
```

The function argument to **signal**—and the returned value—may also have two special values, **SIG_IGN** and **SIG_DFL**. A call to **signal** of the form **signal(sig, SIG_IGN)** means that signal **sig** is to be ignored. A call to **signal** of the form **signal(sig, SIG_DFL)** means that signal **sig** is to receive its "default" handling, which usually means ignoring some signals and terminating the program on other signals.

The **ssignal** function (found in UNIX System V) works exactly like **signal** but is used only in conjunction with **gsignal** for user-defined software signals. Handlers supplied to **ssignal** return integer values that become the return value of **gsignal**.

The **raise** and **gsignal** functions cause the indicated signal (or software signal) to be raised in the current process. The **kill** function causes the indicated signal to be raised in the specified process; it is less portable.

When a signal is raised for which a handler has been established by **signal** or **gsignal**, the handler is given control. ISO C (and most other implementations) either reset the associated handler to **SIG_DFL** before the handler is given control or in some other way block the signal; this is to prevent unwanted recursion. (Whether this happens for the signal **SIGILL** is implementation-defined for historical and performance reasons.) The handler may return, in which case execution continues at the point of interruption, with the following caveats:

1. If the signal was raised by **raise** or **gsignal**, then those functions return to their caller.
2. If the signal was raised by **abort**, then ISO C programs are terminated. Other implementations may return to the caller of **abort**.
3. If the handled signal was **SIGFPE** or another implementation-defined computational signal, then the behavior upon return is undefined.

Signal handlers should refrain from calling library functions other than **signal** itself, since some signals could arise from library functions and since library functions (other than **signal**) are not guaranteed to be reentrant.

ISO C defines the macros listed in Table 19–2 to stand for certain standard signals. These signals are common to many implementations of C.

Table 19–2 Standard signals

Macro name	Signal meaning
SIGABRT	abnormal termination, such as is caused by the **abort** facility
SIGFPE	an erroneous arithmetic operation such as an attempt to divide by zero
SIGILL	an error caused by an invalid computer instruction
SIGINT	an attention signal, as from an interactive user striking a special keystroke
SIGSEGV	an invalid memory access
SIGTERM	a termination signal, from a user or another program

The **psignal** function (not in ISO C) prints on the standard error output the string **prefix** (which is customarily the name of the program) and a brief description of signal **sig**. This function may be useful in handlers that are about to call **exit** or **abort**.

References **exit** 19.3; **longjmp** 19.4

19.7 sleep, alarm

ISO C facilities	Traditional and alternate facilities
	`void sleep(unsigned seconds);`
	`unsigned alarm(unsigned seconds);`

The **`alarm`** function sets an internal system timer to the indicated number of seconds and returns the number of seconds previously on the timer. When the timer expires, the signal **`SIGALRM`** is raised in the program. If the argument to **`alarm`** is 0, then the effect of the call is to cancel any previous **`alarm`** request. The **`alarm`** function is useful for escaping from various kinds of deadlock situations.

The **`sleep`** function suspends the program for the indicated number of seconds, at which time the sleep function returns and execution continues. Sleep is typically implemented using the same timer as **`alarm`**, and if the sleep time exceeds the time already on the **`alarm`** timer, **`sleep`** will return immediately after the **`SIGALRM`** signal is handled. If the sleep time is shorter than the time already on the **`alarm`** timer, then **`sleep`** will reset the timer just before it returns so that **`SIGALRM`** will be received when expected.

Implementations will generally terminate **`sleep`** when any signal is handled; some supply the number of unslept seconds as the return value of **`sleep`** (of type **`unsigned`**).

Some implementations may define these functions as taking arguments of type **`unsigned long`**. These functions are not part of ISO C, since they are more properly the concern of an operating systems standard such as POSIX.

References **`signal`** 19.6

20

Miscellaneous Functions

The facilities in this section allow the C programmer to interrogate, and in some cases modify, the environment in which the program is running. The function **main**, which programmers must define to establish an entry point in their C programs, is also described, as are the functions **bsearch** and **qsort**, which provide general searching and sorting capabilities.

Table 20–1 Chapter summary

Name	Section	Name	Section	Name	Section
bsearch	20.5	**getcwd**	20.3	**main**	20.1
ctermid	20.2	**getenv**	20.4	**qsort**	20.6
cuserid	20.2	**getwd**	20.3		

20.1 main

ISO C facilities	Traditional and alternate facilities

`int main(void);`
`int main(`
`  int argc,`
`  char *argv[]);`
	`int main(void);`
	`int main(`
	`  int argc,`
	`  char *argv[]);`
	`int main(`
	`  int argc,`
	`  char *argv[],`
	`  char *env[]);`
	`extern char *environ[];`

The function **main** is not a library function; it is a function that the programmer defines to designate the entry point of his program and to serve as a vehicle for obtaining information about the program's execution environment. Among all the source files making up a C program, there must be exactly one definition of **main**. Most C implementations, including ISO C, permit **main** to be defined with zero or two parameters, customarily called **argc** and **argv**. Some implementations provide an optional third parameter, **env**. The arguments to **main** are set up by the execution environment and are not directly under control of the C programmer.

The parameter **argc** is the count of the number of "program arguments" or "options" supplied to the program when it was invoked by a user or another program.

The parameter **argv** is a vector of pointers to strings representing the program arguments. The first string, **argv[0]**, is the name of the program itself; if the name is not available, **argv[0][0]** must be **'\0'**.. The string **argv[*i*]**, *i*=1, …, **argc**–1, is the *i*th program argument. ISO C requires that **argv[argc]** be a null pointer, but it is not so in some older implementations. The vector **argv** and the strings to which it points must be modifiable, and their values must not be changed by the implementation or host system during program execution.

Example

The following short program prints out its name and arguments.

```
#include <stdio.h>
int main(int argc, char *argv[])
{
    int i;
    printf("Name: "); printf("%s\n", argv[0]);
    printf("Arguments: ");
    for( i=1; i<argc; i++)
        printf("%s ",argv[i]);
    printf("\n");
    return 0;
}
```

Some implementations permit a third argument to **main**, **env**, which points to a null-terminated vector of "environment values," each one a pointer to a null-terminated string of the form **"name=value"**. When the environment pointer is not a parameter to **main**, it might be found in a global variable. Some UNIX implementations use the global variable **environ** to hold the environment pointer. However, it is more portable to use the ISO C facility **getenv** to access the environment (section 20.3).

Example

Assuming **envp** holds the environment pointer, this code prints out the environment contents:

```
char *envp[];
...
for(i=0; envp[i] != NULL; i++) printf("%s\n",envp[i]);
```

20.2 ctermid, cuserid

ISO C facilities	Traditional and alternate facilities

```
#include <stdio.h>
char *ctermid(char *s);
char *cuserid(char *s);
#define L_ctermid ...
#define L_cuserid ...
```

The function **ctermid** computes a file name that corresponds to the controlling terminal for the current process. This file name can be passed to **fopen** to establish an I/O connection with the terminal. The concept of treating I/O devices such as terminals as files is central to UNIX but may be less natural in other systems. However, many C implementations provide a similar facility.

The argument **s** may be null, in which case the file name is stored in an internal buffer whose address is returned as the value of the call. The next call to **ctermid** might overwrite the buffer. If **s** is not null, it is assumed to point to a character array at least **L_ctermid** characters long, into which the name is stored. The value of **s** is returned.

The function **cuserid** retrieves the name of the user who "owns" the current process. The argument **s** may be null, in which case the user name is stored in an internal buffer whose address is returned as the value of the call. The next call to **cuserid** will overwrite the buffer. If **s** is not null, it is assumed to point to a character array at least **L_cuserid** characters long, into which the name is stored. The value of **s** is returned.

20.3 getcwd, getwd

ISO C facilities	Traditional and alternate facilities
	#include <sys/param.h> **char *getcwd(char *buf, int size);** **char *getwd(char *pathname);** **#define MAXPATHLEN ...**

The functions **getcwd** or **getwd** (depending on the implementation) are used to determine the "current working directory," which is generally the file system directory in which file I/O will take place if a specific directory is not specified in a file name.

The **getcwd** function returns a pointer to the current working directory name. If the argument **buf** is null, then **size** bytes of storage are allocated by **malloc**, the working directory name is copied into that storage, and its address is returned. If the argument **buf** is not null, it should point to at least **size** characters of space into which the working directory name will be copied and the address **buf** will be returned. In some implementations, **size** must be larger than the longest pathname to be returned (e.g., 2 bytes longer). If an error occurs, a null pointer is returned and **errno** is set.

The **getwd** function copies into the character array at **pathname** the working directory name. The array should be at least **MAXPATHLEN** characters long. If an error occurs, a null pointer is returned and a message is placed in **pathname**.

References **errno** 11.2; **malloc** 16.1

20.4 getenv

ISO C facilities	Traditional and alternate facilities
#include <stdlib.h> **char * getenv(** **const char *name);**	 **char * getenv(** **char *name);**

The **getenv** function takes as its single argument a pointer to a string which is interpreted as a name understood by the execution environment. The function returns a pointer to another string, which is the "value" of the argument **name**. If the indicated name has no value, a null pointer is returned. The returned string should not be modified by the programmer, and it may be overwritten by a subsequent call to **getenv**. The set of (*name*,*value*) bindings may also be made available to the **main** function (section 20.1) as the (non-ISO) **env** parameter.

20.5 bsearch, qsort

ISO C facilities	Traditional and alternate facilities
`#include <stdlib.h>`	

`void *bsearch(`
`  const void *key,`
`  const void *base,`
`  size_t count,`
`  size_t size,`
`  int (*compar)(`
`    const void *the_key,`
`    const void *a_value));`
	`char *bsearch(`
	`  char *key,`
	`  char *base,`
	`  unsigned count,`
	`  int size,`
	`  int (*compar)(`
	`    char *the_key,`
	`    char *a_value));`

`void qsort(`
`  void *base,`
`  size_t count,`
`  size_t size,`
`  int (*compar)(`
`    const void *element1,`
`    const void *element2));`
	`void qsort(`
	`  char *base,`
	`  unsigned count,`
	`  int size,`
	`  int (*compar)(`
	`    char *element1,`
	`    char *element2));`

The function **bsearch** searches an array of **count** elements whose first element is pointed to by **base**. The size of each element in characters is **size**. **compar** is a function whose arguments are a pointer to the key and a pointer to an array element; it returns a negative, zero, or positive value depending if the key is less than, greater than, or equal to the element. The array must be sorted in ascending order (according to **compar**) at the beginning of the search. **bsearch** returns a pointer to an element of the array that matches the **key**, or a null pointer if no such element is found.

The function **qsort** sorts an array of **count** elements whose first element is pointed to by **base**. The size of each element in characters is specified by **size**. **compar** is a function that takes as arguments pointers to two elements and returns –1 if the first element is "less than" the second, 1 if the first element is "greater than" the second, and 0 if the two elements are "equal." The array will be sorted in ascending order (according to **compar**) at the end of the sort.

Example

The function **fetch** below uses **bsearch** to search **Table**, a sorted array of structures. The function **key_compare** is supplied to test the key values. Notice that **fetch** first embeds the key in a dummy element (**key_elem**); this allows **key_compare** to be used with both **bsearch** and **qsort** (section 20.6):

```
#include <stdlib.h>
#define COUNT 100
struct elem {int key; int data; } Table[COUNT];
```

```
int key_compare(const void * e1, const void * e2)
{
    int v1 = ((struct elem *)e1)->key;
    int v2 = ((struct elem *)e2)->key;
    return (v1<v2) ? -1 : (v1>v2) ? 1 : 0;
}

int fetch(int key)
/* Return the data item associated with key in
  the table, or 0 if no such key exists. */
{
    struct elem *result;
    struct elem key_elem;
    key_elem.key = key;
    result = (struct elem *)
            bsearch(
                (void *) &key_elem, (void *) &Table[0],
                (size_t) COUNT, sizeof(struct elem),
                key_compare);
    if (result == NULL)
        return 0;
    else
        return result->data;
}
```

Example

The function **sort_table** below uses **qsort** to sort the table in the above example. The same function, **key_compare**, is used to compare table elements:

```
void sort_table(void)
/* Sorts Table according to the key values */
{
    qsort(
        (void *)Table,
        (size_t) COUNT,
        sizeof(struct elem),
        key_compare );
}
```

20.6 C++ COMPATIBILITY

20.6.1 main

In C++, the **main** function must not be called recursively, nor can its address be taken. C++ imposes more restrictions on program start-up, so implementations may handle **main** as a special case. If you need to manipulate the **main** function, simply create a second function, call it from **main**, and use it in place of **main** in your program.

A

The ASCII Character Set

		0			0x20		0x40		0x60	
		0			040		0100		0140	
Hex.	Octal	Dec.	Char.	Name	Dec.	Char.	Dec.	Char.	Dec.	Char.
0	0	0	^@	NUL	32	SP	64	@	96	`
1	1	1	^A	SOH	33	!	65	A	97	a
2	2	2	^B	STX	34	"	66	B	98	b
3	3	3	^C	ETX	35	#	67	C	99	c
4	4	4	^D	EOT	36	$	68	D	100	d
5	5	5	^E	ENQ	37	%	69	E	101	e
6	6	6	^F	ACK	38	&	70	F	102	f
7	7	7	^G	BEL, \a	39	'	71	G	103	g
8	010	8	^H	BS, \b	40	(	72	H	104	h
9	011	9	^I	TAB, \t	41	)	73	I	105	i
0xA	012	10	^J	LF, \n[a]	42	*	74	J	106	j
0xB	013	11	^K	VT, \v	43	+	75	K	107	k
0xC	014	12	^L	FF, \f	44	,	76	L	108	l
0xD	015	13	^M	CR, \r	45	-	77	M	109	m
0xE	016	14	^N	SO	46	.	78	N	110	n
0xF	017	15	^O	SI	47	/	79	O	111	o
0x10	020	16	^P	DLE	48	0	80	P	112	p
0x11	021	17	^Q	DC1	49	1	81	Q	113	q
0x12	022	18	^R	DC2	50	2	82	R	114	r
0x13	023	19	^S	DC3	51	3	83	S	115	s
0x14	024	20	^T	DC4	52	4	84	T	116	t
0x15	025	21	^U	NAK	53	5	85	U	117	u
0x16	026	22	^V	SYN	54	6	86	V	118	v
0x17	027	23	^W	ETB	55	7	87	W	119	w
0x18	030	24	^X	CAN	56	8	88	X	120	x
0x19	031	25	^Y	EM	57	9	89	Y	121	y
0x1A	032	26	^Z	SUB	58	:	90	Z	122	z
0x1B	033	27	^[	ESC	59	;	91	[	123	{
0x1C	034	28	^\	FS	60	<	92	\	124	|
0x1D	035	29	^]	GS	61	=	93	]	125	}
0x1E	036	30	^^	RS	62	>	94	^	126	~
0x1F	037	31	^_	US	63	?	95	_	127	DEL

[a] The use of '\012' for '\n' is common, but some systems use other values, such as '\023'.

B

Syntax of the C Language

This appendix summarizes the grammar for the ISO C language. The productions are listed in alphabetical order and are accompanied by the section numbers in this book where they are first presented. The topmost production of the grammar is *translation-unit*.

abstract-declarator : 5.12
pointer
pointer$_{opt}$ *direct-abstract-declarator*

add-op : one of 7.6.2
`+ -`

additive-expression : 7.6.2
multiplicative-expression
additive-expression add-op multiplicative-expression

address-expression : 7.5.6
`&` *cast-expression*

array-declarator : 4.5.3
declarator `[` *constant-expression*$_{opt}$ `]`

assignment-expression : 7.9
conditional-expression
unary-expression assignment-op assignment-expression

assignment-op : one of 7.9
```
=    +=   -=   *=   /=   %=
<<=  >>=  &=   ^=   |=
```

bit-field : 5.6
 declarator$_{opt}$ **:** *width*

bitwise-and-expression : 7.6.6
 equality-expression
 bitwise-and-expression **&** *equality-expression*

bitwise-negation-expression : 7.5.5
 ~ *cast-expression*

bitwise-or-expression : 7.6.6
 bitwise-xor-expression
 bitwise-or-expression **|** *bitwise-xor-expression*

bitwise-xor-expression : 7.6.6
 bitwise-and-expression
 bitwise-xor-expression **^** *bitwise-and-expression*

break-statement : 8.8
 break ;

c-char : 2.7.3
 any source character except the apostrophe **'**,
 backslash ****, or newline character
 escape-character

c-char-sequence : 2.7.3
 c-char
 c-char-sequence *c-char*

case-label : 8.7
 case *constant-expression*

cast-expression :
 unary-expression 7.5
 (*type-name* **)** *cast-expression*

character-constant : 2.7.3
 ' *c-char-sequence* **'**
 L' *c-char-sequence* **'**

character-escape-code : one of 2.7.5
 a b f n r t v \\ ' " ?

character-type-specifier : 5.1.3
 char
 signed char
 unsigned char

comma-expression : 7.10
assignment-expression
comma-expression **,** *assignment-expression*

component-declaration : 5.6
type-specifier component-declarator-list **;**

component-declarator : 5.6
simple-component
bit field

component-declarator-list : 5.6
component-declarator
component-declarator-list **,** *component-declarator*

component-selection-expression : 7.4.2
direct-component-selection
indirect-component-selection

compound-statement : 8.4
{ *inner-declaration-list*$_{opt}$ *statement-list*$_{opt}$ **}**

conditional-expression : 7.8
logical-or-expression
logical-or-expression **?** *expression* **:** *conditional-expression*

conditional-statement : 8.5
if-statement
if-else-statement

constant : 2.7
integer-constant
floating-constant
character-constant
string-constant

constant-expression : 4.5.3
expression

continue-statement : 8.8
continue ;

decimal-constant : 2.7.1
nonzero-digit
decimal-constant digit

declaration : 4.1
declaration-specifiers initialized-declarator-list **;**

declaration-list : 8.4, 9.1
declaration
declaration-list declaration

declaration-specifiers : 4.1
storage-class-specifier declaration-specifiers$_{opt}$
type-specifier declaration-specifiers$_{opt}$
type-qualifier declaration-specifiers$_{opt}$

declarator : 4.5
pointer-declarator
direct-declarator

default-label : 8.7
`default`

digit : one of 2.5
`0 1 2 3 4 5 6 7 8 9`

digit-sequence : 2.7.2
digit
digit digit-sequence

direct-abstract-declarator : 5.12
`(` *abstract-declarator* **`)`**
direct-abstract-declarator$_{opt}$ **`[`** *constant-expression*$_{opt}$ **`]`**
direct-abstract-declarator$_{opt}$ **`(`** *parameter-type-list*$_{opt}$ **`)`**

direct-component-selection : 7.4.2
postfix-expression **`.`** *name*

direct-declarator : 4.5
simple-declarator
`(` *declarator* **`)`**
function-declarator
array-declarator

do-statement : 8.6.2
`do` *statement* **`while`** **`(`** *expression* **`)`** **`;`**

dotted-digits : 2.7.2
digit-sequence **`.`**
digit-sequence **`.`** *digit-sequence*
`.` *digit-sequence*

enumeration-constant : 5.5
identifier

enumeration-constant-definition : 5.5
enumeration-constant
enumeration-constant **=** *expression*

enumeration-definition-list : 5.5
enumeration-constant-definition
enumeration-definition-list **,** *enumeration-constant-definition*

enumeration-tag : 5.5
identifier

enumeration-type-definition : 5.5
enum *enumeration-tag*$_{opt}$ **{** *enumeration-definition-list* **}**

enumeration-type-reference : 5.5
enum *enumeration-tag*

enumeration-type-specifier : 5.5
enumeration-type-definition
enumeration-type-reference

equality-expression : 7.6.5
relational-expression
equality-expression equality-op relational-expression

equality-op : one of 7.6.5
== **!=**

escape-character : 2.7.5
**** *escape-code*

escape-code : 2.7.5
character-escape-code
octal-escape-code
hex-escape-code

exponent : 2.7.2
e *sign-part*$_{opt}$ *digit-sequence*
E *sign-part*$_{opt}$ *digit-sequence*

expression : 7.10
comma-expression

expression-list : 7.4.3
assignment-expression
expression-list **,** *assignment-expression*

expression-statement : 8.2
expression **;**

field-list : 5.6
    component-declaration
    field-list component-declaration

floating-constant : 2.7.2
    digit-sequence exponent floating-suffix$_{opt}$
    dotted-digits exponent$_{opt}$ *floating-suffix*$_{opt}$

floating-suffix : one of 2.7.2
    f F l L

floating-type-specifier : 5.2
    float
    double
    long double

following-character : 2.5
    letter
    underscore
    digit

for-expressions : 8.6.3
    (*expression* $_{opt}$ **;** *expression* $_{opt}$ **;** *expression* $_{opt}$ **)**

for-statement : 8.6.3
    for *for-expressions statement*

function-call : 7.4.3
    postfix-expression **(** *expression-list*$_{opt}$ **)**

function-declarator : 4.5.4, 9.1
    direct-declarator **(** *parameter-type-list* **)**
    direct-declarator **(** *identifier-list*$_{opt}$ **)**

function-definition : 9.1
    function-specifier compound-statement

function-specifier : 9.1
    declaration-specifiers$_{opt}$ *declarator declaration-list*$_{opt}$

goto-statement : 8.10
    goto *identifier ;*

hex-digit : one of 2.7.1
    0 1 2 3 4 5 6 7 8 9
    A B C D E F a b c d e f

hex-escape-code : 2.7.5
    x *hex-digit*
    hex-escape-code hex-digit

hexadecimal-constant : 2.7.1
  0x *hex-digit*
  0X *hex-digit*
  hexadecimal-constant hex-digit

identifier : 2.5
  underscore
  letter
  identifier following-character

identifier-list : 4.5.4, 9.1
  identifier
  identifier-list **,** *identifier*

if-else-statement : 8.5
  if (*expression* **)** *statement* **else** *statement*

if-statement : 8.5
  if (*expression* **)** *statement*

indirect-component-selection : 7.4.2
  postfix-expression **->** *name*

indirection-expression : 7.5.7
  ***** *cast-expression*

initialized-declarator : 4.1
  declarator $initializer\text{-}part_{opt}$

initialized-declarator-list : 4.1
  initialized-declarator
  initialized-declarator-list **,** *initialized-declarator*

initializer : 4.6
  expression
  { *initializer-list* $,_{opt}$ **}**

initializer-list : 4.6
  initializer
  initializer-list **,** *initializer*

integer-constant : 2.7.1
  decimal-constant $integer\text{-}suffix_{opt}$
  octal-constant $integer\text{-}suffix_{opt}$
  hexadecimal-constant $integer\text{-}suffix_{opt}$

integer-type-specifier : 5.1
  signed-type-specifier
  unsigned-type-specifier
  character-type-specifier

iterative-statement : 8.6
  do-statement
  while-statement
  for-statement

label : 8.3
  named-label
  case-label
  default-label

labeled-statement : 8.3
  label **:** *statement*

letter : one of 2.5

A	**B**	**C**	**D**	**E**	**F**	**G**	**H**	**I**	**J**	**K**	**L**	**M**
N	**O**	**P**	**Q**	**R**	**S**	**T**	**U**	**V**	**W**	**X**	**Y**	**Z**
a	**b**	**c**	**d**	**e**	**f**	**g**	**h**	**i**	**j**	**k**	**l**	**m**
n	**o**	**p**	**q**	**r**	**s**	**t**	**u**	**v**	**w**	**x**	**y**	**z**

logical-and-expression : 7.7
  bitwise-or-expression
  logical-and-expression **&&** *bitwise-or-expression*

logical-negation-expression : 7.5.4
  ! *cast-expression*

logical-or-expression : 7.7
  logical-and-expression
  logical-or-expression **||** *logical-and-expression*

long-suffix : one of 2.7.1
  l L

mult-op : one of 7.6.1
  *** / %**

multiplicative-expression : 7.6.1
  cast-expression
  multiplicative-expression mult-op cast-expression

named-label : 8.10
  identifier

nonzero-digit : one of 2.7.1
  1 2 3 4 5 6 7 8 9

null-statement : 8.11
  ;

octal-constant : 2.7.1
  0
  octal-constant octal-digit

octal-digit : one of 2.7.1
  0 1 2 3 4 5 6 7

octal-escape-code : 2.7.5
  octal-digit
  octal-digit octal-digit
  octal-digit octal-digit octal-digit

parameter-declaration : 4.5.4, 9.1
  declaration-specifiers declarator
  declaration-specifiers abstract-declarator$_{opt}$

parameter-list : 4.5.4, 9.1
  parameter-declaration
  parameter-list **,** *parameter-declaration*

parameter-type-list : 4.5.4, 9.1
  parameter-list
  parameter list **, ...**

parenthesized-expression : 7.3.3
  (*expression* **)**

pointer : 4.5.2, 5.12
  ***** *type-qualifier-list*$_{opt}$
  ***** *type-qualifier-list*$_{opt}$ *pointer*

pointer-declarator : 4.5.2
  pointer direct-declarator

postdecrement-expression : 7.4.4
  postfix-expression **--**

postfix-expression : 7.4
  primary-expression
  subscript-expression
  component-selection-expression
  function-call
  postincrement-expression
  postdecrement-expression

postincrement-expression : 7.4.4
  postfix-expression **++**

predecrement-expression : 7.5.8
  -- *unary-expression*

preincrement-expression : 7.5.8
++ *unary-expression*

primary-expression : 7.3
identifier
constant
parenthesized-expression

relational-expression : 7.6.4
shift-expression
relational-expression relational-op shift-expression

relational-op : one of 7.6.4
< **<=** **>** **>=**

return-statement : 8.9
return *expression* $_{opt}$ **;**

s-char-sequence : 2.7.4
s-char
s-char-sequence s-char

s-char : 2.7.4
any source character except the double quote **"**,
backslash ****, or newline character
escape-character

shift-expression : 7.6.3
additive-expression
shift-expression shift-op additive-expression

shift-op : one of 7.6.3
<< **>>**

signed-type-specifier : 5.1.1
short *or* **short int** *or* **signed short** *or* **signed short int**
int *or* **signed int** *or* **signed**
long *or* **long int** *or* **signed long** *or* **signed long int**

simple-component : 5.6
declarator

simple-declarator : 4.5.1
identifier

sizeof-expression : 7.5.2
sizeof (*type-name* **)**
sizeof *unary-expression*

statement : ch. 8
  expression-statement
  labeled-statement
  compound-statement
  conditional-statement
  iterative-statement
  switch-statement
  break-statement
  continue-statement
  return-statement
  goto-statement
  null-statement

statement-list : 8.4
  statement
  statement-list statement

storage-class-specifier : one of 4.3
  auto **extern** **register** **static** **typedef**

string-constant : 2.7.4
  " *s-charr-sequence*$_{opt}$ **"**
  L" *s-char-sequence*$_{opt}$ **"**

structure-tag : 5.6
  identifier

structure-type-definition : 5.6
  struct *structure-tag*$_{opt}$ **{** *field-list* **}**

structure-type-reference : 5.6
  struct *structure-tag*

structure-type-specifier : 5.6
  structure-type-definition
  structure-type-reference

subscript-expression : 7.4.1
  postfix-expression **[** *expression* **]**

switch-statement : 8.7
  switch **(** *expression* **)** *statement*

top-level-declaration : 9.1
  declaration
  function-definition

top-level-declaration-list : 9.1
  top-level-declaration
  top-level-declaration-list top-level-declaration

translation-unit : 9.1
top-level-declaration
translation-unit top-level-declaration

type-name : 5.12
declaration-specifiers abstract-declarator$_{opt}$

type-qualifier : 4.4
const
volatile

type-qualifier-list : 4.5.2
type-qualifier
type-qualifer-list type qualifier

type-specifier : 4.4
enumeration-type-specifier
floating-point-type-specifier
integer-type-specifier
structure-type-specifier
typedef-name
union-type-specifier
void-type-specifier

typedef-name : 5.10
identifier

unary-expression : 7.5
postfix-expression
sizeof-expression
unary-minus-expression
unary-plus-expression
logical-negation-expression
bitwise-negation-expression
address-expression
indirection-expression
preincrement-expression
predecrement-expression

unary-minus-expression : 7.5.3
- *cast-expression*

unary-plus-expression : 7.5.3
+ *cast-expression*

underscore : 2.5
_

union-tag : 5.7
identifier

union-type-definition : 5.7
  union *union-tag*$_{opt}$ **{** *field-list* **}**

union-type-reference : 5.7
  union *union-tag*

union-type-specifier : 5.7
  union-type-definition
  union-type-reference

unsigned-suffix : one of 2.7.1
  u U

unsigned-type-specifier : 5.1.2
  unsigned short int$_{opt}$
  unsigned int$_{opt}$
  unsigned long int$_{opt}$

void-type-specifier : 5.9
  void

while-statement : 8.6.1
  while (*expression* **)** *statement*

width : 5.6
  expression

C

Answers to the Exercises

This appendix contains solutions to the exercises in Chapters 2–9.

CHAPTER 2 ANSWERS

1. Reserved words, hexadecimal constants, wide string constants, and parentheses are lexical tokens. Comments and whitespace serve only to separate tokens. Trigraphs are removed before token recognition.
2. The number of tokens for each string is:
   (a) 3 tokens
   (b) 2 tokens; **-** is an operator, not part of the constant
   (c) 1 token
   (d) 3 tokens; the second one is **"FOO"**
   (e) 1 token
   (f) 4 tokens; ****** is not a single operator
   (g) not a token; same as **"X\\"**, which is an unterminated string constant
   (h) not a token; identifiers cannot have **$**
   (i) 3 tokens; ***=** is an operator
   (j) either none or 3; **##** is not a lexical token, but it happens to be a preprocessor token
3. The result is `***/`; the comments are identified below between parentheses. Quotation marks inside a comment do not have to balance.

```
/**/*/*"*/*/*"//*//**/*/
(--) (---) (-----)(--)
```

4. The order is:
   1. converting trigraphs
   2. processing line continuation
   3. removing comments
   4. collecting characters into tokens
5. Some possible objections:
   (a) difficult to identify (read) the multiple words in the identifier; use upper case or underscores
   (b) the identifier's spelling is very close to a reserved word

(c) lowercase **l** ("ell") and uppercase **O** ("oh") are easily mistaken for **1** (one) and **0** (zero)

(d) closely resembles a numeric literal (the first letter is an "oh")

(e) if the compiler accepted this identifier, it would be an extension

6. (a) For example: `x = a //*divide*/ b;`

   (b) Assuming an ISO C implementation that distinguished only the first 31 characters of identifiers, an ISO C program that spelled the same identifier differently after the 31st character would be flagged as an error in C++.

   (c) For example, the declaration: **int class = 0;**

   (d) The expression **sizeof('a')==sizeof(char)** will be different in C and C++, assuming **sizeof(char)!=sizeof(int)**.

CHAPTER 3 ANSWERS

1. (a) The space before the left parenthesis is not permitted in ISO or traditional C. Instead of a macro with one parameter, **ident** will be a macro with no parameters that expands to "**(x) x**".

   (b) The **=** and **;** characters are not necessary and are probably wrong. In some traditional C compilers the space after **#** might cause problems.

   (c) This definition is all right.

   (d) This definition is all right; you can define reserved words as macros.

2.

	ISO C	*Traditional C*
(a)	**b+a**	**b+a**
(b)	**x 4** (two tokens)	**x4** (one token)
(c)	**"a book"**	**# a book**
(d)	**p?free(p):NULL**	**p?p?p?p?...:NULL:NULL:NULL** (infinitely)

3. The result after preprocessing (ignoring whitespace) is these three lines:

```
int blue = 0;
int blue = 0;
int red = 0;
```

4. Because the arguments and body are not parenthesized, the result of expanding the macro could be misinterpreted in a larger expression. A safer definition would be

```
#define DBL(a)    ((a)+(a))
```

5. The macro is expanded in the following steps:

```
M(M)(A,B)
MM(A,B)
A = "B"
```

6. This solution depends on the presence of **defined** and **#error**:

```
#if !defined(SIZE) || (SIZE<1) || (SIZE>10)
#error "SIZE not properly defined "
#endif
```

7. In the preprocessor command **#include </a/file.h>**, the sequence **/a/file.h** is considered a token (a single file name); it would not be a token to the compiler.

8. Presumably the programmer wishes to print an error when **x==0**. However, **x==0** is a run-time test, whereas **#error** is a compile-time command. If this program were compiled, the error message would always appear and halt compilation, regardless of the value of **x**.

CHAPTER 4 ANSWERS

1. The function will return the value of its argument each time it is called. Only if the **static** storage class specifier is used on the declaration of **i** inside **P** will the return value change in successive calls.

2. The declarations of **f** as a function, integer variable, type name, and enumeration constant all conflict with each other; eliminate all but one of those declarations. The use of **f** as both a structure tag and a union tag conflict; eliminate the union so that **f** is also declared as a structure component. The use of **f** as a label does not conflict with any other declarations except in a few older C implementations.

3.

Code	***int i;***	***long i;***	***float i;***
`int i;`	(defined)		
`void f(i)`		(defined)	
`    long i;`		(defined)	
`{`			
`    long l = i;`		(used)	
`    {`			
`        float i;`			(defined)
`        i = 3.4;`			(used)
`    }`			
`    l = i+2;`		(used)	
`}`			
`int *p = &i;`	(used)		

4. (a) **`extern void P(void);`**
   (b) **`register int i;`**
   (c) **`typedef char *LT;`**
   (d) **`extern Q(int i, const char *cp);`**
   (e) **`extern int R( double *(*p)(long i) );`**
   (f) **`static char STR[11];`** (Note: leave room for the null character.)
   (g) **`const char STR2[] = INIT_STR2;`** Braces around **INIT_STR2** are optional. Also acceptable would be: **`const char *STR2=INIT_STR2;`** (No braces.)
   (h) **`int *IP = &i;`**

5. **`int m[3][3] = {{1,2,3},{1,2,3},{1,2,3}};`**

CHAPTER 5 ANSWERS

1. Note that none of these types should involve type **int**, since the size of **int** might be no larger than **short** anyway.
   (a) **long** or **unsigned long** (**unsigned short** might not handle 99999)
   (b) a structure containing two components: type **short** (for the area code) and type **long** (for the local number) (or the unsigned versions of these types)
   (c) **char** (any variant)
   (d) **signed char** in ISO C; **short** in other implementations (**char** might be unsigned)
   (c) **signed char** in ISO C; **short** in other implementations (**char** might be unsigned) (characters are guaranteed to have positive values in type **signed char**)
   (f) **double** would work, but less space would be occupied by using type **long** and storing the balance as a number of cents

2. The type of **UP_ARROW_KEY** is **int** and has the value **0x86** (134). If the computer uses a **signed** type for **char**, the values for the extended characters will be negative, so if the argument to **is_up_arrow** really is **0x86**, the **return** statement test will be **-122==134**, which is false instead of true. The correct way to write the function is to coerce the character code to be of type **char** or coerce the argument to be of type **unsigned char**. That is, use one of the following return statements:

```
return c == (char) UP_ARROW_KEY;
return (unsigned char) c == UP_ARROW_KEY;
```

The first solution is probably better, since it allows the most freedom in defining a value for **UP_ARROW_KEY**.

3. (a) legal
   (b) legal
   (c) illegal; cannot dereference a **void *** pointer
   (d) illegal; cannot dereference a **void *** pointer

4. (a) ***(iv + i)**
   (b) ***(*(im+i)+j)**

5. 13. The cast is not necessary in ISO C, but it makes the intent clearer and may be needed in some older compilers.

6. **x.i = 0;**
   x.F.s = 0; (0 and 1 are the only legal values.)
   x.F.e = 0; x.F.m = 0;
   x.U.d = 0.0; (or **x.U.p = NULL;** , but not **x.U.a[0] = '\0';**, which leaves some elements of **a** undefined)

7. The sketches are shown below. The number of bits occupied by each field is indicated, and markers along the bottom indicate word boundaries. Note particularly the order of the bit fields.

Big-endian, right-to-left bit packing

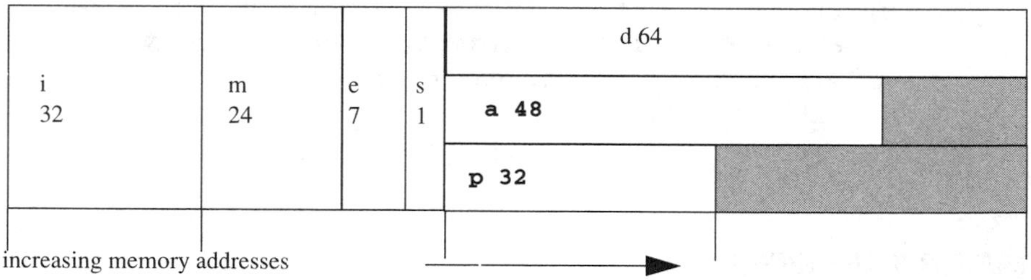

Little-endian, right-to-left bit packing

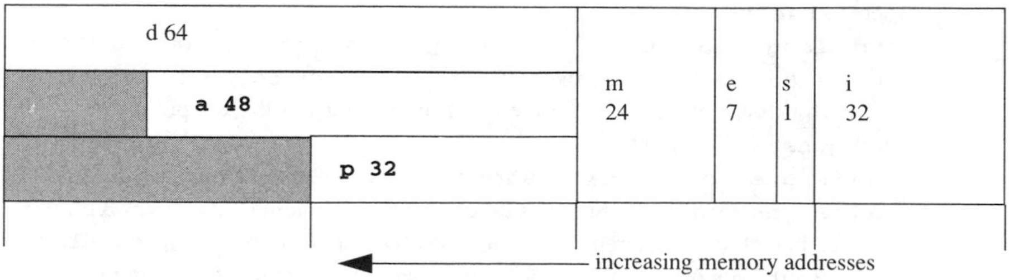

8.
```
typedef int *fpi(); /* type definition */
fpi *x;             /* variable declaration */
int *fpi()          /* function; can't use typedef in header */
{
    return (fpi *)0;
}
```

CHAPTER 6 ANSWERS

1. All the casts are permitted in ISO and traditional C except (c) and (e), which are disallowed in ISO C.
2. In this solution, we assume the traditional C compiler allows mixed pointer assignments but otherwise follows ISO rules. However, for some traditional C compilers the answers will be the same as for question 1.
   (a) Permitted in ISO and traditional C.
   (b) Disallowed in ISO C; permitted in traditional C.
   (c) Disallowed in ISO C; permitted in traditional C.
   (d) Disallowed in ISO C and traditional C.
   (e) Disallowed in ISO C; permitted in traditional C.
   (f) Permitted in ISO and traditional C.
3. (a) **unsigned**
   (b) **unsigned long** in traditional C; **long** or **unsigned long** in ISO C
   (c) **double**
   (d) **long double** in ISO C;
   (e) **int *** (the usual unary conversions are applied to **int []**)
   (f) **short (*)()**, because the usual unary conversions are applied first. Here is a plausible situation in which this could happen:
```
extern short f1(), f2(), (*pf)();
extern int i;
pf = (i>0 ? f1 : f2);   /* binary conv on f1 and f2 */
```
4. It is permitted (if wasteful) for an implementation to use 32 bits to represent type **char**. Regardless of the representation, the value of **sizeof(char)** is always 1. The range of type **int** cannot be smaller than that of type **char**; it can be the same or it can be arbitrarily larger.
5. There is not necessarily any relationship between them. They could be the same or one could be larger than the other.
6. The value 128 can be expressed as the 32-bit hexadecimal number 00000080_{16}. Since computer A is a big-endian, the bytes are stored in the order 00_{16}, 00_{16} 00_{16}, 80_{16}. On the little-endian computer, the bytes are reassembled from the low-order end, yielding 80000000_{16}, or –2,147,483,648. The result is the same if A is the little-endian and B is the big-endian.

CHAPTER 7 ANSWERS

1. (a) **char ***
   (b) **double** (**float** in ISO C)
   (c) **float**
   (d) **int**

(e) `double` (`float` in ISO C)
(f) `int`
(g) `int`
(h) `int`
(i) illegal
(j) `float`

2. (a) `p1+=1; p2+=1; *p1=*p2;`
   (b) `*p1=*p2; p1-=1; p2-=1;`

3. (a) `#define low_zeroes(n)   (-1<<n)`
   (b) `#define low_ones(n) (~low_zeroes(n))`
   (c)
```
#define mid_zeroes(width,offset) \
        (low_zeroes(width+offset) | low_ones(offset))
```
   (The `+` operator could be used in place of `|`.)
   (d) `#define mid_ones(width,offset (~mid_zeroes(width,offset))`

4. The expression `j++==++j` is legal but its result is undefined in ISO C, because `j` is modified twice in the same expression. Depending on which operand of `==` is evaluated first, the result could be 0 or 1, although the final value of `j` is likely to be 2. On the other hand, `j++&&++j` is legal and defined; its result is 0, and `j` has the value 1 at the end of the expression.

5. (a) allowed, since the types are compatible
   (b) not allowed (the referenced type on the left does not have enough qualifiers)
   (c) allowed, since only one type specifies a size
   (d) allowed, since qualification is irrelevant if the right side is not an lvalue
   (e) not allowed, only because `float` is not compatible with its promoted type (`double`)
   (f) allowed, since the referenced types are compatible

6. No. The assignment is illegal because each structure definition creates a new type. If the definitions are in different source files, the types are compatible, but this is a technicality that permits programs compiled in separate pieces to have well-defined behavior.

CHAPTER 8 ANSWERS

1. (a)
```
n = A;
L1:
if (n>=B) goto L2;
sum+=n;
n++;
goto L1;
L2:;
```
   (b)
```
L:
if (a<b) {
   a++;
   goto L;
}
```
   (c)
```
L:
sum += *p;
if (++p < q) goto L;
```

2. The value of **j** is 3. "**j** is undefined" is incorrect; although the program jumps into a block, the fact that **i** has storage class **static** means that it will be properly initialized before the program begins.

3. The value of **sum** is 3. **i** takes on the values 0, 1, ... each time around the loop. When **i** is 0, 1, and 3, **sum** is incremented and the **continue** statement causes another loop iteration. When **i** is 2, **sum** is not altered but the loop is continued. However, when **i** is 4, the **break** within the **switch** causes control to reach the **break** statement in the loop, which causes termination of the loop. Therefore **case 5:** is never executed.

CHAPTER 9 ANSWERS

1. (a) valid prototype
   (b) legal declaration, but not a prototype; must have a parameter type list within parentheses
   (c) illegal declaration; must have at least one parameter declaration before ellipsis
   (d) illegal declaration; must have at least one type specifier, storage class specifier, or type qualifier before each parameter name
   (e) valid prototype; parameter name is not necessary
   (f) legal definition, but not a prototype; must have parameter types within parentheses
2. (a) not compatible; prototype's parameter type is not compatible with the usual argument conversions, which is required when the definition is not in prototype form
   (b) not compatible; it does not matter that the prototype appears in the definition
   (c) compatible; the parameter names do not have to be the same
   (d) not compatible; the two prototypes do not agree in the use of the ellipsis
   (e) compatible; neither is a prototype, so promoted argument types are passed
   (f) compatible
3. (a) not legal; cannot convert **short *** to **int *** under the assignment conversions
   (b) legal; **s** will be converted to type **int** and **ld** will be unchanged
   (c) legal; **ld** will be converted to type **short**
   (d) legal; the first parameter is unchanged, the second is converted to type **int**, and the third is unchanged
   (e) legal; the parameter is converted to type **int** before the call, and back to type **short** at the beginning of the called function
   (f) legal, but probably wrong; the parameter is unchanged but will be interpreted as being of type **int** by the caller
4. The call is governed by the prototype appearing on the first line. The latter declaration does not hide the former, because **P** has external linkage.
5. (a) OK; the value will be converted to type **short** before being returned
   (b) OK; the value will be converted to type **short** before being returned
   (c) illegal; the expression cannot be converted to the type of the return value
   (d) illegal; the expression cannot be converted under the assignment conversion rules

Index

B

C

T

X

Y